# Access 97

## A COMPREHENSIVE APPROACH

**Kathleen Stewart**
Moraine Valley Community College
Palos H

Mc Graw Hill **Glenco**
**McGra**

New York, New York   Columbus, Ohio   Wo

This program has been prepared with the assistance of Gleason Group, Inc., Norwalk, CT.

*Editorial Director:* Pamela Ross

*Developmental Editor:* Robert Schneider, Douglas Cross

*Copy Editor:* Beth Conover

*Composition:* PDS Associates, Creative Ink

Screens were captured using CaptureEze 97 from Application Techniques, Inc., Pepperell, MA.

## Glencoe/McGraw-Hill

A Division of The **McGraw·Hill** Companies

**Access 97: A Professional Approach**
*Student Edition*
ISBN  0-02-803324-8

**Access 97: A Comprehensive Approach**
*Student Edition*
ISBN  0-02-803353-1

**Access 97: A Professional Approach**
*Annotated Instructor's Edition*
ISBN  0-02-803328-0

**Access 97: A Comprehensive Approach**
*Teacher's Annotated Edition*
ISBN  0-02-803357-4

# Contents

## UNIT 1

# Understanding Access Basics

## UNIT 3

# Getting Information from a Database    *221*

# Appendices

# Preface

*Access 97* has been written to help you master Microsoft Access for Windows. The text is designed to take you step-by-step through the features in Access that you are likely to use in both your personal and business life.

## Case Study

Learning about the features of Access is one thing, but applying what you've learned is another. That's why a *Case Study* runs throughout the text. It offers you the opportunity to learn Access within a realistic business context. Take the time to read the Case Study about Carolina Critters, a fictional manufacturing company set in Charlotte, North Carolina. All of the work for this course will deal with this business.

## Organization of the Text

The text includes four *units*. Each unit is divided into smaller *lessons*. There are 13 lessons, each building on previously learned procedures. This building block approach, together with the Case Study and the features listed below, enables you to maximize your learning process.

## Features of the Text

- ☑ *Objectives* are listed for each lesson
- ☑ The *estimated time* required to complete the lesson is stated
- ☑ Within a lesson, each *heading* corresponds to an objective
- ☑ *Exercises* that walk you through all procedures in a lesson are titled for easy reference
- ☑ *Key terms* are italicized and defined as they are encountered
- ☑ Extensive *graphics* display screen contents
- ☑ *Toolbar buttons* and *keyboard keys* are shown in the text when they are used

☑ *Large toolbar buttons in the margins* provide easy-to-see references

☑ Lessons contain important *Notes* and useful *Tips*

☑ A *Command Summary* lists the commands learned in the lesson

☑ *Using Help* introduces you to a Help topic related to the content of a lesson

☑ *Concepts Review* includes True/False, Short Answer, and Critical Thinking questions to focus on lesson content

☑ *Skills Review* provides skill reinforcement for each lesson

☑ *Lesson Applications* ask you to apply your skills in a more challenging way

☑ *Unit Applications* give you the opportunity to use all of the skills you learned throughout the unit

☑ Appendices

☑ Glossary

☑ Index

# *Conventions Used in the Text*

This text uses a number of conventions to help you learn the program and save your work.

- Text that you are asked to key appears either in **boldface** or as a separate figure.

- Filenames appear in **boldface**.

- You will be asked to save files, tables, reports, etc. with your initials.

- Menu letters you can key to activate a command are shown as they appear on screen, with the letter underlined (example: "Choose Print from the File menu."). Dialog box options are also shown this way (example: "Click Frame Slides in the Print dialog box.").

# If You Are Unfamiliar with Windows

If you're unfamiliar with Windows, you'll want to work through *Appendix A: "Windows Tutorial"* before beginning Lesson 1. You may also need to review *Appendix B: "Using the Mouse," Appendix C: "Using Menus and Dialog Boxes,"* and *Appendix E: "File Management"* if you've never used a mouse or Windows before.

# Screen Differences

As you read about and practice each concept, illustrations of the screens have been provided to help you follow the instructions. Don't worry if your screen has a somewhat different appearance than the screen illustration. These differences result from variations in system and computer configurations.

# Acknowledgments

We would like to thank the many reviewers of this text, and those students and teachers who have used this book in the past, for their valuable assistance.

# Installation Requirements

To work with this textbook, you need Microsoft Access 97 installed on an IBM or IBM-compatible microcomputer's hard drive (or on a network). To properly install Access, refer to the Access manual that came with the program. Use the following checklist to evaluate the Access installation requirements.

## Hardware

- ☑ Personal computer with a 486 or higher processor
- ☑ Hard disk drive
- ☑ 3.5-inch diskette drive
- ☑ 12 MB of RAM (with an additional 38 MB of free hard-disk space)
- ☑ 32 MB of hard disk space required for a "Typical" installation, 42 MB required for a "Custom" installation
- ☑ VGA or higher-resolution video monitor (SVGA 256-color recommended)
- ☑ Printer (laser or ink-jet recommended)
- ☑ Mouse

## Software

- ☑ Access 97 or Microsoft Office 97
- ☑ Windows 95

# CASE STUDY

There's more to learning a database program like Microsoft's Access then simply keying data in an existing database or running a pre-existing query. You need to know how to use Access in a real-world situation. That's why all the lessons in this book relate to everyday business tasks.

As you work through the lessons, imagine yourself working as an intern for Carolina Critters, a fictional company that manufactures stuffed animals, located in Charlotte, North Carolina.

# CAROLINA CRITTERS

CASE STUDY

# Carolina Critters, Inc.

7216 N. Tryon St.
Charlotte, NC 28216
(704) 555-5959

Carolina Critters, Inc. was formed in 1946 by Hector Fuentes, upon his return from serving in the U.S. Navy in World War II. Hector's son, Carlos, took over the company in 1962 and ran it until 1994, when his daughter Lisa assumed the presidency. Originally producing only stuffed "teddy bears" and a dog, modeled on Franklin Delano Roosevelt's

dog, the company has branched out over the years. It now has 5 product lines and 25 products, producing over $25 million in annual sales. Today, the stuffed animals from Carolina Critters—ranging from traditional teddy bears and cats and dogs, to dinosaurs and endangered species—are sold in department stores and toy stores across the nation.

# Working As an Intern

**Y**ou'll be working as an intern at Carolina Critters. This involves working in each of the departments for a few weeks. Carolina Critters believes it is important for new employees to gain experience working in all areas of the company. In this "trial period" you have the opportunity to demonstrate your skills.

Carolina Critters expects that any incoming employee will have a solid foundation of skills.*

**Basic Skills**

Reading, writing, arithmetic/mathematics, listening, and speaking

**Thinking Skills**

Creative thinking, decision making, problem solving, being able to visualize problems and solutions, knowing how to learn, and reasoning

**Personal Qualities**

Responsibility, self-esteem, sociability, self-management, and integrity/honesty

## Keys to Successful Job-Performance*

**1. Resources: Identifies, organizes, plans, and allocates resources**

A. *Time*—Selects goal-relevant activities, ranks them, allocates time, and prepares and follows schedules

B. *Money*—Uses or prepares budgets, makes forecasts, keeps record, and makes adjustments to meet objectives

C. *Material and Facilities*—Acquires, stores, allocates, and uses materials or space efficiently

D. *Human Resources*—Assesses skills and distributes work accordingly, evaluates performance and provides feedback

**2. Interpersonal: Works with others**

A. *Participates as a Member of a Team*—Contributes to the group effort

B. *Teaches Others New Skills*

C. *Serves Clients/Customers*—Works to satisfy customers' expectations

D. *Exercises Leadership*—Communicates ideas to justify a position, persuades and convinces others, responsibly challenges existing procedures and policies

E. *Negotiates*—Works toward agreements involving exchanges of resources, resolves differing interests

F. *Works with Diversity*—Works well with men and women from diverse backgrounds

**3. Information: Acquires and uses information**

A. *Acquires and Evaluates Information*

B. *Organizes and Maintains Information*

C. *Interprets and Communicates Information*

D. *Uses Computers to Process Information*

**4. Systems: Understands complex relationships**

A. *Understands Systems*—knows how social, organizational, and technological systems work and operates effectively with them

B. *Monitors and Corrects Performance*—Distinguishes trends, predicts impacts on system operations, diagnoses systems' performance and corrects malfunctions

C. *Improves or Designs Systems*—Suggests modifications to existing systems and develops new or alternative systems to improve performance

**5. Technology: Works with a variety of technologies**

A. *Selects Technology*—Chooses procedures, tools or equipment including computers and related technologies

B. *Applies Technology to Task*—Understands overall intent and proper procedures for setup and operation of equipment

C. *Maintains and Troubleshoots Equipment*—Prevents, identifies, or solves problems with equipment, including computers and other technologies

* These skills and competencies were identified by the Secretary of Labor and the Secretary's Commission on Achieving Necessary Skills (SCANS). They are included in the report *What Work Requires of Schools: A SCANS Report for America 2000*, published in June, 1991, by the U.S. Department of Labor.

3

# CAROLINA CRITTERS

# Key People at Carolina Critters

In your work as an intern, you'll have a chance to meet many of the people who work at Carolina Critters, Inc. You will certainly interact with the four people profiled here. In fact, you'll be doing most of your work for James McCluskie, the Vice-President and Chief Financial Officer.

### James McCluskie
*Vice-President, Chief Financial Officer*

Hector Fuentes was President of Carolina Critters when Jim McCluskie started working in the Accounting Department almost 40 years ago. Jim remembers times in the Christmas season when everyone, including Hector Fuentes, was packing and shipping products to get them to market. Now a grandfather, Jim is looking forward to retirement when he and his wife, Ginny, can live year around in their cabin on Lake Norman, North Carolina.

### Lisa Fuentes
*President*

As Lisa says, "I've always worked at Carolina Critters." She formally started in the Sales Department when she was 23 years old. She became the Sales and Marketing Manager after three years, and took over from her father, Carlos, in 1994. Lisa is an avid outdoor person and can often be found on weekends riding her horse, Rusty, on trails in the Uwharrie National Forest.

### Frances Falcigno
*Sales and Marketing Manager*

Fran Falcigno took over for Lisa Fuentes as Sales and Marketing Manager in 1994. Before that,

Fran worked in the Sales Department and was based in New York. She loved the move to Charlotte and found that it provides her with ample opportunity to increase her collection of hand-crafted country quilts and vintage toys.

### Luis Gutierrez
*Manufacturing Manager*

Luis has been with Carolina Critters for over twenty years, working his way up through the Manufacturing Department. Before working at Carolina Critters, Luis had served in the Air Force. He still likes to fly and has been building and flying small reproduction aircraft as a hobby.

4

# Carolina Critters, Inc.

**Method
of
Manufacturing**

Carolina Critters, Inc. uses an unusual method of manufacturing. Carolina Critters doesn't buy each individual component for a stuffed animal (such as material for the outer shell, plastic joints for arms and legs, felt pads for paws, specially-made eyes, extruded plastic components for the nose or claws, clothes, stuffing, and so on). Instead, it has approached a small number of suppliers and contracted with them for "kits" containing all the pre-cut, pre-weighed, pre-formed materials required to manufacture a specific stuffed animal. For example, Robinson Mills, Inc., a supplier in Passaic, New Jersey, provides the kit for "Professor Bear" (pictured here with some of the components included in the kit).

# What is a Database?

A *database* is a collection of information (or "data") that is organized to make retrieving specific information easy. Access is a software application used to create and manage a computerized database. In Access, a database consists of the following elements (called "objects"): tables, queries, reports, forms, macros, and modules. The following diagram sketches out the relationships between the first four objects (which are discussed in this text).

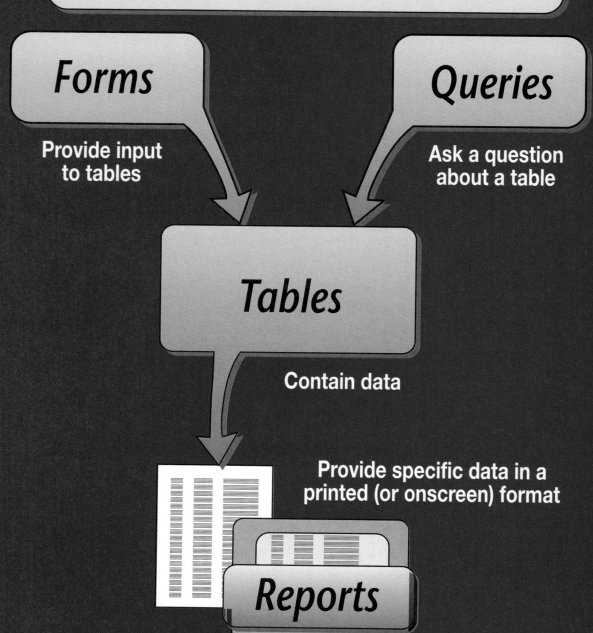

**Forms**

Provide input
to tables

**Queries**

Ask a question
about a table

**Tables**

Contain data

Provide specific data in a
printed (or onscreen) format

**Reports**

# The Carolina Critters Database

In this text you will be dealing with only one database—the database for Carolina Critters, Inc. In every unit of the text you will be using a slightly different version of the database. The diagram below shows some of the specific objects in the database you will be using for the last unit of the text.

## Forms

Employee Information Form
Kit Suppliers Form
New Customer Entry Form
Sales Campaigns Form
Sales Order Entry Main Form
Sales Order Entry Subform
Sales Review Main Form
Sales Review Subform

## Queries

Animals by Product Group
CC Invoice Main Query
CC Invoice Subreport Query
CC Payroll Main Query
CC Payroll Subreport Query
CC Product List Main Query
CC Product List Subreport Query
CC Sales Review Main Query

CC Sales Review Subreport Query
CC Shipments Main Query
CC Shipments Subreport Query
Delivery Dates
Employees by Job Code
Inventory by Animal
Order Summary by Animal

## Tables

Carriers
Customers
Employees
Job Codes
Kit Contents
Kit Suppliers
Payroll Information

Product Lines
Sales Campaigns
Sales Order Line Items
Sales Orders
Sales Representatives
Stuffed Animals

## Reports

CC Invoice Main Report
CC Payroll Main Report
CC Products Main Reports
CC Sales Review Main Report
CC Sales Review Subreport
CC Shipments Main Report
Current Customers
Current Kit Suppliers

Employees by Job Code
Employee's Date of Hire
Inventory Value
Kit Contents
Kit Costs
Order Summary
Sales Campaign
Stuffed Animal Products

# Preview

As you learn Microsoft Access, you'll be producing printouts of reports, tables, and forms. You'll learn all of the important Access features, from creating and editing tables, to developing forms and queries, and fine-tuning your reports for a professional appearance. By "working" as an intern at Carolina Critters, Inc., you'll gain experience that you can apply to real-world business.

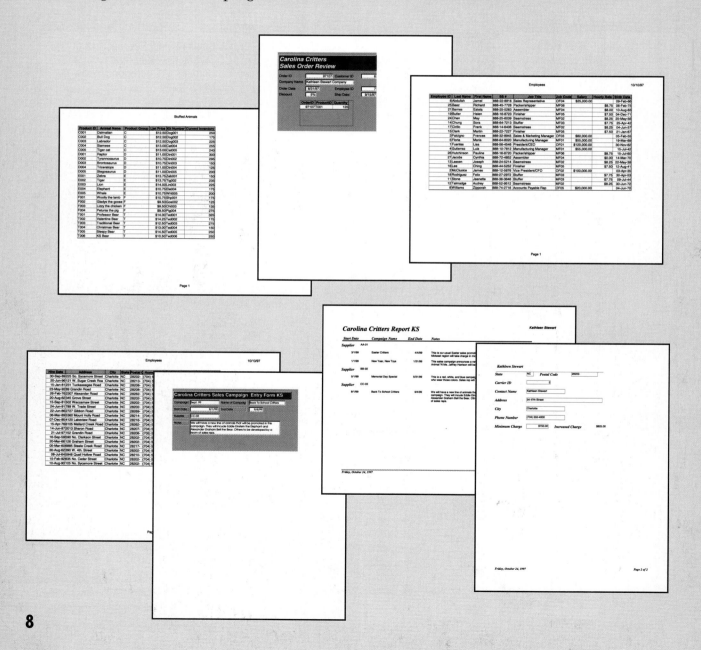

# Understanding Access Basics

LESSON

# 1

# Getting Started with a Database

OBJECTIVES

After completing this lesson, you will be able to:

1. Start Access and copy a database.
2. Identify parts of the Access screen.
3. Select objects in the Database window.
4. Open a table and navigate in the table.
5. Open multiple tables.
6. Edit records in a table.
7. Print a table.
8. Close a database and exit Access.

 Estimated Time: 1¾ hours

**M**icrosoft Access is *database software* that tracks information for businesses or individuals. It's included in Microsoft Office and is also available as a stand-alone program.

You use and are also part of many databases. The telephone book is a database that displays information about people, companies, associations, and other groups. You are part of your school's database because the school keeps track of when you enrolled, what courses you've taken, what grades you received, where you live, and other information.

Access is actually a specific type of database software called a *relational database management system* (RDBMS). In a relational database you eliminate duplication of data by specifying relationships between data. This allows you to compile and analyze data quickly and efficiently.

# *Starting Access*

An Access database can contain several different objects. (An *object* is an element of a database.) Database objects include tables, queries, reports, forms, macros, and modules. You use objects to store, display, select, or perform an action in your database.

In this lesson, you work with tables. *Tables* are the most basic database objects. (They are similar to a table in word processing or a worksheet in a program like Excel.) All the data in your database is stored in tables. Within each table, data is stored as a record. A *record* contains data about one thing (a person, for example, or a product) stored in a row in a table. Each data element within a record is called a *field*. Fields are stored in columns in a table.

Your school, for example, has a table of students' names, social security numbers, and addresses. A student's name, social security number, and address, collectively, is a record of information about a single student. A student's name, separately, is a field.

**FIGURE 1-1**
Tables, records, and fields

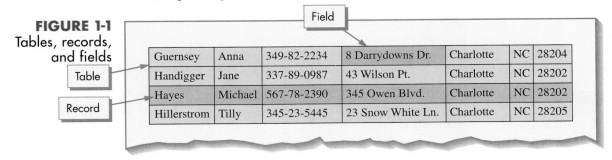

| Table | Record | | | | | | |
|---|---|---|---|---|---|---|---|
| Guernsey | Anna | 349-82-2234 | 8 Darrydowns Dr. | Charlotte | NC | 28204 |
| Handigger | Jane | 337-89-0987 | 43 Wilson Pt. | Charlotte | NC | 28202 |
| Hayes | Michael | 567-78-2390 | 345 Owen Blvd. | Charlotte | NC | 28202 |
| Hillerstrom | Tilly | 345-23-5445 | 23 Snow White Ln. | Charlotte | NC | 28205 |

Your school probably has another table that lists available courses. Another table might list which students are enrolled in which courses. All the information is not stored in one big table. Your school's database consists of small, manageable tables that are all somehow related. That's the basic concept of a relational database management system.

**EXERCISE** 1-1 **Start Access and Copy a Database**

**FIGURE 1-2**
Shortcut icon to start Access

Shortcut to
Msaccess.exe

There are several ways to start Access, depending on how your system is set up. For example, you can use the Windows 95 taskbar, the Microsoft Office Shortcut bar, My Computer, or Windows Explorer. If a shortcut is available to start Access, you can double-click the shortcut icon on your desktop.

 **NOTE:** Windows offers great flexibility in starting its applications. If you have problems, ask your instructor for help.

**1.** Turn on your computer. Windows 95 loads.

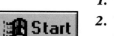

**2.** Using the left mouse button, click the Start button  on the Windows taskbar and point to Programs. The Programs menu appears.

**FIGURE 1-3**
Starting Access
from the Windows
taskbar

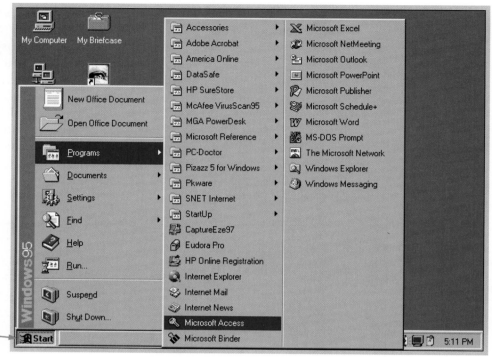

**3.** Click Microsoft Access. (You may have to point first to a program group that contains Microsoft Access, such as Microsoft Office.) In a few seconds, the program is loaded and the Access dialog box appears prompting you to create a new database or open an existing database.

**FIGURE 1-4**
When Access
starts, a dialog
box appears.

**4.** The dialog box may list several recently opened database names. Click to select More Files and click OK to see the default location for all databases.

**5.** The Open dialog box opens, showing the files available in your default folder. Locate the filename **CC1.mdb.**

**NOTE:** If the file CC1.mdb is not located in your default folder, ask your instructor where you can find the file. You may need to use the Look in drop-down box to go to the folder containing the file.

6. Once you locate the file, click once to select it. Then point at the selected filename, click the right mouse button, and choose Copy from the shortcut menu.

**NOTE:** Access automatically saves changes you make to data in a database. Since you will make changes throughout this course, you need a database that shows your changes. In this text, when you begin a unit you are told to copy a database template and rename the database using your initials. This distinguishes your database (and the changes you make to it) from the original and from other students' databases.

7. Move the pointer to an unused white area of the filename section of the Open dialog box, click the right mouse button, and choose Paste from the shortcut menu. A file named "Copy of CC1.mdb" appears.

**FIGURE 1-5**
Copying a database

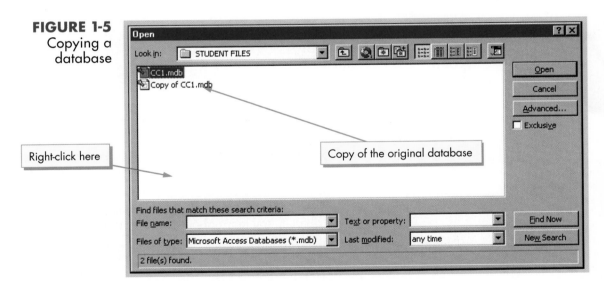

8. Select the filename **Copy of CC1.mdb**. Click the right mouse button and choose Rename from the shortcut menu. Key *[your initials]*CC1.mdb and press Enter.
9. Double-click *[your initials]*CC1.mdb to open the file. The Access screen and Database window appear. The Database window is the base for operations you perform when working with your database.

UNIT 1 ■ UNDERSTANDING ACCESS BASICS

**FIGURE 1-6**
Access screen

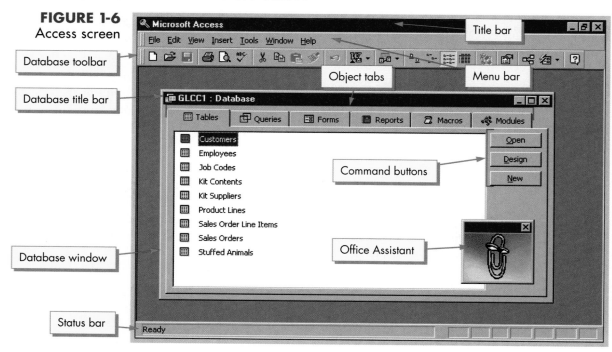

**TABLE 1-1** **Parts of the Access Screen**

| PART OF SCREEN | PURPOSE |
|---|---|
| Title bar | Contains the program name (Access). |
| Database title bar | Contains the name of the database (GL1CC1.mdb). |
| Menu bar | Displays the names of menus you use to perform various tasks. You can use the mouse or the keyboard to open menus. |
| Database toolbar | A row of buttons you use to execute commands with your mouse. Access opens with the Database toolbar displayed by default. You learn about the other toolbars later. |
| Database window | Displays a tab for each object in the database. It also includes Command buttons to Open or Design an existing object or create a New one. |
| Object tabs | Tabs for each type of object in the database. By selecting a tab, you can work with the database's tables, queries, forms, reports, macros, or modules. |
| Status bar | Displays information about the current task. Indicators on the status bar show the current mode of operation. |
| Office Assistant | Provides tips as you work and suggests Help topics related to the work you're doing. |

14

## EXERCISE 1-2 Display Database Properties

**1.** Move the pointer to <u>F</u>ile on the menu bar. Click the left mouse button to open the menu.

**FIGURE 1-7**
Properties dialog box–Contents tab

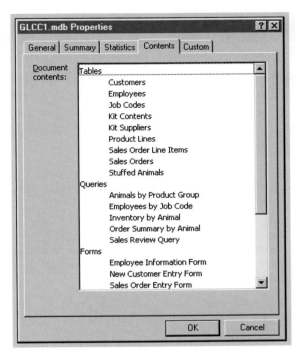

**TIP:** Navigating in Access is like navigating in Windows 95. (If you don't know how to use Windows 95, see Appendices A through E).

**2.** Move the pointer down to Database Proper<u>t</u>ies and click the left mouse button. This opens the Properties dialog box.

**3.** Click the Contents tab at the top of the dialog box to see a list of the tables, queries, forms, reports, macros, and modules in the current database.

**4.** Click OK to close the dialog box.

**TABLE 1-2** **Properties Dialog Box Tabs**

| TAB | PURPOSE |
|-----|---------|
| General | Contains the date the database was created, last modified, and last opened. Also contains the filename, size, location of the database, and attributes. |
| Summary | Displays the database title, author, company, category, key-words, and comments. |
| Statistics | Contains the date the database was created, last modified, printed, and last opened. |
| Contents | Displays a list of the tables, queries, forms, reports, macros, and modules that the database contains. |
| Custom | Used to assign a custom property for a file. You can add a name, type, and value for the custom property. |

# *Identifying Parts of the Access Screen*

Some parts of the Access screen, such as toolbar buttons, are identified by name when you point to them with the mouse.

**EXERCISE** **1-3** **Identify Buttons, Menus, and Menu Items**

**FIGURE 1-8**
Identifying a
toolbar button

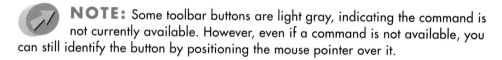

**1.** Position the pointer over the New Database button 🗋 on the Database toolbar. A *ScreenTip* (a box with the button name) appears below the button. You click this button to open a blank database or choose from a list of sample databases.

**2.** Move the mouse pointer (but don't click) over the Open Database button 🖼 on the toolbar. You click this button to open an existing database.

> **NOTE:** Some toolbar buttons are light gray, indicating the command is not currently available. However, even if a command is not available, you can still identify the button by positioning the mouse pointer over it.

**3.** Point to other toolbar buttons to identify them by name.

> **TIP:** The menu bar shows which commands have corresponding keyboard shortcuts. Keyboard shortcuts appear on the menu to the right of the menu command. (Your computer may also show the keyboard shortcut in the ScreenTip for a button.) Notice that you can print a table by choosing Print from the File menu, by clicking the Print button on the toolbar, or by pressing Ctrl+P.

**4.** Move the pointer to Edit on the menu bar and click the left mouse button. This opens the Edit menu. Click Edit to close the menu.

> **NOTE:** When you are told to "click" a menu option or a toolbar button, use the left mouse button. From this point forward, use the left mouse button unless you are told explicitly to use the right mouse button.

**5.** Click View to open the View menu. Without clicking the mouse button, move the pointer down to the Arrange Icons menu option. The right-pointing arrow indicates a cascading menu. This cascading menu displays options for arranging the icons in the Database window.

**FIGURE 1-9**
Displaying menu
options

**6.** Click a blank area of the screen to close the menu. Be careful not to click a menu option or toolbar button.

**7.** Hide the Office Assistant by clicking its Close button ⊠.

# Selecting Objects in the Database Window

When you open a database, the Database window appears within the Access program window. At the top of the Database window, notice the Object tabs. You use these tabs to choose the specific type of elements or objects in the database. When a tab is selected, you see the names of all the tables, queries, forms, and so on that are in the database. For example, if you select the Tables tab, all the tables in the database are displayed.

There are six types of objects in an Access database:

- *Tables* store information about a person, place, or thing. A table consists of record*s*, which contain fields that are used for data entry. The information in a table appears in rows (records) and columns (fields), similar to a spreadsheet.

- *Queries* are used to find answers to questions about a database. You can design queries to show only certain fields from one or more tables. You can specify criteria or conditions that must be met for a record to be included. You can use a query to calculate totals or averages from other information already in the table.

- *Forms* allow you to view, edit, or add records in a convenient and attractive way. You can design a form to look like a paper form so those who enter the data are already familiar with the layout. With most forms, you can usually see an entire record at one time.

- *Reports* are used to print data from a table or query on paper. You can group your data, calculate totals, apply different formats, and add graphics to make the report attractive and easy to read.

- *Macros* run a series of commands. You can write macros for repetitive activities and to automate the procedures you use most often.

- *Modules* contain Visual Basic for Applications (VBA) code. They are more sophisticated than macros.

# EXERCISE 1-4 View Table Properties

The Table Properties dialog box displays characteristics of a particular table, including the table name, the description, the date the file was created, and the last time the file was updated.

1. Click the Tables tab, if necessary. All the tables in the current database are shown.

2. Click to select the Customers table. Click the Properties button 🗗 on the right side of the Database toolbar to open the Customers Properties dialog box. Notice the date the file was created and modified. Also notice the description. In later lessons you learn how to change and add descriptions.

**FIGURE 1-10**
Customers
Properties
dialog box

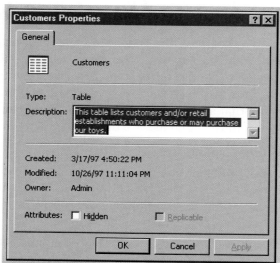

3. Click OK to close the dialog box.

4. Click the Employees table. Click the right mouse button and choose Properties from the shortcut menu. This opens the Employees Properties dialog box.

5. Click the Close button ☒ in the upper right corner of the Employees Properties dialog box to close the dialog box.

# EXERCISE 1-5 Datasheet and Design Views

Tables can be viewed in two ways:

● You can view a table in Datasheet View. This is the view that appears when you first open a table. This view resembles a spreadsheet with rows and columns. Each record is displayed in its own row. Each field of the record is shown in its own column. You can enter data, edit data, find records, resize rows and columns, and move rows and columns in Datasheet View.

● You can also view a table in Design View. This is the view you use to modify and create tables. The records in a table do not appear in this view; instead a grid appears listing the field names, the type of data contained in each field (for example, number, text, currency, and so on), and a description of the field. Design View also includes field properties, including formatting options, default values, validation rules, and other characteristics for each field in the table. (You find out more about data types and field properties in later lessons.)

1. Click the Tables tab, if necessary. Click the Customers table. Click the Open command button on the right side of the Database window. This opens the Customers table in Datasheet View. This view resembles a spreadsheet containing the customer records. Click the Maximize button ⬚ to maximize the table window.

**FIGURE 1-11**
Customers table
datasheet

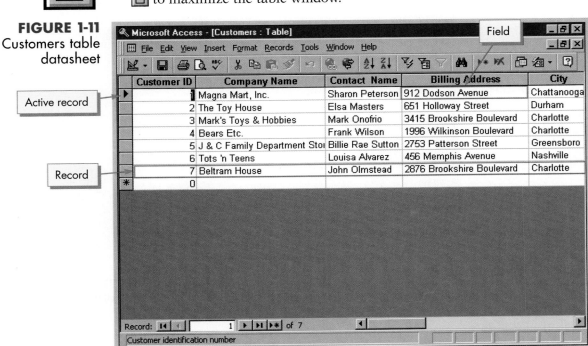

2. With the Customers datasheet displayed, click the down arrow of the View button 🔲 on the left side of the Database toolbar. The icon for the current view (Datasheet View) is indented.

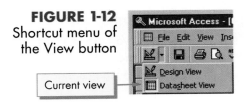

**FIGURE 1-12**
Shortcut menu of
the View button

3. Choose Design View from the shortcut menu. This displays the Customers table in Design View. Customer records don't appear in this view. This view shows the field names, data types, and descriptions. The field name (CustomerID, CompanyName, etc.) appears in the left column in Design View and at the top of each column in Datasheet View.

**TIP:** The buttons on the toolbar change depending on the view. Right--click in a blank area of the toolbar to open a shortcut menu that shows which toolbar is active. You can also access other toolbars from this menu. To close the shortcut menu, click outside the menu.

**FIGURE 1-13**
Customers table in
Design View

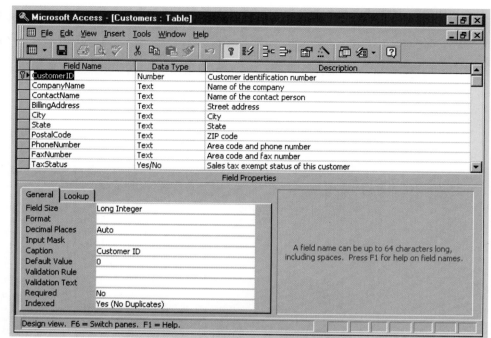

4. Choose Close from the File menu to close the Customers table.

5. Double-click Employees (or the table icon to the left of Employees). The Employees table opens in Datasheet View.

**NOTE:** Double-clicking a table's name or its table icon is another way to open a table.

6. Click the View button ![icon] (the button itself and not the down arrow). This displays the Employees table in Design View.

**NOTE:** The View button is a "toggle button" that you use to switch between Design and Datasheet Views. When there are two views for an object, you can click the icon to switch views. The face of the button changes depending on the current view.

7. Click the View button ![icon] again to return to Datasheet View.

# *Working with Tables*

In Access you can use the mouse, keyboard, and scroll bars to move the pointer in a table. You can also use navigation buttons to help you quickly move to a specific record.

● Scroll bars frame the right and lower borders of the table window. You can use the scroll bars to bring different parts of your table into view.

**NOTE:** When you scroll a window, you are simply changing what you see on the screen. You are not moving the pointer. The pointer marks where your next action will occur. To move the pointer you click the mouse button, use the navigation buttons, or press Tab or Enter.

● Navigation buttons are in the lower left corner of the table window. These buttons include First Record, Previous Record, Next Record, Last Record, and New Record.

## EXERCISE  1-6  Scroll Through a Table

*1.* If necessary, click the Maximize button ▢ to maximize the Employees table window in Datasheet View. In the vertical scroll bar, click below the scroll box to move down one screen. This action has the same effect as pressing PgDn.

**FIGURE 1-14**
Using scroll bars

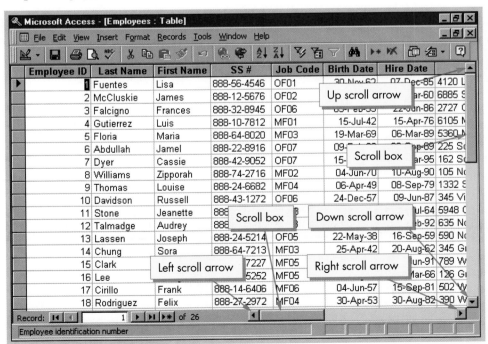

2. Drag the scroll box to the top of the vertical scroll bar.

3. Click the down scroll arrow on the scroll bar twice to move down two lines.

4. Click the right scroll arrow on the horizontal scroll bar once, then click the left scroll arrow once to return to the original horizontal position.

5. Click the up scroll arrow on the vertical scroll bar twice to bring the top of the table into full view. Notice that throughout this scrolling movement, the insertion point remains at the top of the table.

**TABLE 1-3**   **Scrolling Through a Table**

| TO MOVE THE INSERTION POINT | DO THIS |
| --- | --- |
| Up one line | Click the up scroll arrow. |
| Down one line | Click the down scroll arrow. |
| Up one screen | Click the scroll bar above the scroll box. |
| Down one screen | Click the scroll bar below the scroll box. |
| To any relative position | Drag the scroll bar up or down. |
| To the right | Click the right scroll arrow. |
| To the left | Click the left scroll arrow. |

# EXERCISE   1-7   Use Navigation Buttons

The navigation buttons are located in the lower left corner of a table window. You can use these buttons to move the pointer to a specific record, form, or page.

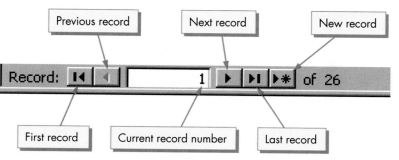

**FIGURE 1-15**
Navigation buttons

1. With the Employees table open, click the Next Record navigation button  once. This button appears as a right-pointing arrow. The next Employee ID is now highlighted. This button moves the pointer one record at a time.

2. Click the Previous Record button ◄ once. This button appears as a left-pointing arrow. The pointer moves to the previous record. This button moves one record at a time.

3. Click the Last Record button ▶|. This button appears as a right-pointing arrow with a vertical line to the right of the arrow. The pointer moves to the last record in the table.

4. Click the First Record button |◄. This button appears as a left-pointing arrow with a vertical line to the left of the arrow. The pointer moves to the first record in the table.

 **TIP:** Another way to move to a specific record is to double-click in the Specific Record box (between the navigation buttons), key the desired record number, and press Enter.

5. Click the Close button ⊠ to close the Employees table.

6. Open the Customers table and maximize the window, if necessary. Click the New Record button ▶*. This button appears as a right-pointing arrow with an asterisk to the right of the arrow. This moves the pointer to the end of the table to enter a new record.

7. As with most Windows programs, you can also use keyboard shortcuts with Access (see Table 1-4). For example, press Tab twice. This moves the pointer to the "Contact Name" field. Press Shift + Tab once. This moves the pointer back to the "Company Name" field.

**TABLE 1-4**   **Keyboard Navigation Shortcuts**

| PRESS | TO DO THIS |
| --- | --- |
| Tab | Move to the next field. |
| Shift + Tab | Move to the previous field. |
| PgUp | Move up one screen. |
| PgDn | Move down one screen. |
| Ctrl + Home | Return to the first record. |
| Ctrl + End | Move to the last record. |

**NOTE:** Whenever keyboard combinations (such as Ctrl + Delete ) are shown in this text, remember to hold down the first key without releasing it and press the second key. Release the second key and then release the first key. An example of the entire sequence is: Hold down Ctrl, press Delete, release Delete, and release Ctrl. With practice, this sequence becomes easy.

**EXERCISE** **1-8** **Increase and Decrease Column Widths**

To make your table easier to read, you can increase or decrease column widths. If a field heading or entry is longer than the column, you can adjust the column to accommodate the field heading or field entry. You can also make the column smaller if the field entry is small.

*1.* In the Customers table, place the pointer on the vertical border between the Company Name and Contact Name field names at the tops of the second and third columns. Notice the pointer changes to a double-headed arrow with a wide vertical bar.

**FIGURE 1-16**
Resizing columns

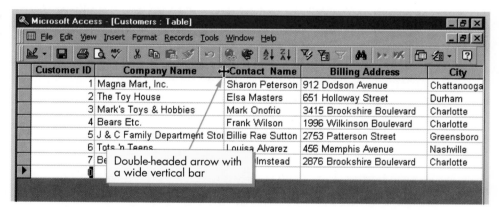

*2.* Drag the pointer to the right until there is enough space for the word "Stores." Release the button.

 **TIP:** You can automatically adjust the width of the left column to the widest text by double-clicking the border between the field names (column titles).

*3.* Place the pointer between the Billing Address and City field names. Use the scroll bars to bring the columns into view, if necessary.

*4.* When the pointer changes to a double-headed arrow with a wide vertical bar, drag the pointer to the left making the Address column smaller until it just accommodates the longest Billing Address.

**TIP:** The layout of a table is the way it appears on the screen. It includes the size of the columns, the height of the rows, the fonts, the arrangement of the columns, colors, and other settings.

**5.** Close the Customers table. A dialog box appears prompting you to save the layout of the Customers table. Click <u>Y</u>es to accept the changes.

**EXERCISE** **1-9** **Freeze Fields in a Table**

Most tables contain more fields than you can view at one time, so you need to scroll the window often. If there is a field that you want to see on screen all the time, you can freeze that field at the left edge of the screen.

**1.** Open the Employees table in Datasheet View and maximize the window, if necessary.

**2.** Move the pointer to the Employee ID title. When the pointer changes to a down-pointing arrow, left click. The column is selected.

**TIP:** To select more than one column, select the first column, then press and hold [Shift] while clicking the other column.

**3.** Choose Free<u>z</u>e Columns from the <u>F</u>ormat menu. Then click anywhere in the table to deselect the column. Notice that the right vertical border of the frozen column is slightly heavier than the other vertical lines.

**4.** Click the right scroll arrow several times. The Employee ID column doesn't scroll.

**5.** To unfreeze all the columns, choose Unfreeze <u>A</u>ll Columns from the <u>F</u>ormat menu.

**6.** Select the SS# column by clicking the SS# title when the pointer is a down-pointing arrow.

**7.** Choose Free<u>z</u>e Columns from the <u>F</u>ormat menu. The SS# column moves to the left edge of the table.

**8.** Click the right scroll arrow several times. The SS# column doesn't scroll.

**9.** Choose Unfreeze <u>A</u>ll Columns from the <u>F</u>ormat menu.

**10.** Close the Employees table. A dialog box appears prompting you to save the layout of the Employees table The layout now shows the SS# field at the left edge. Click <u>N</u>o.

**NOTE:** If you freeze a column other than the first column, Access moves that column to the first column on the left. If you do not save the layout when you close the table, the columns return to their original position.

# *Working with Multiple Tables*

You can open more than one table so you can compare or contrast data in those tables. When you work with multiple tables, you can tile the windows to better see the data.

**EXERCISE** **1-10** **Open Multiple Tables**

1. Open the Customers table.
2. Choose *[your initials]***CC1** Database from the <u>W</u>indow menu. This returns you to the Database window.
3. Open the Employees table.

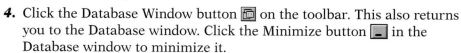

4. Click the Database Window button 🔳 on the toolbar. This also returns you to the Database window. Click the Minimize button 🔳 in the Database window to minimize it.
5. Choose Ti<u>l</u>e Horizontally from the <u>W</u>indow menu. The two tables now appear tiled horizontally on the screen.

**FIGURE 1-17**
Tables appear
tiled horizontally.

Minimized
Database
window

6. Close the Customers and Employees tables.
7. Click the Restore button 🔳 in the minimized Database window.

# *Editing Records in a Table*

Access saves changes to a record as soon as you move the insertion point away from the record. If you move to the next record, your changes are saved. If you move to the previous record, your changes are saved. You generally do not need to use the Save command when you edit or add records. To save the data in a record while you are editing it, click Save Record on the Records menu.

You can determine if a record was saved by the shape of the Record Selector. The Record Selector marks the current record or where the insertion point is located. The Record Selector has three shapes.

- A pencil appears when you add or edit text. This indicates the record has not been saved.

- A triangle indicates the record has been saved.

- An asterisk always appears to mark the new record as the last record in the table.

**EXERCISE** ▌1-11▐ **Delete Text**

With basic text editing, as with most tasks in Access, keyboard shortcuts are available. Table 1-5 summarizes the keyboard shortcuts you may find most helpful.

**TABLE 1-5**   **Basic Text Editing**

| KEY | RESULT |
|---|---|
| Backspace | Deletes characters to the left of the insertion point. |
| Ctrl + Backspace | Deletes the word to the left of the insertion point. |
| Delete | Deletes characters to the right of the insertion point. |
| Ctrl + Delete | Deletes all the characters to the right of the insertion point to the end of the line. |

1. Open the Employees table in Datasheet View and maximize the window, if necessary.

2. In the Employees table, move the insertion point to the right of the last name for Employee #8 "Williams." (Use the mouse to position the I-beam and click to place the insertion point.)

3. Press Backspace five times to delete five characters and key **son**. Notice the Record Selector changes to a pencil symbol when you edit text. "Williams" is changed to "Wilson."

**FIGURE 1-18**
Record Selector

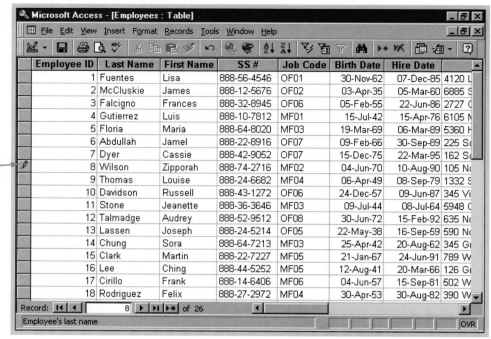

Pencil

**4.** Use the scroll bar to view the Address field. In Employee #2's record, move the insertion point between the "6" and the "8" in the Address field.

**5.** Press Delete once and key **1**. The "6885" changes to "6185"

**6.** In Employee #5's record, move the insertion point to the left of the word "Holly" in the Address field.

**7.** Press Ctrl+Backspace (hold down Ctrl and press Backspace). The words "Holly Road" remain.

**8.** In Employee #13's record, move the insertion point to the right of "Clarkson" in the Address field.

**9.** Press Ctrl+Delete to delete "Street." Press the spacebar once and key **Road**.

## EXERCISE 1-12 Insert Text

When editing a table, you can insert text or use Overtype mode to key over existing text. Use Insert to switch between Insert and Overtype mode.

**1.** With the Employees table open, scroll the table so you can see the Employee ID and Last Name fields.

**2.** In Employee #9's record, move the insertion point to the right of "s" in "Thomas" in the Last Name field. Key a hyphen, then key **Smith**. When you are adding the second name, part of the first name may scroll out of view. Don't worry, the data is still there.

3. In Employee #10's record, move the insertion point to the left of "Russell" in the First Name field.

4. Press ⌈Insert⌉ to switch to Overtype mode. You know you are in Overtype mode when the letters "OVR" appear on the status bar.

**FIGURE 1-19**
Overtype mode

Overtype mode indicator

5. Key **Raymond** over the old text.

6. Close the Employees table.

7. Open the Customers table in Datasheet View. You are still in Overtype mode.

8. In the "Bears Etc." record, move the insertion point to the left of "Frank Wilson" in the Contact Name field.

9. Key *[your first name & last name]* over the old text. Delete extra characters, if necessary.

 **NOTE:** By keying your actual first and last name in this field, your table will be differentiated from other students when it is printed. In this text you are often asked to key a unique identifier such as your name or initials in a particular field so you can identify your material when it is printed.

 **TIP:** When using Overtype mode, you may have to delete extra characters from the previous entry if the entries are not the same length.

10. Press ⌈Insert⌉ to turn off Overtype mode.

# *Printing a Table*

Once you create a table, it's easy to print it. You can use any of these methods:
- Click the Print button 🖶 on the Database toolbar
- Choose <u>P</u>rint from the <u>F</u>ile menu
- Press ⌈Ctrl⌉+⌈P⌉

The menu and keyboard methods open the Print dialog box, where you choose printing options. Clicking 🖶 sends the document directly to the printer, using Access's default settings. It doesn't open the Print dialog box.

## EXERCISE 1-13 Change Page Setup

**FIGURE 1-20**
Page Setup dialog box with default margin settings

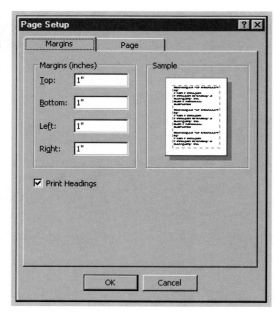

**FIGURE 1-21**
Page Setup dialog box - Page tab

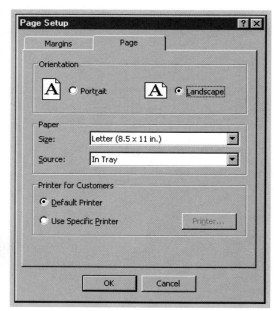

When printing tables, you can set the print layout or page orientation to portrait (vertical) or landscape (horizontal). Landscape orientation is often useful if a table contains many fields and you want to fit the table on one printed page.

1. With the Customers table open, choose Page Setup from the File menu to open the Page Setup dialog box. The Margins tab opens by default. This dialog box displays the default margin settings.

2. Click the Page tab. This dialog box displays the orientation, paper, and printer default settings.

3. Click the Landscape option button. Click OK to close the dialog box.

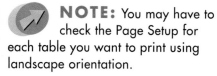 **NOTE:** You may have to check the Page Setup for each table you want to print using landscape orientation.

4. Click the Print Preview button 📷 to see how your table will print. You can also see how many pages will print. See Figure 1-22 on the next page.

5. Click the Next Page button ▶.

**FIGURE 1-22**
Preview of
Customers table

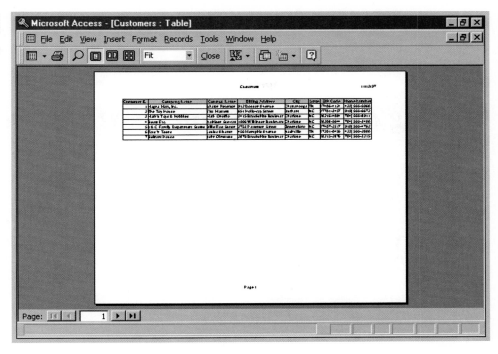

**NOTE:** Access *tiles* pages when tables are too wide for the printed page. This means only the columns that fit on a page print on that page. Columns are not cut in the middle.

*6.* Click <u>C</u>lose to return to the Customers table.

**EXERCISE 1-14 Print a Table**

**FIGURE 1-23**
Print dialog box

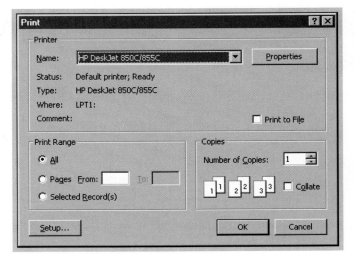

*1.* To print the Customers table, choose <u>P</u>rint from the <u>F</u>ile menu. The Print dialog box appears, displaying the Access default settings and showing your designated printer.

**2.** Click OK or press ⌨Enter⌨ to accept the settings. A printer icon appears on the taskbar as the table is sent to the printer.

**3.** Close the Customers table.

# Closing a Database and Exiting Access

When you finish working on a database, you can close it and open another database or you can exit the program.

There are four ways to close a database and exit Access:

- Use the Close buttons ⊠ in the upper right corner of the window.

**FIGURE 1-24**
Close buttons

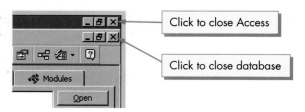

- Use the <u>F</u>ile menu.
- Use the Database Control icon, located in the **upper left corner of the window.** Then choose <u>C</u>lose from the **Database Control menu.**

**FIGURE 1-25**
Control menu

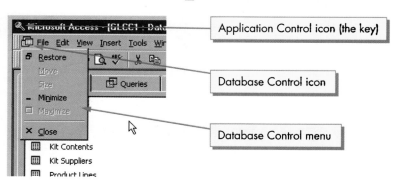

- Use keyboard shortcuts. ⌨Ctrl⌨+⌨W⌨ or ⌨Ctrl⌨+⌨F4⌨ closes a database and ⌨Alt⌨+⌨F4⌨ exits Access.

**EXERCISE** **1-15** **Close a Database and Exit Access**

**1.** Choose <u>C</u>lose from the <u>F</u>ile menu to close the database.

**NOTE:** When no database is open, there is no Database window on the screen. If you want to start a new database, you can click the New Database button 🗋.

**2.** Click the Close button ⊠ in the upper right corner of the screen to exit Access and display the Windows desktop.

**COMMAND SUMMARY**

| FEATURE | BUTTON | MENU | KEYBOARD |
|---|---|---|---|
| Open | 🖼 | File, Open Database | Ctrl + O |
| Database Properties | | File, Database Properties | |
| Table Properties | 🗗 | View, Properties | Alt + Enter |
| Table View | 📖 | View, Datasheet View | |
| Column Width | | Format, Column Width | |
| Freeze Columns | | Format, Freeze Columns | |
| Unfreeze Columns | | Format, Unfreeze All Columns | |
| Tile Windows | | Window, Tile Horizontally | |
| | | Window, Tile Vertically | |
| Page Setup | | File, Page Setup | |
| Save | 💾 | File, Save | Ctrl + S |
| Print Preview | 🔍 | File, Print Preview | |
| Print | 🖨 | File, Print | Ctrl + P |
| Close a document | ⊠ | File, Close | Ctrl + W or Ctrl + F4 |
| Exit Access | ⊠ | File, Exit | Alt + F4 |

**USING HELP**

The Office Assistant is your guide to Access online Help. The Office Assistant provides tips based on the kind of work you're doing and directs you to relevant Help topics. It may amuse you with its animated movements. If you find it annoying, you can hide it or choose another character.

**Get acquainted with the Office Assistant:**

1. Start Access, if necessary. Click Cancel in the opening Access dialog box.
2. If the Office Assistant is not displayed, click the Office Assistant button  on the toolbar.
3. If necessary, click the Office Assistant figure for a balloon with the question "What would you like to do?"
4. Key **How do I use Office Assistant?** in the text box and click <u>S</u>earch. The Office Assistant locates Help topics related to your question.
5. Review the displayed topics and click "See More" to display additional related topics.
6. Click the topic "Ways to get assistance while you work." An Access Help window with the same topic is displayed. This window provides a general overview of Help.

**FIGURE 1-26**
Getting Help while you work

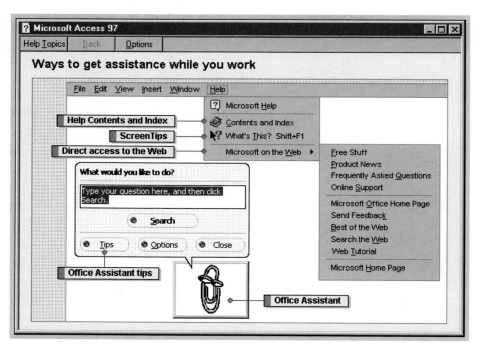

7. Click the topic Office Assistant to display a descriptive box. Review the description and then click the box to close it. Click the topic Office Assistant tips and review the description.
8. Explore other topics in the Help window. Click the window's close button to close Help. Close the Office Assistant.

# Concepts Review

**Each of the following statements is either true or false. Indicate your choice by circling either T or F.**

T  F  *1.* You can only open one table at a time.

T  F  *2.* The Record Selector is a triangle if the record has been saved.

T  F  *3.* The pencil symbol appears only when you add text to a table.

T  F  *4.* You can use the navigation buttons to move to a specific record.

T  F  *5.* Records in a table don't appear in Datasheet View.

T  F  *6.* Pressing Delete deletes characters to the left of the insertion point.

T  F  *7.* The records in a table do not appear in the Design View of the table.

T  F  *8.* Freezing fields allows you to lock fields to keep the fields in view.

**Write the correct answer in the space provided.**

*1.* What menu and menu option open the Print dialog box?

_____

*2.* Which buttons do you use to quickly move to different records in a table?

_____

*3.* Which view displays the records in columns and rows like a spreadsheet?

_____

*4.* What menu contains the command to freeze fields in columns?

_____

*5.* Which navigation button do you use to move to the end of a table and add a record?

_____

**6.** Which navigation button would move you to Record #2 if you are currently at Record #3?

_____

**7.** What dialog box contains the description, creation date, and modification date for a table?

_____

**8.** Which view displays the field names, data types, and field properties?

_____

## CRITICAL THINKING

**Answer these questions on a separate page. There are no right or wrong answers. Support your answers with examples from your own experience, if possible.**

**1.** When editing a table, you can use either Insert or Overtype mode. When would it be more efficient to use Insert mode? When would it be more efficient to use Overtype mode? For everyday use, which mode do you prefer? Why?

**2.** Navigation buttons move you to a specific record. What are the advantages of using the navigation buttons instead of the scroll bars? When would it be more advantageous to use the scroll bars?

# Skills Review

## EXERCISE 1-16

**Identify parts of the Access screen.**

**1.** Start Access by following these steps:

   **a.** Click the Start button 🏁 Start on the Windows taskbar.

   **b.** Point to <u>P</u>rograms and click Microsoft Access (you may have to point first to the program group that contains Microsoft Access).

**2.** Locate your file, *[your initials]*CC1.mdb, and double-click to open it.

**3.** Move the pointer to the Open Database button 📂 and display the button's name. Point to the Print Preview button 🔍 to identify it.

**4.** Click <u>F</u>ile on the menu bar. Move the pointer down the File menu without clicking the mouse button. Notice the cascading menu for the Get External <u>D</u>ata option.

5. Close the menu by clicking <u>F</u>ile on the menu bar or by clicking in a blank area of the screen.

## Select objects in a Database window and navigate in a table.

1. View the Table Properties dialog box by following these steps:
   a. Click the Employees table.
   b. Click the right mouse button.
   c. Choose Properties from the shortcut menu.
   d. Click OK to close the dialog box.

2. Change from Datasheet View to Design View by following these steps:
   a. Double-click the Customers table to open it.
   b. Click the View button 🔲 once to change to Design View.
   c. Click the View button 🔲 again to return to Datasheet View.
   d. Click the Close button ⊠ in the upper right corner of the table window to close the Customers table.

3. Navigate in a table by following these steps:
   a. Open the Employees table.
   b. Click the Maximize button 🔲.
   c. Drag the scroll box on the vertical scroll bar to the bottom of the scroll bar.
   d. Click the up scroll arrow on the scroll bar twice to move up two lines.
   e. On the vertical scroll bar, click above the scroll box.
   f. Click the Next Record navigation button ▶ twice to move the pointer forward two records.
   g. Click the Previous Record button ◀ once to move back one record.
   h. Click the Last Record button ▶| to move to the last record in the table.
   i. Click the First Record button |◀ to move to the first record in the table.

4. Increase and decrease column widths by following these steps:
   a. Place the pointer on the vertical border between the Last Name and First Name field names.
   b. Drag the pointer to the right until all the last names fit in the column.
   c. Place the pointer between the Birth Date and Hire Date field names.
   d. Drag the pointer to the left making the Birth Date column smaller, until the column just accommodates the Birth Date title.

*e.* Close the Employees table.

   *f.* When the dialog box appears, click Yes to accept the changes to the layout.

**5.** Freeze fields in a table by following these steps:

   *a.* Open the Customers table.

   *b.* Click the Customer ID field name. Press and hold Shift and click the Company Name field name.

   *c.* Choose Freeze Columns from the Format menu.

   *d.* Scroll to view the Fax Number field.

   *e.* To unfreeze the columns, choose Unfreeze All Columns from the Format menu.

   *f.* Close the Customers table. Click No in the dialog box asking if you want to save changes to the layout.

## EXERCISE 1-18

## Open multiple tables and edit records in a table.

**1.** Open multiple tables by following these steps:

   *a.* Open the Kit Suppliers table.

   *b.* Choose *[your initials]***CC1**: Database from the Window menu.

   *c.* Open the Kit Contents table.

   *d.* Click the Database Window button 🔳. Click the Minimize button 🔳 to minimize the Database window.

   *e.* Choose Tile Horizontally from the Window menu.

   *f.* Close the Kit Supplies and Kit Contents tables.

   *g.* Click the Restore button 🔳 for your Database window.

**2.** Delete text in a table by following these steps:

   *a.* Open the Customers table and maximize the window. Move the insertion point to the right of "Wilkinson" in the Billing Address of "Bears Etc."

   *b.* Hold down Ctrl and press Delete to delete "Boulevard." Add a space and key **Avenue**

   *c.* Move the insertion point between the "l" and "s" in "Elsa Masters" in the Contact Name for "The Toy House."

   *d.* Press Delete once and key **l**. "Elsa" is changed to "Ella."

   *e.* Move the insertion point to the left of the "C" in "J & C Family Department Stores" in the Company Name field.

   *f.* Press Ctrl + Backspace to delete "J &." Key **K** and add a space.

3. Insert text in a table by following these steps:

   *a.* Move the insertion point to the right of the "t" in "Magna Mart, Inc." in the Company Name field.

   *b.* Press [Insert] to switch to Overtype mode.

   *c.* Press the spacebar to add a space and then key **Corporation** over the old text.

   *d.* Press [Insert] again to turn off Overtype mode.

   *e.* Close the Customers table and save the layout, if prompted.

## EXERCISE 1-19

### Print a table, close a database, and exit Access.

1. Open the Employees table and maximize the window, if necessary.

2. Click the Last Record button [▶|]. Switch to Overtype mode.

3. Move to the Last Name field and key *[your last name]* over the text. Delete any remaining characters.

4. Move to the First Name field and key *[your first name]* over the text. Delete any remaining characters. Turn off Overtype mode.

5. Change page orientation by following these steps:

   *a.* Choose Page Setup from the File menu.

   *b.* Click the Page tab.

   *c.* Click the Landscape option button.

   *d.* Click OK to close the dialog box.

6. Preview your table before printing by following these steps:

   *a.* Click the Print Preview button [🔍].

   *b.* Click the Next Page button [▶].

   *c.* Click Close to return to the Employees table.

7. Print a table by following these steps:

   *a.* Choose Print from the File menu.

   *b.* Click OK or press [Enter] to accept the settings.

   *c.* Close the Employees table.

8. Close the database and exit Access by following these steps:

   *a.* Choose Close from the File menu to close the database.

   *b.* Click the Close button [✕] to exit Access.

# Lesson Applications

**Start Access, add a properties description, and edit text in a table. Print a table.**

1. Start Access, if necessary, and open your database file.
2. Open the Properties dialog box for the Kit Suppliers table.
3. Key the following Description:

   **Table contains the supplier name, contact, address, and phone number of the companies supplying kits for Carolina Critters.**

4. Click OK to close the dialog box.
5. Open the Kit Suppliers table and make the corrections shown in Figure 1-27. Key your name as the Contact Name for Robinson Mills, Inc. (Not all the columns of the table appear in the following figure.)

    **TIP:** You may want to adjust the column width of the Contact Name column when changing data in that field.

**FIGURE 1-27**

| Suppli | Supplier Name | Contact Name | Address | City | Postal Code |
|---|---|---|---|---|---|
| AA-01 | Mills Fabric & Notion Supply | Mary Smith | 1642 Industrial Drive | McHenry | 60050- *1642* |
| BB-02 | Laramie Fabric Works | John Anders | ~~1019~~ Grant Street | Denver | 80203- *2218* |
| CC-03 | ~~Colby~~ Manufacturing ~~Company~~ *Inc.* | Perry Johnson | 625 E. South Street | Raleigh | 27601- *0625* |
| DD-04 | Robinson Mills, Inc. | ~~Susan Aldona~~ | 481 Lafayette Avenue | Passaic | 07055- *0481* |

*(Handwritten corrections: Waterman over Mary; Peter over John; Kay over Perry; 2218; Cosby over Colby; Your Name replacing Susan Aldona)*

6. Change the page orientation to Landscape.
7. Print the table and close it. Save changes to the layout.

**Open multiple tables. Edit text and adjust columns.**

1. Open the Stuffed Animals table.
2. Open the Product Lines table.
3. Minimize the Database window and tile the two tables horizontally.

4. Look at the two tables. What product line is a "Tiger?" What product line is "Woolly the Lamb?" Write your answer on a separate sheet of paper.

 **TIP:** Line Code and Product Group are the same thing.

5. Close the Stuffed Animals table.

6. In the Product Lines table, make the Line Code column smaller to accommodate the column title. Close and save the layout of the table.

7. Restore the Database window.

8. Open the Kit Contents table.

9. Make the Kit Number, Supplier, and Cost columns smaller to accommodate the column titles.

10. Change to Design View. What kind of data type is the Cost field? Write your answer on the same piece of paper you used for your answers in step 4.

11. Close and save the layout of the table. Write your name on your answer sheet and turn it in to your instructor.

## EXERCISE 1-22

### Edit and print a table.

1. Open the Sales Orders table and make the corrections shown in Figure 1-28.

**FIGURE 1-28**

*9/10/98*    *9/20/98*

| Order ID | Customer ID | Employee ID | Order Date | Ship Date | Discount |
|----------|-------------|-------------|------------|-----------|----------|
| 97101 | 1 | 6 | 9/ 9/98 | 9/17/98 | 10% ~~5%~~ |
| 97102 | 2 | 7 | 9/24/98 | 10/ 1/98 | 10% |
| 97103 | 5 | 7 | ~~10/14/98~~ | ~~10/21/98~~ | 15% ~~0%~~ |
| 97104 | 4 | 7 ~~6~~ | 10/23/98 | 11/ 1/98 | 5% ~~0%~~ |
| 97105 | 3 | 6 | ~~12/24/98~~ | ~~12/28/98~~ | 2% |

*1/2/99*

*Your Birthday in 1999*

 **NOTE:** You must enter percents as decimals (for example, key 5% as **.05**; 10% as **.1**).

2. Preview the table.

3. Print the table and close it.

**EXERCISE 1-23**

## Edit and print a table.

1. Open the Employees table.
2. Make the Postal Code column larger to accommodate the column title.
3. Add the entries shown in Figure 1-29. (Not all the columns of the table appear in the following figure.)

FIGURE 1-29

| Employee ID | Last Name | First Name | City | State | Postal Code |
|---|---|---|---|---|---|
| 1 | Fuentes | Lisa | Charlotte | NC | 28216- 1933 |
| 2 | McCluskie | James | Charlotte | NC | 28217- 5324 |
| 3 | Falcigno | Frances | Charlotte | NC | 28269- 3024 |
| 4 | Gutierrez | Luis | Charlotte | NC | 28262- 2202 |
| 5 | Floria | Maria | Charlotte | NC | 28214- 1807 |
| 6 | Abdullah | Jamel | Charlotte | NC | 28202- 1121 |
| 7 | Dyer | Cassie | Charlotte | NC | 28208- 4411 |
| 8 | Williams | Zipporah | Charlotte | NC | 28202- 1141 |
| 9 | Thomas-Smith | Louise | Charlotte | NC | 28205- 2546 |
| 10 | Davidson | Russell | Charlotte | NC | 28202- 1051 |
| 11 | Stone | Jeanette | Charlotte | NC | 28210- 5006 |
| 12 | Talmadge | Audrey | Charlotte | NC | 28202- 1212 |
| 13 | Lassen | Joseph | Charlotte | NC | 28202- 1216 |
| 14 | Chung | Sora | Charlotte | NC | 28202- 1114 |
| 15 | Clark | Martin | Charlotte | NC | 28202- 1337 |
| 16 | Lee | Ching | Charlotte | NC | 28202- 1330 |
| 17 | Cirillo | Frank | Charlotte | NC | 28202- 1133 |
| 18 | Rodriguez | Felix | Charlotte | NC | 28202- 1548 |
| 19 | Butler | Helen | Charlotte | NC | 28208- 4454 |
| 20 | Abrams | Sidney | Charlotte | NC | 28216- 5572 |
| 21 | Barnes | Estela | Charlotte | NC | 28208- 4417 |
| 22 | Fishman | Norman | Charlotte | NC | 28202- 1321 |
| 23 | Fernandez | Victor | Charlotte | NC | 28202- 1044 |
| 24 | Chen | May | Charlotte | NC | 28262- 9712 |
| 25 | Baez | Richard | Charlotte | NC | 28213- 6649 |
| 26 | Hutchinson | Pauline | Charlotte | NC | 28207- 2642 |

4. Change the page orientation to Landscape and print the table.
5. Close the table and save the layout.
6. Exit Access.

# Adding and Editing Data

## LESSON 2

**OBJECTIVES**

After completing this lesson, you will be able to:

1. Add and delete records in a table.
2. Copy and paste records in a table.
3. Add and delete records in a form.
4. Change views in a form.
5. Print a form.
6. Edit records in a form.

 Estimated Time: 1½ hours

In Lesson 1, you were introduced to tables, one of the objects in a database. In this lesson you are introduced to forms, another database object. Forms, like tables, allow you to enter and view information. Forms differ from tables because information is displayed in a way that is easy to read.

In this lesson, you learn how to add and edit data in tables and forms. You use the copy and paste commands to copy data from one record to another, saving time and ensuring accuracy.

## Adding and Deleting Records in Tables

Access makes it easy to add records to a table or to remove records that are no longer necessary. For example, when a new student is enrolled in your school, a record has to be added to your school's database. If a course is no longer offered, the school may be able to delete the course from its list of courses.

# EXERCISE  2-1  Add Records to a Table

You can add records to a table in Datasheet View. At the end of the table a blank new record is marked by an asterisk in the Record Selector. You can move to this new record by clicking the New Record navigation button ▶✱ or the New Record button ▶✱ on the toolbar.

You can also enter records using the Data Entry command. You do not see the other records in the table.

1. Open Access, if necessary. Open the *[your initials]*CC1.mdb database.

2. Open the Customers table and maximize the window. Click the New Record navigation button ▶✱. The triangular arrow called the *record pointer* indicates the current record.

3. Key the following to create a new record, pressing Tab between field entries:

Customer ID:　　　　**8**

Company Name:　　　**ABC Toys, Inc.**

**FIGURE 2-1**
Pencil icon appears in the Record Selector when adding a record

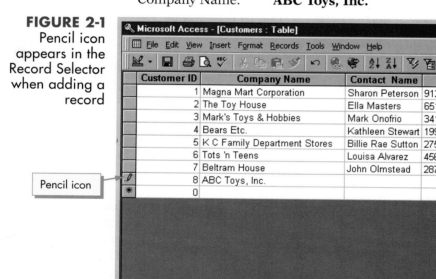

Contact Name:　　　**Suzanne Parker**
Billing Address:　　**9218 Park West Boulevard**
City:　　　　　　　**Knoxville**
State:　　　　　　　**TN**

|  |  |
|---|---|
| Postal Code: | **39723-9218** |
| Phone Number: | **(423) 555-1897** |
| Fax Number: | **(423) 555-1899** |

 **NOTE:** Access formats some fields for you automatically. For example, you don't have to key the hyphen in the Postal Code field or the parentheses, space, or hyphen in phone numbers. Characters that you don't have to key are shown in blue.

**4.** The Tax Exempt field is a Yes/No field. When you leave it blank, it means "No." Press Tab to leave it blank. Access saves the entry and moves the record pointer to the next row so you can add another record.

**5.** Choose Data Entry from the Records menu. Key the following to add another record:

|  |  |
|---|---|
| Customer ID: | 9 |
| Company Name: | **Children's Hospital** |
| Contact Name: | **Paul Scheider** |
| Billing Address: | **5274 West First Avenue** |
| City: | **Durham** |
| State: | **NC** |
| Postal Code: | **27702-5274** |
| Phone Number: | **(919) 555-1000** |
| Fax Number: | **(919) 555-1050** |
| Tax Exempt?: | *Click the box for a check mark to indicate "Yes" and press* Tab. |

 **NOTE:** In this text, *red italic* indicates a keying instruction related to a specific field.

**6.** Choose Remove Filter/Sort from the Records menu to view all records.

## EXERCISE 2-2 Delete Records from a Table

As you are working with your table, you may want to delete records you no longer need.

**1.** In the Customers table, click the Record Selector to select the row for "Mark's Toys & Hobbies."

**FIGURE 2-2**
Dialog box
confirming deletion

**2.** Press Delete. A dialog box
appears prompting you to
confirm the deletion.

**NOTE:** You cannot undo a
deleted record.

**3.** Click Yes. Access deletes the
record and saves the table.

**4.** Click anywhere in the Company Name field for "K C Family Department
Stores" to move the insertion point.

**5.** Choose Delete Record from the Edit menu. Click Yes to confirm the
deletion.

**6.** Close the Customers table.

# Using AutoCorrect, Copy, and Paste

Access corrects commonly misspelled words automatically as you key text,
correcting "teh," for example, to "the." However, the AutoCorrect feature does
more than just correct misspellings.

**EXERCISE** **2-3** **Correct Errors with AutoCorrect**

**FIGURE 2-3**
AutoCorrect
dialog box

AutoCorrect options

Words that are
corrected
automatically

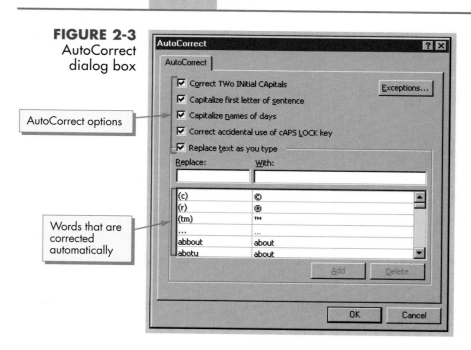

**1.** Choose AutoCorrect
from the Tools menu
and look at the
options available in
the AutoCorrect
dialog box.

**2.** Scroll down the list
of entries and notice
the words that
Access corrects
automatically. Make
sure the Replace Text
as You Type option is
checked.

**NOTE:** Microsoft Office products share AutoCorrect, so changes you make in Access affect Word and Excel.

**TABLE 2-1** AutoCorrect Options

| OPTIONS | DESCRIPTION |
|---|---|
| Correct Two Initial Capitals | Corrects words keyed with two initial capital letters, such as "ACcess" or "THis." |
| Capitalize first letter of sentence | Corrects first letter of sentence keyed without a capital letter. |
| Capitalize Names of Days | Corrects a day spelled without an initial capital letter. |
| Correct Accidental Use of Cap Locks Key | Corrects words typed with Shift pressed and Caps Lock on, such as cAPS. |
| Replace Text as You Type | Makes corrections automatically. |

**3.** Click Cancel to close the dialog box.

**4.** Open the Kit Contents table and maximize the window, if necessary. Click the New Record button ▶✱ on the toolbar.

**5.** Key **Zeb002** in the Kit Number field. Press Tab three times to move to the Kit Contents field.

**6.** In the "Kit Contents" field, key **i want teh kit to contain teh follwoing materials.** Include a period after the sentence. The field scrolls as you key the sentence. Access automatically corrects "i," "teh," and "follwoing."

**7.** Key this sentence with the errors: **TOdya is tuesday.** Include a period at the end of the sentence. Access corrects the capitalization of "Today" and "Tuesday."

**8.** With Caps Lock on, key "The" as you ordinarily would without Caps Lock on. "tHE" is converted to "The."

**9.** Delete the record you just keyed by choosing Delete Record from the Edit menu. Click Yes to confirm the deletion.

**10.** Close the Kit Contents table. Don't save the layout changes to this table. Click No, if prompted.

**EXERCISE** **2-4** **Create an AutoCorrect Entry**

You can create your own AutoCorrect entry for words you often misspell. You can also use AutoCorrect to create shortcuts for text you use repeatedly, such as names or phrases. Examples of these types of AutoCorrect entries are:

- "CC" for "Carolina Critters"
- "ABC" for "ABC Toys, Inc."

**1.** Open the Customers table.

**2.** Choose <u>A</u>utoCorrect from the <u>T</u>ools menu. In the <u>R</u>eplace box key **abc**.

**3.** In the <u>W</u>ith box, key **ABC Toys, Inc.**

**FIGURE 2-4**
Creating your own
AutoCorrect entry

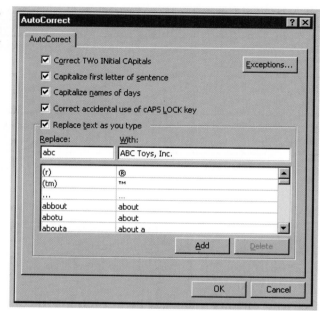

**4.** Click the <u>A</u>dd command button to move the entry into the alphabetized list. Click OK.

**5.** Click the New Record button ▶＊. Key **10** in the Customer ID field and press Tab.

**6.** Key **abc** in the "Company Name" field and press Tab. Access spells out the entry, just as you specified in the AutoCorrect dialog box.

**7.** To remove the "abc" entry, open the <u>A</u>utoCorrect dialog box. Choose the "abc" entry from the list, click the <u>D</u>elete command button, and click OK.

**8.** Click in the record you just added and delete it by choosing Delete <u>R</u>ecord from the <u>E</u>dit menu. Click <u>Y</u>es to confirm the deletion.

## EXERCISE  2-5  Use the Undo Command

Access remembers changes you make in a table and allows you to undo some of these changes. For example, if you accidentally delete some text in a field, you can use the Undo command to reverse the action. There are three ways to undo an action:

- Click the Undo button  on the toolbar.
- Press Ctrl+Z.
- Choose Undo from the Edit menu.

1. In the Customers table, delete the Contact Name of the first record by moving the insertion point to the left of "Sharon Peterson" and pressing Ctrl+Delete.

2. Click the Undo button  on the toolbar. This action restores "Sharon Peterson."

3. Move the insertion point to the left of the word "Avenue" in the billing address of "Bears Etc." Press Insert and key **Road**. Delete any remaining characters. Press Insert again to turn off Overtype mode.

**NOTE:** When you are in Insert mode, "OVR" appears in the status bar at the bottom right of the Access window.

4. Choose Undo Delete from the Edit menu. This restores "Avenue."

**NOTE:** As soon as you move the insertion point away from a record, it is saved.

5. Close the Customers table.

**EXERCISE 2-6 Use Copy and Paste to Edit Records**

You can copy a block of text from one part of a table to another. There are several ways to copy and paste text. The most common methods are:

- Click the Copy and Paste buttons on the toolbar.
- Press Ctrl+C (copy) and Ctrl+V (paste).
- Choose Copy and Paste from the Edit Menu.
- Click the right mouse button and choose Copy and Paste from the shortcut menu.

1. Open the Employees table. Click the New Record button. Key the following to create a new record (leaving the "Job Code" field blank):

Employee ID: **27**
Last Name: **Kwan**

| First Name: | **Sam** |
| SS#: | **888-11-2222** |
| Job Code: | *Leave blank.* |
| Birth Date: | **7/16/72** |

 **NOTE:** When you enter a birth date, use the mm/dd/yy format. Access automatically formats what you enter to match the other dates.

| Hire Date: | **04/04/97** |
| Address: | **111 Westbrook Drive** |
| City: | **Charlotte** |
| State: | **NC** |
| Postal Code: | **28202-3876** |
| Home Phone: | **(704) 555-1111** |
| Emergency Contact: | **John Smith** |
| Emergency Phone: | **(704) 555-1112** |

**2.** Scroll the window to see the "Job Code" field. Select the code "MF04" in any record.

 **3.** Click the Copy button  on the toolbar to transfer a copy of the text to the Clipboard. Notice that the selected text remains in its original position in the table.

**4.** Position the insertion point in the "Job Code" field in the record you just added.

**5.** Right-click and choose Paste from the shortcut menu. A copy of "MF04" is copied into the "Job Code" field.

 **TIP:** Text that you copy to the Clipboard can be pasted repeatedly until you copy new text.

**6.** Close the Employees table.

# *Adding Records with a Form*

A *form* is an Access object in which you can enter, view, sort, edit, and print data. When you key data in a table, you enter the data in rows and columns. If there are many fields, you may not be able to see a complete record. A form, on the other hand, displays one record at a time. Like a table window, the form window contains navigation buttons and scroll bars if necessary to view the whole form.

## EXERCISE 2-7 Navigate in a Form

You move the insertion point in a form much as you do in a table. You see scroll bars (if necessary) and navigation buttons in a form window.

1. Click the Forms tab in the Database window. The window lists the forms in the current database.

2. Double-click the Employee Information Form to open it. Notice the form contains scroll bars. The navigation buttons are at the bottom of the form.

**FIGURE 2-5**
Employee
Information Form

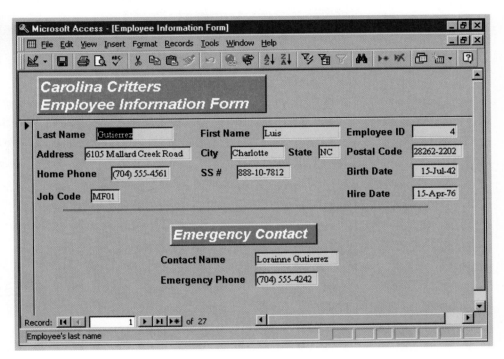

3. Click the Next Record button ▶ until "James McCluskie's" record is highlighted. If you pass the record, click the Previous Record button ◀.

4. Click the Last Record button ▶I. The pointer moves to the last employee, "Zipporah Wilson."

5. Click the First Record button I◀ to move back to the first record, "Luis Gutierrez."

6. You can also use PgUp and PgDn to move through records in a form. Press PgDn several times to move forward through the records. Press PgUp to move backward through the records.

## EXERCISE  2-8  Add Records with a Form

Forms often make it easier to add records because they can be designed to re-produce the appearance of a paper document. You see one record at a time, often enabling you to view all the fields at once.

**1.** With the Employee Information Form open, click the New Record button ►*. A new blank form opens ready for you to add information.

**FIGURE 2-6**
A blank new form opens to add a new record.

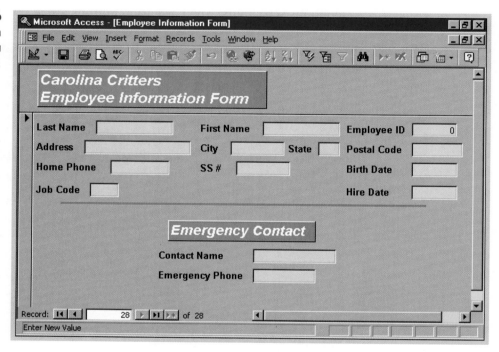

**2.** Key the following to create a new record, pressing Tab between entries:

| | |
|---|---|
| Last Name: | **Woodsik** |
| First Name: | **Sophie** |
| Employee ID: | **28** |
| Address: | **456 Victoria Avenue** |
| City: | **Charlotte** |
| State: | **NC** |
| Postal Code: | **28202-7997** |
| Home Phone: | **(704) 555-1601** |
| SS#: | **888-22-1111** |
| Birth Date: | **01/25/57** |

**NOTE:** Watch the screen as you enter the dates. Notice how Access reformats the date.

| | |
|---|---|
| Job Code: | **OF06** |
| Hire Date: | **05/10/86** |
| Contact Name: | **Howard Woodsik** |
| Emergency Phone: | **(704) 555-1662** |

*3.* Close the form. Click the Tables tab and open the Employees table.

*4.* Click the Last Record button ▶I to see the last record you added, "Sophie Woodsik."

*5.* Close the Employees table.

**EXERCISE  2-9  Add Records with the Data Entry Command**

You can also use the Data Entry command to enter records in a form. You will not be able to see the other records in the form.

*1.* Open the Employee Information Form.

*2.* Choose <u>D</u>ata Entry from the <u>R</u>ecords menu and key the following information:

| | |
|---|---|
| Last Name: | **Willis** |
| First Name: | **Marjorie** |
| Employee ID: | **29** |
| Address: | **7737 Derby Avenue** |
| City: | **Charlotte** |
| State: | **NC** |
| Postal Code: | **28202-6443** |
| Home Phone: | **(704) 555-1828** |
| SS#: | **888-77-1135** |
| Birth Date: | **05/09/53** |
| Job Code: | **MF03** |
| Hire Date: | **07/06/83** |
| Contact Name: | **Ellen Gilroy** |
| Emergency Phone: | **(704) 555-4998** |

*3.* Choose <u>R</u>emove Filter/Sort from the <u>R</u>ecords menu.

*4.* Click the Last Record button ▶I to see the record you entered. Close the Employee Information Form.

# *Changing Views in a Form*

There are two ways to view a form:

- Form View appears when you first open a form. You enter data, edit data, and find records in Form View.
- Design View allows you to create a new form or modify the layout of the existing form. You don't see records in Design View. You see controls, which consist of a label and a text box. The text box holds the information from a field.

You can also switch to the Datasheet View using the View button.

## EXERCISE 2-10 Use Form and Design Views

1. Open the Employee Information Form.
2. Click the down arrow of the View button . The shortcut menu displays three choices–Design View, Form View, and Datasheet View. The indented icon indicates the current view (Form View).

**FIGURE 2-7**
Form View menu

3. Choose Design View from the shortcut menu to display the Employee Information Form in Design View. Notice the employee records do not appear in this view. This view shows controls for the form's labels and text boxes.
4. Click the View button, not the down arrow. The form appears in Form View.

**FIGURE 2-8**
Employee
Information Form
in Design View

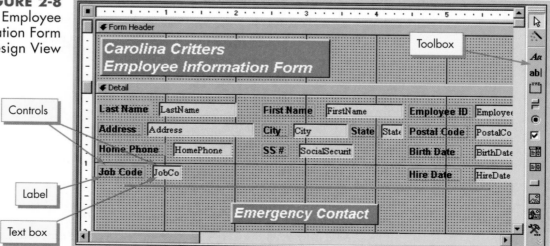

**NOTE:** The View button is a toggle button that switches between Design View and Form View. The face of the button shows the view you can switch to.

# *Printing a Form*

Forms are designed for working at the computer. The design and layout features are optimized for the monitor. Although forms are designed for screen work, you can print them Use any of these methods to print a form:

- Click the Print button 🖨 on the toolbar.
- Choose Print from the File menu.
- Press Ctrl + P.

If you click the Print button 🖨, all the forms are printed with your default print settings. If there are 29 records in the table, all 29 forms print, one for each record.

The menu and keyboard commands open the Print dialog box so you can set a print range or change the page setup. A print range selects certain forms for printing. You use the page setup to set the paper orientation or change the margins.

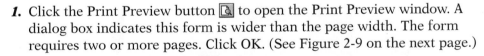

## EXERCISE 2-11 View a Form in Print Preview

It's good practice to preview a form before printing it. Print Preview shows how your form looks on paper. You may want to change settings before you print the actual form.

1. Click the Print Preview button 🔍 to open the Print Preview window. A dialog box indicates this form is wider than the page width. The form requires two or more pages. Click OK. (See Figure 2-9 on the next page.)

2. Click the Two Pages button 🔳. This displays two pages. The gray bar on the second page is the part of the form that is wider than the page width. (See Figure 2-10 on the next page.)

3. Click the Zoom button 🔍. This enlarges the form. Click 🔍 again to reduce the form.

 **NOTE:** When you move the insertion point to the form, the insertion point changes to a magnifying glass with a plus or minus sign (depending on the magnification). You can change the magnification by moving the insertion point to the form and clicking anywhere in the preview.

**FIGURE 2-9**
Preview of Employee
Information Form

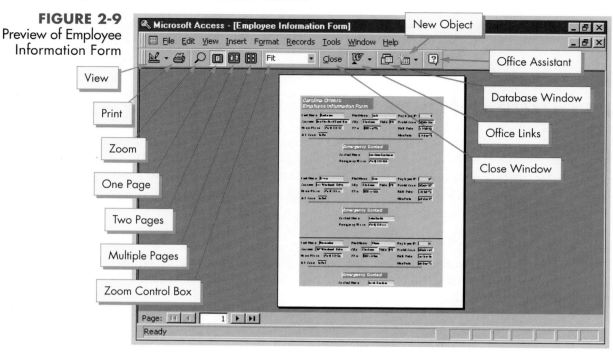

**NOTE:** The preview of the Employee Information Form shows three records. The size of the form determines the number of records that print per page.

**FIGURE 2-10**
Viewing two pages

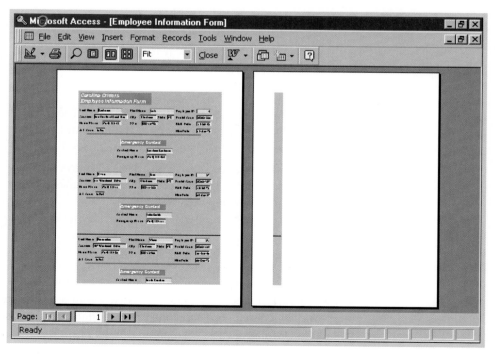

**TABLE 2-2**    **Print Preview Toolbar Buttons**

| BUTTON/NAME | FUNCTION |
|---|---|
| ☒ View | Click the arrow to switch to another view. |
| 🖨 Print | Prints the form in the Print Preview window. |
| 🔍 Zoom | Enlarges or reduces magnification of a form. This button toggles between enlarging and reducing a form. |
| ▣ One Page | Displays one page at a time. |
| ▦ Two Pages | Displays two pages at a time. |
| ▦ Multiple Pages | Displays multiple pages. |
| Fit ▾ Zoom Control Box | Allows you to choose a magnification to reduce or enlarge a form. |
| ☒ Close | Closes Print Preview window and returns to Design View or Database window. |
| 🗗 Office Links | Opens a drop-down list of related Office commands. |
| 🗗 Database Window | Opens the Database window. |
| 🖩 New Object | Opens a drop-down list of new objects you can create. |
| ❓ Office Assistant | Opens the Office Assistant. |

**FIGURE 2-11**
Zoom Control
options

4. To enlarge a form without full magnification, click the down arrow next to the Zoom Control box and choose 50%.

5. Close Print Preview by clicking the Close button.

## EXERCISE  2-12  Change Page Setup

When printing forms, you may want to change the print layout or orientation to landscape. This is helpful if the form you want to print doesn't fit on one printed page.

1. With the Employee Information Form open, choose Page Setup from the File menu to open the Page Setup dialog box.

2. Click the Page tab. This tab displays the orientation, paper, and the default printer.

3. Click the Landscape option button. Click OK to close the dialog box.

# EXERCISE  Print a Form

1. If you only want to print a form for one record (employee), you have to select the form you want to print. Move to the form with your name.

2. Click in the Record Selector area to select the record.

> **NOTE:** The Record Selector is the narrow bar to the left of the labels and text boxes. It appears darker when you select a record.

3. Choose <u>P</u>rint from the <u>F</u>ile menu to open the Print dialog box. The dialog box displays the default settings and shows your designated printer.

**FIGURE 2-12**
Print dialog box

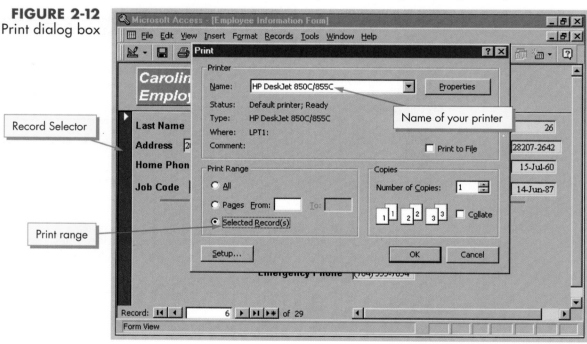

4. Click Selected <u>R</u>ecord(s) as the Print Range.

5. Click OK or press Enter to accept the settings. A printer icon appears on the taskbar as the form is sent to the printer.

6. Close the Employee Information Form.

# *Editing Records in a Form*

You can edit records in a form using the same tools you used to edit tables. For example, Backspace deletes a single character and the keyboard combination Ctrl + Delete deletes an entire line.

## EXERCISE 2-14 Delete Text

1. Open the Sales Order Review form. Click the Next Record button ▶ at the bottom of your screen to move to "The Toy House" record.

 **NOTE:** The Sales Order Review form is actually two forms in one. It uses two tables for its data.

2. Move the insertion point to the left of "Toy" in the Company Name field.

3. Press Ctrl + Backspace. Notice the current record pointer changes to the pencil symbol when editing text. "The Toy House" is now changed to "Toy House."

4. Move the insertion point between the numbers "0" and "2" in the Order ID field at the top of the form.

5. Press Delete once and key **7**. The Order ID is now changed to "97107."

6. Move the insertion point to the right of the "7" in the Employee ID field and click.

7. Press Backspace and key **6**. The Employee ID is now "6."

8. Move the insertion point to the first character in the Order Date field.

9. Press Ctrl + Delete. Key [*your birth date*] using mm/dd/yy format.

10. Close the Sales Review form. Click the Tables tab and open the Customers table. Notice the change to "Toy House" (it used to be "The Toy House"). Close the Customers table.

11. Open the Sales Orders table and notice OrderID "97107." There is no Order ID "97102." Close the Sales Orders table.

## EXERCISE 2-15 Delete Records in a Form

As with tables you can delete records you no longer need in a form. You can delete the record on the screen from the Edit menu. You can also select the record and press Delete.

1. Click the Forms tab and open the Employee Information Form. Move to the record for "Martin Clark." Click the Record Selector to select the record.

2. Press Delete. Notice the next record is now displayed.

 **NOTE:** You cannot use ↶ to restore a deleted a record.

3. Click Yes to confirm the deletion.

# EXERCISE 2-16 Insert Text

When editing a form, you can insert text or use Overtype mode to key over existing text. Use Insert to switch between Insert and Overtype modes. You can also insert text using the Copy and Paste commands.

1. With the Employee Information Form open, move forward to the record of "May Chen."
2. Select "OF06" in the Job Code field. Click the Copy button 🖻 on the toolbar.
3. Move back to "Estela Barnes'" record. If necessary, highlight the text in the Job Code field.
4. Click the Paste button 🖺 on the toolbar. Estela Barnes now has the job code of "OF06."
5. Move back to the record for "Jamel Abdullah." If necessary, move the insertion point to the left of OF07 in the Job Code field.
6. Press Insert to switch to Overtype mode. Key **MF04** over the old text.
7. With Overtype mode on, move the insertion point between "0" and "4" in the Job Code field. Key **5**. The Job Code is now "MF05."

 **TIP:** In Overtype mode the insertion point is wider than normal. It may appear the insertion point is on the "4" rather than between "0" and "4."

8. Press Insert again to turn off Overtype mode.
9. Close the form and open the Employees table. Notice the changes to Estela Barnes' and Jamel Abdullah's records. Close the Employees table.

## COMMAND SUMMARY

| FEATURE | BUTTON | MENU | KEYBOARD |
|---|---|---|---|
| Undo | ↶ | Edit, Undo | Ctrl+Z |
| Copy | 🖻 | Edit, Copy | Ctrl+C |
| Paste | 🖺 | Edit, Paste | Ctrl+V |
| Delete record | ⋈ | Edit, Delete Record | |
| Zoom | 🔍 | View, Zoom | |
| New record | ▶* | Insert, New Record | |
| Form View | 🔙 | View, Form View | |
| Form Design View | 🔙 | View, Design View | |
| Data Entry | | Records, Data Entry | |
| Remove Data Entry | | Records, Remove Filter/Sort | |

## USING HELP

Access' online Help is like an interactive teaching tool. One way to explore online Help is to display a list of Help topics. You choose a topic and Access displays information or provides a demonstration.

To display the list of Help topics, choose <u>C</u>ontents and Index from the <u>H</u>elp menu.

**Follow these steps to display a Help topic window about previewing forms:**

*1.* Choose <u>C</u>ontents and Index  from the <u>H</u>elp menu to display the Help Topics window. Click the Contents tab, if necessary.

**FIGURE 2-13**
Help Topics
window

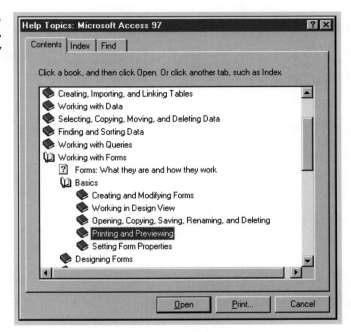

*2.* Browse through the list of topics, each of which is represented by a book icon 📘.

*3.* Double-click the topic "Working with Forms" (you can double-click the icon or the text).

*4.* Double-click the topic "Basics."

*5.* Double-click "Printing and Previewing," then double-click "Preview a form."

*6.* Maximize the window and read the information, scrolling as necessary.

*7.* Click ⊠ when you finish.

UNIT 1 ■ UNDERSTANDING ACCESS BASICS

# Concepts Review

## TRUE/FALSE QUESTIONS

Each of the following statements is either true or false. Indicate your choice by circling **T** or **F**.

**T  F  1.** The pencil appears in the Record Selector after a record is saved.

**T  F  2.** You can use the Undo button  to restore a record after you delete it.

**T  F  3.** When you enter data on a form, you also have to update the table associated with the form.

**T  F  4.** You can't change the page orientation for a form.

**T  F  5.** You can create an AutoCorrect entry for words you misspell often.

**T  F  6.** You can only add records in a table.

**T  F  7.** Access automatically saves a record when you close its form.

**T  F  8.** You click the New Record button to add a record to a form.

## SHORT ANSWER QUESTIONS

Write the correct answer in the space provided.

**1.** What view does a table have to be in to add records?

_____

**2.** What icon appears in the Record Selector when adding records?

_____

**3.** What do you click to add a record to a table or form?

_____

**4.** What do you use to change the magnification to 50% in Print Preview?

_____

**5.** What button do you click to change a form to Design View?

_____

**6.** What option do you choose in the Print dialog box to print a single form?

_____

**7.** What dialog box allows you to change page orientation?

_____

**8.** Which function will the keyboard combination Ctrl+Z perform?

_____

## CRITICAL THINKING

**Answer these questions on a separate page. There are no right or wrong answers. Support your answers with examples from your own experience, if possible.**

**1.** You can work with records in Datasheet View or Form View. Which do you prefer and why? When might it be better to use Form View? When might it be better to use Datasheet View?

**2.** When you delete a record from a table, it cannot be recovered. Can you think of applications when you might never delete records, even though the record is inactive?

# Skills Review

## EXERCISE 2-17

**Add, delete, copy, and paste records in a table.**

**1.** Start Access, if necessary, and open your file *[your initials]***CC1.mdb**.

**2.** Add a record by following these steps:

**a.** Open the Kit Suppliers table and maximize the window. Click the New Record button ▸*.

**b.** Key the following, pressing Tab between field entries:

| | |
|---|---|
| Supplier ID: | **EE-05** |
| Supplier Name: | **Southern Fabrics, Inc.** |
| Contact Name: | **Randolph C. Petersen** |
| Address: | **2600 Patterson Street** |
| City: | **Greensboro** |
| Postal Code: | **27407-2600** |
| Phone Number: | **(910) 555-6625** |
| Fax Number: | **(910) 555-6626** |

**c.** Close the Kit Suppliers table.

    ***d.*** Open the Customers table.

    ***e.*** Choose <u>D</u>ata Entry from the <u>R</u>ecords menu. Key the following to add another record:

| | |
|---|---|
| Customer ID: | **10** |
| Company Name: | **Penny's Dolls and Toys** |
| Contact Name: | **Jody Mentor** |
| Billing Address: | **756 Gulf Street** |
| City: | **Mitford** |
| State: | **CT** |
| Postal Code: | **06460-7560** |
| Phone Number: | **(203) 555-1897** |
| Fax Number: | **(203) 555-7854** |
| Tax Exempt | *Leave blank and press Tab.* |

    ***f.*** Choose <u>R</u>emove Filter/Sort from the <u>R</u>ecords menu. Close the Kit Suppliers table.

**3.** Delete a record by following these steps:

    ***a.*** Open the Stuffed Animals table. Maximize the window.

    ***b.*** Scroll to find the "Betsy the cow" record and click anywhere in the record.

    ***c.*** Choose Delete <u>R</u>ecord from the <u>E</u>dit menu.

    ***d.*** Click <u>Y</u>es to confirm the deletion.

    ***e.*** Close the Stuffed Animals table.

**4.** Correct errors automatically by following these steps:

    ***a.*** Open the Customers table and click the New Record button ▶*.

    ***b.*** Key **11** in the Customer ID field.

    ***c.*** Press `Tab` to move to the Company Name field.

    ***d.*** Key **Teh Hobby Comany** in the Company Name field and press `Tab`. Access automatically corrects "teh" and "Comany."

    ***e.*** Turn on Caps Lock. In the City field, key **Charlotte** as you ordinarily would without Caps Lock. Press `Tab`. "cHARLOTTE" becomes Charlotte.

    ***f.*** Key the following to finish the record.

| | |
|---|---|
| Contact Name: | **Jerry Adams** |
| Billing Address: | **3258 Brookshire Boulevard** |
| State: | **NC** |
| Postal Code: | **28216-4004** |
| Phone Number: | **(704) 555-8011** |

| | |
|---|---|
| Fax Number: | **(704) 555-8012** |
| Tax exempt?: | *Leave blank.* |

**g.** Close the Customers table.

**5.** Create an AutoCorrect entry by following these steps:

**a.** Open the Employees table.

**b.** Choose <u>A</u>utoCorrect from the <u>T</u>ools menu. In the R<u>e</u>place box, key **ch**. In the <u>W</u>ith box, key **Charlotte**. Click the <u>A</u>dd button and click OK.

**c.** Click the New Record button ▶∗ and key the following, pressing ⌗Tab⌗ between entries:

| | |
|---|---|
| Employee ID: | **30** |
| Last Name: | **Jones** |
| First Name: | **Bertha** |
| SS#: | **888-18-2694** |
| Job Code: | **MF06** |
| Birth Date: | **08/10/72** |
| Hire Date: | **07/16/96** |
| Address: | **392 West 4th Street** |

**d.** Key **ch** in the City field and press ⌗Tab⌗. Access spells out the entry.

**e.** Key the following to finish the record:

| | |
|---|---|
| State: | **NC** |
| Postal Code: | **28202-3229** |
| Home Phone: | **(704) 555-4141** |
| Emergency Contact: | **Mary Jones** |
| Emergency Phone: | **(704) 555-4136** |

**f.** Remove the "ch" entry by opening the <u>A</u>utoCorrect dialog box, choosing "ch" entry from the list, clicking the Delete command button, and clicking OK.

**g.** Close the Employees table.

**6.** Undo actions by following these steps:

**a.** Open the Product Lines table.

**b.** Double-click "Endangered" to select it and press ⌗Delete⌗.

**c.** Click the Undo button ↶ on the toolbar.

**d.** Move the insertion point to the left of the word "Dogs" in the first record. Press ⌗Insert⌗ and key **Critters**. Press ⌗Insert⌗ again to turn off Overtype mode.

**e.** Choose <u>U</u>ndo Typing from the Edit menu. This action restores "Dogs."

**f.** Close the Product Lines table.

7. Copy and paste to edit records by following these steps:

   **a.** Open the Customers table. Click the New Record button ▶* and key the following, leaving the "Company Name" and "City" fields blank:

   | | |
   |---|---|
   | Customer ID: | **12** |
   | Company Name: | *Leave blank.* |
   | Contact Name: | **Frank Peterson** |
   | Billing Address: | **1012 Dobson Avenue** |
   | City: | *Leave blank.* |
   | State: | **TN** |
   | Postal Code: | **37406-4124** |
   | Phone Number: | **(423) 555-7765** |
   | Fax Number: | **(423) 555-7766** |
   | Tax Exempt?: | *Leave blank.* |

   **b.** Select "Magna Mart Corporation" in the "Company Name" field of the first record and click the Copy button 📋.

   **c.** Position the insertion point in the "Company Name" field in the record you just added.

   **d.** Right-click and choose Paste from the shortcut menu.

   **e.** Double-click to select "Chattanooga" in the "City" field of the first record and press Ctrl + C.

   **f.** Position the insertion point in the "City" field in the record you just added. Press Ctrl + V.

   **g.** Close the Customers table.

## EXERCISE 2-18

## Navigate in a form and add records with a form.

1. Navigate in a form by following these steps:

   **a.** Click the Forms tab and open the Employee Information Form. Click the Next Record button ▶ until the record of "Frank Cirillo" is current.

   **b.** Click the Last Record button ▶| to move to the last employee, "Marjorie Willis."

   **c.** Click the First Record button |◀ to move to the first record, "Luis Gutierrez."

   **d.** Press PgDn three times to move to the fourth record.

   **e.** Press PgUp two times to move back two records.

   **f.** Press Ctrl + End to move to the last record.

   **g.** Press Ctrl + Home to move to the first record.

**2.** Add records with a form by following these steps:

    ***a.*** Click the New Record button ▶✱ and key the following:

| | |
|---|---|
| Last Name: | **Adams** |
| First Name: | **William** |
| Employee ID: | **31** |
| Address: | **6825 Steele Creek Road** |
| City: | **Charlotte** |
| State: | **NC** |
| Postal Code: | **28217-3599** |
| Home Phone: | **(704) 555-5122** |
| SS#: | **888-22-5554** |
| Birth Date: | **12/22/61** |
| Job Code: | **MF04** |
| Hire Date: | **10/31/80** |
| Contact Name: | **Cynthia Adams** |
| Emergency Phone: | **(704) 555-5122** |

    ***b.*** Close the Employee Information Form.

    ***c.*** Open the Employees table. Click the Last Record button ▶❙ to see the record you added, "William Adams." Close the Employees table.

**3.** Add records with a form using the Data Entry command by following these steps:

    ***a.*** Open the Employee Information Form and choose <u>D</u>ata Entry from the <u>R</u>ecords menu.

    ***b.*** Key the following information:

| | |
|---|---|
| Last Name: | **Clark** |
| First Name: | **Morton** |
| Employee ID: | **32** |
| Address: | **7345 High Bridge Terrace** |
| City: | **Charlotte** |
| State: | **NC** |
| Postal Code: | **28217-4466** |
| Home Phone: | **(704) 555-1189** |
| SS#: | **888-22-7779** |
| Birth Date: | **12/24/67** |
| Job Code: | **OF05** |
| Hire Date: | **8/16/75** |

Contact Name:     **Melanie Clark**

Emergency Phone:  **(704) 326-4188**

*c.* Choose <u>R</u>emove Filter/Sort from the <u>R</u>ecords menu to see all records. Close the Employee Information Form.

4. Change between Form View and Design View by following these steps:

*a.* Open the New Customer Entry Form.

*b.* Click the down arrow of the View button 🖼 and choose Design View from the shortcut menu.

*c.* Click 🖼 again to return to Form View. Close the form.

## EXERCISE 2-19

## Change print setup and print a form.

1. View a form in Print Preview by following these steps:

*a.* With the Sales Order Review form open and maximized, click the Print Preview button 🔍.

*b.* Click anywhere on the page to enlarge the form. Click again to reduce the form.

*c.* To enlarge the form without full magnification, click the down arrow next to the Zoom Control box and choose 75%.

*d.* Close Print Preview by clicking the <u>C</u>lose button.

2. Change the print setup by following these steps:

*a.* Choose Page Set<u>u</u>p from the <u>F</u>ile menu. Click the Page tab.

*b.* Click the <u>L</u>andscape option button. Click OK to close the dialog box.

3. Print a form by following these steps:

*a.* To print a form for one record, move to the "Magna Mart" record.

*b.* Click in the Record Selector area to select the form.

*c.* Choose <u>P</u>rint from the <u>F</u>ile menu.

*d.* Click Selected <u>R</u>ecord(s) to select the "Magna Mart" form.

*e.* Click OK or press ⌐Enter¬ to print the form. Close the Sales Order Review form.

## EXERCISE 2-20

## Edit records in a form.

1. Delete text in a form by following these steps:

**a.** Open the Employee Information Form and move to "Norman Fishman's" record.

    **b.** Move the insertion point to the right of "North" in the Address field.

    **c.** Press `Ctrl`+`Backspace`. "45 North Irvin Avenue" changes to "45 Irvin Avenue." Delete the extra space between "45" and "Irvin."

    **d.** Move the insertion point to the left of "Fishman" in the Emergency Contact field.

    **e.** Press `Ctrl`+`Delete` and key **Taylor**. "Betty Fishman" is changed to "Betty Taylor."

    **f.** Close the Employee Information Form.

    **g.** Open the Employees table to see the changes to "Norman Fishman." Close the Employees table.

**2.** Delete records in a form by following these steps:

    **a.** Open the Employee Information Form and move to "Helen Butler's" record.

    **b.** Choose Delete Record from the Edit menu.

    **c.** Click Yes to confirm the deletion. Close the Employee Information Form.

**3.** Insert text in a form by following these steps:

    **a.** Click the Tables tab and open the Sales Order Line Items table. Look for Order ID 97107. This order doesn't yet exist. Close the table.

    **b.** Click the Forms tab and open the Sales Order Review form.

    **c.** Move to the "Bears Etc." record.

    **d.** Highlight "C003" in the Product ID field at the bottom of the form. Click the Copy button 🖺.

    **e.** Move back to "Toy House'" record. Place the insertion point in the ProductID field for Order 97107. Click the Paste button 🖺.

    **f.** Press `Tab` and key **10** in the Quantity field.

    **g.** Close the Sales Order Review form.

    **h.** Open the Sales Order Line Items table and see the new OrderID "97107." Close the Sales Order Line Items table.

**4.** Close the database.

# Lesson Applications

## EXERCISE 2-21

**Add records in a table.**

1. Open the Kit Suppliers table, maximize the window, and add the following new supplier:

   | | |
   |---|---|
   | Supplier ID: | **FF-06** |
   | Supplier Name: | **Northeast Fabric Supply** |
   | Contact Name: | **Patrice Davis** |
   | Address: | **562 Industrial Parkway** |
   | City: | **Wallingford** |
   | Postal Code: | **06492-5223** |
   | Phone Number: | **(203) 555-6332** |
   | Fax Number: | **(203) 555-6331** |

2. Print the Kit Suppliers table, landscape, and close the table.

## EXERCISE 2-22

**Add, delete, and edit records in a form.**

1. Open the Employee Information Form. Delete the records for Luis Gutierrez and Joseph Lassen, and close the form.

2. Open the Employees table and make the corrections shown in Figure 2-14. (Not all the columns of the table appear in the figure.)

    **TIP:** Freezing the Last Name and First Name columns may be helpful.

**FIGURE 2-14**

| Employee ID | Last Name | First Name | Job | Address |
|---|---|---|---|---|
| 7 | Dyer | ~~Cassie~~ *Cassandra* | OF07 | 162 ~~South~~ Summit Avenue |
| 8 | Wilson | Zipporah | MF02 | 105 North Sycamore Street |
| 9 | Thomas-Smith | Louise | ~~MF04~~ | 1332 Shamrock ~~Drive~~ *Street* |
| 10 | Davidson | Raymond | OF06 *OF05* *North* | 345 Victoria Avenue |
| 11 | Stone | Jeanette | ~~MF03~~ *MF06* | 5948 Quail Hollow Road |

70

3. Close the Employees table.

4. Open the New Customer Entry Form and add the following new customer:

| | |
|---|---|
| Customer ID: | **13** |
| Company Name: | **Bears Etc. #2** |
| Billing Address: | **190 Wilkinson Boulevard** |
| City: | **Charlotte** |
| State: | **NC** |
| Postal Code: | **28208-5644** |
| Phone Number: | **(704) 555-3600** |
| Fax Number: | **(704) 555-3601** |
| Contact Name: | *Key your first and last name.* |
| Tax Exempt?: | *Leave blank.* |

5. Print this record, portrait, and close the New Customer Entry Form.

6. Look at the Customers table. View the record you just added, then close the table.

## EXERCISE 2-23

### Copy and paste records in a table.

1. Open the Kit Suppliers table and start a new record.

2. Key **GG-07** in the Supplier ID field.

3. Select "Cosby Manufacturing Company" in the Supplier Name field and copy it. Paste it to the Supplier Name field for the new record.

4. Enter your name as the contact name for the new record.

5. Select any address and paste it to the new record.

6. Repeat these steps to copy and paste information for the new record. You can select data from any record for each field.

7. Print the table, landscape, and close the Kit Suppliers table.

# Finding Data, Sorting Records, and Using Filters

**OBJECTIVES**

After completing this lesson, you will be able to:

1. Find text in tables and forms.
2. Replace text.
3. Sort records in a table and form.
4. Use filters to sort tables and forms.
5. Create an advanced filter.
6. Use multiple criteria to filter a form.

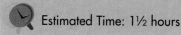 Estimated Time: 1½ hours

The Find, Replace, Sort, and Filter commands in Access are similar to the Find, Replace, Sort, and Filter commands in most word processing programs.

- Find and Replace commands search all the records of a table for text or data you specify. For example, to search for a particular employee, you enter the employee's name in the Find dialog box and Access searches the entire table for the record.

- Sort commands arrange the records in a table or form in a particular sequence. For example, you can sort all records in the Employees table alphabetically by last name.

- Filter commands display only records that meet conditions you specify. For example, you can display only customers in Charlotte, North Carolina.

# *Using the Find Command*

Finding records can be time consuming if you have to scroll through a table with several thousand records. You can use the Find command to locate a record quickly.

There are three ways to use Find:

- Choose Find from the Edit menu.
- Press Ctrl + F.
- Click the Find button .

The Find command can search an entire field, part of a field, or the start of a field. Searches are not case sensitive, which means Access finds uppercase and lowercase versions of the text.

## EXERCISE   3-1   Find a Record

**FIGURE 3-1**
Edit menu

1. Open the file *[your initials]***CC1.mdb**.
2. Open the Customers table and maximize the window.
3. Choose Find from the Edit menu to open the Find dialog box.
4. Key **Charlotte** in the Find What box.
5. If necessary, choose All from the Search drop-down list. (This is the default option and should already be chosen.) The All option tells Access to start at the current record, continue to the end of the table, and wrap back to any records that precede the current record.

**NOTE:** To see more of the table text during a search, drag the Find dialog box by its title bar to the bottom right corner of the screen.

**FIGURE 3-2**
Find dialog box

**TABLE 3-1**     Find Dialog Box Options

| OPTIONS | DESCRIPTION |
| --- | --- |
| Match Case | Finds text that matches uppercase and lowercase exactly as you enter it. |
| Search Fields as Formatted | Finds data that is based on the display format. This option searches to locate a date that is stored as the number "1/25/97," but is displayed as "25-Jan-97." This is the slowest search. |
| Search Only Current Field | Searches the records in the current field. This option is checked by default because it speeds the search. |
| Search All | Searches the entire table in both directions, forward and backward. |
| Search Up | Searches the table in Up (backward) direction only. |
| Search Down | Searches the table in Down (forward) direction only. |
| Match Any Part of Field | Matches characters anywhere in the field. |
| Match Whole Field | Finds records in which the entire value in the Find What box is a match. |
| Match Start of Field | Finds records in which the Find What entry matches the beginning of the field. |

6. Since you want to search all the fields in the table, click Search Only Current Field to deselect the option.
7. Click Find First. Access moves the pointer to the first occurrence of "Charlotte."
8. Click Find Next to move to the next occurrence of "Charlotte."
9. Continue clicking Find Next until Access displays a message saying the search is complete.
10. Click OK in the message box.
11. Click Close to close the Find dialog box.

 **NOTE:** The Find dialog box remains open until you close it.

**EXERCISE** 3-2 **Find Records Using the Matching Case Option**

The Find command includes options for fine-tuning how words or phrases are matched to what you type in the Find What box. One of these options is Match Case, which you use to conduct a case-sensitive search.

74

**1.** Move to the end of the table by pressing ⌨Ctrl+⌨End.

**2.** Click the Find button .

> **NOTE:** Notice that "Charlotte" is still in the Find What box from your last search. Since the entry is highlighted, all you have to do is key the new text to start a new search.

**3.** Key **Durham** in the Find What box.

**4.** Click the Match Case check box to select it. Choose Up from the Search drop-down list box to reverse the search direction since the pointer is at the end of the table.

**FIGURE 3-3**
Choosing options in the Find dialog box.

**5.** Click Find Next to begin the search.

**6.** Click Find Next until a message box appears telling you the search is complete. Click OK.

**7.** Key **durham** in the Find What box. The Match Case option is still selected.

**8.** Choose Down from the Search drop-down list box.

**9.** Click Find Next to begin the search. Notice that this time there are no matches.

**10.** Click OK in the message box that says the search is finished.

**11.** Close the Find dialog box.

**12.** Close the Customers table.

# EXERCISE 3-3 Find Records Using Wildcards

When you use the Find command, you are actually specifying *criteria*. Criteria are text strings or expressions that Access uses to find matching records. Up to this point, you have only used text as criteria (the words "Charlotte" and "Durham").

When you use text as your criteria, you can use *wildcard* characters, which are helpful when you are not quite sure of the spelling, the number, or some other element. Access uses the same wildcards as most Search commands:

- A question mark (?) represents a single character. Mar? is a criterion that would find "Mary," "Mark," or "Mart"—all four-character words that start with "Mar."

- An asterisk (*) represents any number of characters. Mar* is a criterion that would find "March," "Martin," "Marigold," or "Marblestone"—all words that start with "Mar" regardless of how many letters follow.

- The number sign (#) represents a single number. If you are looking for all the ZIP codes that start with "200," you could use a Find criterion of 200##.

1. Open the Employee Information Form.

2. Click the Find button 🔍.

3. Key **MF*** in the Find What box.

4. Click the Match Case check box to deselect it, if necessary.

5. Choose All from the Search drop-down list.

6. Click Find First to find the first occurrence that matches the search criteria.

7. Continue clicking Find Next until the finished message appears. Notice that any employee with the job code "MF" appears (for example, "MF01," "MF02," and "MF03" are matches).

8. Click OK in the message box and close the Find dialog box.

9. Close the Employee Information Form.

10. Open the Stuffed Animals table and click 🔍.

11. Key **T?????** in the Find What box.

12. Click Find Next to begin the search and continue to click Find Next. Access finds all the records that begin with "T" followed by five characters. Notice that Access ignores words that include more than five characters after the "T," such as "Tiger" or "Triceratops." Each question mark (?) represents one character.

13. Click OK in the message box and close the Find dialog box.

14. Close the Stuffed Animals table.

# Using the Replace Command

The Replace command finds matching text and substitutes replacement text. You can replace all instances of matching text at once, or you can find and confirm each replacement.

There are two ways to use the Replace command:

- Choose Replace from the Edit menu.
- Press Ctrl + H.

EXERCISE 3-4 **Replace Text Using Find Next**

1. Open the Customers table.
2. Choose Replace from the Edit menu.
3. Key **Boulevard** in the Find What box.
4. Press Tab to move to the Replace With text box and key **Avenue**. Since you want to search all the text in a field and all the fields in the table, click Match Whole Field and Search Only Current Field, if necessary, to deselect those options.

**FIGURE 3-4**
Replace dialog box

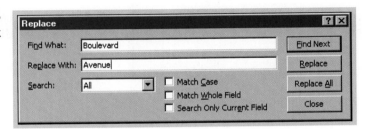

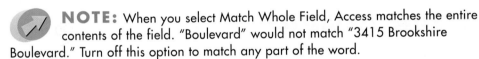 **NOTE:** When you select Match Whole Field, Access matches the entire contents of the field. "Boulevard" would not match "3415 Brookshire Boulevard." Turn off this option to match any part of the word.

5. Click Find Next to start the search.
6. Click Replace to replace the first occurrence of "Boulevard" with "Avenue."
7. Click Replace again to replace the next occurrence. Continue clicking Replace until Access indicates that it can't find the text you specified.
8. Click OK in the message box.
9. Close the Replace dialog box.
10. Close the Customers table.

EXERCISE 3-5 **Replace Text Using Replace All**

The Replace All option in the Replace dialog box replaces all occurrences of text in a table or form without confirmation.

1. Open the Kit Suppliers table.

2. Click the Address field name at the top of the fifth column to select the Address field.

3. Press Ctrl+H to open the Replace dialog box.

4. Key **Street** in the Find What text box. Press Tab and key **Road** in the Replace With text box. Select the Search Only Current Field option. Make sure the Match Case and Match Whole Field options aren't selected.

**NOTE:** If you use Replace All with both Match Whole Field and Search Only Current Field off, you change all occurrences of "Street" to "Road" throughout the table. Not only would all the addresses be changed, but an employee named "Della Street" would become "Della Road." A town named "Streeter" would become "Roader."

**FIGURE 3-5**
Access warns that you cannot undo changes.

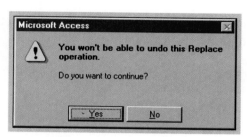

5. Click the Replace All command button. Access warns that you cannot undo the changes.

6. Click Yes to continue and close the Replace dialog box. Notice that all occurrences of "Street" in the Address field were changed to "Road."

7. Close the Kit Suppliers table.

# Sorting Records

Records are displayed in tables and forms in an order determined by the *primary key*, which is a field in a table that must be different for every record. Access shows the records alphabetically or numerically, depending on the primary key. If no primary key is assigned, Access displays records in the order in which they were keyed.

You can arrange records in different orders to find information more quickly. For example, records in the Customers table are in order by the CustomerID number, but when you plan sales calls it may be more helpful to see them in order by ZIP Code. The Stuffed Animals table is arranged by ProductID, but you may need to see them in order by price or inventory on hand if you are planning a special sales promotion.

There are three ways to sort data:

- Choose Sort from the Records menu.
- Click the Sort Ascending button ⬆ or Sort Descending button ⬇.
- Click the right mouse button and select Sort Ascending or Sort Descending from the shortcut menu.

## EXERCISE 3-6 Sort a Single Column

The simplest way to sort a table is to sort based on a single field.

1. Open the Employees table and maximize the window, if necessary. Place the pointer anywhere in the Last Name field and click.

2. Click the Sort Ascending button  on the toolbar to sort the Last Name field alphabetically in ascending order (A to Z).

3. Click the Sort Descending button to sort the field in descending order (Z to A).

4. Close the Employees table. Click No when Access asks if you want to save changes to the design.

> **NOTE:** If you save the design changes after sorting a table, the records are saved in the new order.

5. Open the Sales Order Review form, place the pointer in the Company Name field, and click.

**FIGURE 3-6**
Records menu

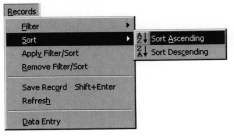

6. Choose Sort from the Records menu and choose Sort Ascending. Scroll through the records. The records are sorted alphabetically in ascending order by company name.

7. Close the Sales Order Review form.

## EXERCISE 3-7 Sort Multiple Columns

You can sort a table by more than one field. For example, you may want to view customers by city and alphabetically by name within the city. Access requires that sorted fields are located next to each other and that the main sort column is on the far left. You may need to move some columns temporarily.

1. Open the Customers table. Place the pointer at the top of the State field and click when the pointer changes to a down-pointing arrow. This selects the entire column.

2. Point to the State field name and drag the column to the left. As you drag the column, a wide vertical line shows where the column could be

inserted. When the wide vertical line is located to the left of the Company Name field, release the mouse button. The State column is now to the left of the Company Name column.

**FIGURE 3-7**
A wide vertical line shows where the column will be inserted.

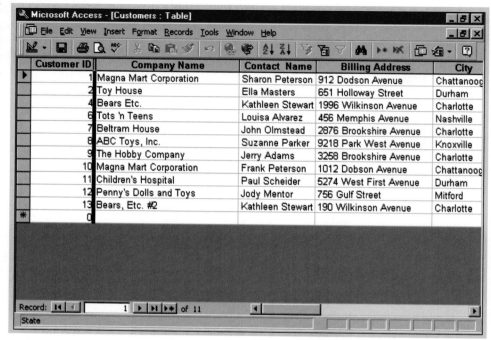

3. Press Shift, point to the Company Name field, and click when the pointer changes to a down-pointing arrow. This selects both columns.

4. Click the Sort Ascending button ⬇. This sorts by state and then company name within each state.

5. Close the Customers table. Click No when Access asks if you want to save changes to the design.

# Using Filters

A *filter* shows a subset of the table with records that match the criteria that you set. For example, if you want to view all the stuffed animals in the D Product Group, you can create a filter that removes the unnecessary records.

There are four types of filters:

- Filter By Selection

   Use Filter By Selection to display only those records that include text you select. This selection is available as a button, as a menu command (under <u>R</u>ecords, <u>F</u>ilter), and from a shortcut menu when you right-click.

- Filter By Form

  Selecting Filter By Form causes a blank datasheet or form to appear. In the datasheet you specify a field (or multiple fields), how the fields are to be sorted, and any additional criteria. Use the <u>A</u>pply Filter/Sort command (or the Apply Filter button ▼) to perform the filter. Filter By Form is available as a button and as a menu command (under <u>R</u>ecords, <u>F</u>ilter).

- Filter By Input

  Use Filter by Input to display records that match an exact value in the current field. It is available only from a shortcut menu when you right-click.

- Filter Excluding Selection

  Use Filter Excluding Selection to exclude all records that match a selected value. Filter Excluding Selection is available as a menu command (under <u>R</u>ecords, <u>F</u>ilter) and from a shortcut menu when you right-click.

> **NOTE:** After you use the Apply Filter button ▼, it turns into the Remove Filter button ▼. Clicking the Remove Filter button displays all records in the table again.

---

**EXERCISE**  **Use Filter By Selection**

---

When you create a Filter By Selection, you simply highlight text within a field that you want to establish as criteria. Table 3-2 shows the effect of text selection on the filter.

**TABLE 3-2**  **Selecting Text for a Filter By Selection**

| SELECT | TO DISPLAY |
|---|---|
| Entire field | Records containing the exact match of the text selected. |
| Part of the field starting with the first character | Records that start with the same character(s) as the selected text. |
| Characters anywhere in the field (except the beginning or the end) | Records in which all or part of the field matches the selected text. |

1. Open the Stuffed Animals table.

2. In the List Price column, select the first occurrence of $12.50.

3. Click the Filter By Selection button . Access displays only products with list prices of $12.50.

**FIGURE 3-8**
Filter By Selection displays products with a list price of $12.50.

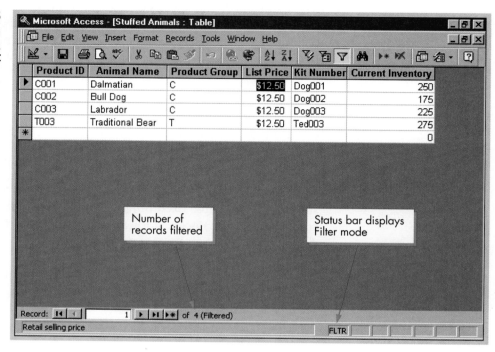

4. Click the Remove Filter button 🔽 to display all the records in the Stuffed Animals table again.

> **NOTE:** The Remove Filter button is the same as the Apply Filter button except that the Remove Filter button appears depressed when a filter is in effect.

5. Move to the first record and select the characters "Dog" in the Kit Number field.

6. Choose Filter from the Records menu. Then choose Filter By Selection. Only the records with Kit Numbers that begin with "Dog" are displayed.

**FIGURE 3-9**
Filtering results when selecting part of a field.

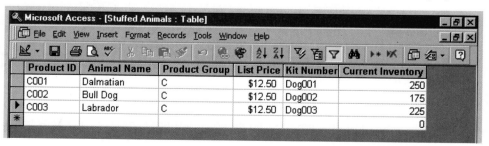

**NOTE:** If the table contained an entry of "Doggie," the filter would also display that record because it contains the characters "Dog."

**7.** Choose <u>R</u>emove Filter/Sort from the <u>R</u>ecords menu to display all the records in the Stuffed Animals table.

**8.** Close the Stuffed Animals table. Click <u>Y</u>es to save the changes to the table.

---

**EXERCISE** 3-9 **Use Filter By Form**

---

A Filter By Form is more sophisticated than a Filter By Selection because you can use it to set criteria for more than one field. When you use a Filter By Form, a blank datasheet is displayed. You use an expression in a Filter By Form or select from a drop-down list of values. In the following exercise, you use a Filter By Form to view all employees who have job code MF05.

**1.** Open the Employees table and click the Filter By Form button ▣. A blank Filter by Form window appears.

**2.** Click in the Job Code field. A drop-down list arrow appears.

**3.** Click the arrow. The drop-down list displays all the values in the Job Code field. Choose MF05 from the list. Quotation marks appear around "MF05" and the value is entered in the field.

**FIGURE 3-10**
Job Code field
drop-down list

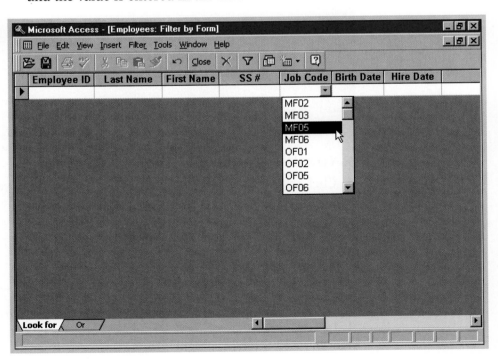

4. Click the Apply Filter button 🝥. The records with the job code of MF05 appear.

5. Click the Remove Filter button 🝥. Close the Employees table. Click Yes to save the changes to the table.

6. Open the Employees Information Form and click the Filter By Form button 🝥. A blank form appears.

7. Click in the Job Code field to display the drop-down list arrow.

8. Choose MF06 from the drop-down list.

9. Click the Apply Filter button 🝥. The first record matching the criteria appears in the form.

**FIGURE 3-11**
Results of the Filter
By Form

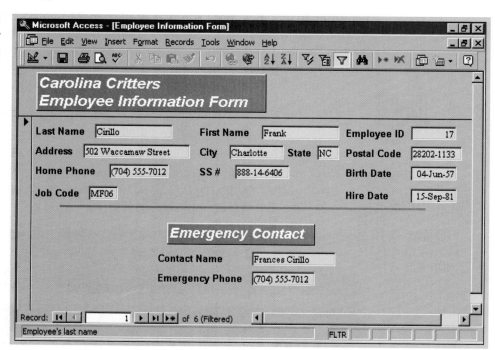

10. View the next record that fits the criteria.

11. Click the Remove Filters button 🝥. Close the Employees Information Form.

# EXERCISE 3-10  Use Filter By Input

Use Filter By Input to search for an exact value in the current field. The Filter By Input command is available from a shortcut menu displayed by clicking the right mouse button in a field.

**FIGURE 3-12**
Use Filter By Input

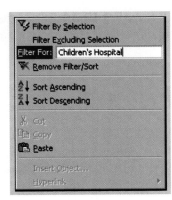

1. Open the Customers table.
2. Click in the Company Name field.
3. Click the right mouse button. In the Filter For: box, key **Children's Hospital**. Click anywhere outside the menu or press Enter.

   **NOTE:** You must key the exact value. Keying "Children's," for example, will not return any records. The value must also be in the current field.

4. The Children's Hospital record is displayed. Click the Remove Filter button ▽ and close the table. Do not save the changes.

## EXERCISE 3-11 Use Filter Excluding Selection

Use Filter Excluding Selection to exclude records that match a value. For example, you may want to view the records of all kits except those of a certain supplier.

1. Open the Kit Contents table.
2. In the Supplier ID field, select "AA-01" in any record.
3. Click the right mouse button. Click Filter Excluding Selection.

**FIGURE 3-13**
Use Filter
Excluding Selection

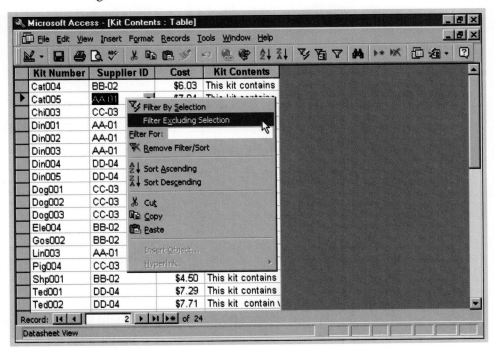

**4.** All records except those with Supplier ID AA-01 are displayed. Click the Remove Filter button 🔽 and close the table. Do not save the changes.

# Creating an Advanced Filter/Sort

You use the Filter window to create an Advanced Filter/Sort. The upper pane of the Filter window displays a list of fields in the table. The lower pane displays a grid in which you can specify field names, sort orders, and criteria expressions.

 **TIP:** The design grid in a Filter window is sometimes called the QBE (Query By Example) grid.

**EXERCISE** **3-12** **Use the Filter Window**

**1.** Open the Sales Orders table.
**2.** Choose Filter from the Records menu. Choose Advanced Filter/Sort. The Filter window appears.

**FIGURE 3-14**
Filter window

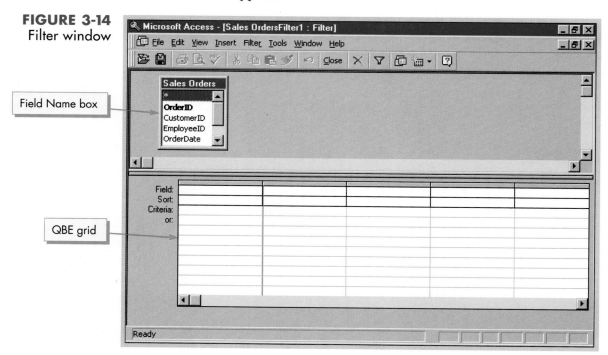

**3.** Select the OrderID field from the Field Name box in the upper pane and drag it to the Field row in the design grid in the lower pane. (When the pointer reaches the lower pane, it turns into a field symbol until you drop it into the design grid.)

**4.** Select the CustomerID field in the Field Name box and drag it to the second column in the Field row in the lower pane.

**FIGURE 3-15**
Adding fields and criteria to the Filter window.

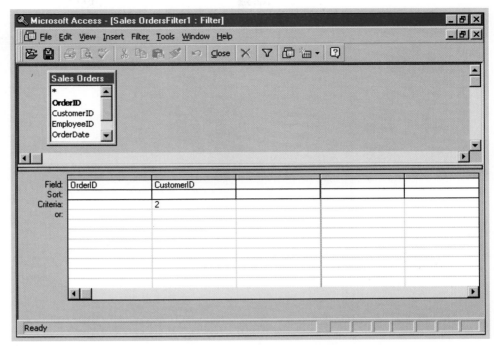

**5.** Click the Criteria row under the CustomerID field in the lower pane. Key **2**.

**6.** Click the Apply Filter button 🟨. The record for Customer #2 is displayed.

**7.** Click the Remove Filter button 🟨.

**8.** Close the Sales Orders table. Click <u>Y</u>es to save the changes.

## EXERCISE 3-13 Create an Advanced Filter

**1.** Open the Employees table and maximize the window, if necessary. Review the current arrangement of the records to see their order.

**2.** Click anywhere in the Employee ID column and click the Sort Ascending button 🔼.

**3.** Choose <u>F</u>ilter from the <u>R</u>ecords menu. Then choose <u>A</u>dvanced Filter/Sort.

 **NOTE:** You may see the sort condition and criteria from the Filter By Form you completed in Exercise 3-12. The filter was saved with the table.

**4.** Click the Clear Grid button ☒.

**5.** You can adjust the size of the panes so you see more space in the top pane. Then you can resize the Field Name box. Place the pointer on the horizontal border between the two panes and it changes to the split pointer.

**FIGURE 3-16**
Resizing the Filter
Window panes

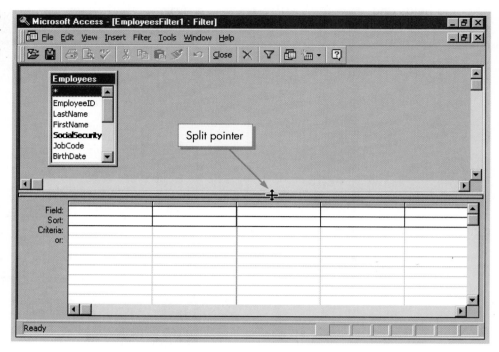

**6.** Drag the border down to make the upper pane slightly taller than the lower pane. Then drag the border for the Field Name box to make it taller so you can see more of the field names.

**7.** Drag JobCode in the Field Name box to the first column in the QBE grid.

**8.** Click in the Criteria row beneath the JobCode field and key **OF06**. (See Figure 3-17 on the next page.)

**9.** Click the Apply Filter button ▽. The records of the employees whose Job Code is OF06 are listed.

**10.** Click the Remove Filter button ▽.

**11.** Choose <u>F</u>ilter from the <u>R</u>ecords menu, then choose <u>A</u>dvanced Filter/Sort.

**12.** Click the Clear Grid button ☒.

**13.** Drag LastName in the Field Name box to the first column in the QBE grid.

**14.** Click in the Criteria row beneath LastName and key **W\***.

**15.** Click the Apply Filter button ▽. The records for employees whose last name starts with a "W" are listed.

**FIGURE 3-17**
Filter window for
OF06 JobCode.

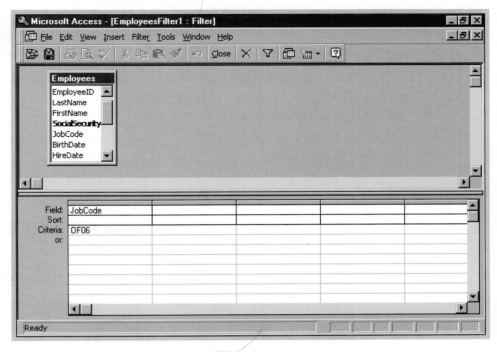

16. Click the Remove Filter button .

17. Sort the records again in ascending order by the EmployeeID.

18. Close the Employees table and save the changes.

> **NOTE:** Filters are saved with the table until you create another filter. You can click the Apply Filter button to display the results of a saved filter.

# *Using Multiple Criteria*

You may need to use more than one condition or criterion to find records. For example, you may need to find all the stuffed animals that belong to either Product Group D or E. This is considered an *"Or"* condition. An "Or" condition finds records that match *either* one of the criteria you specify. When you write "Or" conditions in a Filter By Form, you use two or more blank datasheet windows.

Another possible use of multiple criteria is an *"And"* condition. Suppose you need to find all stuffed animals in Product Group D that cost $10.75. A record would have to meet *both* conditions. "And" conditions are more restrictive and usually find fewer matching records than "Or" conditions. When you prepare "And" conditions in a Filter By Form, you place the conditions on one blank datasheet.

**EXERCISE** **3-14** Create a Filter Using Multiple Criteria

1. Open the Stuffed Animals table and maximize the window, if necessary.
2. Click the Filter By Form button 🖺.
3. Click the Clear Grid button ✕.
4. Click in the Product Group field and choose D from the drop-down list.
5. Click the Or tab at the bottom of the window. This opens a second blank form for the second criteria. (Remember, an "Or" condition uses two or more datasheets to list criteria.)

**FIGURE 3-18**
Click the Or tab to open a new blank datasheet.

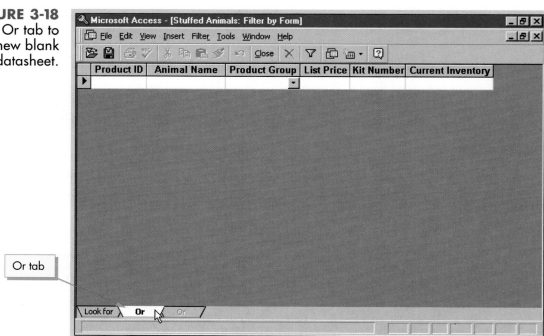

6. Click in the Product Group field and choose E from the drop-down list.
7. Click the Apply Filter button 🟅. The stuffed animals from either Group D or E are listed.
8. Click the Remove Filter button 🟅.
9. Click the Filter By Form button 🖺.
10. Click the Clear Grid button ✕.
11. Click in the Product Group field and choose E from the drop-down list.
12. Click the List Price field and choose 10.75. This is an "And" condition so the two criteria are on the same datasheet.

**FIGURE 3-19**
An "And"
condition uses only
one datasheet.

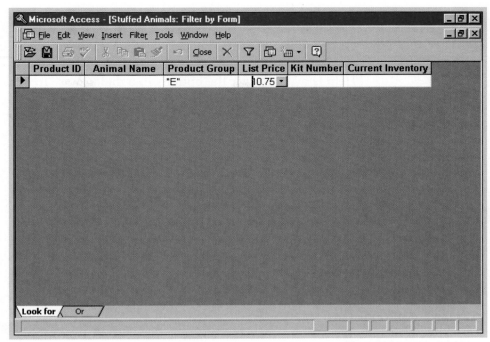

13. Click the Apply Filter button . Stuffed animals from Group E with a list price of $10.75 are listed.

14. Click the Remove Filter button.

15. Close the Stuffed Animals table and save the changes.

**COMMAND SUMMARY**

| FEATURE | BUTTON | MENU | KEYBOARD |
|---|---|---|---|
| Find | 🔍 | Edit, Find | Ctrl + F |
| Replace | | Edit, Replace | Ctrl + H |
| Sort, Ascending | ↕ | Records, Sort, Ascending | |
| Sort, Descending | ↕ | Records, Sort, Descending | |
| Filter By Selection | | Records, Filter, Filter By Selection | |
| Filter By Form | | Records, Filter, Filter By Form | |
| Filter Excluding Selection | | Records, Filter, Filter Excluding Selection | |
| Apply Filter | | Records, Apply Filter/Sort | |
| Remove Filter | | Records, Remove Filter/Sort | |

## USING HELP

Help is available for the options in a dialog box. To explore an option before choosing it, click the Help button in the dialog box. The mouse pointer changes to a question mark and you can click the option to display a pop-up description. You can also right-click on the option and click What's This to display the pop-up description.

**Try exploring options in the Find dialog box:**

1. Open the Employees table.

2. Open the Find dialog box.

3. Point to Find What option  (the title itself, not the box). Click the right mouse button and click What's This? A pop-up box appears with the description of the option.

**FIGURE 3-20**
Click the right mouse button on a screen element to get Help.

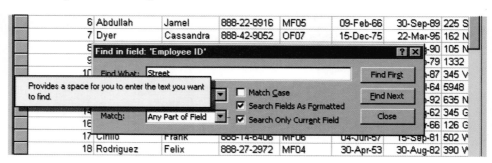

4. Click the pop-up box with the left mouse button to close the box. (To copy or print the description, click the right mouse button and select from the shortcut menu.)

5. Close the Find dialog box

6. Choose What's This from the Help menu.

7. Point to the Filter By Form button and click the left mouse button. Click the pop-up box to close it.

8. Close the Employees table.

# Concepts Review

Each of the following statements is either true or false. Indicate your choice by circling **T** or **F**.

T  F  **1.** The results of all types of filters are displayed in a form.

T  F  **2.** The keyboard command to find text is Ctrl+H.

T  F  **3.** You can use filters to apply multiple criteria or conditions.

T  F  **4.** You can use the asterisk (*) wildcard to replace a single character when finding records.

T  F  **5.** To narrow your search, you can use the Match Case option to find words with the same capitalization.

T  F  **6.** When using the Sort command to sort multiple columns, the columns must be next to each other.

T  F  **7.** If no primary key is present, records are sorted in the order in which they were keyed.

T  F  **8.** You can sort by several columns, selecting one column at a time.

Write the correct answer in the space provided.

**1.** How do you reposition or move the Find and Replace dialog boxes?

_____

**2.** What command do you use to change every occurrence of a word in a table without confirmation?

_____

**3.** What do you call a sort from lowest to highest number or from A to Z?

_____

**4.** How do you add fields to a QBE grid in the Filter window?

_____

**5.** What button is used to apply a filter?

_____

6. Where do you key the text you want to find in the Find dialog box?

_____

7. What do you use in place of characters when you don't know the exact spelling of a name?

_____

8. What Search option do you select when you want to search an entire table?

_____

## CRITICAL THINKING

**Answer these questions on a separate page. There are no right or wrong answers. Support your answers with examples from your own experience, if possible.**

1. The Replace All option is very powerful and can be very useful. It can also lead to occasional problems if you haven't thought through a specific Replace All operation. Describe what types of errors might occur and discuss some precautions you might take when using Replace All.

2. When sorting by multiple columns, how could you sort data that would be helpful? How would a different sort arrangement change the usefulness of the table?

# Skills Review

## EXERCISE 3-15

**Find and replace records.**

1. Start Access, if necessary, and open the file *[your initials]*CC1.mdb.
2. Find a record by following these steps:
   a. Open the Stuffed Animals table.
   b. Click the Find button 🔍.
   c. Key **10.75** in the Find What box..
   d. Choose All from the Search drop-down list, if necessary. Make sure the Match Case and Search Only Current Field options are not selected.
   e. Click the Find First command button. The first occurrence of $10.75 is highlighted.
   f. Click Find Next to move to the next occurrence. Continue clicking Find Next until you see the message box telling you Access finished searching the records. Click OK.

*g.* Close the Find dialog box and close the Stuffed Animals table.

**3.** Find a record using the Match Case option by following these steps:

      *a.* Open the Kit Contents table and click the Find button 🔍.

      *b.* Key **dd-04** in the Find What box. Click the Match Case check box to select it.

      *c.* Click Find Next to begin the search. Access tells you it finished searching the records without finding a match. Click OK.

      *d.* Edit the text in the Find What box to **DD-04**. Click Find Next.

      *e.* Continue clicking Find Next. Click OK when Access finishes searching the table. Close the Find dialog box and close the Kit Contents table.

**4.** Find a record using wildcards by following these steps:

      *a.* Open the Stuffed Animals table and click the Find button 🔍.

      *b.* Key **Ted\*** in the Find What box. Deselect the Match Case check box, if necessary. Choose All from the Search drop-down list.

      *c.* Click Find First. Click Find Next and continue clicking Find Next. Click OK when Access finishes searching the table.

      *d.* Close the Find dialog box and close the Stuffed Animals table.

      *e.* Open the Employee Information Form and click the Find button 🔍.

      *f.* Edit the Find What box by keying **OF??**

      *g.* Click Find Next. Continue clicking Find Next. Click OK when Access finishes searching the form.

      *h.* Close the Find dialog box and close the Employee Information Form.

**5.** Replace text using Find Next by following these steps:

      *a.* Open the Stuffed Animals table.

      *b.* Choose Replace from the Edit menu.

      *c.* Key **9.50** in the Find What text box. Press Tab to move to the Replace With text box and key **10.95**.

      *d.* Click Find Next to start the search.

      *e.* Click Replace to replace the first occurrence.

      *f.* Click Replace again to replace the next occurrence and continue clicking Replace. Click OK when Access can't find the text you specified.

      *g.* Close the Replace dialog box and close the Stuffed Animals table.

**6.** Replace text using Replace All by following these steps:

      *a.* Open the Employees table.

      *b.* Press Ctrl+H to open the Replace dialog box.

      *c.* Key **MF04** in the Find What text box. Key **MF05** in the Replace With text box.

**d.** Click Replace <u>A</u>ll. Click <u>Y</u>es to continue.

**e.** Close the Replace dialog box and close the Employees table.

EXERCISE 3-16

## Sort records in forms and tables.

**1.** Sort a single column by following these steps:

**a.** Open the Stuffed Animals table and place the pointer in the Animal Name field of the first record and click.

**b.** Click the Sort Ascending button.

**c.** Click the Sort Descending button.

**d.** Close the Stuffed Animals table. Click <u>N</u>o when Access asks if you want to change the design of the table.

**e.** Open the Employee Information Form. If necessary, place the pointer in the Last Name field and click.

**f.** Choose <u>S</u>ort from the <u>R</u>ecords menu and choose Sort <u>A</u>scending.

**g.** View several records to check the order.

**h.** Close the Employee Information Form.

**2.** Sort multiple columns by following these steps:

**a.** Open the Kit Contents table.

**b.** Select the Supplier column.

**c.** Press Shift, point to the Cost column, and click when the pointer changes to a down-pointing arrow.

**d.** Click.

**e.** Close the Kit Contents table. Click <u>Y</u>es to save changes to the table.

EXERCISE 3-17

## Use filters to search for records in tables and forms.

**1.** Use Filter By Selection by following these steps:

**a.** Open the Employees table.

**b.** Select MF06 in the Job Code field.

**c.** Choose <u>F</u>ilter from the <u>R</u>ecords menu, then choose Filter By <u>S</u>election.

**d.** Choose <u>R</u>emove Filter/Sort from the <u>R</u>ecords menu.

**e.** Close the Employees table and save the changes.

**2.** Use Filter By Form by following these steps:

***a.*** Open the Customers table.

   ***b.*** Click the Filter By Form button ▣.

   ***c.*** Click the Clear Grid button ✕.

   ***d.*** Move to the State field and click inside the field. Click the down arrow and choose NC from the drop-down list.

   ***e.*** Click the Apply filter button ▽.

   ***f.*** Click ▽. Close the Customers table and save the changes.

   ***g.*** Open the Sales Order Review form and click the Filter By Form button ▣.

   ***h.*** Move to the Employee ID field and click inside the field. Choose 6 from the drop-down list.

   ***i.*** Click the Apply Filter button ▽.

   ***j.*** Click the Next Record button ▶ to see the next record that fits the criteria.

   ***k.*** Click the Remove Filter button ▽. Close the Sales Order Review form.

**3.** Use Filter By Input by following these steps:

   ***a.*** Open the Kit Contents table.

   ***b.*** Click in the Kit Number field.

   ***c.*** Click the right mouse button. In the Filter For: box, key **Chi003**. Click anywhere outside the menu or press Enter to view the Chi003 record.

   ***d.*** Click the Remove Filter button ▽ and close the table. Don't save the changes.

**4.** Use Filter Excluding Selection by following these steps:

   ***a.*** Open the Sales Order Line Items table and briefly review it.

   ***b.*** Click in the Product ID field.

   ***c.*** Find "C003" in any record and select it.

   ***d.*** Click the right mouse button. Click Filter Excluding Selection. All records except those with Product ID C003 are displayed.

   ***e.*** Click the Remove Filter button ▽ and close the table. Don't save the changes.

## EXERCISE 3-18

## Use advanced filters to search for multiple records in tables and forms.

   **1.** Use the Filter window by following these steps:

   ***a.*** Open the Employees table.

   ***b.*** Choose <u>F</u>ilter from the <u>R</u>ecords menu and then choose <u>A</u>dvanced Filter/Sort. Maximize the window, if necessary.

***c.*** Click the Clear Grid button ⊠.

   ***d.*** Place the pointer on the horizontal border between the two panes to display the split pointer. Drag the border down to make the top pane taller than the bottom pane. Drag the border for the Field Name box to make it taller so you can see more field names.

   ***e.*** Drag JobCode from the Field Name box to the Field row in the first column in the QBE grid

   ***f.*** Click in the Criteria row beneath JobCode and key **MF03**.

   ***g.*** Click the Apply Filter button ▽.

   ***h.*** Click the Remove Filter button ▽.

2. Create an advanced filter by following these steps:

   ***a.*** Choose <u>F</u>ilter from the <u>R</u>ecords menu. Choose <u>A</u>dvanced Filter/Sort.

   ***b.*** Click the Clear Grid button ⊠.

   ***c.*** Drag LastName to the Field row in the first column in the QBE grid. Drag JobTitle to the Field row in the second column.

   ***d.*** In the Sort row for the LastName field, click and select Ascending.

   ***e.*** In the Criteria row for the JobCode field, key **MF05**.

   ***f.*** Click the Apply Filter button ▽.

   ***g.*** Click the Remove Filter button ▽.

   ***h.*** Close the Employees table and save the changes.

3. Create a filter using multiple criteria by following these steps:

   ***a.*** Open the Kit Contents table.

   ***b.*** Click the Filter By Form button ▦. Click the Clear Grid button ⊠, if necessary.

   ***c.*** Move to the Supplier ID field and click. Choose CC-03 from the drop-down list.

   ***d.*** Click the Or tab at the bottom of the window.

   ***e.*** Choose AA-01 in the Supplier ID field and click the Apply Filter button ▽.

   ***f.*** Click the Remove Filter button ▽.

   ***g.*** Click the Filter By Form button ▦. Click the Clear Grid button ⊠.

   ***h.*** Move to the Supplier ID field and click. Choose CC-03 from the drop-down list.

   ***i.*** Move to the Cost field and click. Choose 6.73 from the drop-down list.

   ***j.*** Click the Apply Filter button ▽.

   ***k.*** Click the Remove Filter button ▽.

   ***l.*** Close the Kit Contents table and save the changes.

4. Close the database.

# Lesson Applications

## Find and replace records in a table.

1. Start Access, if necessary, and open the file *[your initials]*CC1.mdb. Open the Customers table.

2. Find all occurrences of Chattanooga and replace it with **Memphis**.

 **TIP:** Make sure all the check boxes are deselected in the Replace dialog box.

3. Close the Customers table.

4. Open the Kit Contents table.

5. Sort by Kit Number in descending order and use the Replace command to make the corrections to the Kit Contents table shown in Figure 3-21. Check Search Only Current field in the Replace dialog box. (Not all the rows of the table appear in the following figure.)

**FIGURE 3-21**

| Kit Number | Supplier | Cost | Kit Contents |
|---|---|---|---|
| Zeb001 | BB-02 | $6.71 | This kit contains |
| Whl005 | AA-01 | $4.24 | This kit contains |
| Tig002 | CC-03 | $6.73 | This kit contains |
| Ted005 | AA-01 | $8.05 | This kit contains |
| Ted004 | AA-01 | $6.97 | This kit contains |
| Ted003 | DD-04 | $6.71 | This kit contains |
| Ted002 | DD-04 | $7.71 | This kit contains |
| Ted001 | DD-04 | $7.29 | This kit contains |

*Bear*

6. Close the Replace dialog box. Then close the Kit Contents table and save the changes.

7. Open the Stuffed Animals table.

**8.** Sort by Kit Number in descending order and use the Replace command to make the corrections to the Stuffed Animals table shown in Figure 3-22. (Not all the rows of the table appear in the following figure.)

**FIGURE 3-22**

| Product ID | Animal Name | Product Group | List Price | Kit Number | Current Inventory |
|---|---|---|---|---|---|
| E002 | Tiger | E | $13.75 | Tig002 | 235 |
| T005 | Sleepy Bear | T | $14.50 | ~~Ted~~005 | 250 |
| T004 | Christmas Bear | T | $13.00 | ~~Ted~~004 | 150 |
| T003 | Traditional Bear | T | $12.50 | ~~Ted~~003 | 275 |
| T002 | Valentine Bear | T | $14.25 | ~~Ted~~002 | 175 |
| T001 | Professor Bear | T | $14.00 | ~~Ted~~001 | 325 |
| F001 | Woolly the lamb | F | $10.75 | Shp001 | 175 |

*Bear*

**9.** Close the Replace dialog box.

**10.** Key your initials in uppercase letters after "Zebra" in the first record. Key your birthdate (in the format mm/dd/yy) after "Whale."

**11.** Print the table.

**12.** Close the Stuffed Animals table and save the design.

## EXERCISE 3-20

**Use a filter to sort records in a table. Sort records in a form.**

**1.** Open the Stuffed Animals table.

**2.** Create a Filter By Selection to show all the products in Product Group E.

**3.** Remove the filter.

**4.** Create a Filter By Selection to show all the products in Product Group T. Remove the filter.

**5.** Use Filter Excluding Selection to show all products other than those in Product Group D. Remove the filter.

**6.** Use a filter to see how many Brontosauruses are in stock

**7.** Close the Stuffed Animals table and save the changes.

**8.** Open the Employees table.

9. Create a Filter By Selection to view the employees with a Job Code of MF05.

10. Print the filter results, landscape. Circle your last name in the records. Remove the filter.

11. Close the Employees table and save the changes.

12. Open the Employee Information Form.

13. Sort the records by Employee ID in ascending order.

14. Find the record with your name using Filter By Input. Remove the filter.

15. Close the Employee Information Form.

## EXERCISE 3-21

### Use multiple criteria in a filter.

1. Open the Kit Contents table.

2. Use a Filter By Form to find the kits from Suppliers BB-02 or DD-04.

3. Remove the filter.

4. Close the Kit Contents table and save the changes.

5. Open the Stuffed Animals table.

6. Use a Filter By Form to display all products that are either in Product Group E or have a List Price of $11.00.

7. Print the table, portrait.

8. Remove the filter. Close the Stuffed Animals table and save your changes.

## EXERCISE 3-22

### Use an Advanced Filter.

1. With the Employees table open, create an Advanced Filter using the Hire Date and Job Code fields.
   - Sort the Hire Date in ascending order.
   - Set the criteria for the Job Code as **MF05**

2. Apply the filter.

3. Print the results of the filter, landscape.

 **TIP:** Employee #26 has your name.

**4.** Remove the filter.

**5.** Create another Advanced Filter using the same fields (Hire Date and Job Code). Edit the criteria for the Job Code to **MF06** and apply the filter. Which employee with job code **MF06** has worked at Carolina Critters the longest?

**6.** Remove the filter.

**7.** Sort the Birth Date field in ascending order. Which employee is the oldest? Sort the Birth Date field in descending order. Which employee is the youngest?

**8.** Remove the filter.

**9.** Close the Employees table and save the changes.

**10.** Exit Access.

# Unit 1 Applications

## APPLICATION 1-1

Add and edit records in a table. Sort records in ascending and descending order. Print a table.

1. Open the file **[your initials]CC1.mdb**.

2. Open the Employees table and maximize the window.

3. Sort the records by Employee ID. Select the Employee ID and Last Name columns and freeze them.

4. Make the corrections to the Employees table shown in Figure U1-1. (Not all the columns and rows of the table appear in the figure.)

**FIGURE U1-1**

| Employee ID | Last Name | First Name | SS # | Job Code | Birth Date |
|---|---|---|---|---|---|
| 5 | Floria | Maria | 888-64-8020 | MF03 | 19-Mar-69 |
| 6 | Abdullah | Jamel | 888-22-8916 | MF05 | 09-Feb-66 |
| 7 | Dyer | Cassandra | 888-42-~~9052~~ *9079* | ~~OF07~~ *MF03* | ~~15-Dec-75~~ *79* *10* |
| 8 | Wilson | Zipporah | 888-74-2716 | MF02 | 04-Jun-70 |
| 9 | Thomas-Smith | Louise | 888-24-6682 | MF05 | 06-Apr-49 |

5. Increase the width of the Address column to accommodate the text in the column. Scroll down to view all the Addresses.

6. Increase the width of the Emergency Contact and Emergency Phone columns to accommodate the field names.

7. Decrease the width of the City column to accommodate the text in the column.

8. Unfreeze the columns.

9. Close the Employees table and save the layout.

10. Open the Stuffed Animals table and sort the table by Product ID in ascending order. Move to the last record.

11. Make the corrections to the Stuffed Animals table shown in Figure U1-2. (Not all the rows of the table appear in the following figure.)

**FIGURE U1-2**

| Product ID | Animal Name | Product Group | List Price | Kit Number | Current Inventory |
|---|---|---|---|---|---|
| T003 | Traditional Bear | T | $12.50 | Bear003 | 275 |
| T004 | Christmas Bear | T | $13.00 | Bear004 | 150 |
| ~~T005~~ | Sleepy Bear | T | ~~$14.50~~ | ~~Bear005~~ | 250 |

*T006*      *13.95*      *Bear006*

12. Close the Stuffed Animals table. Save the layout changes.

13. Open the Kit Contents table. Sort the table by Kit Number in ascending order. Make the corrections to the table shown in Figure U1-3. (Not all the rows of the table appear in the figure.)

**FIGURE U1-3**

| Kit Number | Supplier ID | Cost | Kit Contents |
|---|---|---|---|
| Bear003 | DD-04 | $6.71 | This kit contains |
| Bear004 | AA-01 | $6.97 | This kit contains |
| ~~Bear005~~ | ~~AA-01~~ | ~~$8.05~~ | This kit contains |

*Ted006*      *DD-04*      *$7.98*

14. Add the following new record:

    Kit Number: **Anm001**

    Supplier ID: **AA-01**

    Cost: **$8.05**

    Kit Contents: *Key your first and last name.*

15. Sort the Kit Number field in ascending order.

16. Print the table in landscape orientation.

17. Close and save the Kit Contents table.

## APPLICATION 1-2

**Add and delete records in a form and table. Add a new record. Copy and paste text in records.**

1. Open the Employee Information Form.

2. Use the Find command to move to Raymond Davidson's record. Select and delete the record.

**3.** Add the following new record:

| | |
|---|---|
| Last Name: | **Jacobs** |
| First Name: | **Cynthia** |
| Employee ID: | **33** |
| Address: | **152 Grandin Road** |
| City: | **Charlotte** |
| State: | **NC** |
| Postal Code: | **28208-4679** |
| Home Phone: | **(704) 555-2266** |
| SS#: | **888-72-4852** |
| Birth Date: | **03/14/70** |
| Job Code: | **MF04** |
| Hire Date: | **07/21/97** |
| Contact Name: | **Dorothy Jacobs** |
| Emergency Phone: | **(704) 555-2266** |

**4.** Sort the Last Name field in ascending order.

**5.** Close the Employee Information Form.

**6.** Open the Kit Suppliers table.

**7.** Add the following new record leaving the Supplier Name, Address, City, and Postal Code fields blank:

| | |
|---|---|
| Supplier ID: | **HH-08** |
| Supplier Name: | *Leave blank.* |
| Contact Name: | **John Ellsworth** |
| Address: | *Leave blank.* |
| City: | *Leave blank.* |
| Postal Code: | *Leave blank.* |
| Phone Number: | **(303) 555-2696** |
| Fax Number: | **(303) 555-1996** |

**8.** Copy the Supplier Name, Address, City, and Postal Code from the "Mills Fabric & Notion Supply" record and paste them in the new record. Copy one field at a time.

**9.** Change the Supplier Name to **Hilton Fabrics & Notion Supply** and the Address to **1647 Industrial Street**.

**10.** Print the table in landscape orientation.

**11.** Close the Kit Suppliers table.

## APPLICATION 1-3

**Add records in a form. Edit records in a table. Copy and paste records in a table.**

1. Open the Sales Order Review form and add the following new record:

| | |
|---|---|
| Order ID: | **97108** |
| Customer ID: | **4** |
| Company Name: | **Bears Etc.***[your initials]* |
| Order Date: | **08/31/98** |
| Employee ID: | **7** |
| Discount: | **.05** |
| Ship Date: | *Your Birth Date* |
| Order ID: | **97108** |
| Product ID: | **T001** |
| Quantity: | **125** |

2. Print the form for the record you just created.

3. Close the Sales Order Review form.

4. Open the Stuffed Animals table.

5. Add the following new record, leaving the Animal Name and List Price fields blank:

| | |
|---|---|
| Product ID: | **F006** |
| Animal Name: | *Leave blank.* |
| Product Group: | **F** |
| List Price: | *Leave blank.* |
| Kit Number: | **Lam001** |
| Current Inventory: | **200** |

6. Copy the Animal Name and List Price from the "Woolly the lamb" record and paste them in the new record.

7. Change the Animal Name to **Woolsey the lamb**.

8. Sort the Product ID in ascending order.

9. Close and save the Stuffed Animals table.

10. Open the Kit Contents table.

11. Add the following new record leaving the Kit Contents field blank:

| | |
|---|---|
| Kit Number: | **Lam001** |
| Supplier ID: | **CC-03** |
| Cost: | **$4.50** |
| Kit Contents: | *Leave blank.* |

12. Decrease the width of the Supplier ID and Cost columns to accommodate the title text.

13. Sort the Kit Number field in ascending order.

14. Close and save the Kit Contents table.

## APPLICATION 1-4

**Use filters to sort records. Edit records using find and replace.**

1. Open the Kit Suppliers table.

2. Change the Supplier ID of "Robinson Mills, Inc." to **II-09**.

3. Close the Kit Suppliers table.

4. Open the Kit Contents table.

5. Replace all occurrences of DD-04 with **II-09**. Make sure all the check boxes are deselected in the Replace dialog box.

6. Create a Filter By Form to show the Kit Numbers supplied by Supplier II-09.

7. Remove the filter.

8. Close and save the Kit Contents table.

9. Open the Employee Information Form.

10. Use a wildcard character to create a Filter By Form that shows all employees with a Job Code of "OF." Do not select one of the existing Job Codes from the drop-down list. Scroll through the filtered forms, then remove the filter.

11. Use the same wildcard character to create another Filter By Form that shows all employees with a Job Code of "MF." Scroll through the filtered forms and remove the filter.

12. Close the Employee Information Form.

13. Open the Customers table.

14. Use Filter By Input to display all Customers located in Charlotte.

15. Print the results of the filter in landscape orientation.

16. Remove the filter. Close and save the Customers table.

17. Open the Stuffed Animals table.

18. Create a Filter Excluding Selection that displays all products except those with a Product Group of "E."

19. Remove the filter. Close and save the Stuffed Animals table.

## APPLICATION 1-5

### Add a record. Create an advanced filter.

1. Open the Employees table and maximize the window, if necessary.

2. Add a new record for yourself. You will be Employee #34. Enter your first and last name. For your Social Security number, start with **888** and use the rest of your own number.

3. In the Job Code field, copy one of the existing fields.

4. Key the dates in the format: mm/dd/yy. Key your birth date. Key today's date as your Hire Date.

5. For the Street Address, key **127 Cherry Hill Street**.

6. Key your city, state, postal code, and phone. Your emergency contact is the person who should be called if something happens to you.

7. Return the pointer to the first record when you finish your record.

8. Choose Filter from the Records menu and choose Advanced Filter/Sort. Clear the grid.

9. If necessary, maximize the window. Size the panes to see more space in the upper pane. Size the field name box to make it taller.

10. Drag the LastName, FirstName, and Address fields to the QBE grid.

11. Sort the last name field in ascending order.

12. In the Criteria row for the address field, key **\*Road**. Apply the filter and view the results.

13. Remove the filter.

14. Design another Advanced Filter/Sort. Do not clear the grid.

15. Add another criteria for the address field. In the Or row for the Address field, key \***Street**. Apply the filter.

16. Print the results of the filter in landscape orientation.

17. Remove the filter. Close and save the Employee table.

18. Close the database and exit Access.

# UNIT 2

# Building a Database

# Adding Tables to a Database

OBJECTIVES

After completing this lesson, you will be able to:

1. Create a table using the Table Wizard.
2. Make changes to a table in Design View.
3. Add a default value and an input mask to a field.
4. Create a table in Design View.
5. Add a validation rule for a field in a table.
6. Delete a table and compact a database.

 Estimated Time: 1¾ hours

In the first unit, you worked with tables and forms. You learned how to navigate through records, how to edit data, and how to add records. In this lesson, you learn to add new tables to a database using the:

- Table Wizard
- Design View

## *Creating Tables Using a Wizard*

The Table Wizard is the easiest way to create common business and personal tables. The *Table Wizard* is an automated template or sample design for a table. First, you select the type of table you want to create, such as customers, employees, invoices, or medical records. Then the Table Wizard provides a list of field names. You select field names, modifying them to fit your needs. After you name the table, you can start adding records.

# EXERCISE 4-1 Add Fields in Table Wizard

1. Make a copy of **CC2.mdb** and rename it *[your initials]***CC2.mdb**. Open the file.

**FIGURE 4-1**
New Table
dialog box

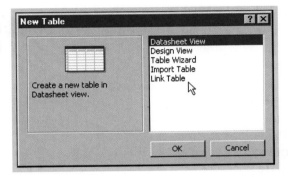

2. Click the Tables tab, if necessary. Click the <u>N</u>ew command button. The New Table dialog box opens.

3. Click Table Wizard and click OK. The first dialog box of the Table Wizard opens with sample tables and fields.

4. Below the list of Sample Tables, click the Business option button (if necessary).

5. In the Samples Tables list, select Customers. Notice that the Sample Fields list changes to show field names that are appropriate for a customer table.

**FIGURE 4-2**
Table Wizard
dialog box

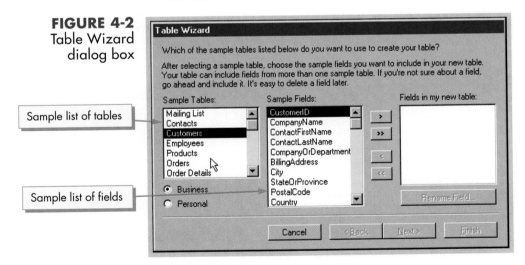

Sample list of tables

Sample list of fields

 **NOTE:** The Sample Tables and Sample Fields lists are not in alphabetical order.

**TABLE 4-1**  **Sample Field Buttons**

| BUTTON | PURPOSE |
|--------|---------|
| ➤ | Adds one Sample Field to the "Fields in my new table" list. |
| ➤➤ | Adds all the Sample Fields to the "Fields in my new table" list. |
| ◄ | Removes one Sample Field from the "Fields in my new table" list. |
| ◄◄ | Removes all the Sample Fields from the "Fields in my new table" list. |

**6.** Select the CustomerID field and click the ➤ button. The CustomerID field is added to the "Fields in my new table" list.

**7.** Move the following Sample Fields to the "Fields in my new table" list by clicking the ➤ button. You can also double-click the Sample Field name to move it.

**CompanyName**
**ContactFirstName**
**BillingAddress**
**StateOrProvince**
**PostalCode**
**ContactTitle**
**PhoneNumber**
**FaxNumber**

 **NOTE:** If you move a Sample Field to your field list by mistake, you can move it back to the Sample Fields list by clicking the ◄ button.

**8.** You can add Sample Fields from more than one Sample Table. In the Samples Table list, select Contacts. Find and add the LastMeetingDate to your list.

**FIGURE 4-3**
Table Wizard dialog box with fields you added.

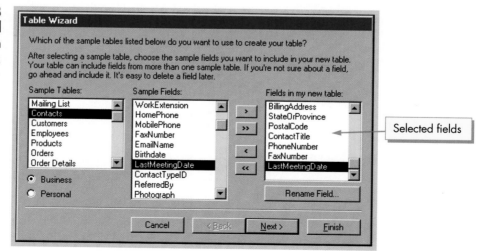

**EXERCISE** **4-2** **Rename Table Fields**

You can rename Sample Fields by clicking the Rename Field button. You can also rename a sample field in Table Design View.

**1.** Select the CustomerID field in your list on the right.

**2.** Click the Rename Field button. The Rename Field dialog box opens with the field highlighted and ready to be renamed.

**FIGURE 4-4**
Rename field
dialog box

**3.** Key **ProspectiveID** in the Rename field text box. Do not insert a space between "Prospective" and "ID." Click OK. ProspectiveID replaces CustomerID in the "Fields in my new table" list.

**4.** Select the ContactFirstName field in your list. Click Rename Field.

**5.** In the Rename Field dialog box, key **ContactName**. Click OK.

**6.** Rename StateOrProvince to **State**. Click OK.

**7.** Rename ContactTitle to **EmployeeID**. Click OK.

**EXERCISE** **4-3** **Complete the Table in the Table Wizard**

**1.** After renaming the fields, click Next. The next dialog box asks what you want to name your new table. Access enters a default name based on the sample table you selected.

 **NOTE:** When a wizard dialog box has a Back button, you can use it to return to the previous dialog box to view or change your choices.

**2.** Key **Prospective Customers** in the "What do you want to name your table?" text box. (See Figure 4-5 on the next page.)

**3.** Read the paragraph about the primary key. Then select "Yes, set a primary key for me."

**4.** Click Next. A dialog box tells you about relationships between tables. For now, do not identify any relationships between this new table and the tables already in your database. (See Figure 4-6 on the next page.)

**FIGURE 4-5**
Naming the table

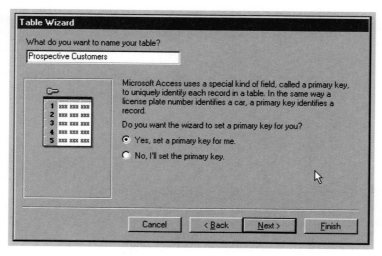

**FIGURE 4-6**
Creating table
relationships

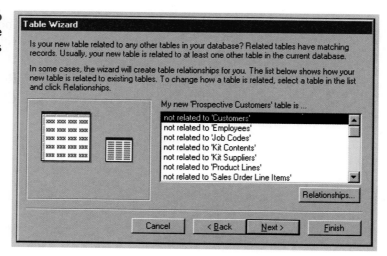

**5.** Click <u>N</u>ext. Access has all the information required to create a table. Now you can:

- Modify the table design.

    This opens the table in Design View so you can make more changes to the design.

- Enter data directly into the table.

    This is the default selection and opens the table so you can enter records.

- Enter data into the table using a form the wizard creates for you.

    This option opens an AutoForm, a simple form for the table you just created. You can then enter records in the form.

**6.** Select "Enter data directly into the table," if necessary. Click <u>F</u>inish. The completed table appears, ready for you to enter data.

**7.** Maximize the window. Add the following three records to the new table:

 **NOTE:** The ProspectiveID field is an AutoNumber field. Access automatically assigns sequential numbers to each new record. You cannot enter data in this field.

| | |
|---|---|
| ProspectiveID: | *Press* Tab |
| CompanyName: | **Crafts & More** |
| ContactName: | **Caroline Morgan** |
| BillingAddress: | **22651 45th Avenue** |
| State: | **WA** |
| PostalCode: | **98032-2265** |
| EmployeeID: | **6** |
| PhoneNumber: | **(206) 555-1919** |
| FaxNumber: | **(206) 555-1199** |
| LastMeetingDate: | **04/30/97** |

| | |
|---|---|
| ProspectiveID: | *Press* Tab |
| CompanyName: | **Bears & Such** |
| ContactName: | **Wayne Fitch** |
| BillingAddress: | **141 Route 1** |
| State: | **VA** |
| PostalCode: | **24472-0141** |
| EmployeeID: | **7** |
| PhoneNumber: | **(703) 555-2734** |
| FaxNumber: | **(703) 555-2735** |
| LastMeetingDate: | **05/09/97** |

| | |
|---|---|
| ProspectiveID: | *Press* Tab |
| CompanyName: | **The Doll and Bear Barn** |
| ContactName: | **Theodora Alexander** |
| BillingAddress: | **365 Main Street** |
| State: | **CT** |
| PostalCode: | **06085-0365** |

EmployeeID:      **7**

PhoneNumber:     **(860) 555-9116**

FaxNumber:      **(860) 555-9117**

LastMeetingDate:   **10/15/97**

**8.** Close the Prospective Customers table.

 **NOTE:** When you use a wizard, many fields are formatted for you, such as the PostalCode, telephone, and date fields.

# *Making Changes in Design View*

You modify the design of a table in Design View, even if you used the Table Wizard to create the table. Design View shows the field names, the data type, an optional description, and properties for each field.

You already worked with field names. The *data type* identifies the type of information in the field (such as alphabetic data or numeric data). The field description is optional and may be helpful to you or others who use the table. *Field properties* are various settings and attributes that affect how a field looks and what it does. Field properties depend on the data type.

 **NOTE:** All Access objects (tables, queries, reports, and forms) have properties stored in a Properties sheet.

**TABLE 4-2**

| Table Design View Elements | |
|---|---|
| **PROPERTY** | **PURPOSE** |
| Field Name | Identifies the data in the field. The name should describe the data and can be up to 64 characters. You can use most letters, numbers, and spaces in a field name. |
| Data Type | Identifies the type of data that you can enter and the type of operations that can be performed on that data. You can select one of nine data types from a drop-down list. |
| Description | Optional explanation of the field that appears in the status bar when the insertion point is in the field. |
| Field Properties | Characteristics or attributes of a field that control how the data is stored and displayed. |

**EXERCISE** | **4-4** | **View Table Design and Edit Field Properties**

You can now use the Design View to design the table you created using the Table Wizard. Notice that next to the field name there is a small key symbol that indicates this field is the primary key.

*1.* Open the Prospective Customers table and maximize the window. Click the View button ![] to switch to Design View. A window with two sections appears. The lower half of the window displays the Field Properties of the current field. It includes two tabs, General and Lookup. The lower half of the window also includes a special Help window that displays definitions and hints related to the field, row, or column in which the pointer is located.

**NOTE:** The General tab includes properties for all the fields in the table; the Lookup tab includes additional properties for text fields. These tabs are often referred to as the Field Properties Sheet or the Properties Sheet.

**FIGURE 4-7**
Prospective
Customers table in
Design View

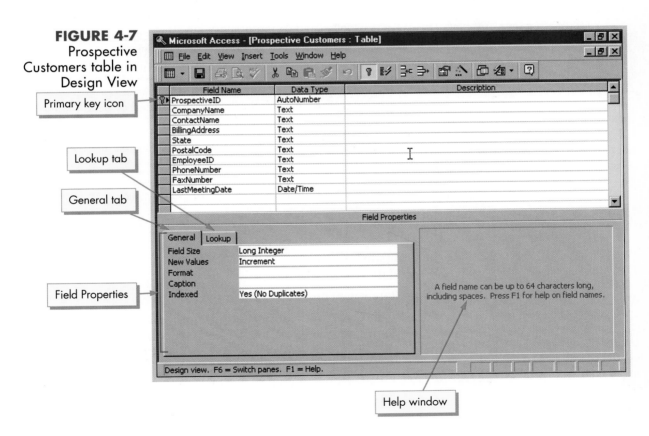

**TABLE 4-3**  **Access Data Types**

| SETTING | TYPE OF DATA |
| --- | --- |
| Text | Stores alphanumeric data, such as names, addresses, or social security numbers. If a field has numbers that aren't used in calculations (phone numbers, policy numbers), you should design them as text fields. A text field can hold up to 255 characters. |
| Memo | Holds descriptive text such as sentences and paragraphs. A memo field cannot be sorted or used in filters. It can be up to 64,000 characters long. |
| Number | Restricted to numbers with or without a decimal point. Data in a number field can be used in arithmetic calculations. |
| Date/Time | Stores formatted dates or times and allows these values to be used in date and time calculations. |
| Currency | Holds monetary values that can be used in arithmetic calculations. |
| AutoNumber | Causes Access to assign the next consecutive number when you add a record. It is sometimes known as a "counter" and is usually used as the primary key. |
| Yes/No | Restricted to one of two values, usually "Yes" or "No," "True" or "False." Often called a "logical field." |
| OLE Object | Stores pictures, sound clips, or graphics created in another application. An OLE field cannot be sorted or used in filters. |
| Hyperlink | Stores an Internet address. The data is displayed as Office 97 hyperlink text so when you click it, Access immediately goes to that Internet site/page. |
| Lookup Wizard | Creates a field that displays values from another table or from a list of values you type. The Lookup Wizard helps you set the data type. |

2. Click the CompanyName row. The Field Properties are different because this is a Text data type.

3. Click in the State row. This is a Text data type.

4. Click in the PostalCode row. Notice that this, too, is a Text data type, however it uses an input mask of "00000\-999." (Look in the third row of the General tab.) The input mask formats the data as you enter it.

**NOTE:** An input mask in the General Tab of the Field Properties Sheet uses predefined codes, but you can enter most input masks using a wizard. You do not need to memorize the codes.

**TABLE 4-4**   Field Properties

| PROPERTY | PURPOSE |
| --- | --- |
| Field Size | Sets the size of a text field and can be up to 255 characters. Access uses only the space it needs, even when the size is larger than the data. |
| Format | Defines the appearance of number and date fields. For example, you can set dates to appear like "May 5, 1999" or "05/05/99." |
| Input Mask | Displays formatting characters such as the parentheses around an area code or the hyphen in a social security number. |
| Caption | Sets a label for a field other than the field name. The label appears as the column title in the table and as the label for the controls in forms and reports. |
| Default Value | Assigns a value automatically to all new records in a table. If all employees live in Illinois, you can set "IL" as the default value for the State field. |
| Validation Rule | Checks the data for the field to verify it conforms to the rule you entered. The following is an example of a validation rule: "C or E or F or D or T." This rule doesn't allow any character except "C," "E," "F," "D," or "T." |
| Validation Text | Displays an error message if you violate the validation rule. For the rule mentioned above, you might enter "You must enter C, D, E, F, D, or T for our products." |
| Required | Does not allow you to enter a record if this field is empty. Set this property to "Yes" to require entry in a field. |
| Allow Zero Length | Allows you to leave text and memo fields empty without those fields being given a value of zero (0). If this property is set to "No" and you leave a text field blank, Access assigns a zero to the field. A zero is different from blank; this could affect the results of calculations and queries. |
| Indexed | Increases the speed of searches and queries, but may slow general operations. Set this to "Yes" for fields that you use often to find or sort records. |

5. Click in the PhoneNumber row. Notice the input mask for this field.

6. Click in the LastMeetingDate row. This is a Date/Time data type with an input mask that helps you enter the date and a format that displays the date in a particular way.

7. Click in the State field. Make sure the General tab is displayed in the Field Properties. This text field is 20 spaces wide.

8. Double-click the number "20" in the Field Size row for the State. Key **2** to make this field narrower.

9. Click in the Billing Address field. Make sure the General tab is displayed. This text field is 255 spaces wide.

10. Double-click the number "255" in the Field Size row. Key **50** to make this field narrower. Text fields should be wide enough to hold most data, but not so wide that they waste space.

11. Click in the Description column for ContactName. Key **Person to call at this location.**

12. Close the table. Since you changed the design of the table, Access reminds you to save it. Click <u>Y</u>es.

**FIGURE 4-8**
Access warns that some data may be lost.

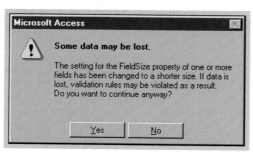

13. Because you changed field sizes, Access warns that some data may be lost. It would be cut off or truncated if you make the field size too small. Click <u>Y</u>es.

14. Open the Prospective Customers table. Maximize the window, if necessary.

15. Click anywhere in the ContactName column. Read the description in the status bar.

**NOTE:** When you changed the field size of the State field, you changed the internal size of the field, not the display size. The field requires less space in the database file, but is displayed in a wider column onscreen.

## EXERCISE 4-5 Insert a Field

If you forgot to include a field while designing a table or find that you have new data, you can insert a field into the table. This is done in Design View.

1. Click the View button  to return to the Design window.

2. Click anywhere in the State row. Click the Insert Rows button 

**NOTE:** When you insert a row, it is placed before the row where the insertion point is located.

3. Click in the Field Name column of the new row if necessary.

**FIGURE 4-9**
Inserting a row

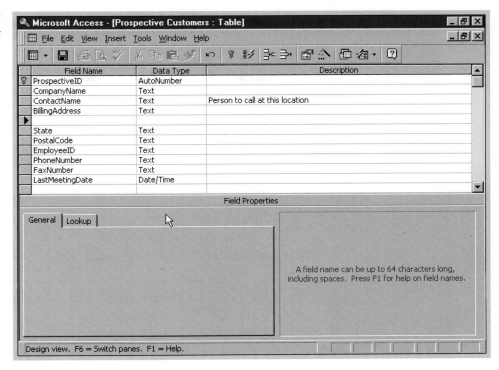

4. Key **City** as the field name. Press Tab. Text is the default data type.

5. Press Tab again. In the Description column, key **City where the new customer is located.**

6. Click anywhere in the EmployeeID row. Choose Rows from the Insert menu.

7. Key **WebPage** as the field name. Press Tab. Choose Hyperlink.

8. Press Tab again. In the Description column, key **Company Web Page Address.**

9. Click anywhere in the LastMeetingDate row. Click the Insert Rows Button ⧉. Key **Comments** as the field name.

10. Press Tab. Choose Memo from the drop down list.

11. Press Tab. Key **General comments about new customer.**

12. Click the View button ⧉ to return to the datasheet. Access asks you to save the table because you made changes. Click Yes.

**FIGURE 4-10**
Access displays a message box asking you to save the table.

*13.* Key the following cities and Internet address in the appropriate columns. Text in a Hyperlink field is formatted as an Internet address. (These addresses are not real, so do not try to access them.)

| Crafts & More: | **Seattle** | **www.crafts.com** |
| Bears & Such: | **Norfolk** | **www.Bear_n_Such.net** |
| The Doll and Bear Barn: | **Hartford** | **www.DollAndBearBarn.org** |

*14.* Click in the Comments field for Record #1.

*15.* Press [Shift]+[F2] to open the Zoom Window. You can use this text-editing window to enter long text.

*16.* Key **This company will order all small stuffed animals.** Click OK to close the Zoom window.

*17.* Click in the Comments field for Record #2 and press [Shift]+[F2].

*18.* Key **This company will order only small teddy bears.** Do not click OK.

 **NOTE:** If you click OK and close the Zoom window before you are ready, press [Shift]+[F2] to open it again.

*19.* Select all the text in the Zoom window. Point at it and click the right mouse button. Select Copy from the shortcut menu. Click OK to close the Zoom window now.

*20.* Click in the Comments field of Record #3. Click the right mouse button and select Paste.

*21.* Close the table.

# *Adding Default Values and Input Masks*

Two field properties that speed data entry are default values and input masks. In addition to allowing you to work faster, these properties increase accuracy.

A *default value* sets the same data for all new records. When all employees live in the same state, you can set that state to appear automatically in each new record. The telephone area code might also be an appropriate use for a default value. If you add the Default Value property to a field after you enter records, those records are not changed.

An *input mask* adds formatting characters to a field so you don't have to enter them. The input mask ensures all the fields are the same and saves you keying time. The input mask for a telephone number looks like this: (___)___-____. (The data is not underlined, that's just the way the predefined code looks.) There is an Input Mask Wizard for telephone numbers, social security numbers, and a few other common fields. You can also use special Access formatting characters to design your own input mask.

# EXERCISE 4-6  Add a Default Value

1. Select the Employees table. Click the <u>D</u>esign button to open the table in Design View. Maximize the window.

2. Click anywhere in the City row.

3. Click in the Default Value row in the General tab. This is where you key text that is entered automatically for all new records.

4. Key **Charlotte**.

**FIGURE 4-11**
Adding a
default value

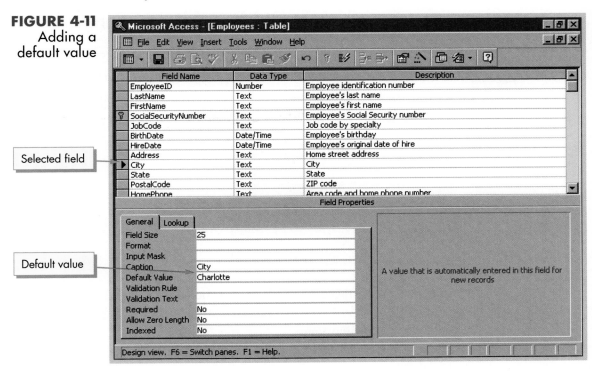

5. Click the View button to return to Datasheet View and click <u>Y</u>es to save the table. Add the following record. The City field is entered for you.

| | |
|---|---|
| Employee ID: | **29** |
| Last Name: | **Sullivan** |
| First Name: | **Thomas** |
| SS#: | **888-33-1587** |
| Job Code: | **MF04** |
| Birth Date: | **06/15/62** |
| Hire Date: | **10/22/95** |
| Address: | **495 West 4th Street** |

City:                    **Charlotte**

State:                   **NC**

Postal Code:             **28202-0495**

Home Phone:              **(704) 555-9889**

Emergency Contact:       **Elizabeth Sullivan**

Emergency Phone:         **(704) 555-9889**

**6.** Close the Employees table.

---

**EXERCISE**    4-7  ### Delete a Field and Add a Field with an Input Mask

**1.** Open the Prospective Customers table in Design View.

**2.** Click in the FaxNumber row. Click the Delete Rows button ▤.

**3.** The message box warns that you will lose the data in the field. Click <u>Y</u>es.

**FIGURE 4-12**
A message warns
you that data will
be permanently
deleted.

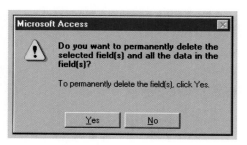

**4.** Change to Datasheet View and save the table. Scroll the window to confirm that you removed the Fax Number field.

**5.** Return to Design View.

**6.** Click in the LastMeetingDate row and click the Insert Rows button ▤.

**7.** Key **FaxNumber** as the field name. Press [Tab]. This is a Text data type.

**8.** Double-click 50 in the Field Size row in the General properties tab. Key **30** to match the PhoneNumber field.

**9.** Click in the Description column for the FaxNumber row. Key **Customer's fax number**

**10.** Click in the Input Mask row in the Field properties area. The Build button ⌷ appears.

> **NOTE:** You can enter your own input mask or start the Input Mask Wizard when you click the Build button ⌷.

**FIGURE 4-13**
Input Mask row

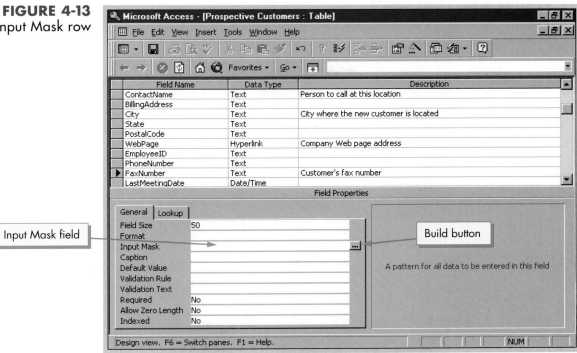

Input Mask field

Build button

11. Click the Build button [...].

12. Before the Input Mask Wizard starts, save the changes you just made. Click Yes.

13. The Input Wizard lists several common masks and shows how the data is displayed. Select the Phone Number mask and click Next.

**FIGURE 4-14**
Input Mask Wizard
with common
masks

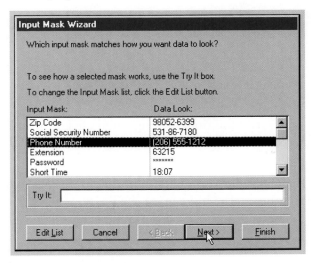

14. The wizard asks if you want to change the input mask. You can also see the Access codes used to build the mask. Click Next.

**FIGURE 4-15**
The wizard gives
you the option to
change the Input
Mask.

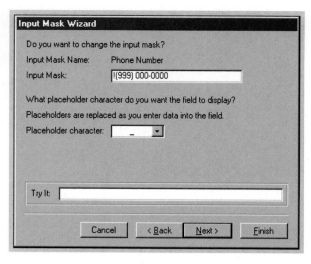

**15.** The wizard asks how you want to store the data within Access. Select "Without the symbols in the mask," if necessary. (This option uses less space internally within Access.)

**FIGURE 4-16**
The wizard asks
you how to store
the data.

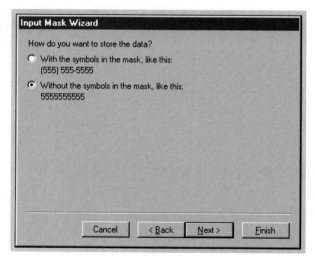

**16.** Click Next, read the final message, and click Finish. The input mask with its Access codes appears in the General properties tab.

**17.** Change to Datasheet View and save the table.

**18.** Key the missing fax numbers. With the input mask you don't have to key the parentheses, the hyphen, or the space.

Crafts & More:             **(206) 555-1199**

Bears & Such:             **(703) 555-2734**

The Doll and Bear Barn:  **(860) 555-9177**

**19.** Close the Prospective Customers table.

# Creating Tables in Design View

You can also create a new table in Design View. You enter the field names, data types, descriptions, and field properties, just as you did using the Table Wizard. You use the same data types and field properties, even the same field names and descriptions, that you used with the Table Wizard.

When you design your own table, you should set a primary key. This is a field in the table that holds unique data for each record. Social security numbers are often used as a primary key field, because no two people have the same number. Don't use a person's name as a primary key, because it's possible that two people have the same name.

 **TIP:** It is possible to create a table without a primary key, but it's not good practice. Access uses the primary key to determine how you relate tables. Although you haven't used relationships yet, you learn the importance of this capability as you learn more about Access.

**EXERCISE 4-8 Create a Table in Design View**

1. Click the Tables tab and click <u>N</u>ew.
2. Select Design View in the New Table dialog box and click OK. Maximize the window, if necessary. No field names appear in the Design window.
3. The insertion point is in the first row in the Field Name column. Key **ProductType**
4. Press Tab. In the Data Type field "Text" is the default setting.
5. Press Tab. In the Description field, key **Name of the animal group**
6. Press F6 to move to the General tab in the property sheet or double-click in the Field Size row.

 **TIP:** In all Windows applications, you can move from one pane to another by pressing F6.

7. Enter **15** as the field size.
8. Click in the Caption row and key **Product Type** with a space between the words.
9. Press F6 and Tab or click in the Field Name column in the second row in the upper pane.
10. Key **ProductCode** and press Tab. This is also a Text data type.
11. Press Tab again and as the Description key **Product line code letter**

127

12. Set the Field Size in the General tab of the Properties sheet to **1**.

13. Set the Caption to **Line Code** with a space between the words.

14. Click in the Indexed row of the Properties sheet. Click the drop-down arrow and select No.

15. Press F6 and Tab or click in the Field Name column in the third row in the upper pane.

16. Key **Details** and press Tab.

17. Click the drop-down arrow for the Data Type and select Memo. You don't specify a size for a Memo field, but it can hold up to 64,000 characters.

18. Press Tab. In the Description column, key **Additional information about this product line.**

19. Click anywhere in the ProductType row. Click the Primary Key button 🔑. The primary key means the data entered in this field must be unique for each record.

20. Click the Save button 💾. The Save As dialog box opens with "Table1" as the name.

 **TIP:** If you don't identify a primary key, you see a message box asking if you want to do so when you save the table.

21. Key **Product Type** as the table name. Click OK. The Design window remains open.

**FIGURE 4-17**
Completed Product
Type table

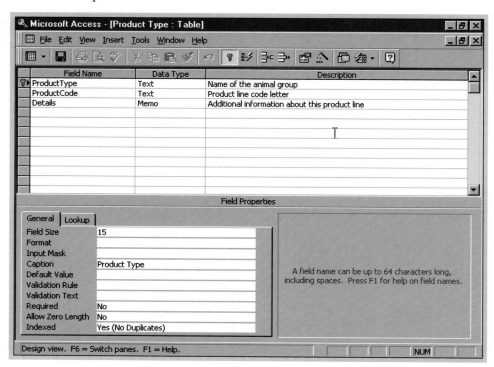

# *Adding Validation Rules and Validation Text*

A *validation rule* sets a specific requirement for the data you enter into a field. For example, you could set a validation rule in an Inventory field that doesn't allow you to enter a number greater than 100. If you enter a number with a value of 105, you break the rule and cannot complete the record. You see an error message when you try to move the insertion point away from the record. *Validation text* is the message you see when you break a validation rule.

 **NOTE:** Some validation rules are automatic. For example, you cannot enter alphabetic characters in a Number field.

## EXERCISE 4-9 Add Validation Rules and Validation Text

1. Click in the Product Code row. Then click in the Validation Rule row in the lower pane. Although there is a Build button here, don't click it. You key the validation rule.

2. Key **C or D or E or F or T** in the Validation Rule row.

3. Click in the Validation Text row. In the Validation Rule row Access automatically enters quotation marks around the codes, but not around the word "or." These quotes are necessary, but you usually don't need to key them yourself.

4. In the Validation Text row, key **You must enter C, D, E, F, or T for our product codes.** Key the period. (See Figure 4-18 on the next page.)

5. Change to the Datasheet View. Click <u>Y</u>es to save the changes.

6. Add the following two new records, one with an error, to check your validation rule.

 **TIP:** To view the entire Details field, press Shift + F2 to open the Zoom window.

| | |
|---|---|
| Product Type: | **Cats & Dogs** |
| Line Code: | **C** |
| Details: | **This line was purchased in 1997 from Olmstead Toys in Chicago. It includes 12 animals and will be expanded to 14 by next fall.** |
| Product Line: | **Lizards** |
| Line Code: | **R** |

**FIGURE 4-18**
Validation rule and
validation text for
Product Code field

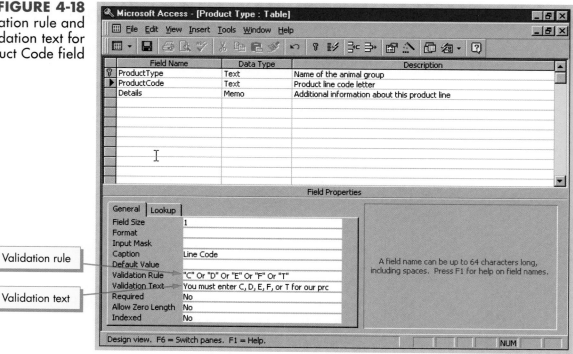

Validation rule

Validation text

**FIGURE 4-19**
Validation text
appears

**7.** Access displays the validation text, alerting you that the value entered in the field violates the validation rule you established. Click OK.

**8.** Change the R to **D**.

**9.** Key the Details for the Lizards Product Type.

Details:  **This line was developed in-house by several employees. It has 3 animals and may be sold to a competitor soon.**

**10.** Close the table.

# Deleting Tables and Compacting Databases

Just as you can add a table to your database, you can also delete it. (If you set relationships between tables, you must first remove those relationships. You learn about relationships in Lesson 8.)

When you make changes in a database, it expands and uses disk space poorly. Unfortunately when you delete records or tables from the database, it doesn't automatically recover the space. The Compact command recovers this space and resaves your database in a more efficient way.

**EXERCISE** **4-10** Delete a Table

**FIGURE 4-20**
Message box
verifying delete

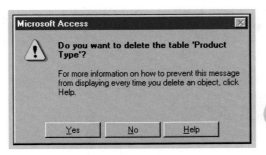

1. In the Tables tab, select the Product Type table, but don't open it.
2. Press ⌈Delete⌋.

**NOTE:** You can also select <u>D</u>elete from the <u>E</u>dit menu.

3. Click <u>Y</u>es to delete the table and close the message box.

**EXERCISE** **4-11** Compact a Database

1. Choose Database <u>U</u>tilities from the <u>T</u>ools menu. Choose <u>C</u>ompact Database. The database is compacted and resaved using the same name.

**COMMAND SUMMARY**

| FEATURE | BUTTON | MENU | KEYBOARD |
|---|---|---|---|
| Insert Row | 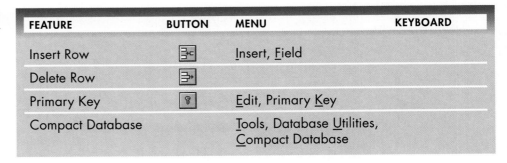 | Insert, <u>F</u>ield | |
| Delete Row | | | |
| Primary Key | | <u>E</u>dit, Primary <u>K</u>ey | |
| Compact Database | | <u>T</u>ools, Database <u>U</u>tilities, <u>C</u>ompact Database | |

**USING HELP**

Access offers several ways to display information about a particular Help topic. For example, once you open the Help Topics dialog box, you can locate a topic using the Contents or Index tab.

● Use the Contents tab in the same way you use a table of contents in a book. The Contents tab displays the contents of Help in outline form.

- Use the Index tab in the same way you would use the index of a book to look up a topic. Key a topic and then scroll through the alphabetical index.

**Display a Help screen to learn about primary keys using the Help Index:**

***1.*** Choose <u>C</u>ontents and Index from the <u>H</u>elp menu.

***2.*** Click the Index tab.

***3.*** In the first box, key **primary keys**. As you're keying the word, the box below scrolls within the index of alphabetized topics.

***4.*** Click "setting" under "primary keys." Click <u>D</u>isplay.

***5.*** In the Topics Found dialog box, double-click "Tables: What they are and how they work." Access displays a graphic window about tables. There are three layers to this help window.

***6.*** Read the first screen. You can click one of the boxed terms to open a description or definition. Then click anywhere to close it.

***7.*** Click the **2** in the top left corner below the Help Topics button. Read this screen.

***8.*** Click the **3** below the Help Topics button. Click the Choose a primary key box.

***9.*** Read the definition. When you finish browsing the Help window, click <u>C</u>lose to close Help.

**FIGURE 4-21**
Using the Help
Index

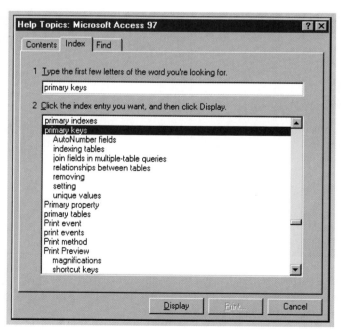

***10.*** Close your database.

# Concepts Review

Each of the following statements is either true or false. Indicate your choice by circling **T** or **F**.

T  F  *1.* After you create a table, you can make changes in Design View.

T  F  *2.* You can rename fields in Design View and when creating a table using the Table Wizard.

T  F  *3.* Access automatically generates validation text after you create a validation rule.

T  F  *4.* You can reduce the size of a database by compacting it.

T  F  *5.* A default value can save time and ensure accuracy by automatically entering data.

T  F  *6.* Properties for a field are always the same, no matter what the data type.

T  F  *7.* You cannot add a field after creating a table.

T  F  *8.* The default size for a text field is 50.

Write the correct answer in the space provided.

*1.* What can you use to automatically format data as you type?

_____

*2.* What property sets a specific requirement for what is entered in a field?

_____

*3.* What are the characteristics of a field called?

_____

*4.* What kind of data type would you normally assign to a phone number field?

_____

*5.* What button do you click to start the Input Mask Wizard?

_____

**6.** What view do you have to be in to modify a table?

_____

**7.** What field property automatically assigns a value when you add a new record to a table?

_____

**8.** What menu and menu option do you use to insert a field when modifying a table?

_____

## CRITICAL THINKING

**Answer these questions on a separate page. There are no right or wrong answers. Support your answers with examples from your own experience, if possible.**

**1.** You learned how to create tables using two different methods. Which way do you prefer? Why? What are some of the advantages of using the other method?

**2.** Besides saving keystrokes, what are some of the other advantages of a default value? Can you think of fields that might be set with default values?

# Skills Review

## EXERCISE 4-12

**Create a table using a wizard and make changes in Design View. Add a default value and an input mask.**

**1.** Open your file *[your initials]*CC2.mdb.

**2.** Create a table using the Table Wizard by following these steps:

    **a.** Click the Tables tab, if necessary. Click the New button.

    **b.** Click Table Wizard and click OK.

    **c.** Select Business, if necessary.

    **d.** In the Sample Tables list, click Employees.

    **e.** Click the EmployeeID field and click the ▶ button.

    **f.** Add the following sample fields with the ▶ button or by double-clicking.

**SocialSecurityNumber**

**FirstName**

**LastName**

**Title**

**Region**

**DateHired**

3. Rename table fields by following these steps:

   *a.* In the "Fields in my new table" list, select the Title field.

   *b.* Click the Rename Field button.

   *c.* Key **JobTitle** in the <u>R</u>ename Field text box and click OK.

4. Complete the table in Table Wizard by following these steps:

   *a.* Click <u>N</u>ext. Key **Sales Representatives** to name your table.

   *b.* Select "Yes, set a primary key for me."

   *c.* Click <u>N</u>ext. Click <u>N</u>ext again to bypass the Relationships dialog box.

   *d.* If necessary, select "Enter data directly into the table." Click <u>F</u>inish.

   *e.* Maximize the window and add the following records:

| | |
|---|---|
| Employee ID: | *Press* Tab |
| Social Security Number: | **888-13-6464** |
| First Name: | **Jeffrey** |
| Last Name: | **Harrison** |
| Job Title: | **Sales Rep II** |
| Region: | **North** |
| Date Hired: | **01/16/97** |
| | |
| Employee ID: | *Press* Tab |
| Social Security Number: | **888-22-8916** |
| First Name: | **Jamel** |
| Last Name: | **Abdullah** |
| Job Title: | **Sales Rep I** |
| Region: | **East** |
| Date Hired: | **09/30/89** |
| | |
| Employee ID: | *Press* Tab |
| Social Security Number: | **888-42-9052** |
| First Name: | **Cassie** |
| Last Name: | **Dyer** |

| | |
|---|---|
| Job Title: | **Sales Rep II** |
| Region: | **West** |
| Date Hired: | **03/22/95** |
| | |
| Employee ID: | *Press* Tab |
| Social Security Number: | **888-42-9056** |
| First Name: | **Dianne** |
| Last Name: | **Clark** |
| Job Title: | **Sales Rep I** |
| Region: | **South** |
| Date Hired: | **09/27/67** |

**5.** Identify and change field properties by following these steps:

**a.** Change to Design View.

**b.** In the upper pane, click in the FirstName row.

**c.** Press F6 or double-click the Field Size entry.

**d.** Key **25** as the field size.

**e.** Click in the LastName row in the upper pane.

**f.** Press F6 or double-click the Field Size entry.

**g.** Key **25** as the field size.

**h.** Change the field size for the JobTitle to **25**.

**i.** Click in the Region row. In the Description column, key **Sales rep's territory.**

**6.** Add fields in Design View by following these steps:

**a.** Click in the Region field. Click the Insert Rows button ▣◄.

**b.** Key **Salary** as the field name. Press Tab.

**c.** Choose "Currency" as the Data Type. Press Tab.

**d.** For the Description, key **Sales rep's base pay**.

**7.** Add a default value by following these steps:

**a.** Click in the JobTitle row.

**b.** Key **Sales Rep** in the Default Value row.

**c.** Change to Datasheet View. Save the table. Click <u>Y</u>es again to continue.

**d.** Add the following record. You need not key the dollar sign or the comma for the salary field.

| | |
|---|---|
| Employee ID: | *Press* Tab |
| Social Security Number: | **888-22-1688** |
| First Name: | **Maggie** |

| | |
|---|---|
| Last Name: | **Miller** |
| Job Title: | *Press* Tab. |
| Salary: | **$22,000** |
| Region: | **North** |
| Date Hired: | **08/21/91** |

*e.* Key the salaries for the other reps. Sales Rep II makes **$28,000**. Sales Rep I makes **$25,000**.

*f.* Close the Sales Representatives table.

## EXERCISE 4-13

### Create a table in Design View.

1. Create a table in Design View by following these steps:

*a.* In the Tables window, click New.

*b.* Select Design View and click OK.

*c.* Key **WarehouseID** as the first field name. Press Tab.

*d.* Display the drop-down list and choose "Number." Press Tab.

*e.* Key **Internal warehouse number** in the Description column.

*f.* Click in the Caption row and key **Warehouse Number**.

*g.* Click in the Field Name column for the second row and key **Location**.

*h.* Press Tab. This field is a Text data type (the default). Press Tab again.

*i.* Key **County location of the warehouse** as the Description.

*j.* Click in the Caption row and key **County Location**.

*k.* Click in the Field Name column for the third row and key **ShipmentDate**.

*l.* Press Tab. Select Date/Time as the data type. Press Tab again.

*m.* Key **Date of last shipment received** as the Description.

*n* Click in the Caption row and key **Shipment Date**.

*o.* Click in the Input Mask row. Click the Build button. Click Yes to save the table.

*p.* Key **Warehouses** as the table name and click OK.

*q.* Click No to continue without setting the primary key.

*r.* Select the Short Date mask and click Next.

*s.* You don't need to change the mask. Click Next. Then click Finish.

*t.* Click in the Field Name column for the fourth row and key **Details**. Press Tab.

*u.* Select Memo as the data type. Press Tab.

*v.* Key **Additional information about this warehouse** as the Description.

*w.* Click in the Caption row and key **Comments**.

**2.** Click anywhere in the ShipmentDate field. Click the Primary Key button 🔑 to set the date as the primary key.

 **NOTE:** This means we have only one shipment per date to one of our three warehouses.

## EXERCISE 4-14

### Add a validation rule and validation text. Add records.

**1.** Add a validation rule and validation text by following these steps:

*a.* Click the WarehouseID row. Click the Validation Rule row.

*b.* Key **1 or 2 or 3** in the Validation Rule row.

*c.* Click in the Validation Text row. Key **You must enter 1, 2, or 3 for our warehouse numbers.** Key the period.

*d.* Change to Datasheet View and click Yes to save the table.

*e.* Make the columns wide enough so you can see the captions at the top of each column.

*f.* Add new records, one with an error, to check the validation rule:

| | |
|---|---|
| Warehouse Number: | **1** |
| County Location: | **Harrison** |
| Shipment Date: | **10/25/97** |
| Comments: | *Leave blank.* |

| | |
|---|---|
| Warehouse Number: | **2** |
| County Location: | **DuPage** |
| Shipment Date: | **12/02/97** |
| Comments: | **Be aware of winter weather conditions.** |

| | |
|---|---|
| Warehouse Number: | **3** |
| County Location: | **Jackson** |
| Shipment Date: | **01/23/98** |
| Comments: | *Leave blank.* |

Warehouse Number:     **4**

 **NOTE:** The Validation message tells you to enter 1, 2, or 3 for the warehouse number.

**g.** Click OK. Change the Warehouse Number to **3** and complete the record:

County Location:     **Jackson**

Shipment Date:       **03/02/98**

Comments:            *Leave blank.*

**2.** Delete a field by following these steps:

    **a.** Switch to Design View.

    **b.** Click in the Location row

    **c.** Click the Delete Rows button ➡️. Click <u>Y</u>es to confirm the deletion.

    **d.** Switch to the Datasheet View and save the table.

    **e.** Close the Warehouses table.

## EXERCISE 4-15

## Delete a table and compact a database.

**1.** Delete a table by following these steps:

    **a.** In the Tables tab, select the Warehouses table, but don't open it.

    **b.** Press Delete.

    **c.** Click <u>Y</u>es to delete the table.

**2.** Delete the Prospective Customers table.

**3.** Compact a database by following these steps:

    **a.** Choose Database <u>U</u>tilities from the <u>T</u>ools menu.

    **b.** Choose <u>C</u>ompact Database.

# Lesson Applications

## Create a table using the Table Wizard. Change a table in Design View.

1. Start Access and open your database file, if necessary.

2. Create a new table using the Table Wizard.

3. Add the following fields from the Products sample table:
   **ProductID**
   **ProductName**
   **CategoryID**
   **UnitsOnOrder**
   **UnitPrice**

4. Add the **Promised-byDate** field from the Orders sample table.

5. Rename the following fields:
   ProductName:      **AnimalName**
   CategoryID:       **ProductGroup**
   UnitPrice:        **ListPrice**

6. Name the table **New Products**.

7. Select the option to have Access assign the primary key. There are no relationships.

8. Select the option to modify the table design and click <u>F</u>inish.

9. Change the data type of the ProductID to Text and change the field size to 15.

10. Add the caption **Animal Name** to the AnimalName field.

11. Add the caption **Product Group** to the ProductGroup field.

12. Change the data type of the ProductGroup to Text and change the field size to 1.

13. Add the description **Number of prospective orders for new items** to the UnitsOnOrder field.

14. Add the caption **List Price** to the ListPrice field.

15. Add the description **Date of promised completion of prototype** to the Promised-byDate field.

16. Change to Datasheet View and save the table. Maximize the window, if necessary. Key the following records:

| | |
|---|---|
| Product ID: | **E006** |
| Animal Name: | **Sea lion** |
| Product Group: | **E** |
| Units On Order: | **125** |
| List Price: | **$11.50** |
| Promised-by Date: | **07/16/98** |

| | |
|---|---|
| Product ID: | **F008** |
| Animal Name: | **Rooster** *Key your last name.* |
| Product Group: | **F** |
| Units On Order: | **100** |
| List Price: | **$9.95** |
| Promised-by Date: | **10/22/98** |

| | |
|---|---|
| Product ID: | **T007** |
| Animal Name: | **Patriot bear** |
| Product Group: | **T** |
| Units On Order: | **200** |
| List Price: | **$13.95** |
| Promised-by Date: | **06/22/98** |

**17.** Resize each column to accommodate the text or title.

**18.** Print the table in landscape orientation. Close and save the table.

## EXERCISE 4-17

### Change a table in Design View. Add a default value and input mask.

**1.** Open the Kit Suppliers table in Design View.

**2.** Insert a field between the City and PostalCode fields. Name the field **State** and choose Text as the data type. Set the Field Size at **2**.

**3.** Change to Datasheet View and save the table.

**4.** Key the following states in the appropriate columns:

| | |
|---|---|
| Mills Fabric & Notion Supply: | **IL** |
| Laramie Fabric Works: | **CO** |
| Cosby Manufacturing Company: | **NC** |
| Robinson Mills, Inc.: | **NJ** |
| Southern Fabrics, Inc | **NC** |
| Northeast Fabrics Supply | **CT** |

5. Close the table.

6. Open the Employees table in Design View.

7. Key **NC** as the default value for the State field.

8. Change to Datasheet View and save the table.

9. Add the following record:

| | |
|---|---|
| Employee ID: | **30** |
| Last Name: | *Key your last name.* |
| First Name: | *Key your first name.* |
| Social Security Number: | **888-***Key the last 6 digits of your SS#.* |
| Job Code: | **MF03** |
| Birth Date: | *Key your birth date.* |
| Hire Date: | **10/15/96** |
| Address: | **2625 Gibbon Road** |
| City: | **Charlotte** |
| State: | **NC** |
| Postal Code: | **28269-2625** |
| Home Phone: | **(704) 555-6114** |
| Emergency Contact: | **Steve Smith** |
| Emergency Phone: | **(704) 555-6115** |

10. Print the table in landscape orientation.

11. Close the table.

12. Open the Sales Representatives table in Design View.

13. Change the Format property of the Date/Hired field Medium Date.

14. Switch to Datasheet View. Save the table.

15. Look at the Date Hired column.

16. Close the table.

## EXERCISE 4-18

**Create a table in Design View. Add an input mask, a validation rule, and validation text.**

1. Create a new table in Design View.

2. Add the following fields, with the data types and properties shown:

| Field Name | Data Type | Field Size | Properties |
|---|---|---|---|
| CarrierID | Text | 4 | Primary Key |
| CarrierName | Text | 30 | |
| ContactName | Text | 50 | |
| Address | Text | 35 | |
| City | Text | 20 | |
| State | Text | 2 | |
| ZIPCode | Text | 15 | Input Mask |

 **NOTE:** Name the table "Carriers."

| | | | |
|---|---|---|---|
| DeliveryMethod | Text | 15 | Validation Rule: **Air or Truck or Rail**; Validation Text: **You must enter Air, Truck, or Rail as the Delivery Method.** |

**NextDayDelivery: Yes/No**

3. Switch to the Datasheet View and save the table.

4. Add the following records. For the NextDayDelivery field, click in the box to mark it as "Yes." Otherwise, leave the box unchecked.

CarrierID: **A101**
CarrierName: **Seaboard Shipping**
ContactName: **Jonathan Martin**
Address: **4513 West Greenberg Lane**
City: **Charlotte**
State: **NC**
ZIPCode: **28202-4513**
DeliveryMethod: **Truck**
NextDayDelivery: **Yes**

CarrierID: **B202**
CarrierName: **US Rail**
ContactName: *Key your name.*
Address: **334 Hilltop Drive**
City: **Chattanooga**
State: **TN**
ZIPCode: **37406-0334**
DeliveryMethod: **Rail**
NextDayDelivery: **No**

| | |
|---|---|
| CarrierID: | **C301** |
| CarrierName: | **All Air Ways** |
| ContactName: | **Pamela Olmstead** |
| Address: | **56 South Boulevard A** |
| City: | **Lancaster** |
| State: | **PA** |
| ZIPCode: | **17603-0056** |
| DeliveryMethod: | **Air** |
| NextDayDelivery: | **Yes** |

5. Adjust columns for the best fit.

6. Print the table in landscape orientation.

7. Close the table. Save the changes.

## EXERCISE 4-19

### Create a table in Design View. Delete a table. Compact the database.

1. Create a new table in Design View.

2. Add the following fields and field properties:

| Field Name | Data Type | Description | Properties |
|---|---|---|---|
| **EmployeeID** | **Number** | **Employee's identification number** | |
| **SocialSecurityNumber** | **Text** | **Employee's social security number** | Primary Key; Input Mask |

 **NOTE:** Name the table "Payroll Information."

| | | |
|---|---|---|
| **MonthlySalary** | **Currency** | **Employee's monthly salary** |
| **HourlyRate** | **Currency** | **Employee's hourly rate** |
| **FederalTax** | **Currency** | **Federal income tax** |
| **StateTax** | **Currency** | **State or local tax** |
| **FICA** | **Currency** | **Social Security deductions** |
| **Savings** | **Currency** | **Personal savings deductions** |
| **OtherInformation** | **Memo** | **Comments** |

3. Enter a caption with a space between the words for each field that has more than one word.

4. Switch to the Datasheet View and save the table.

**5.** Maximize the window, if necessary, and add the following records:

| | |
|---|---|
| Employee ID: | **4** |
| Social Security Number: | **888-10-7812** |
| Monthly Salary: | **$4,500** |
| Hourly Rate: | *Leave blank.* |
| Federal Tax: | **$987** |
| State Tax: | **$234** |
| FICA: | **$433** |
| Savings: | **$125** |
| Other Information: | **Employee has claimed no exemptions.** |

| | |
|---|---|
| Employee ID: | **17** |
| Social Security Number: | **888-14-6406** |
| Monthly Salary: | *Leave blank.* |
| Hourly Rate: | **$7.75** |
| Federal Tax: | **$273** |
| State Tax: | **$113** |
| FICA: | **$101** |
| Savings: | **$50** |
| Other Information: | **Employee participates in our 403(b) program.** |

| | |
|---|---|
| Employee ID: | **3** |
| Social Security Number: | **888-32-8945** |
| Monthly Salary: | **$6,500** |
| Hourly Rate: | *Leave blank.* |
| Federal Tax: | **$1,975** |
| State Tax: | **$378** |
| FICA: | **$623** |
| Savings: | **$200** |
| Other Information: | **Employee has asked to change his exemptions in six months.** |

| | |
|---|---|
| Employee ID: | **30** |
| Social Security Number: | **888**-*Key the last 6 digits of your SS#.* |
| Monthly Salary: | *Leave blank.* |
| Hourly Rate: | **$7.75** |
| Federal Tax: | **$300** |

| State Tax: | **$113** |
|---|---|
| FICA: | **$101** |
| Savings: | **$25** |
| Other Information: | **Employee is part-time and a student.** |

6. Sort the records in ascending order by Employee ID.

7. Adjust columns for the best fit.

8. Print the table in landscape orientation.

9. Close and save the table.

10. Delete the New Products table.

11. Compact the database.

12. Exit Access.

# Adding Forms to a Database

**LESSON 5**

**OBJECTIVES**

After completing this lesson, you will be able to:

1. Create an AutoForm.
2. Create a form using the Form Wizard.
3. Work with the controls on a form.
4. Create a form header.
5. Add a calculated control to a form.
6. Create a form in Design View.
7. Change the format of a form.

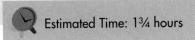 Estimated Time: 1¾ hours

You've used both tables and forms to enter and edit data. When you use a table, all the records are displayed in rows. If a table has many fields, you cannot see the entire record at once and need to scroll. It's often better to view one record at a time in a form.

In addition to this advantage of forms, there are several other benefits of using forms to work with data:

- You can arrange data in an attractive format that may include special fonts, colors, shading, and images.
- You can design a form to match paper forms you use to enter data.
- You can calculate totals and other arithmetic expressions in a form.
- You can display data from more than one table in a form.

**147**

# Creating an AutoForm

The quickest way to create a form for a table is to use an AutoForm. After you specify a table, Access creates a simple, single-column layout that includes all the fields in the table. Access will give you two options in the dialog box when you use AutoForm. A Columnar AutoForm shows one record at a time with all the fields in a single column or list. A Tabular AutoForm displays each record in a single row with each field in a separate column.

## EXERCISE 5-1 Create an AutoForm

1. Open the file *[your initials]***CC2.mdb**.
2. Click the Forms tab. Then click the <u>N</u>ew button. The New Form dialog box opens.
3. Click AutoForm: Columnar in the list.
4. Click the drop-down arrow to the right of the text box labeled "Choose the table or query where the object's data comes from:" This drop-down list displays the names of tables and queries in the database.

**FIGURE 5-1**
Drop-down list displays existing tables and queries

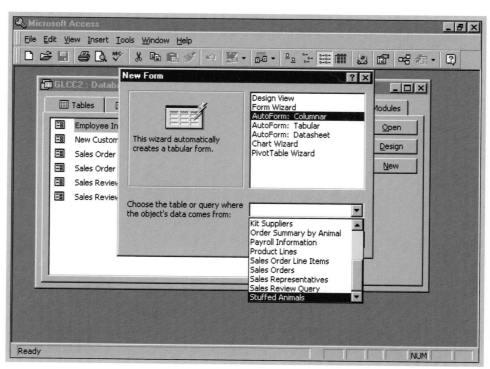

5. Choose "Stuffed Animals" from the drop-down list and click OK.

6. Access creates a simple form displaying the first record of the Stuffed Animals table. The fields are arranged in a single column.

**FIGURE 5-2**
AutoForm with fields displayed in a single column

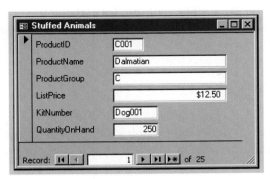

**TIP:** The navigation buttons are at the bottom of the form. These buttons move the pointer from record to record.

## EXERCISE  5-2  **Enter and Edit Data Using a Form**

You use the same tools to enter, find, sort, and display records in a form as you use in tables.

1. Click the New Record button ▶✳. A blank form is displayed. Add the following record, pressing ⌨Tab between fields:

| | |
|---|---|
| ProductID: | **C006** |
| Animal Name: | **Persian cat** |
| Product Group: | C |
| List Price: | **$13.95** |
| Kit Number: | **Cat006** |
| Current Inventory: | **200** |

**NOTE:** The record is saved in the Stuffed Animals table.

2. Click the First Record button ◀ and then the Next Record button ▶ until you locate the Stegosaurus record.

3. Change the List Price field to $**12.50**.

4. Close the form. Access prompts you to save the form before closing it. Click <u>Y</u>es to save the form.

5. In the Save As dialog box, key **Stuffed Animals AutoForm**. Click OK.

# EXERCISE 5-3 Create a Form with a Wizard

You can create the same single-column form using the Form Wizard. The Form Wizard, however, gives you an opportunity to select the fields, the layout, and the style for the form. The layout might be columnar, tabular, or datasheet. The style selects colors and fonts automatically.

**1.** Click the Forms tab if necessary. Then click <u>N</u>ew.

**2.** In the New Form dialog box, select Form Wizard.

**3.** Display the drop-down list of tables and queries in the database. Select Stuffed Animals. Click OK.

 **NOTE:** If you make a mistake selecting the table, you can select it in the first Form Wizard dialog box.

**4.** The dialog box asks which fields to use on the form. Click the ⏩ button to move all the fields to the right.

**5.** Highlight KitNumber in the <u>S</u>elected Fields list. Click the ◀ button to move it back to the list on the left.

**FIGURE 5-3**
Selected fields to be included on the form

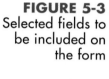

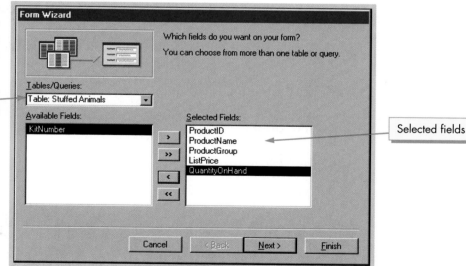

**6.** Click <u>N</u>ext. The dialog box asks you to choose a layout. Select <u>C</u>olumnar (the default), if necessary.

**7.** Click <u>N</u>ext. The next dialog box lists several styles. As you click each choice, you see a preview of the style. Select each style to see the preview.

8. Click Standard as the style for your form. Then click <u>N</u>ext.

9. The dialog box asks what title you want for the form. Key **Stuffed Animals Form** for the title.

10. Select "<u>O</u>pen the form to view or enter information." Click <u>F</u>inish.

11. The form is the same as your AutoForm, except the KitContents field isn't included. Close the form.

# *Working with Controls on a Form*

Controls contain all the information on a form. A *control* displays data, performs an action, or adds a design element. The three types of controls are bound, unbound, and calculated.

- A *bound control* is linked to the table or query; it has a data source. Use bound controls to enter or change the data in the table.

- An *unbound control* displays labels, titles, lines, rectangles, or other design elements. It has no data source and isn't linked to the table.

- A *calculated control* uses an expression as its source of data. A calculated control might use field names, arithmetic operators, constant numbers, or functions. In the AutoForm you created for the Stuffed Animals table, you might use a calculated control with this expression: ListPrice*QuantityOnHand. The * symbol is an operator that represents multiplication. This expression calculates the value of the inventory.

A control has two parts—the unbound control (the label) and the bound control (the text box). You can select the control as a whole, or you can select either the bound or the unbound part.

To change a control, select it by clicking it. A selected control displays small dark squares known as *selection handles*.

As you move the pointer over the top or bottom borders of a selected control, an open-hand pointer appears. The pointer moves the *entire control* (the text box and the label).

If you place the pointer on the top left selection handle of a control, a hand with a pointing finger appears. This pointer moves the *individual* bound (text box) or unbound (label) part of the control. You can also size the controls by placing the pointer on a handle until it is a double-headed arrow.

A form is divided into sections, with each section having its own controls. Almost all forms have a Detail section. This section displays the records. Many forms have a Form Header and/or Footer, which can hold a title, an image, or other information. A header or footer appears once at the top or bottom of the form.

## EXERCISE 5-4 Move and Size Form Controls

**1.** Select the Stuffed Animals Form and click <u>D</u>esign. Maximize the window.

**FIGURE 5-4**
Elements in the
Design window

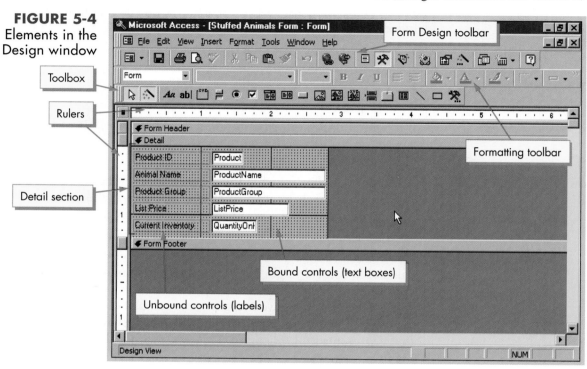

**NOTE:** The Toolbox may float in the Design window. To move it, drag it by its title bar to the top of the window to anchor or dock it with the other toolbars at the top of the window.

**2.** Move the pointer to the right edge of the Detail section. When the pointer changes to a double-headed arrow, drag the pointer to the right until the window reaches the 4½-inch mark on the horizontal ruler.

**3.** Click either the label or the text box for the Animal Name control. Selection handles appear around the borders of the control.

**4.** Place the pointer on either the top or bottom border of the control (but not on the handles). The pointer changes to an open hand. If you don't see the open hand, move the pointer slowly over the top or bottom border.

**5.** Drag the Animal Name control up and to the right so it is next to the Product ID control.

**NOTE:** If you make an error sizing or moving a control, click the Undo button and try again.

**FIGURE 5-5**
Moving a control

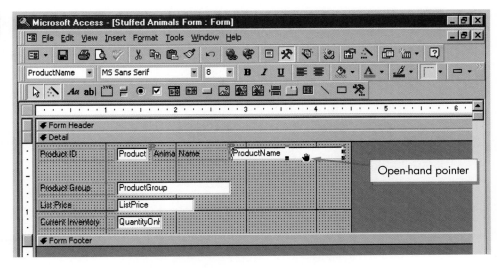

6. Drag the Product Group control so it is just below the Animal Name control. Leave two rows of dots on the design grid between the two controls.

7. Select the List Price control. Press [Shift] and select the Current Inventory control. Both controls are selected.

8. Point at the top or bottom border of either of the two selected controls until you see the open-hand pointer. Drag the controls just below the Product Group control. Leave two rows of dots on the grid as space.

9. Click an unused part of the form to deselect both controls.

10. Select the Current Inventory control and drag it so there are two rows of dots between it and the List Price control.

11. Select the Animal Name text box. Point at the middle selection handle at the right edge of the text box. The pointer changes to a horizontal double-headed arrow.

12. Drag the right edge of the text box to make it slightly narrower.

13. Click the View button 🔲 to see the form. Scroll through the forms to make sure you can see all the animal names.

14. Return to Design View.

15. Repeat the steps to make the Animal Name text box narrower, if necessary. Check the width in Form View again.

16. Return to Design View. Select the Product Group text box. Point at the middle selection handle at the right edge of the text box. Drag the right edge to make it narrower.

**17.** Check the form in Form View. Scroll through the forms and return to Design View.

**18.** Select the Animal Name label. Point at the middle right handle of the label. When the pointer is the double-headed arrow, drag the control to make it as wide as the words "Animal Name."

**19.** Select the Animal Name text box. Point at the top left handle of the bound control (text box).

**20.** When the pointer is a hand with a pointing finger, drag the control closer to its label.

**FIGURE 5-6**
Moving bound
control only

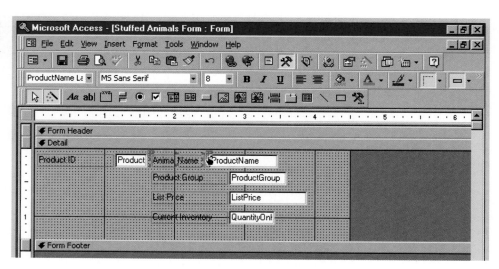

**21.** Return to Form View and click the Save button 🔲 to save your changes.

# EXERCISE  5-5  Align Controls

After you move and size controls on a form, you may notice they aren't vertically or horizontally aligned. Use the Align command to align the controls. This command requires that you select at least two controls. For each control, you must select both the text box and the label.

**1.** Return to Design View.

**2.** Select the Product ID control text box. Press Shift and select the Product ID label. Press Shift and select the Animal Name text box. Press Shift and select the Animal Name label. (See Figure 5-7 on the next page.)

**3.** Choose Align from the Format menu. Choose Top from the cascading menu to align the top borders of the controls.

**FIGURE 5-7**
Selecting multiple
controls

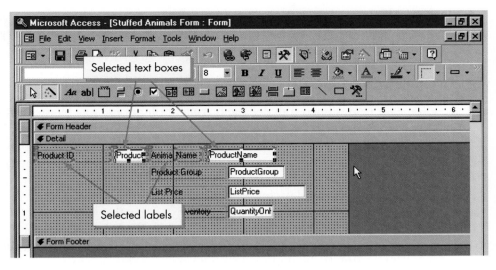

**TABLE 5-1**  **Alignment Options**

| CHOOSE | TO DO THIS |
|--------|-----------|
| Left | Vertically align the left edges of the controls with the control that is the farthest to the left. |
| Right | Vertically align the right edges of the controls with the control that is the farthest to the right. |
| Top | Horizontally align the top edges of the controls with the control that is the highest. |
| Bottom | Horizontally align the bottom edges of the controls with the control that is the lowest. |
| To Grid | Align the upper most corner of the selected control to the grid. |

**4.** Click anywhere in the unused portion of the form to deselect the controls.

**5.** Select the Product ID control text box. Press Shift and select the Product ID label. Continue to hold Shift while selecting the labels and text boxes for List Price and Current Inventory.

**6.** Choose Align from the Format menu. Choose Left from the cascading menu to align the left edges of the controls.

**7.** Click anywhere in the unused portion of the form to deselect the controls.

**8.** Save your changes. Return to Form View and close the form.

**155**

# EXERCISE 5-6 Work with Control Properties

A control on a form is an object and all Access objects have properties. You checked the database properties in Lesson 1. You set field properties when you designed a table. Each control on a form has its own properties sheet, too. A properties sheet lists all the characteristics or attributes for that control.

A label control might include properties that display the text in 18-point bold italic. A text box control might set the edge of the control at the 1.5-inch mark on the ruler and display the data in Currency format. The properties for a particular control depend on the type of control.

For a bound control, many properties are "inherited" from the underlying table. For example, if you used the Yes/No checkbox for a field in the table, that control has the Yes/No checkbox in the form. If you set the Currency format in the table, that control inherits the Currency format in the form. Many properties are automatically set and adjusted in the form as you move and size the controls.

 **NOTE:** A form inherits properties from a table, but a table does not inherit properties from a form.

*1.* Select the Employee Information Form and click Design.

**FIGURE 5-8**
Text Box control properties for Last Name field

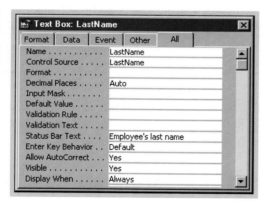

*2.* Right-click the Last Name text box (not the label). Choose Properties from the shortcut menu. The Text Box properties sheet opens. It has five tabs.

*3.* Click the All tab. The properties sheet is a window you can size and move. Drag the border of the window to make it taller. Scroll to view the list of properties for the text box.

*4.* Close the properties sheet.

 *5.* You can also use the Properties button 🖻 on the toolbar to view the properties sheet. Click the Job Code label (not the text box), then click the Properties button 🖻. Scroll through the list of properties. Notice that the properties for a label are different than the properties for a text box.

⭐ **TIP:** You can double-click an unselected control to open its properties sheet.

**FIGURE 5-9**
Job Code label
properties

6. Change the Width property to **3**. This makes the label 3 inches wide. Close the properties sheet.

7. Since the label is too wide, click the Undo button. Then save and close the form.

## EXERCISE 5-7 Set Tab Order

Tab order determines where the insertion point goes when you press Tab while working in Form View. The usual order is left-to-right, top-to-bottom. When you move controls, however, the tab order is adjusted and may not be what you expect. You can reset or change the tab order.

1. Open the Stuffed Animals Form. Maximize the window, if necessary.

2. Press Tab to move from field to field. The order is left-to-right, top-to-bottom. Finish so the pointer is in the Product ID field on any record.

 **NOTE:** If your tab order is not left-to-right, top-to-bottom, you may have already made a change that adjusted the tab order.

3. Switch to Design View.

4. Select the Product ID control. Place the pointer on the top or bottom border to display the open-hand pointer.

5. Drag the Product ID control down and to the right so it is next to the Current Inventory control.

6. Select the Current Inventory control and drag the control up where the Product ID control was. It's OK if the controls overlap. (See Figure 5-10 on the next page.)

7. Switch to Form View.

8. Press Tab to move from field to field. After moving the controls, the tab order is changed.

**FIGURE 5-10**
Dragging the
Current Inventory
control

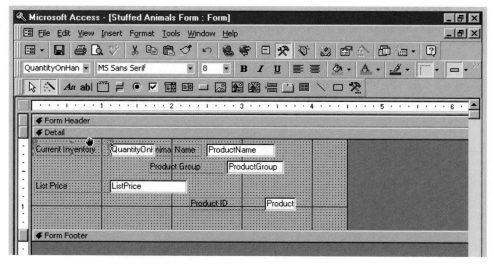

**FIGURE 5-11**
Tab Order
dialog box

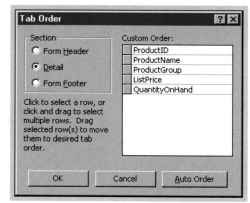

9. Switch to Design View.

10. Click anywhere in the Detail section of the form. Select Tab Order from the View menu. The Tab Order dialog box opens.

11. With the controls rearranged, the old tab order is no longer left-to-right, top-to-bottom. Click Auto Order to set the tab order left-to-right, top-to-bottom. Click OK.

12. Return to Form View.

13. Check the tab order. Close the form, but don't save the changes.

# Creating a Form Header

You've been working in the Detail section of the form where the field controls are stored. The Form Header, another section of the form, appears at the top of the form. In the Form Header, you can add a label, an image, clip art, or even a photograph.

**EXERCISE** 5-8 **Open the Form Header**

1. Select the Stuffed Animals AutoForm and click Design.

**2.** Maximize the window, if necessary. Place the pointer on the border between the Form Header and Detail sections. The pointer changes to a horizontal bar with a double-headed arrow.

**FIGURE 5-12**
Adding a Form
Header

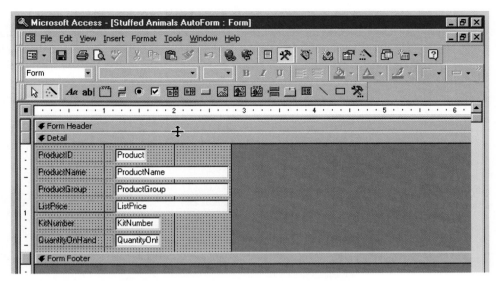

**3.** Drag the border down until the Form Header is about 1 inch tall.

 **TIP:** Each square of the grid is 1 inch by 1 inch.

**4.** Click the Label button [Aa] in the toolbox. The pointer changes to a crosshair cursor with the letter "A."

**5.** Drag the pointer down and right to draw a box approximately 2 inches wide and ½ inch tall at the left edge of the Form Header.

**FIGURE 5-13**
Adding a label to
Form Header

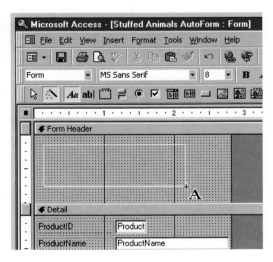

**6.** Key **Stuffed Animals AutoForm** in the label box.

**7.** Click outside the label box to deselect it.

**159**

## EXERCISE  5-9  Format the Header Label

You can set the style for a label much as you format text in a word processor. You can apply bold, italic, and font sizes to the text. You can also use the properties sheet to apply other special effects such as a background color, a raised or sunken appearance, and different colors for the text. The Formatting toolbar includes buttons to set many of these changes. Changes you make from the toolbar are automatically recorded in the properties sheet.

**1.** Click the Stuffed Animals AutoForm label in the Form Header to select it. The Formatting toolbar displays the current font name and font size list boxes.

**FIGURE 5-14**
Changing font and
font size

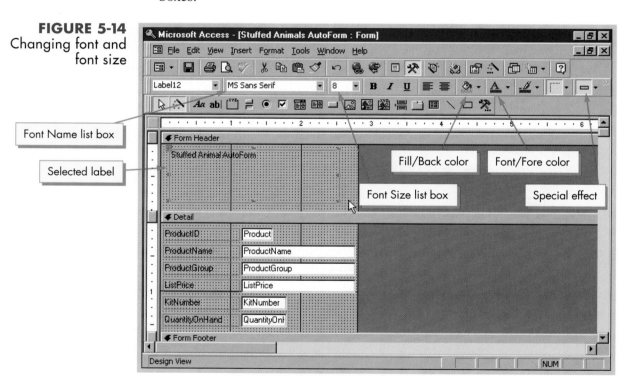

**2.** Click the drop-down arrow next to the Font Name list box. Find and click Times New Roman to change the font in the label to Times New Roman.

**3.** Click the drop-down arrow next to the Font Size list box. Click 18 to change the label to 18 point.

**4.** Place the pointer on the right middle handle and drag the edge of the label to make it wide enough to show the text on one line. The form border automatically extends as you drag the label.

**5.** Click the drop-down arrow next to the Font/Fore Color button  to open a palette of the available colors.

**6.** Select a medium blue to change the label to blue.

**7.** Change to Form View to see the changes.

**8.** Close and save the form.

**FIGURE 5-15**
Color palette

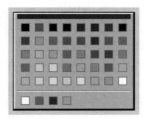

**9.** Open the Stuffed Animals Form in Design View. Maximize the window.

**10.** Place the pointer on the border between the Form Header and Detail sections and drag the border down until the Form Header is about 1 inch tall.

**11.** Click the Label button  in the toolbox. Draw a box approximately 2 inches wide and ½ inch tall at the left edge of the form header.

**12.** Key **Stuffed Animals Form** in the label box and press Enter.

**13.** Click the drop-down arrow for the Font Name and select Times New Roman.

**14.** Click the drop-down arrow for the Font Size and select 18. Size the label to show the text on one line, if necessary.

**15.** Click the drop-down button for the Fill/Back Color . Select a medium green from the color palette.

**TIP:** Individual color buttons in a palette are sometimes called "tiles."

**16.** Click the drop-down arrow for the Foreground Color button . Select white from the palette.

**17.** Save the form. Switch to Form View and view the changes. Close the form.

# Adding a Calculated Control to a Form

Two of the controls in the Stuffed Animals form contain data that, when multiplied, provide important information. The Current Inventory control in the form uses the QuantityOnHand field as its data source. The List Price control uses the ListPrice field. When you multiply the ListPrice by QuantityOnHand, the result is the total dollar value of the stock for that animal.

A calculated control uses an expression instead of a field. An expression might combine arithmetic operators (+ - * /), constants, field names, and/or functions.

Use the Text Box tool to add a calculated control to the form.

# EXERCISE 5-10 Add a Calculated Control to a Form

1. Open the Stuffed Animals Form in Design View. Maximize the window, if necessary.

2. Click the Text Box button [abl] on the toolbar.

3. Position the pointer to the right of the Current Inventory control so the crosshair cursor is at the 3-inch mark on the design grid.

4. Drag the pointer to the right and down to draw a box that is approximately 1½ inches wide and the same height as the Current Inventory control.

**FIGURE 5-16**
Adding a text box

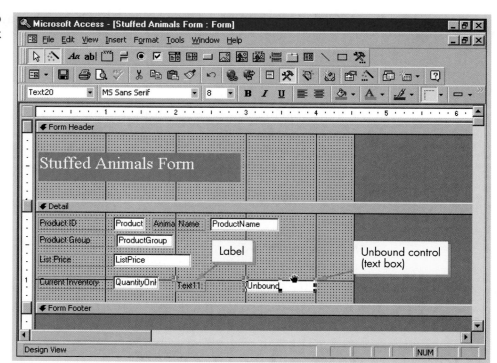

**NOTE:** The default label for text boxes that you add to a form is "Text" followed by two numbers.

5. Drag to select the default label "TextNN." (The NN could be any number.) Key **Total Value** as the new label.

6. Select the Unbound control and click the Properties button [icon] to open its properties sheet. Click the All tab, if necessary.

7. The Control Source determines where the data comes from. Click the Control Source row. The drop-down arrow displays a list of the fields in the underlying table. Do not select a field name now.

**FIGURE 5-17**
Control Source row

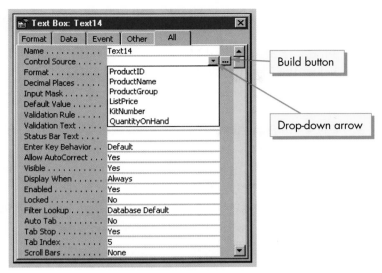

**8.** Click the Build button ![...] to open the Expression Builder, which allows you to enter field names, operators, functions, constants, and other elements with minimum keying.

**FIGURE 5-18**
Expression Builder
with an expression

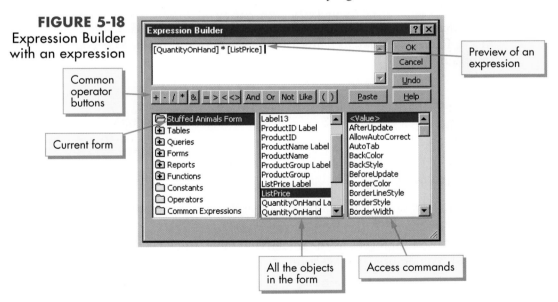

**9.** In the middle panel, double-click the QuantityOnHand field. Do not select the QuantityOnHand label. The field name is displayed in the Preview window with brackets.

 **NOTE:** You can double-click the field names or select them and click the Paste button.

10. Click the * symbol once for multiplication. It appears in the Preview window.

11. Find and double-click the ListPrice field in the middle panel. Do not select the ListPrice label.

12. Click OK to close the Expression Builder. The expression is entered in standard Access format in the Control Source row of the properties sheet.

13. Click the Format row in the properties sheet. Click the drop-down arrow. Choose Currency.

14. Delete "TextXX" in the Name row in the properties sheet and key **Total Value** as the name of the control.

15. Close the properties sheet. The calculated control appears on the form.

16. Change to Form View. Check several records.

17. Close and save the form.

# Creating a Form in Design View

You can start with a blank form window and add fields anywhere on the form. You don't need to use the AutoForm or the Form Wizard. Using Design View for a form is similar to using Design View for a table in that you start from scratch.

**EXERCISE** 5-11 **Create a Form in Design View**

1. Click the Forms tab, if necessary. Click <u>N</u>ew.

2. Select Design View.

3. Click the drop-down arrow for the option "Choose the table or query where the object's data comes from."

4. Choose Employees as the underlying table. Click OK. A blank form opens with an empty Detail section.

 5. Click the Field List button . A small window listing the fields in the Employees table appears. (See Figure 5-19 on the next page.)

6. Select the FirstName field in the Field List window. To add a field to the Detail section, drag it from the window to the form. The pointer changes to a small field box icon as you drag. Place the LastName field at the top of the form at the 1-inch mark on the design grid.

> **NOTE:** Drag the bottom border of the Field List window to make it taller.

**FIGURE 5-19**
New blank form
ready to be
designed

Toolbox

Detail section

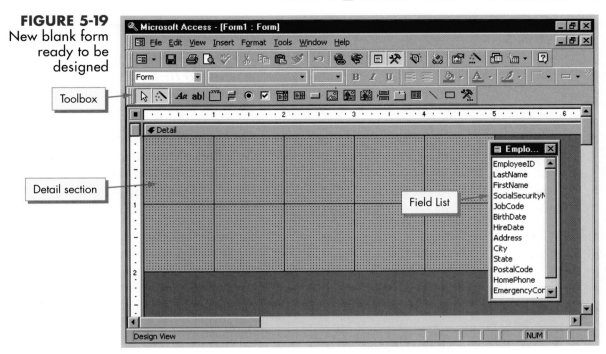

**7.** Repeat these steps to place the LastName and HireDate fields. Place each
field at the 1-inch mark, leaving two rows of dots between the fields.

**FIGURE 5-20**
Placement of fields

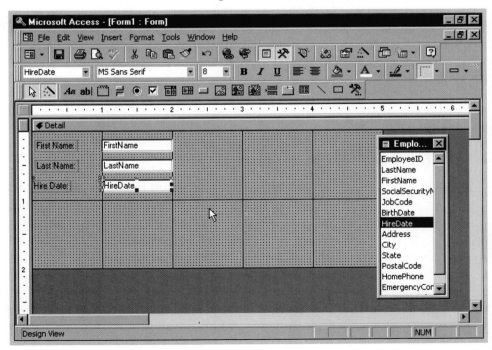

**8.** Save the form. Name it **Hire Dates**.

## EXERCISE 5-12 Move and Align Controls

You move and size controls on a form that you designed just as you do on an AutoForm or a Wizard form. You should also align controls and check the tab order when you design a form.

1. Select the FirstName control text box (not the label).

2. Place the pointer on the top left selection handle to display the pointing-finger pointer. Drag the text box control closer to its label.

3. Select the LastName control text box (not the label) and drag it closer to its label. Try to align the control with the FirstName text box.

4. Repeat these steps for the HireDate text box.

5. Select the FirstName text box. Press [Shift] and select the other two text boxes.

6. Choose Align from the Format menu. Choose Right to align the borders of the text box controls.

7. Select the FirstName label. Press [Shift] and select the other two labels.

8. Choose Align from the Format menu. Choose Left to align the left borders of the labels.

9. Deselect the controls.

10. Change to Form View and check your form. Then return to Design View.

11. Click in the Detail section of the form. Select Tab Order from the View menu. The Tab Order dialog box opens.

12. The current order is correct, so click Cancel.

13. Return to Form View and check the tab order.

14. Return to Design View. Close the Field List window and save the form.

# Formatting a Form

When you create a form, the Form Header is not displayed. You can open it, add a label, and apply styles, colors, and fonts. You can change the border styles and background colors for controls. You can even change the background color for an entire section of the form. In addition to your own formatting, you can use the AutoFormat command to apply a style template to the form.

## EXERCISE 5-13 Open the Form Header/Footer

1. Choose Form Header/Footer from the View menu. The Form Header and Form Footer sections open.

2. Drag the bottom border of the Form Header to make the section about 1 inch tall.

3. Click the Label button . Draw a box approximately 2 inches wide and ½ inch tall at the left edge of the Form Header.

4. Key **Hire Dates for Employees** and press Enter.

5. Change the font and size to Arial, 20 point. Click the Bold button **B** and the Italic button **I**. Size the label to show the title. Save the form.

6. Place the pointer on the border between the Form Footer and Detail sections. Drag the border up until the empty space below the controls is about the same height as the empty space above the controls.

**FIGURE 5-21**
Hire Dates form

7. Save the form again.

# EXERCISE 5-14 Set a Special Effect

You can apply special effects to a control. These effects change the appearance of the border or the background of the control.

1. Select the First Name, Last Name, and Hire Date labels. Do not select the text boxes.

2. Click the drop-down arrow for the Special Effect button ▭ in the toolbar. Place the pointer on each button in the palette to see its name.

**NOTE:** If you click a button that has a drop-down arrow, you apply the current color or style. You must click the drop-down arrow to see the choices.

3. Select Raised as the special effect for the labels.
4. Change to Form View to see the effect.
5. Return to Design View.

**EXERCISE 5-15 Change Front and Back Colors**

1. Select the label in the Form Header.
2. Click the drop-down arrow for the Fill/Back color button ▣. Select red.
3. While the label is still selected, click the drop-down arrow for the Font/Fore button ▣. Select white.
4. While the label is still selected, click the drop-down arrow for ▣. Select Raised to match the labels in the Detail section.
5. Click the Detail bar at the top of the Detail section. This selects the entire section.
6. Since red is the current background color, you do not need to display the palette. Click the Fill/Back color button ▣.
7. Change to Form View. This form would be difficult to look at all day! Return to Design View.

 **NOTE:** You cannot undo some color changes.

8. Click the drop-down arrow for the Fill/Back Color button ▣ and select light gray to return to the original look of the form. You may need to try a few grays before you get the right match.
9. Save the form.

**EXERCISE 5-16 Use AutoFormat**

1. Select AutoFormat from the Format menu. (See Figure 5-22 on the next page.)
2. The AutoFormat dialog box lists the names of the style templates that you can use for forms. Click each AutoFormat name. As you click each name, the preview changes to give you an idea of the design.

**FIGURE 5-22**
AutoFormat
dialog box

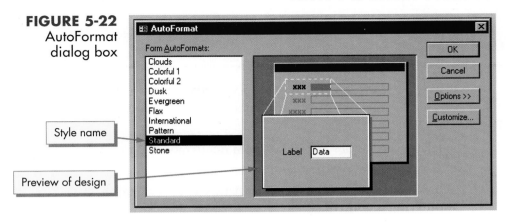

Style name

Preview of design

**NOTE:** You can still apply formatting after using an AutoFormat.

**3.** Choose Colorful 1 and click OK. The form is reformatted. Change to Form View to see the changes.

**4.** Return to Design View. Click the AutoFormat button 🖺 and try another AutoFormat.

**5.** Close the form without saving the changes.

**6.** Compact the database. Close the database.

## COMMAND SUMMARY

| FEATURE | BUTTON | MENU | KEYBOARD |
|---------|--------|------|----------|
| View Properties | 🖻 | View, Properties | |
| AutoFormat | 🖺 | Format, AutoFormat, Format | |
| Field List | ▣ | View, Field List | |
| Fill/Back Color | 🎨 | | |
| Font/Fore Color | A | | |
| Special Effect | ▱ | | |
| Tab Order | | View, Tab Order | |
| Label | Aa | | |
| Text Box | abl | | |
| Field List | ▣ | View, Field List | |
| Align | | Format, Align | |

## USING HELP

To learn how to do something in Access, you can ask the Office Assistant. You ask a question in your own words and the Office Assistant provides a list of relevant topics.

**Use the Office Assistant to find out more about modifying a control:**

***1.*** Click the Office Assistant icon in the toolbar.

***2.*** Where it says "Type your question here, then click Search," key **modifying a control.**.

***3.*** Click the <u>S</u>earch button. Access displays a list of topics.

***4.*** Move the cursor over the suggested answers. Notice that the button changes color. Click the triangle next to See MoreÖ. Click the ForeColor Property topic.

**FIGURE 5-23**
Using the Answer
Wizard

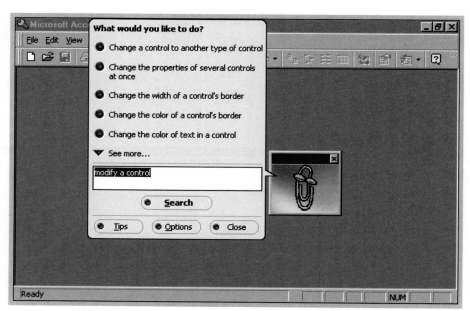

***5.*** When you finish browsing the Help window, close Help and the Office Assistant.

# Concepts Review

## TRUE/FALSE QUESTIONS

Each of the following statements is either true or false. Indicate your choice by circling either **T** or **F**.

**T   F**   **1.** When you update data on a form, you also need to update the underlying table.

**T   F**   **2.** A form contains one section.

**T   F**   **3.** You use Design View to create a form from scratch.

**T   F**   **4.** An AutoForm creates a form that includes all the fields in a selected table.

**T   F**   **5.** The pointer changes to an open hand when you place it on the top left selection handle.

**T   F**   **6.** You can use AutoFormat to select a style template for a form.

**T   F**   **7.** You can only change the form background in Form View.

**T   F**   **8.** Field properties that are assigned when you create a table are inherited when a form is created.

## SHORT ANSWER QUESTIONS

Write the correct answer in the space provided.

**1.** What section on a form contains the record information?

_____

**2.** What section appears at the top of a form where you can add a company logo?

_____

**3.** Which tool do you use to add a calculated control to a form?

_____

**4.** What type of control is linked to a table or query?

_____

5. What do you use to create a simple single column form that uses all the fields in a table?

_____

6. What determines how the insertion pointer moves in a form when you enter or edit data?

_____

7. What button changes text color in a label?

_____

8. What does your pointer look like when you move a label or text box separately?

_____

## CRITICAL THINKING

**Answer these questions on a separate page. There are no right or wrong answers. Support your answers with examples from your own experience, if possible.**

1. In this lesson you learned how to create forms using an AutoForm, the wizard, and Design View. Which do you prefer? Why? When would you use a wizard? Design View? What are the differences?

2. You have edited, added, and searched records in a table and a form. What commands are the same? What commands are different? Describe differences or similarities between a table and a form.

# Skills Review

## EXERCISE 5-17

**Create an AutoForm.**

1. Create an AutoForm by following these steps:
   a. Open the file *[your initials]*CC2.mdb.
   b. Click the Forms tab and the New button.
   c. Click AutoForm: Columnar.

 **NOTE:** The AutoForm uses the AutoFormat that was last used at your workstation.

> ***d.*** Click the drop-down arrow for "Choose the table or query where the object's data comes from."
>
> ***e.*** Choose Kit Suppliers. Click OK.

**2.** Enter and edit data using a form by following these steps:

> ***a.*** Click the New Record button. Add the following record, pressing Tab between each field:

| | |
|---|---|
| Supplier ID: | **GG-07** |
| Supplier Name: | **Johnson Fabric Centers** |
| Contact Name: | **Hank Johnson** |
| Address: | **565 Main Street** |
| City: | **Abbott** |
| State: | **TX** |
| Postal Code: | **77621-0565** |
| Phone Number: | **(817) 555-1885** |
| Fax Number: | **(817) 555-1886** |

> ***b.*** Move to the Cosby Manufacturing Company record.
>
> ***c.*** Edit the address field to **628 South Street**.

**3.** Click the Save button 🖫. Key **Kit Suppliers Entry Form** in the Form Name box. Click OK.

**4.** Close the form.

## Modify controls in Design View.

> **1.** Move and size controls by following these steps:
>
> ***a.*** Open the Kit Suppliers Entry Form in Design View. Maximize the window, if necessary.
>
> ***b.*** Move the pointer to the right edge of the form. Drag the edge of the form to the right until the form is 4.5 inches wide.
>
> ***c.*** Select the Supplier ID control. Place the pointer on a border to display the open-hand pointer.
>
> ***d.*** Drag the Supplier ID control to the 3-inch mark on the horizontal ruler.
>
> ***e.*** Select the Supplier Name control and drag it up to where the ID control was located.
>
> ***f.*** Select the remaining controls. Drag them below the Supplier Name control. Deselect the controls.

*g.* Select the Supplier ID text box. Move the pointer to the top left handle. When the pointer changes to the pointing finger, drag the control to the 3¾-inch mark on the horizontal ruler.

    *h.* Change to Form View to see if the controls are wide enough for the text. Return to Design View.

    *i.* Save the form.

**2.** Align controls by following these steps:

    *a.* Use ⸢Shift⸣+click to select all the text boxes except the Supplier ID.

    *b.* Choose A̲lign from the Fo̲rmat menu. Choose R̲ight from the cascading menu.

    *c.* Deselect the controls.

    *d.* Check Form View to see if the controls are wide enough. If not, resize them in Design View.

    *e.* Save and close the form.

**3.** Review control properties by following these steps:

    *a.* Open the New Customer Entry Form in Design View. Maximize the window, if necessary.

    *b.* Right-click the Company Name text box and choose Properties from the shortcut menu.

    *c.* Click the All tab, if necessary.

    *d.* Review the properties, then close the properties sheet.

    *e.* Select the Contact Name label and click the Properties button 🗇.

    *f.* Review the properties. Notice the differences between label and text box properties.

    *g.* Close the properties sheet. Save and close the form.

**4.** Change and set tab order by following these steps:

    *a.* Open the Kit Suppliers Entry Form in Form View.

    *b.* Press ⸢Tab⸣ to move from field to field.

    *c.* Switch to Design View.

    *d.* Choose Tab Orde̲r from the V̲iew menu.

    *e.* Select the Contact Name field. Drag it to the top of the list. Click OK.

    *f.* Change to Form View. Press ⸢Tab⸣ to move from field to field.

    *g.* Return to Design View.

    *h.* Choose Tab Orde̲r from the V̲iew menu.

    *i.* Click A̲uto Order. Click OK.

    *j.* Return to Form View. Press ⸢Tab⸣ to move from field to field.

**5.** Close the form without saving your changes.

**EXERCISE 5-19**

## Create a form with the Form Wizard. Add a Form Header. Add a calculated control.

1. Create a form with the Form Wizard by following these steps:
   a. Click the Forms tab and <u>N</u>ew.
   b. In the New Form dialog box, select Form Wizard.
   c. Display the drop-down list of tables and queries. Select Kit Suppliers. Click OK.
   d. Click the ⟫ button to move all the fields to the right.
   e. Find and select the PostalCode field in the Selected Fields list. Click the ⟨ button to move it back to the list on the left
   f. Click <u>N</u>ext. Select <u>C</u>olumnar as your layout, if necessary.
   g. Click <u>N</u>ext. Click Colorful 1 as the style. Then click <u>N</u>ext.
   h. Key **Kit Suppliers Form** for the title. If necessary, select "<u>O</u>pen the form to view or enter information." Click <u>F</u>inish.

2. Add a Form Header by following these steps:
   a. Switch to Design View. Maximize the window, if necessary.
   b. Place the pointer on the border between the Form Header and Detail sections. When the pointer is a horizontal bar with a double-ended arrow, drag the border down until the Form Header section is about 1 inch tall.
   c. Click the Label button [Aa]. Position the pointer at the upper left corner of the header.
   d. Drag the pointer down and right to draw a box about ½ inch tall and almost as wide as the form.
   e. Key **Kit Suppliers for Carolina Critters** and press Enter.

3. Format a Form Header by following these steps:
   a. Select the label in the Form Header.
   b. Click the drop-down arrow for the Font Size list box. Select 20.
   c. Size the control so the title fits on one line.
   d. Switch to Form View to see the changes. Close and save the form.

4. Add a calculated control to a form by following these steps:
   a. Open the Stuffed Animals Form in Design View.
   b. Place the pointer on the border between the Form Footer and Detail sections. Drag the border down to make the Detail section about 1 inch taller.

*c.* Click the Text Box button abl.

*d.* Position the pointer beneath the control with the calculation.

*e.* Draw a box that is approximately the same size as the Total Value control.

*f.* Select the text in the label ("TextNN"). Key **Discount** as the new label.

*g.* Right-click the Unbound control and open its properties sheet. Click the All tab, if necessary.

*h.* Click the Control Source row. Click the Build button ...].

*i.* In the middle panel, double-click the ListPrice field.

*j.* Click the * button.

*k.* Key **.15** in the Preview window after the * symbol.

*l.* Click OK.

*m.* Click the Format row in the properties sheet. Click the drop-down arrow. Choose Currency.

*n.* Delete the default name in the Name row. Key **Discount**.

*o.* Close the properties sheet.

*p.* Drag the calculated control you just added next to the List Price control.

*q.* Move, align, and size the controls as you think they should be.

*r.* Change to Form View to check your work. Then save and close the form.

## EXERCISE 5-20

**Create a form in Design View. Move and align controls. Set colors and special effects.**

*1.* Create a form in Design View by following these steps:

*a.* Click the Forms tab and click <u>N</u>ew.

*b.* Choose Design View.

*c.* Choose "Product Lines" from the drop-down list of tables and queries. Click OK. Maximize the window.

*d.* Click the Field List button 回, if necessary.

*e.* Drag the Product Line field to the 1-inch mark on the horizontal ruler about ½ inch from the top of the Detail section.

*f.* Drag the Product Group field below the Product Line control.

*g.* Save the form. Key **Product Lines** in the Form <u>N</u>ame box. Click OK.

*2.* Move and size fields by following these steps:

**a.** Select the Product Line text box. Move the pointer to the top left handle. When the pointing finger is displayed, drag the text box to the 1¼-inch mark on the horizontal ruler.

   **b.** Select the Product Group text box and drag it to the 1¼-inch mark on the ruler.

   **c.** Select the Product Line and the Line Code labels.

   **d.** Choose Align from the Format menu. Then choose Left.

   **e.** Select the Product Line and the Product Group text boxes.

   **f.** Choose Align from the Format menu. Then choose Left.

   **g.** Drag the bottom edge of the Detail section to the 1-inch mark on the vertical ruler.

   **h.** Switch to Form View to see your changes.

   **i.** Return to Design View. Save the form.

**3.** Change the background color and special effect by following these steps:

   **a.** Click the Detail bar to select the section.

   **b.** Click the drop-down arrow for Fill/Back Color and select a pale yellow.

   **c.** Select the Product Line and Product Group labels.

   **d.** Select Raised from the Special Effect palette.

   **e.** Switch to Form View to see your changes.

   **f.** Save and close the form.

   **g.** Compact the database and close it.

# Lesson Applications

**Create a form using a wizard. Move and modify controls in a form. Open the Form Header. Add a label.**

1. Start Access, if necessary, and open *[your initials]*CC2.mdb.

2. Open the New Customer Entry Form. Notice the style and arrangement of controls. You will create a form similar to this. Close the form.

3. Use the Form Wizard to create a columnar form using all the fields in the Customers table. Use the Standard style and name the form **Customers**.

4. Change to Design View and maximize the window.

5. Make the form at least 5 inches wide.

6. Move the State control to the right of the City control.

7. Size and position the State and City controls to make room for the Postal Code control. Then move the Postal Code control to the right of the State control.

8. Move the Phone Number control below the City control. Use consistent spacing.

9. Move the Fax Number control to the right of the Phone Number control.

10. Move the Tax Exempt control directly below the Phone Number control. Use consistent spacing.

11. Save the form.

12. Change to Form View to see the changes. Check to see if any controls need sizing (too wide or not wide enough).

13. Return to Design View and make any necessary corrections.

14. Reduce the size of the label boxes so they closely fit the label text.

15. Left align the first column of labels. Left align the first column of text boxes at the 1-inch mark on the design grid. Left align the State and Fax Number labels. Left align the State and Fax Number text boxes.

16. Top align the City, State, and Postal Code labels and text boxes. Do the same for the Phone Number and Fax Number controls.

17. Open the Form Header and make it about 1 inch tall.

18. Add a label and key **Carolina Critters.** Press Shift + Enter. Key **Customers Entry Form** on the next line. Press Enter.

19. Make the label 18-point Arial bold italic. Size the label so it is only two lines.

20. With the label selected, change the text color to white. Change the background color of the label to red. Change the special effect to raised.

21. Position the label so it aligns with the controls at the left in the Detail section.

22. Check the alignment of your controls and make changes if necessary.

23. Save the form.

24. Change to Form View and add a new record with the following data:

| | |
|---|---|
| Customer ID: | **12** |
| Company Name: | *Key your initials, then key "& Associates"* |
| Contact Name: | *Key your first and last name.* |
| Billing Address: | *Key your address.* |
| City: | *Key your city.* |
| State: | *Key your state.* |
| Postal Code: | *Key your ZIP code.* |
| Phone Number: | **(200) 555-9876** |
| Fax Number: | **(200) 555-1234** |
| Tax Exempt? | *Click the checkbox to show "Yes"* |

25. Select your record and print it.

26. Save and close the Customers form.

## EXERCISE 5-22

### Create a form in Design View. Modify form controls. Add a form header with a label.

1. Create a new form in Design View for the Employees table. Maximize the window.

2. Open the Field List window. Select the following fields and drag all of them to the 1-incb mark on the horizontal ruler in the Detail section.

**EmployeeID**

**LastName**

**FirstName**

**EmergencyContact**

**EmergencyPhone**

3. Deselect the controls.

4. Position the Employee ID control as the top left control.

5. Position the First Name control below the Employee ID control.

**6.** Position the Last Name control to the right of the First Name control.

**7.** Position the Emergency Contact control below the First Name control.

**8.** Position the Emergency Phone control to the right of the Emergency Contact control.

**9.** Align the labels for Employee ID, First Name, and Emergency Contact at the left. Do the same for the Last Name and Emergency Phone.

**10.** Drag the text box for the Employee ID control so it ends at the 2¼-inch mark on the horizontal ruler. Repeat for the First Name and Emergency Contact text boxes.

**11.** Align the labels and text boxes of the First Name and Last Name controls at the top. Do the same for the Emergency Contact and Emergency Phone text boxes.

**12.** From the Edit menu, choose Select All to select all the labels and text boxes. Set them to Times New Roman 10 point.

**13.** Switch to Form View and determine which controls needs to be sized. Return to Design View and make the adjustments.

**14.** Drag the Last Name and Emergency Phone text boxes to align near the 4-inch mark on the horizontal ruler. Make sure they are aligned properly.

**15.** Move and size other controls as needed so you can see all the data.

**16.** Close the Field List window.

**17.** Select Form Header/Footer from the View menu. Size the header section to be about 1 inch tall.

**18.** Add a label with the text **Emergency Information**. Make it Arial bold italic 24 point. Select colors and a special effect.

**19.** Save the form as **Emergency Information**.

**20.** Switch to Form View and move to your record. Select and print it.

**21.** Close the form.

## EXERCISE 5-23

**Create a form in Design View. Add a calculation to a form. Add a Form Header. Apply a Filter By Form.**

**1.** Create a new form in Design View using the Payroll Information table.

**2.** Use the **EmployeeID, Social Security Number, Monthly Salary,** and **Hourly Salary**. Place these controls at the 1-inch mark.

**3.** While the controls are selected, set them to 10 point. Then size, position, and align the labels and text boxes so you can see all the data.

4. Add a text box below the controls. Set the label and the text box to 10 point.

5. Key **Monthly Pay** as the new label in place of "TextNN."

6. Open the properties sheet for the text box. Click the Control Source and click the Build button.

7. Add the expression **HourlyRate*140**. Close the Expression Builder.

8. Click the Format row and choose Currency.

9. Key **Pay** in the Name row.

10. Close the properties sheet.

11. Move the Monthly Pay control next to the Hourly Rate controls.

12. Save the form as **Monthly Wages**.

13. Open the Form Header and make it about 1 inch tall.

14. Add a label. Key **Carolina Critters** and press Shift+Enter to start a new line. Key **Employee Monthly Wages**. Press Shift+Enter. Key **Confidential (your initials).** Press Enter. This label is three lines long.

15. Format the label as 16-point Arial bold italic. Resize the label and the Form Header as needed.

16. Check the form in Form View and make changes in Design View if necessary.

17. In Form View, create a Filter By Form. In the Hourly Rate field, key **>0** to find records that have an hourly rate. Apply the filter.

18. Print the filtered records. Remove the filter.

19. Save the form and close it.

20. Compact and close your database. Exit Access.

# Adding Reports to a Database

**OBJECTIVES**

After completing this lesson, you will be able to:

1. **Create a report using a wizard.**
2. **Modify the controls in a report.**
3. **Change the Page Footer and print a report.**
4. **Sort and group records in a report.**
5. **Create a report in Design View.**
6. **Add a calculation to a report and use the Format Painter to copy formatting from one control to another.**

 Estimated Time: 1¾ hours

orms are the best way to view records onscreen. If you want a well-designed printed page, however, it's best to use a report. Reports offer several advantages over printing tables or forms. You can:

- Show fields in an attractive format that may include fonts, colors, shading, and images.
- Create a design that shows only certain fields or records.
- Group and sort records.
- Display summaries and totals.
- Show data from more than one table.

In this lesson you learn how to create a report using the Report Wizard and Design View. Design View for a report has the same types of controls as

Design View for a form. Moving and sizing controls is exactly the same as in a form.

# Creating a Report with the Report Wizard

The Report Wizard lets you choose the fields, the layout, and the style for a report. The style selects fonts, lines, and colors automatically.

**EXERCISE**  **Create a Report with the Wizard**

1. Open your file *[your initials]*CC2.mdb.
2. Click the Reports tab and click New.
3. In the New Report dialog box, select Report Wizard.
4. Display the drop-down list of tables and queries. Select Employees and click OK.

>  **TIP:** If you forget to select the table/query for your report in the New Report dialog box, you can select it in the first Report Wizard dialog box.

5. The first Report Wizard dialog box asks which fields to use in the report. Click the Employee ID field. Click the ▶ button to move the field to the right.

>  **TIP:** You can click the ▶ button or double-click the field name to move it to the right. If you move a field to the right by mistake, click the ◀ button to move it back.

6. Move the following fields to the Selected Fields list:
   **LastName**
   **FirstName**
   **SocialSecurityNumber**
   **JobCode**
7. Click Next. The dialog box asks if you want to group the records. You don't use groups in this report. Click Next. (See Figure 6-1 on the next page.)
8. The next dialog box asks if you want to sort the records. You can use up to four fields for sorting in ascending or descending order.

**FIGURE 6-1**
Select grouping
options

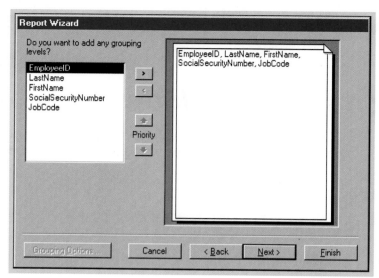

 **NOTE:** The Ascending/Descending button switches between ascending and descending order.

9. Click the drop-down arrow for the first sort field and select LastName.

10. Click the drop-down arrow for the second sort field and select JobCode.

**FIGURE 6-2**
Sorting records

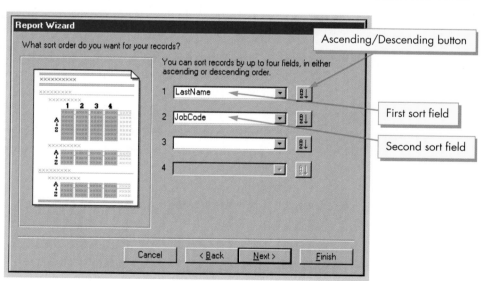

11. Click Next. The dialog box asks which layout and orientation you want. Select Tabular. Select Portrait. Make sure there is a check mark for "Adjust the field width so all fields fit on a page."

12. Click Next. The next dialog box lists styles. The Preview window simulates how a style prints. Preview each style.

**13.** Click Formal as the style for the report and click <u>N</u>ext.

**FIGURE 6-3**
Select report style

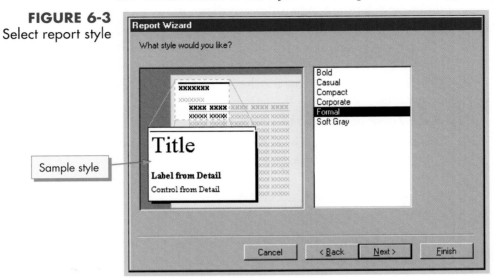

Sample style

**14.** The dialog box asks for a title. Key **Employees by Job Code** as the title. You can also preview a report or modify the design. Select "<u>P</u>review the report" and click <u>F</u>inish.

**15.** A preview of the report appears. The report preview is similar to the print preview in MS Word. Maximize the window.

**FIGURE 6-4**
Report preview

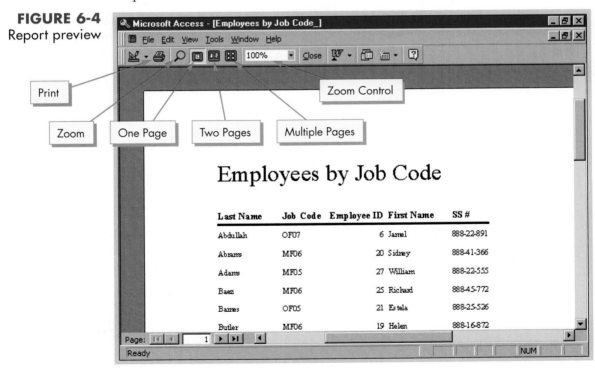

Print

Zoom Control

Zoom    One Page    Two Pages    Multiple Pages

16. As you move the pointer in the page area, it changes to a magnifying glass pointer with a minus sign. Click anywhere in the report to view the entire page.

17. Point anywhere on the page and click again to zoom in. The pointer zooms between a 100 percent view and the fit-to-window size.

18. Click the drop-down arrow for the Zoom Control list and try several of the percentages.

19. Set the Zoom percentage to 100 percent.

20. Click the Close button. The report opens in Design View. The fields are arranged left to right based on the sort order you selected in the Report Wizard.

21. Maximize the window, if necessary.

# Modifying a Report

Reports have the same objects as forms, so you already know how to modify a report. Reports have bound controls (text boxes), unbound controls (labels), and calculated controls.

Similar to a form, a report has a Detail section, a Report Header section, and a Report Footer section. The Detail section contains the records. The Report Header prints once at the top of the report; the Report Footer prints once at the end of the report. There is also a Page Header section and a Page Footer section. Use the Page Header to print a header at the top of every page and the Page Footer to print a footer at the bottom of every page. Headers and footers can contain text, lines, or images.

 **TIP:** Page headers and footers are similar to those used in Word and Excel.

## EXERCISE 6-2 Move and Delete Controls

1. Select the Job Code label in the Page Header section. Move the pointer to the top or bottom edge of the control until the pointer displays an open hand. Then drag the control into the Report Header as shown in Figure 6-5 (on the next page).

2. Select the Job Code text box in the Detail section. Move the pointer to the top or bottom edge of the control until the pointer displays an open hand. Then drag the control into the Report Header. You are moving the Job Title controls out of the way so you can move the other controls.

**FIGURE 6-5**
Moving controls
into the header

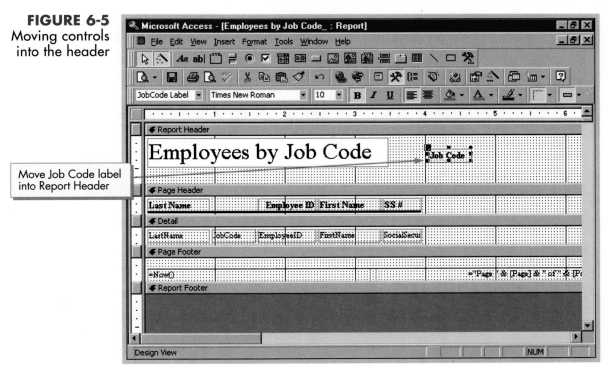

Move Job Code label
into Report Header

 **TIP:** When you move controls from one section to another, it is best to move one control at a time.

*3.* Select the Last Name label in the Page Header section. Press Shift and select the Last Name text box in the Detail section.

 **NOTE:** You must select a control to apply changes to it. A selected control displays selection handles.

*4.* Move the pointer to the top or bottom edge of either control. When the pointer displays an open hand, drag the controls to the right until their right borders touch the 2-inch mark on the design grid. The controls overlap.

*5.* Select the Employee ID label in the Page Header and the Employee ID text box in the Detail section.

*6.* Drag the controls to the left across the Last Name controls until their right borders touch the 1-inch mark on the design grid.

*7.* Select the First Name label in the Page Header section and the First Name text box in the Detail section.

*8.* Move the controls to the left until they end at the 3-inch mark on the design grid.

9. Select the SS# label in the Page Header section and the SocialSecurityNumber text box in the Detail section. Press Delete.

10. Select the Job Code label in the Report Header section. Move the control into the Page Header section so its left edge aligns with the 3¼–inch mark on the horizontal ruler.

11. Move the Job Code text box into the Detail section beside the First Name label, aligning it with the Job Code label.

12. Click the View button  to see if all the data is visible.

13. To return to Design View, click the View 🔲 button.

14. Click 🔲 to save your changes.

# EXERCISE 6-3 Add Fields to a Report

1. Click the Field List button 🔲 to open the Field List window.

2. Size or scroll the window until you see the HireDate field.

3. Drag the HireDate field to the Detail section next to the JobCode text box. The control is added with the text box and the label and overlaps the JobCode control.

**FIGURE 6-6**
Adding a field to your report

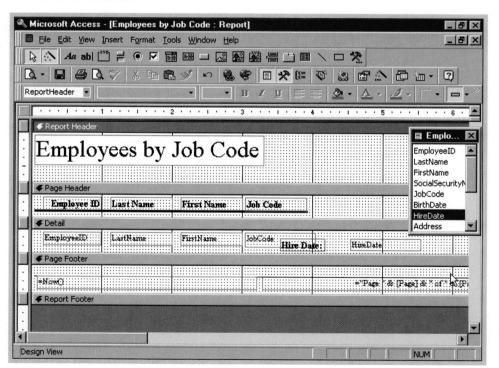

4. Select the Hire Date label, not the text box. Press Delete.

5. Select the Hire Date text box. You can use the open-hand pointer (top/bottom edge) or the pointing-finger pointer (top left handle) in this case because the label is gone. Drag the text box closer to the 4-inch mark in the Detail section.

 **TIP:** Use the grid dots as an aid when you size and align controls.

6. Place the pointer on the right middle handle and make the Hire Date control slightly narrower. Then make it as tall as the Job Code control.

7. Switch to Print Preview to check your work. Then return to the Design window.

8. Close the Field List window.

## EXERCISE 6-4 Copy Labels and Size Objects

You now need a label for the Hire Date field. The quickest way to enter the label so it uses the same format as the other labels is to copy an existing label and edit the text.

1. Select the First Name label in the Page Header section.

2. Click the Copy button 🖹.

3. Click the Paste button 🖺. The copy is placed below the original.

**FIGURE 6-7**
Copying a control

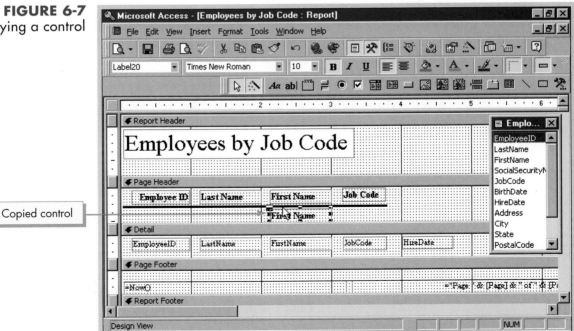

Copied control

**4.** Drag the copied label to the 4-inch mark.

 **NOTE:** The wizard added horizontal lines to both the Page Header and the Page Footer. These design elements make the report more attractive.

**5.** Delete the First Name text in the copied label and key **Hire Date**.

**6.** Change to Print Preview to check the size of the Hire Date controls. Return to Design View and size them if necessary.

**7.** You can resize the horizontal line in the Page Header to reach the Hire Date field now. Select the line.

**8.** Position the pointer on the far right selection handle to display the double-ended arrow.

**9.** Hold ⟨Shift⟩ and drag the end of the line to the 5-inch mark.

**10.** To size the Page Header section, place the pointer on the top of the Detail bar until you see the double-arrow with a horizontal bar. Drag the border up to make the Page Header section shorter. Leave a row of dots below the horizontal line.

**TIP:** Designing a report is a matter of trial and error. Switch back and forth between Report View and Design View often.

**11.** Preview your work. Return to Design View. If you think any controls need to be wider, narrower, or repositioned, make the change.

**12.** Save the report.

## EXERCISE 6-5 Align Controls

After adding, sizing, and moving controls, you need to align them. To align controls, you must have at least two controls selected.

**1.** Select the Employee ID label in the Page Header. Press and hold ⟨Shift⟩ to select each label in the Page Header.

**2.** Choose Align from the Format menu. Choose Top.

**3.** Select each text box in the Detail section.

**4.** Choose Align from the Format menu. Choose Top.

**5.** Select and right align the Hire Date label and text box.

**6.** Switch to Print Preview and check your work. Return to the Design window and adjust the alignment and sizing of the controls until they look professional. Check your work in Print Preview.

**7.** Save the report.

# *Changing the Page Footer*

The Employees by Job Code report was prepared using the Report Wizard. It includes a Report Header, a Page Header, and a Page Footer. The footer prints at the bottom of every page. The wizard added two controls to the Page Footer.

## EXERCISE 6-6 View Properties

1. Change to Print Preview. Zoom to a fit-in-window size so you see the entire page.
2. Point at the footer text at the left and click. This zooms in on that part of the page. The footer displays the current date.
3. Scroll to the right to see the other text in the footer. It shows the page number.
4. Return to Design View.
5. Select the control in the Page Footer that displays =Now(). Right-click the control and select Properties.

 **NOTE:** If the properties sheet shows Line, you selected the horizontal line above the controls. Close the properties sheet and try again.

6. Click the All tab in the properties sheet. This is a text box control. Its Control Source is an Access common expression that displays the current date. The Format is Long Date.
7. Close the properties sheet.
8. Right-click the control in the Page Footer that displays ="Page". . . and select Properties.

 **TIP:** You can select several common expressions in the Expression Builder. You don't need to key them.

9. Click the All tab in the properties sheet. This is a text box control with another common expression as its Control Source.
10. Close the properties sheet.

## EXERCISE 6-7 Delete a Control and Add a Label

1. Select the =Now() control again. Press Delete.

**2.** Click the Label button . Draw a label in the Page Footer where the =Now() was positioned before you deleted it. Draw below the horizontal line. Your label should be about 2 inches wide and the same height as the page number control.

**3.** Key **[*your first and last name*]** and press Enter. The label is selected.

**FIGURE 6-8**
Adding a label in the Page Footer

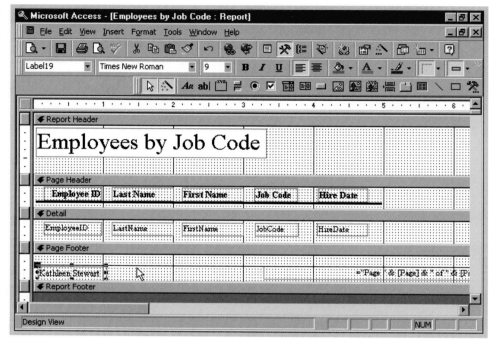

**4.** Click the Bold button **B** to turn off bold for your name. This is the default setting for labels for the Formal style you selected in the wizard.

**5.** Size the control to match the width of your name.

**6.** Click the Print button to print the report.

**TIP:** You can print a report from Print Preview or Design View.

**7.** Save and close the report.

# Sorting and Grouping Records in a Report

You may remember that the Report Wizard asked if you wanted to use groups in the report. A group organizes the records by a particular field. For example, you might want to group the records by job code in the Employees by Job

Code report. All the employees who are tailors would be listed together, all the assemblers/finishers would be listed together, and so on. The records are already sorted by last name, too.

You group records by opening the Group Header/Footer. This creates a new section for a report called the Group section. In the Group Header, you specify a group to use. You can also enter labels for groups. In the Group Footer, you might show subtotals for a particular group. For example, you could show how many employees have a particular job title.

**TABLE 6-1**  Group Properties

| GROUP SECTION | OPTION | ACTION |
|---|---|---|
| Group Header | Yes/No | Display header for this group. |
| Group Footer | Yes/No | Display footer for this group. |
| Group On | Each Value/ Prefix Characters | Select value or range of values that starts a new group. For example, you might group by one year, by every three years, or by every 10 years. |
| Group Interval | # | Interval or number of characters to group. |
| Keep Together | Yes/No | Keep group together on one page. |

# EXERCISE 6-8 Group Records in a Report

1. Open the Employees by Job Code report in Design View.
2. Click the Sorting and Grouping button. The Sorting and Grouping dialog box opens and shows the sorting choices you made in the Report Wizard.
3. Click in the Field/Expression column for the LastName row. The Group Properties show that no Group Header or Footer is used.
4. Click in the Field/Expression column for the Job Title row. No Group Header or Footer is used here either.
5. Click the Group Header row. Click the drop-down arrow and select Yes. Notice the Group icon to the left of the field name. (See Figure 6-9 on the next page.)
6. Close the dialog box. The report now has a JobCode Header.

**FIGURE 6-9**
Sorting and
Grouping
dialog box

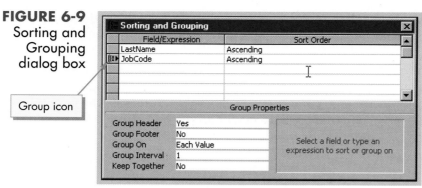

Group icon

# EXERCISE 6-9 Add Fields to the Group Header

Whatever you enter in the Group Header appears at the start of each new group. You would probably want to list the job code at the start of each group. Then you won't need the job code in the Detail section. You could open the Field List window and add the fields to the Group Header. You can also drag the controls already on the report.

1. Select the Job Code label in the Page Header. Drag the field to the left edge of the JobCode Header.

2. Select the Employee ID label in the Page Header, the Job Code label in the Group Header, and the Employee ID text box in the Detail section.

3. Choose Align from the Format menu. Choose Left.

4. Select the Job Code text box in the Detail section and drag its field next to the Job Code label in the Group Header. (See Figure 6-10 on the next page.)

5. Select the Job Code label and the Job Code text box in the Group Header. Align them at the top.

6. Controls should have the same font size to align properly. Select the Job Code text box and make it 10 point like the label.

7. Switch to Print Preview. The Group Header appears, but it doesn't group the records as you would expect. Return to Design View.

8. Click the Sorting and Grouping button 〖≡〗.

9. The major grouping field must be listed first in the dialog box. Click in the record selector area for the JobCode row and drag it to be first.

10. Close the dialog box and switch to Print Preview. The records are grouped by the job title. The job codes are in alphabetical order. The employees within a code are sorted by last name.

**FIGURE 6-10**
Moving controls
into the Group
Header

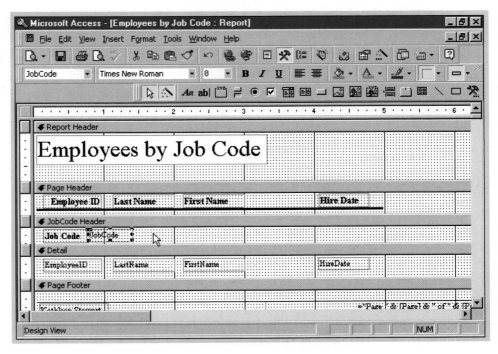

**11.** Return to Design View. Select the Hire Date label and text box and move them closer to the First Name controls. Align controls if necessary.

**12.** Return to Print Preview and print, save, and close the report.

# *Creating a Report in Design View*

You can start with a blank report window and add fields in each section of the report. Using Design View for a report is similar to using Design View for a form.

 **TIP:** You can also use AutoReport, which creates a default report with all the fields, similar to AutoForm. There is a columnar and a tabular AutoReport.

**EXERCISE 6-10 Create a Report in Design View**

**1.** Click the Reports tab, if necessary. Click New.

**2.** Select Design View.

**3.** Choose Stuffed Animals as the underlying table for the object's data. Click OK.

**4.** A blank report opens with empty Page Header and Detail sections. Maximize the window.

**5.** Click the Field List button . Size the Field List window to show all the fields.

**6.** Select the ProductID field in the Field List window and drag it to the 1-inch mark in the Detail section.

**NOTE:** When you drag fields from the Field List, the pointer position marks the left edge of the text box, not the label.

**7.** Select the Product ID label, not the text box. Press Delete.

**8.** Right-click the Product ID text box to open its properties sheet. Click the All tab, if necessary.

**9.** Click the Left row in the All tab to set the ruler location for the left edge of the control. Key **.1** as the location.

**10.** Click the Top row to set the ruler location for the top edge of the control. Key **.125** as the location.

**11.** Click the Width row to set the width of the control. Key **.65** as the width.

**12.** Scroll and click the Height row to set the height of the control. Key **.1667** as the height, if necessary.

**FIGURE 6-11**
Changing property settings

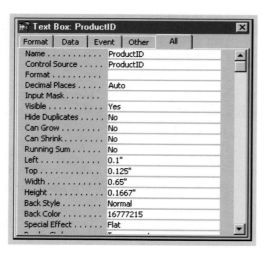

**13.** Close the properties sheet.

**14.** Drag the ProductName field from the Field List window to the 2-inch mark on the horizontal ruler.

**15.** Select and delete the Animal Name label.

16. Open the properties sheet for the ProductName text box. Click the All tab, if necessary.

17. Key the following settings for the ProductName control.

| Left | 1 |
|---|---|
| Top | **.125** |
| Width | 1 |
| Height | **.1667** |

18. Close the properties sheet.

 **TIP:** You can place a field anywhere in the Detail section and then set its location and size in the properties sheet.

19. Add the ListPrice field to the Detail section. Delete the label. Open the properties sheet and key these settings.

| Left | **2.5** |
|---|---|
| Top | **.125** |
| Width | **1** |
| Height | **.1667** |

20. Close the properties sheet and change to Print Preview. Use the Fit zoom size. Notice that there is too much vertical space between the records. Return to Design View.

21. Save your report. Name it **Inventory Value**.

## EXERCISE 6-11 Size and Add Report Sections

The Detail section is 2 inches tall by default. Any white space below the controls in the Detail section appears as space between records in the report. By adjusting the height of the Detail section, you adjust the vertical space between records in the report.

1. Scroll the window to find the top of the Page Footer bar. Place the pointer at the top edge of the bar to display a double-headed arrow with a horizontal bar.

2. Drag the pointer up until there are only two rows of grid dots below the controls in the Detail section.

3. Choose Report Header/Footer from the View menu to open the Report Header and Report Footer sections. The Report Header usually contains the main title. Column titles usually appear in the Page Header.

**4.** Save the report.

# EXERCISE 6-12 Add, Copy, Paste, and Format Labels

You can enter and format one of the column titles and then copy that control and edit the text for the other two labels. The main title in the Report Header is formatted differently than the column titles.

**1.** Click the Label button 🔲. Draw a box in the Report Header that is about 2 inches wide and as tall as the Report Header section.

**2.** Key **Inventory Value** and press Enter.

**3.** Format the label to 18-point Arial bold italic.

**4.** Drag the top of the Page Header bar down to make the Report Header section taller.

**5.** Size the label and the Report Header section so you can see the title. Position it near the left edge of the section.

**6.** Click the Label button 🔲. Draw a box in the Page Header for the Product ID title that is about the same size as the Product ID control.

**7.** Key **Stock No.** as the title and press Enter.

**8.** Format the label to 12-point Arial bold italic.

**9.** Drag the top of the Detail bar down to make the Page Header section slightly taller.

**10.** Size the label to show the title.

**11.** Make sure the label is selected. Click the Copy button 🔲. Then click the Paste button 🔲. The copy is placed below the original.

**12.** Drag the copied label to be the title for the ProductName column.

**13.** Delete **Stock No.** and replace it with **Name** as the column title. Press Enter.

**14.** Copy either label and drag the copy to be the title for the ListPrice column. Replace the text in the copied label with **Price** as the new label.

**15.** Align these labels at the top.

**16.** Drag the top of the Detail bar up until there are two rows of grid dots below the controls in the Page Header section. (See Figure 6-12 on the next page.)

**17.** Draw a label at the left edge of the Page Footer. Key **[*your first and last name*]**. Format the text as 10-point Times New Roman. Size the box to your name.

**18.** Save the report.

**FIGURE 6-12**
Adding labels to
reports

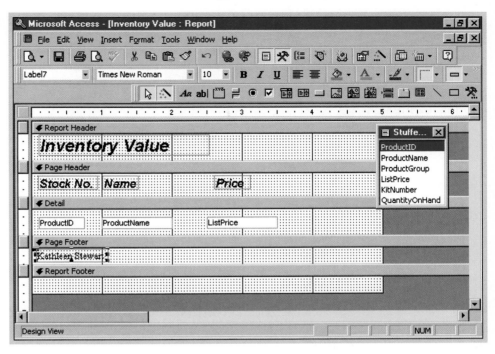

## EXERCISE  6-13  Add Common Expressions

A *common expression* is a control that uses built-in commands to enter dates, times, and page numbers. You can also build your own common expressions using the Access programming language.

*1.* Click the Text Box button [abl] to add a control for the date expression. Draw the text box at the right edge of the Page Footer. It has a label and an unbound control.

*2.* Select and delete the label, not the text box.

*3.* Open the properties sheet for the unbound control. Click the All tab.

*4.* Change the Name of the control to **Date**.

*5.* Click the Control Source row. Click the Build button to open the Expression Builder.

 **TIP:** Access has a Date() expression and a Now() expression. Both show the current date.

*6.* In the list of choices on the left, click Common Expressions. The available expressions appear in the middle panel.

**7.** Double-click "Current Date" in the middle panel. It is previewed in the window. Click OK.

**FIGURE 6-13**
Expression Builder
with the current
date expression

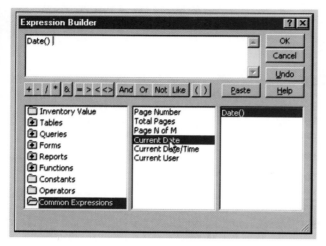

**8.** Click the Format row and its drop-down arrow. Choose Medium Date. Close the properties sheet.

**9.** Change to Print Preview. Look at the report in the Fit size as well as 100 percent. Notice that the ListPrice field inherited the Currency format from the table. Return to Design View.

## EXERCISE 6-14 Format and Align Controls

**1.** Select the three text boxes in the Detail section.

**2.** Change the font to 12-point Times New Roman.

**3.** While all three controls are selected, drag any bottom handle to make them slightly taller. Drag any side handle to make the controls slightly wider.

**4.** Size the Price label so the box just accommodates the text.

**5.** Select the Price label and the List Price text box.

**6.** Choose Align from the Format menu. Choose Right.

**7.** Drag the two controls so their right borders touch the 4-inch mark on the horizontal ruler.

**8.** Size the Name label so the box just accommodates the text.

**9.** Align the Name label and the Product Name text box on the left.

**10.** Drag the two controls so their left borders touch the 1½-inch mark on the horizontal ruler.

11. Select the Stock No. label and its text box. Align them on the left. Place them near the left margin of your report.

12. Select all three labels in the Page Header. Align them on the top.

13. Select all three text boxes in the Detail section. Align them on the top.

14. Change the Date control to the same font and size as your name.

15. Select and align the controls in the Page Footer on the bottom.

16. Check the report in Print Preview. Make sure you can see all the animal names. Make any necessary changes.

17. Return to Design View and save the report.

# *Adding a Calculated Control*

You can use calculated fields in reports just as in forms. In the Inventory Value report, you can compute the total inventory value for each product in stock. You need to multiply the list price by the number in stock.

## EXERCISE 6-15 Adding a Calculated Control

1. In Design View, drag the right border of the report to the 6-inch mark to make the report wider.

2. Click the Text Box button [abl]. Draw a box at the 5-inch mark in the Detail section.

3. Select and delete the label, not the unbound control.

4. Open the properties sheet for the unbound control. Click the All tab.

5. Change the Name of the control to **Current Value**.

6. Click the Control Source row. Click the Build button.

 **NOTE:** The middle panel in the Expression Builder lists the names of all objects currently in the report.

7. In the middle panel, find and double-click the ListPrice field. It is transferred to the preview.

8. Click the * symbol once for multiplication.

9. In the middle panel, click [▤]. All the fields from the table are listed in the rightmost panel. This includes fields not currently in the report.

10. Double-click QuantityOnHand. Click OK.

**FIGURE 6-14**
Expression Builder
with an expression

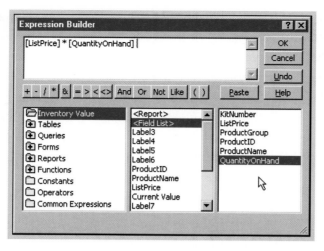

**11.** Click the Format row and select Currency from the drop-down list.

**12.** Close the properties sheet.

**13.** Position the control so it ends at the 5-inch mark.

**14.** Save the report.

**EXERCISE   6-16   Use the Format Painter**

Access has the same Format Painter as Word and Excel. You can copy formats from selected controls to other controls.

**1.** In Design View, select the List Price control in the Detail section.

   **TIP:** You see the name of the control in the Name box in the Formatting toolbar.

   **2.** Click the Format Painter button 🖌. The pointer changes to an arrow with a paintbrush.

**3.** Click the Current Value control you just added. The font and size are copied.

**4.** Align the Current Value control at the top with the List Price control.

**5.** Add a label in the Page Header section for the Current Value column. Key **Value** as the label text.

**6.** Click the Price label and click the Format Painter 🖌. Click the new label to copy the format.

**7.** Size the Value label so the box just accommodates the text.

8. Align the Value label and the Current Value text box on the right.

9. Align the Value label at the top with one of the other labels in the Page Header.

10. Size the Page Header section so there is one row of grid dots below the controls.

11. Size the Detail section so there are two rows of grid dots below the controls.

12. Save and close the report.

13. Compact and close the database. Exit Access.

## COMMAND SUMMARY

| FEATURE | BUTTON | MENU | KEYBOARD |
|---|---|---|---|
| Sorting and Grouping | | View, Sorting and Grouping | |
| Format Painter | | | |
| Zoom | | View, Zoom | |

# Concepts Review

## TRUE/FALSE QUESTIONS

Each of the following statements is either true or false. Indicate your choice by circling **T** or **F**.

T F *1.* A tabular report displays data in rows with column headings, similar to a worksheet.

T F *2.* Use the Text Box button to add a calculated control to a report.

T F *3.* You can modify a report in Print Preview.

T F *4.* You can move controls from one section to another in a report.

T F *5.* A Report Header prints at the top of every page.

T F *6.* You cannot change the name of a control.

T F *7.* Common expressions include calculations such as [ListPrice]*[Quantity].

T F *8.* You add a new section to a report when you group records.

## SHORT ANSWER QUESTIONS

Write the correct answer in the space provided.

*1.* What section of a report includes the data from the records?

*2.* What pointer should you display to move a control (both the bound and unbound controls)?

*3.* In what menu are the Page Header and Report Header options listed?

*4.* What is the name of the dialog box you use to select fields, common expressions, or arithmetic operators?

*5.* What does the expression =Date() display?

6. What tool should you use to add a calculated control to a report?

_____

7. Is a label a bound or an unbound control?

_____

8. What button on the toolbar copies the font and colors from one control to another?

_____

## CRITICAL THINKING

**Answer these questions on a separate page. There are no right or wrong answers. Support your answers with examples from your own experience, if possible.**

1. Look at your Inventory Value report. How would you use the sorting and grouping option? Why?

2. In this lesson you learned how to change the size and position of labels and text boxes on your report using the properties sheet. What are the advantages of using the properties sheet this way? What are the disadvantages?

# Skills Review

## EXERCISE 6-17

**Create a report using the Report Wizard.**

1. Create a form with the Report Wizard by following these steps:

   a. Open the file *[your initials]*CC2.mdb.

   b. Click the Reports tab and click New.

   c. Click Report Wizard in the list.

   d. Choose Customers from the drop-down list of tables and queries and click OK.

   e. Add the following field names to the list by clicking the > button or by double-clicking:

   **Customer ID**

   **CompanyName**

ContactName

BillingAddress

City

State

PostalCode

**f.** Click <u>N</u>ext. Do not add any grouping and click <u>N</u>ext.

**g.** Click the drop-down arrow for the first sort level. Select CompanyName. Click <u>N</u>ext.

**h.** For the layout, select Tabular. For the orientation, select Landscape. Click <u>N</u>ext.

**i.** For the style, select Soft Gray. Click <u>N</u>ext.

**j.** Key **Current Customers** as the title for the report.

**k.** Select the option to "Preview the report." Click <u>F</u>inish.

## EXERCISE 6-18

### Size, align, add, and delete fields.

**1.** Move and size the controls by following these steps:

**a.** Return to Design View for the Current Customers report. Maximize the window.

**b.** Select the ContactName text box in the Detail section and the Contact Name label in the Page Header.

**c.** Place the pointer on the right middle handle of either control to display a double-headed arrow. Drag the pointer to the left until the right edge of the controls touches the 3¾-inch mark on the ruler.

**d.** Select the BillingAddress text box in the Detail section and the Billing Address label in the Page Header.

**e.** Display the open-hand pointer and drag the controls to the 4-inch mark on the ruler.

**f.** Scroll the window and select the City text box in the Detail section and the City label in the Page Header.

**g.** Drag the right-middle handle of either control to the 7-inch mark on the ruler.

**h.** Change to Print Preview to check the width of the City column. It is too narrow. Return to Design View.

***i.*** Drag the right middle handle of either selected control to the right to make the controls about ¼ inch wider.

***j.*** Display the open-hand pointer and drag the City controls to the 6-inch mark on the ruler.

***k.*** Select the State text box in the Detail section and the State label in the Page Header.

***l.*** Display the open-hand pointer and drag the controls to the 7-inch mark on the ruler.

***m.*** Repeat these steps to move the PostalCode controls to the 7½-inch mark.

***n.*** Save the report.

**2.** Change the font, size, and color by following these steps:

***a.*** Click the label in the Report Header.

***b.*** Change the font to 36-point Times New Roman.

***c.*** Size the label so you can see the text.

***d.*** Click the drop-down arrow for the Font/Fore Color button ▣. Select black.

***e.*** Save the report. Change to Print Preview to see your work. Then return to Design View.

**3.** Display control properties by following these steps:

***a.*** Right-click the label in the Report Header. Select Properties.

***b.*** Click the All tab, if necessary.

***c.*** Change the name of the control to **Current Customers Label**.

***d.*** Scroll the list in the properties sheet to find the Font Italic row. Click the drop-down arrow and select Yes.

***e.*** Close the properties sheet.

***f.*** Preview your work and return to Design View and save your changes.

**4.** Delete a field by following these steps:

***a.*** Select the CustomerID text box in the Detail section and the CustomerID label in the Page Header.

***b.*** Press Delete to delete both controls.

**5.** Add a field by following these steps:

***a.*** If the Field List window is not open, click the Field List button ▣.

***b.*** Drag the border or scroll the Field List window until you see the TaxStatus field.

**c.** Drag the TaxStatus field to the Detail section where the CustomerID text box was located before you deleted it.

    **d.** Select the label for this new field, not the checkbox. Press ⌴Delete⌴.

 **NOTE:** You can verify which control is selected in the Select Object area of the Formatting toolbar.

    **e.** Drag the checkbox so it appears vertically centered in relation to the other text boxes in the Detail section.

    **f.** Save your changes.

**6.** Copy a label by following these steps:

    **a.** Click the Contact Name label in the Page Header.

    **b.** Click the Copy button 🖹. Click the Paste button 🖺.

    **c.** Delete "Contact Name" in the copied label. Key **Exempt?** in the label box.

    **d.** Size the control to just accommodate the text.

    **e.** Drag the control to be the title for the checkbox.

    **f.** Select the Exempt? and Contact Name labels in the Page Header.

    **g.** Choose Align from the Format menu. Choose Bottom.

    **h.** Close the Field List window.

    **i.** Drag the top edge of the Detail bar to make the Page Header shorter. Leave one row of grid dots below the gray horizontal line.

    **j.** Change to Print Preview. Then save and close the report.

## EXERCISE 6-19

**Sort and group records in a report. Delete and add controls. Print a report.**

**1.** Group records in a report by following these steps:

    **a.** Open the Stuffed Animal Products report in Design View and maximize the window.

    **b.** Click the Sorting and Grouping button 🖽.

    **c.** Click the drop-down arrow for Field/Expression in the first row.

    **d.** Select ProductGroup. Select Ascending as the Sort Order.

*e.* Click the Group Header row in the Group Properties section. Select Yes.

*f.* Set the remaining properties as:

| | |
|---|---|
| Group Footer: | **No** |
| Group On: | **Each Value** |
| Group Interval: | **1** |
| Keep Together: | **No** |

*g.* Click the drop-down arrow for Field/Expression in the second row.

*h.* Select ProductID and Ascending. Do not turn on the Group Header.

*i.* Close the Sorting and Grouping dialog box.

*j.* Change to Print Preview to see the changes. Return to Design View and save the report.

**2.** Add fields to a Group Header by following these steps:

*a.* Click the Field List button 📋, if necessary.

*b.* Drag the ProductGroup field name to the 1-inch mark in the ProductGroup Header section.

*c.* Drag the control so the left edge of the label touches the 1-inch mark.

*d.* Select the label of the new control and change the font to 12-point Times New Roman bold.

*e.* Point at the top left handle of the text box and drag it to the right, away from the label.

*f.* Size the label so you can see all the text.

*g.* Select the ProductGroup text box and change the font to 12-point Times New Roman bold. Size the text box appropriately.

*h.* Align the label and text box in the Group Header at the top.

*i.* Select the ProductID label in the Page Header, the ProductGroup label in the Group Header, and the ProductID text box in the Detail section.

*j.* Align the controls at the left.

*k.* Change to Print Preview to check your work. Return to Design View and save the report.

**3.** Delete and add controls by following these steps:

*a.* Select the Now() control in the Page Footer. Press Delete.

*b.* Click the Label button 🅰 and draw a label box at the left edge of the Page Footer.

*c.* Key *[your first and last name]* and press Enter.

**d.** Change the font to 12-point Times New Roman.

**e.** Click the Bold button **B** to turn off bold.

**f.** Size the label to see your whole name, if necessary.

**g.** Preview your work and return to Design View.

**h.** Save and print the report. Close the report.

## EXERCISE 6-20

### Create a report in Design View. Copy formats in a report.

**1.** Create a report in Design View by following these steps:

**a.** Click the Reports tab, if necessary. Click <u>N</u>ew.

**b.** Click Design View and choose the Kit Suppliers table from the drop-down list. Click OK.

**c.** Maximize the window. Display the Field List, if necessary.

**d.** Drag the SupplierName field to the 1-inch mark on the horizontal ruler and the ¼-inch mark on the vertical ruler (about three rows of grid dots) in the Detail section.

**e.** Drag the Address field to the 1-inch mark on the horizontal ruler about two rows of grid dots below the Supplier Name controls.

**f.** Drag the City field to the 1-inch mark about two rows of grid dots below the Address controls.

**g.** Size the SupplierName text box to be about 2 inches wide.

**h.** Size the Address text box to be the same width.

**i.** Select all the labels and all the text boxes. Change the font to 10 point.

**j.** Change to Print Preview. Zoom in and out as necessary to determine which controls are not wide enough.

**k.** Return to Design View and size the controls appropriately.

**l.** Save the report. Name it **Our Kit Suppliers**.

**2.** Add and format a Report Header/Footer by following these steps:

**a.** Choose Report <u>H</u>eader/Footer from the <u>V</u>iew menu.

**b.** Click the Label button **Aa** and draw a label box at the left edge of the Report Header about 2 inches wide.

**c.** Key **Kit Suppliers for Carolina Critters** in the label box. Press Enter.

**d.** Change the font to 20-point Arial bold.

**e.** Position the pointer on the top edge of the Page Header bar and drag the border down to make the Report Header taller.

**f.** Size the label until you can see all the words.

**g.** Click the drop-down arrow for the Font/Fore Color button 🅰 and select white.

**h.** Click the drop-down arrow for the Fill/Back Color button 🔲 and select red.

**i.** Click the drop-down arrow for the Special Effect button 🔲 and select Raised.

**j.** Click the Label button 🅰🅰 and draw a label box at the left edge of the report footer.

**k.** Key *[your first and last name]* and press Enter.

**l.** Change the font to 12-point Times New Roman.

**m.** Size the label and the Report Footer to show your name.

**n.** Drag the top border of the Page Footer bar so the Detail section shows two rows of grid dots below the controls.

**o.** Drag the top border of the Detail section up to close the Page Header section.

**p.** Repeat these steps to close the Page Footer section.

**q.** Save your report.

**3.** Copy label formats and modify controls by following these steps:

**a.** Make sure your name label is selected.

**b.** Double-click the Format Painter button 🖌 to lock it.

**c.** Click each control in the Detail section.

**d.** Click the Format Painter button 🖌 again to unlock it.

**e.** Click anywhere in the unused portion of the Detail section to deselect all controls.

**f.** Select the SupplierName, Address, and City text boxes.

**g.** Open the properties sheet for any selected control.

**h.** Click the All tab. Set the Left edge at 1.5 inches. Leave the Top entry blank. Set the Width at 2.5 inches. Set the Height at .2 inches. Close the properties sheet.

**i.** Select the Supplier Name, Address, and City label boxes.

**j.** Open the properties sheet for any selected control.

**k.** Click the All tab. Set the Left edge at .25 inches. Leave the Top entry blank. Set the Width at 1.25 inches. Set the Height at .2 inches. Close the properties sheet.

**l.** Preview your work and print a copy.

**m.** Save and close the report.

**n.** Compact the database and close it.

# Lesson Applications

## Create a report using the Report Wizard. Delete a control and add a label.

1. Start Access, if necessary, and open *[your initials]***CC2.mdb.**
2. Use the Report Wizard to create a report for the Employees table.
3. Select the LastName, FirstName, EmergencyContact, and EmergencyPhone fields for the report.
4. Do not add grouping levels. Sort the records by Last Name in ascending order.
5. Use a tabular layout with a portrait orientation. Select the Casual style.
6. Title the report **Emergency Phone Numbers**. Preview the report.
7. In Print Preview, look at the report in several zoom sizes. View page 2.
8. Return to Design View.
9. Delete the "=Now()" text box in the Page Footer. Add a label in its place and key **[*your first and last name*]**. The label must be below the horizontal line.
10. Save and print the report. Then close it.

## Create a report in Design View. Modify controls.

1. Create a report in Design View for the Employees table.
2. Drag the FirstName field to the 1-inch mark in the Detail section, two rows of grid dots down.
3. Delete the First Name label.
4. Drag the LastName field to the 2½-inch mark in the Detail section, two rows of grid dots down. Delete the label.
5. Drag the LastName text box so its left edge touches the right edge of the FirstName text box.
6. Drag the BirthDate field to the 3½-inch mark in the Detail section, two rows of grid dots down. Delete the label.
7. Drag the BirthDate text box so its left edge touches the right edge of the LastName text box.

8. Select all three text boxes and change them to 11-point Times New Roman.

9. Draw a label in the Page Header for the title **First Name**. Format it as 12-point Arial bold.

10. Copy and paste the First Name label. Change the text to **Last Name** and position the label over the second column. Copy and paste either label to create the third label **Birthday**.

11. Align the controls in both sections as needed.

12. Size the Page Header so there are two rows of grid dots below the labels. Size the Detail section to show one row of grid dots below the controls.

13. Open the Report Header. Draw a label and enter the title **Employee Birthdays**. Format it as Arial 18-point bold italic. Size the label as needed.

14. Size the Report Header to show three rows of grid dots below the label.

15. In the Page Footer, draw a label for your name. Use the Format Painter to copy the format from one of the text boxes to your name.

16. Preview your work. Return to Design View and make changes, if necessary.

17. Save the report as **Employee Birthdays**. Print the report and close it.

## EXERCISE 6-23

### Sort and group records in a report. Add a calculated control for the group.

1. Open the Inventory Value report in Design View. Maximize the window, if necessary.

2. Display the Field List window, if necessary.

3. Use the Sorting and Grouping dialog box to place ProductGroup in the Field/Expression list. Turn on the Group Header and the Group Footer.

4. Drag the ProductGroup field to the Group Header. Use the Format Painter to copy the format from one of the labels in the Page Header to the new text box and label.

5. Preview your report. Then size and align the Group Header controls. Show one row of grid dots above and below these controls.

6. Draw a text box in the ProductGroup Footer, beneath the calculated control in the Detail section.

7. Change the label to **Group Total**.

8. Copy the format from a label in the Page Header to this new label. Size the label and the section as necessary.

9. Open the properties sheet for the unbound control and click All.

10. Open the Expression Builder for the Control Source.

11. In the left panel, double-click the Functions folder. Then double-click the Built-in Functions folder.

12. Scroll the right panel to find Sum and double-click it. You must replace **<<expr>>** with what should be summed.

13. Click after the first parentheses. Delete **<<expr>>** so the expression reads **Sum()** with the insertion point between the parentheses.

14. In the left panel, click Inventory Value. In the middle panel, double-click ListPrice. Click **\***. Delete **<<expr>>.**

15. In the middle panel, scroll and click 🔳. In the right panel, double-click QuantityOnHand. The final expression is Sum([ListPrice]*[QuantityOnHand]).

16. Click OK to close the Expression Builder.

17. Change the Format to Currency.

18. Close the properties sheet.

19. Copy the format from the List Price control in the Detail section to your new text box.

20. Size, move, or align the controls as needed. Currency amounts should align on the right.

21. Place the pointer on the top edge of the Page Footer bar. Drag the border down to display two rows of grid dots beneath the controls in the Group Footer.

22. Save, print, and close the report.

23. Compact the database and close it.

# Unit 2 Applications

## APPLICATION 2-1

**Add a table using the Table Wizard. Add a validation rule and text. Print a table.**

1. Open the file *[your initials]*CC2.mdb.

2. Create a new table using the Table Wizard. Use all the fields in the Tasks sample table in the Business category. Rename the TaskID field as **Campaign#**. Rename TaskDescription as **Name**.

3. Name the table **Sales Campaigns** *[your initials]* and select "Yes, set a primary key for me." Do not assign any relationships. Modify the table design before entering records.

4. For the Campaign# field: Change the Data Type to Text. Set the Field Size to 10. Enter the caption, **Campaign**. For the Name field: Use Text as the Data type and set the Field Size to 35. Enter the caption, **Name of Campaign**.

5. After the Notes field, add a field named **Supplier**. Make it a Text field with a Field Size of 10. Enter a Validation Rule for the Supplier field, which only allows the following entries: **AA-01, BB-02, CC-03,** or **DD-04**. Enter this Validation Text: **You must assign the supplier to be used for this campaign.**

6. Save the table and key the following records.

 **TIP:** Use Shift+F2 to open the Zoom window for the "Notes" Memo field.

| | |
|---|---|
| Campaign: | **January 99** |
| Campaign Name: | **New Year, New Toys** |
| StartDate: | **1/1/99** |
| EndDate: | **1/31/99** |
| Notes: | **This sales campaign announces a new line of toys purchased from Animals 'N Me. Jeffrey Harrison will be in charge of the campaign.** |
| Supplier: | **AA-01** |
| | |
| Campaign: | **March 99** |
| Campaign Name: | **Easter Critters** |
| StartDate: | **3/1/99** |
| EndDate: | **4/4/99** |

Notes: **This is our usual Easter sales promotion. The new sales rep in the Midwest region will take charge in mid-February.**

Supplier: **AA-02** *(See following Note.)*

 **NOTE:** You won't be able to complete the second record because of the Validation Rule. You must fix the error.

**7.** Change the Supplier to **AA-01**. Enter two more records.

Campaign: **May 99**
Campaign Name: **Memorial Day Special**
StartDate: **5/1/99**
EndDate: **5/31/99**
Notes: **This is a red, white, and blue campaign that will highlight animals who wear those colors. Sales rep will be assigned in mid-April.**
Supplier: **BB-02**

Campaign: **Sept 99**
Campaign Name: **Back To School Critters**
StartDate: **8/1/99**
EndDate: **9/4/99**
Notes: **We will have a new line of animals that will be promoted in this campaign. They will include Eddie Einstein the Elephant and Alexander Graham Bell the Bear. Others to be developed by a team of sales reps.**
Supplier: **CC-03**

**8.** Size all the fields, except the Notes field, so you can see the data. Print the table in landscape orientation. You won't be able to see the entire Notes field. Save and close the table.

## APPLICATION 2-2

**Add a form using the Form Wizard. Modify form controls.**

**1.** Using the Form Wizard, create a form that will display all the fields from the Sales Campaigns table. Use a Columnar layout with the Standard style. Name the form **Sales Campaigns Form** *[your initials]*.

217

2. Add a label to the Form Header containing the text **Carolina Critters Sales Campaign Form**. Format this text to 14-point Arial bold with red text on a white background. Size the label to show the text on one line.

3. Move the Name of Campaign control to the right of the Campaign# control at the 2-inch mark on the horizontal ruler. Align the Campaign# and Name controls at the top.

4. Move the StartDate up leaving 2 rows of grid dots. Move the EndDate to the right of StartDate on the 2-inch mark. Align these controls. Move the Notes and Supplier controls up leaving 2 rows of dots between each.

5. View the changes. Print record 4. Save and close the form.

## APPLICATION 2-3

**Move, size, and align form controls.**

1. Using the **Sales Campaigns Form** *[your initials]* change the Form Header text to read **Carolina Critters Campaign Entry Form** *[your initials]*. Change the text to white letters on a red background. Apply a Raised special effect to the label.

2. Change the Name of Campaign text box to a width of 1.25 inches.

3. Select all the labels in the first column and set the width to .65 inches. Move the Campaign# text box to the .75-inch mark on the horizontal ruler. Select all the text boxes in the first column and align them on the left with the Campaign# text box.

4. Change all the labels in the Detail section to the Etched special effect.

5. Switch the Supplier and Notes controls so Supplier is under StartDate and Notes is under Supplier. Align as necessary.

6. Size the Notes text box so the right edge rests on the 4.5-inch mark on the horizontal ruler.

7. Resave the form. Print record 4 and close the form.

## APPLICATION 2-4

**Create a report using the Report Wizard. Modify report controls.**

1. Using the Report Wizard, create a report for all the fields in the Sales Campaign table. Do not use any grouping. Sort the table by StartDate from earliest to latest. Make it a tabular report in landscape orientation with a Corporate style. Name the report **Carolina Critters Report** *[your initials]*.

2. Delete the Campaign# text box in the Detail section and the label in the Page Header.

3. Change the Name of Campaign label to read **Campaign Name**. Size this label and its text box to be 1.35 inches wide. Drag the controls to align the left edges at the 1.25-inch mark.

4. Move the left edges of the EndDate controls to the 2.75-inch mark on the horizontal ruler. Move the left edge of the Notes controls to the 3.75-inch mark. Make the Notes text box 3.5 inches wide.

5. In the second row in the Sorting and Grouping dialog box, add a Group Header for Supplier. Drag the Supplier row to be first and the StartDate row to be second in the Sorting and Grouping dialog box.

6. Move the Supplier text box and label into the Supplier Header you just created, at its left edge. Format the Supplier text box to be the same as the Supplier label. Align the controls if necessary.

7. Add a label in the Report Header with your first and last name in 10-point Arial. Align it at the right edge of the design grid.

8. Size and align all controls as necessary. Print and save the report.

## APPLICATION 2-5

**Create your own table, form, and report using either a wizard or Design View. Choose the layouts and styles.**

1. Create a table called **Shipping** that includes the following fields:
   **CarrierID**
   **ContactName**
   **Address**
   **City**
   **State**
   **PostalCode**
   **PhoneNumber**
   **DeliveryMethod**
   **MinimumCharge**

2. Set Data Types and Field Sizes as you think necessary. Include a Validation Rule and Validation Text that limits the delivery method to Air, Rail, or Truck.

3. Add three records to the table for different carrier companies. Use your name as the Contact Name on one of the records. Print the table in landscape orientation. Save and close the table.

4. Create a form for the Shipping table using all the fields and your choice of layout options. Change the text and background colors. Size, move, and align controls. Add a Form Header with a title that is formatted to emphasize it. Print the form with the record containing your name. Save and close the form.

5. Create a report for the Shipping table. Do not include the PhoneNumber or DeliveryMethod fields. Do not use groups or sorting. Use a tabular landscape layout. Title the report **Shipping Information**. Size and position the controls so you can add a calculated control to determine a new Minimum Charge if rates are increased by 10%. Print the report. Then save and close it.

6. Compact and close the database.

# Getting
# Information
# from a
# Database

| Inventory Value | | Price | Value |
|---|---|---|---|
| Stock No. | Name | | |
| C001 | Dalmatian | | |
| C002 | | | |

Employees by Job Title

LESSON **7**

# Adding Queries to a Database

**OBJECTIVES**

After completing this lesson, you will be able to:

1. Create a query in Design View.
2. Make changes to the dynaset.
3. Modify a query.
4. Specify selection criteria in a query.
5. Use "AND" and "OR" criteria.
6. Use the Top Values property.
7. Add an expression to a query.

 Estimated Time: 1½ hours

**Q**ueries answer questions about the information in a database. Suppose you had a database of baseball players with all their statistics. You could use a query to learn which batters hit more than 20 home runs. You could refine your query and ask a more specific question, like "Who on the Atlanta Braves hit more than 20 homers and at least 30 doubles?" In the same way, a store manager uses queries to find which products sell best and which are most profitable. So queries change a database from mere rows of records into a dynamic information resource. They can help manage a business, run a hospital, send spaceships to Mars—or settle a baseball argument.

Queries resemble filters. Both allow you to select certain fields, sort records, and specify criteria to find the information you need. But a filter is a temporary snapshot of selected data. A query is more permanent. Queries, like tables or forms, are objects, and have their own tab in the Database window.

You can save a query and name it. You can also use it as the source of records for a report.

# Creating a Query in Design View

When you design a query, you're giving Access a road map for searching through a database and finding the records that answer your question. You can use a wizard to design some types of queries, but often it's better and easier to create a query from scratch in Design View. On the lower pane of the Query Design window is the *design grid*. Here you enter the directions Access needs to find your records.

 **TIP:** The design grid is sometimes called the QBE (Query by Example) grid, which was its name in previous versions of Access.

After you design a query, switch to Datasheet View to see the results. Access searches for records according to the instructions you gave it on the design grid. These resulting records are called a *dynaset*, which looks just like a table.

**NOTE:** All the queries you create in this lesson are *select queries*. A select query retrieves records from one or more tables and displays the results in a datasheet. Most queries are select queries.

**FIGURE 7-1**
Query Design
window

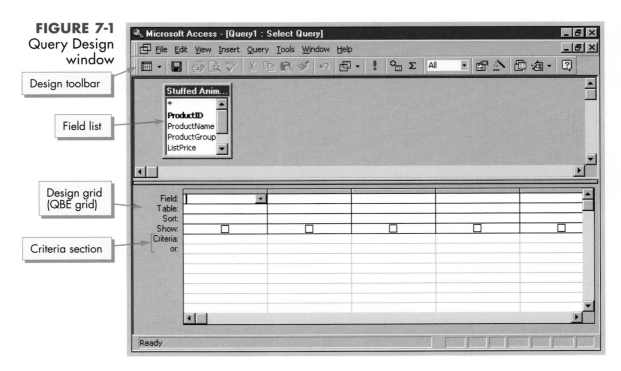

Design toolbar

Field list

Design grid
(QBE grid)

Criteria section

**EXERCISE**  7-1  **Create a Simple Query**

Queries can be simple. For example, you can create a query that includes the fields from a few records of a large table. The field names are placed on the design grid. When you view the results, the dynaset shows only the fields for the specified records.

1. Make a copy of **CC3.mdb** and rename it *[your initials]***CC3.mdb**. Open the file.

2. Click the Queries tab and click the <u>N</u>ew button. The New Query dialog box opens.

3. Select Design View and click OK. The Show Table dialog box opens, and the Query Design window opens behind it.

**FIGURE 7-2**
Show Table
dialog box

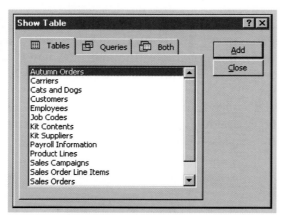

4. If necessary, select the Tables tab in the Show Table dialog box. Choose Stuffed Animals from the list. Click <u>A</u>dd and click <u>C</u>lose. Notice that the Stuffed Animals Field List window appears in the upper pane of the Query Design window. It contains all the fields in the Stuffed Animals table. (Use the vertical scroll bar to inspect them.)

5. In the Query Design window, double-click ProductName in the Stuffed Animals Field List. Notice that ProductName appears in the first cell of the design grid in the Field row. The Table row below the Field row shows the name of the table, Stuffed Animals.

 **TIP:** Another way to add the ProductName field to the design grid is to select it in the field list and drag it to the Field row in the first column.

Notice that in the Show row the option box is checked by default. The ProductName field is shown when you view the results. If you clear the check, the field is not included in the dynaset. In this lesson, all fields in all queries have the Show option selected.

6. Double-click ProductGroup and ListPrice in the Field List window. Notice that each field is added to the next column in the design grid. You finished creating the query. Now you can view its dynaset.

**NOTE:** If you double-click the wrong field name and add it to the design grid, click anywhere in that column and select Edit, Delete Columns to remove it.

**FIGURE 7-3**
Design grid shows fields selected from the Field List window.

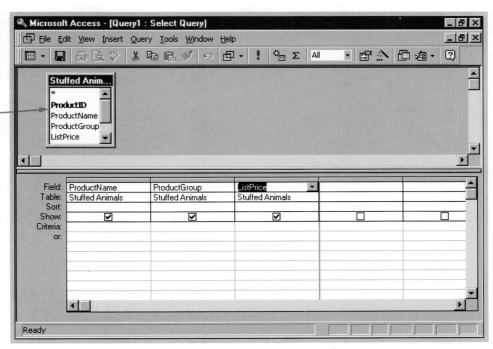

Field List window

---

**EXERCISE** **7-2** **View the Dynaset**

There are several ways to view the dynaset of a query. You can:

- Click the Run button ⬛.
- Choose Run from the Query menu.
- Click the View button 📐 to change to Datasheet View. The View button in a query is a toggle button that works like the View button for a table or form. You can switch between Design and Datasheet Views by clicking 📐.

1. Click the View button 📐 to run the query and see its dynaset in Datasheet View. If necessary, maximize the window. Notice that the dynaset shows all the records with the three fields you entered on the design grid. (See Figure 7-4 on the next page.)

2. Click the Save button 🖫 to save the query. In the text box, Query 1 is the suggested query name.

**FIGURE 7-4**
Query's dynaset
shown in
Datasheet View

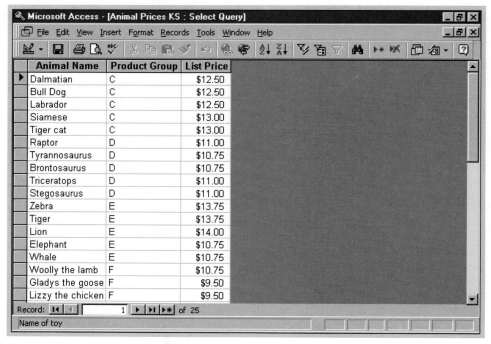

**3.** Key **Animal Prices** *[your initials]* to rename the query. Click OK.

**4.** Click the Database Window button 🗔. Click the Queries tab. Notice that the query was added to your database.

**5.** Choose <u>2</u> Animal Prices *[your initials]* on the <u>W</u>indow menu. Close the query.

# *Making Changes to a Dynaset*

Just like a table or a form, you can enter and modify data in any field of a dynaset. If you create an additional record, the new data is included in the underlying table. If you edit an existing record, the changes are also made in the underlying table.

**EXERCISE** 7-3 **Modify Data**

**1.** Click the Queries tab in the Database window and open the **Animal Prices** *[your initials]* query. When you open the query, you actually run it and display the dynaset.

 **TIP:** You can also double-click the query in the Database window to run it.

2. Change the text in the first record in the Animal Name field from Dalmatian to **Sheepdog**.

3. Close the Animal Prices query.

4. Open the Stuffed Animals table. Notice that the Animal Name in the first record is changed to **Sheepdog**.

**FIGURE 7-5**
Records you edit in a dynaset are also changed in the underlying table.

Edited record

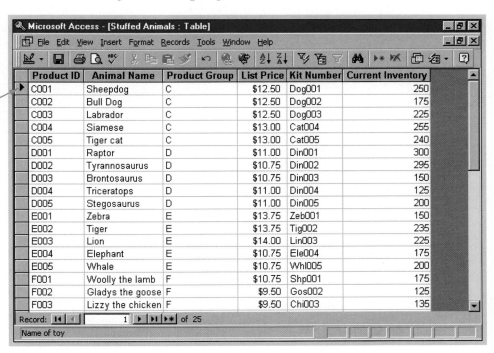

5. Change Sheepdog back to **Dalmatian** and close the table.

# Modifying a Query

You can modify a query after you create it. You can also sort on one field or multiple fields and add or delete fields.

**EXERCISE** **7-4** **Size Elements**

You can resize the Field List window and the columns of the design grid to see more (or less) text of the field names.

1. Click the Queries tab. Open the Animal Prices query in Design View by clicking Design.

2. Move the pointer to the right border of the Stuffed Animals Field List window. Drag the right border to make the field list wider.

3. Move the pointer to the vertical line that separates the ProductName and ProductGroup columns of the design grid. When the pointer is on the line that separates the two column selectors, it changes to a double-headed arrow with a vertical bar (the column-sizing pointer).

4. Drag the border to the left, but don't release the mouse button. As you drag, notice the vertical black line that shows the new width. Return the pointer to its original position and release the button.

**FIGURE 7-6**
Vertical line shows
new width

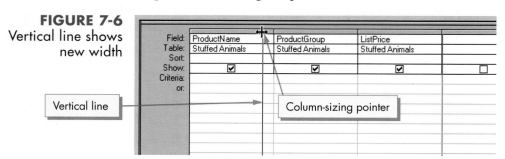

Vertical line

Column-sizing pointer

**TIP:** You can also adjust the height of the panes. Place the pointer on the horizontal border between the panes and it changes to the split pointer. Drag in either direction to resize. If you make the top pane higher, you can make the Field List window taller to see more field names.

**EXERCISE** 7-5 **Sort by One Field**

Just like a table, a query allows you to sort fields in either Ascending or Descending order.

1. On the design grid, click in the Sort row in the first column, which contains the ProductName field.

2. Click the drop-down arrow and select Ascending from the list.

**FIGURE 7-7**
Select a Sort
option on the
design grid.

| Field: | ProductName | ProductGroup | ListPrice | |
|---|---|---|---|---|
| Table: | Stuffed Animals | Stuffed Animals | Stuffed Animals | |
| Sort: | | | | |
| Show: | Ascending | ☑ | ☑ | |
| Criteria: | Descending | | | |
| or: | (not sorted) | | | |

3. Switch to Datasheet View. Notice that the Animal Name field is now alphabetized.

**EXERCISE** **7-6** **Add and Delete Fields**

You can add fields to a query. The fields are added from the Field List window to the design grid.

1. Change to Design View. In the field list, double-click KitNumber. Notice that KitNumber is in the Field row of the fourth column.

 **TIP:** If you make a mistake and want to start from scratch, choose Clear Grid from the Edit menu to clear the design grid.

2. Change to Datasheet View. Notice that the Kit Number field is now part of the dynaset.

3. Switch back to Design View. Move the pointer toward the column selector for ProductGroup on the design grid. The column selector is a small, rectangular box directly above the field row. When the pointer is a down arrow, click to select the column.

**FIGURE 7-8**
Select column when pointer is a down arrow.

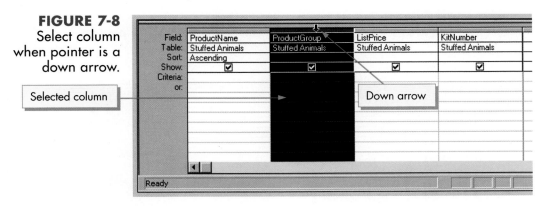

| Field: | ProductName | ProductGroup | ListPrice | KitNumber |
| Table: | Stuffed Animals | Stuffed Animals | Stuffed Animals | Stuffed Animals |
| Sort: | Ascending | | | |
| Show: | ☑ | ☑ | ☑ | ☑ |
| Criteria: | | | | |
| or: | | | | |

Selected column

Down arrow

Ready

4. Press Delete to delete the field from the query.

5. Change to Datasheet View to display the dynaset. Notice that the Product Group field was deleted.

6. Return to Design View.

**EXERCISE** **7-7** **Sort by Multiple Fields**

In Lesson 3 you learned how to sort a table by more than one field. You can also sort on multiple fields in a query. For example, you may want to sort the products you sell by groups and alphabetically by name within the group. The sort order is determined by the order of the sorted field columns on the design grid. The field you want to sort first (the main sort) must be to the immediate left of the field you want to sort second. So you may have to move fields in the design grid to get the sort order you want.

1. Double-click ProductGroup in the Field List window to add the field to the design grid.

2. Move the pointer to the column selector of the ProductGroup field. When the pointer is a down arrow, click to select the column.

3. Move the pointer again to the column selector. Click and keep the button depressed. Notice that a small rectangular box is around the tail of the white-arrow pointer. Drag the entire column to the first column of the design grid and release the button. The ProductGroup column is now in the first column to the left of the ProductName column.

 **TIP:** Before you rearrange field columns, think of the easiest way to reorder them. Sometimes you can eliminate one or two column drags.

 **NOTE:** A thick vertical line marks the new column position.

**FIGURE 7-9**
Move fields to get desired sort order.

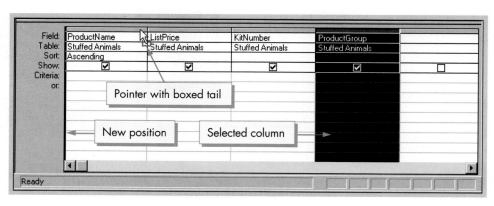

4. Click in the Sort cell of the ProductGroup column. Click the drop-down arrow and select Ascending from the list.

5. The ProductName field should already have an Ascending sort. If it doesn't, click in the Sort cell, click the drop-down arrow, and select Ascending.

6. Change to Datasheet View. Notice that the query is now sorted first by Product Group and then by Animal Name.

# *Specifying Selection Criteria in a Query*

Criteria might be text, numbers, or an expression. You enter criteria in a query to select certain records and exclude others. When you view the results of a query with selection criteria, you see only those records that match the criteria. You might, for example, set criteria that limits the records to products in Group C. Or maybe you'd like a list of stuffed animals that have a list price greater than $10.

## EXERCISE 7-8 Use Criteria in One Field

Criteria can be as simple as a single condition in one field. For example, you may want to include records of products in just one product group, like cats and dogs. Since the product code for cats and dogs is C, you use C as criteria in the ProductGroup field.

1. Return to Design View. In the design grid, find the Criteria row below the Show line. On the Criteria row of the Product Group column, key **C**. Change to Datasheet View. Notice that only those records with a Product Group of "C" (the cats and dogs) are displayed.

**FIGURE 7-10**
Selected records meet the criteria keyed in the design grid.

2. Return to Design View. Notice that Access put quotation marks around the "C" criteria in the design grid.

3. Delete the "C" criteria in the Product Group cell by selecting it and pressing Delete.

 **TIP:** Another way to delete criteria is to click anywhere in the criteria cell. Press F2 to select the entire criteria. Press Delete to remove the criteria.

4. You could also search for all products with a list price between $9.50 and $11. In the Criteria row of the List Price field, key **between 9.50 and 11**. View the dynaset. Notice that only records for those products with prices between $9.50 and $11 are included in the dynaset.

5. Return to Design View. Access capitalized the words in the expression. Delete the criteria for the ListPrice field.

6. Save and close the query.

**231**

# Using "AND" and "OR" Criteria

You can use "AND" and "OR" criteria to refine a query and find specific information. Suppose you wanted to find all the stuffed animals that are bears (product code "T") and cost between $10.50 and $13. In that case, you want to use "AND" criteria, because two conditions must be met. The first condition is that the product must be a bear. The second condition is that the product must cost between $10.50 and $13. With "AND" criteria, only those products that are bears *and* that cost between $10.50 and $13 will be retrieved. When you use "AND" criteria, you enter the conditions on the *same* Criteria row in the design grid.

Suppose, however, you want to see *all* the products that are bears and *all* the products that cost between $10.50 and $13. In that case, use "OR" criteria, because only one condition needs to be met. You want to include products that are bears regardless of cost. You also want to include animals that cost between $10.50 and $13 regardless of whether they're bears or not. With "OR" criteria, all the products that meet either one condition *or* the other condition are included. Animals that meet both conditions are included as well. When you use "OR" criteria, the conditions are placed on *different* Criteria rows in the design grid.

## EXERCISE 7-9 Use "AND" Criteria

Before you use "AND" criteria, follow these steps to create a new query and add five fields to the design grid:

1. Click the Queries tab and click the New button.
2. In the New Query dialog box, choose Design View and click OK. The Show Table dialog box appears with the Query Design window behind it.
3. Select Employees, click Add, and click Close. Maximize the Query Design window so you can see all the fields you add to the design grid.
4. In the Employees field list, double-click the LastName, FirstName, JobCode, BirthDate, and HireDate fields to place them on the design grid.
5. Switch to Datasheet View. Notice that all five fields are in your dynaset.
6. Return to Design View. Now you're ready to use "AND" criteria to find all the employees who have JobCode MF05 *and* were hired after January 1, 1985.
7. In the JobCode column, key **MF05** in the Criteria row.
8. In the HireDate column, key **>1/1/85** in the same Criteria line. (Because you're using "AND" criteria, you enter both conditions in the same Criteria row in the design grid.)

**FIGURE 7-11**
"AND" criteria go
on the same row in
the design grid.

| Field: | FirstName | JobCode | BirthDate | HireDate | |
|---|---|---|---|---|---|
| Table: | Employees | Employees | Employees | Employees | |
| Sort: | | | | | |
| Show: | ☑ | ☑ | ☑ | ☑ | ☐ |
| Criteria: | | "MF05" | | >1/1/85 | |
| or: | | | | | |

**NOTE:** For the condition "hired after January 1, 1985," you use the > (greater than) symbol. (If you wanted to find employees hired before January 1, 1985, you would use <, the less than symbol.)

**9.** View the dynaset.

**10.** Save the query. Name it **MF05 Recent Hires** *[your initials]*.

## EXERCISE 7-10 Use "OR" Criteria

Use "OR" criteria to find all the employees with the Job Code of MF05 *or* who were hired after January 1, 1985.

**1.** Return to Design view. Cut ">#1/1/85#" from the Criteria row of the HireDate column to place it on the Clipboard.

**2.** Paste the date in the Or row of the HireDate column. The Or row is directly below the Criteria row.

**FIGURE 7-12**
"OR" criteria go
on two separate
lines in the Criteria
section of the
design grid.

| Field: | FirstName | JobCode | BirthDate | HireDate | |
|---|---|---|---|---|---|
| Table: | Employees | Employees | Employees | Employees | |
| Sort: | | | | | |
| Show: | ☑ | ☑ | ☑ | ☑ | ☐ |
| Criteria: | | "MF05" | | | |
| or: | | | | >#1/1/85# | |

**3.** Change to Datasheet View. Notice that the dynaset includes records in which either condition is met. Some people have job codes other than MF05, but they were hired after January 1, 1985. Some of the people with job code MF05 were hired before that date. Each record meets one of the OR conditions.

**4.** Save the query.

**TABLE 7-1** Examples of Expressions and How Access Displays Them

| WHAT YOU ENTER | WHAT ACCESS DISPLAYS | ACCESS RETRIEVES RECORDS WHERE |
| --- | --- | --- |
| MF05 | "MF05" | Value is MF05 |
| 15-Aug-98 | #8/15/98# | Date is 15-Aug-98 |
| 1.50 | 1.50 | Value is 1.50 |
| >5000 | >5000 | Value is greater than 5000 |
| <15-Aug-98 | <#8/15/98# | Date is before 15-Aug-98 |
| Between 6 and 12 | Between 6 and 12 | Value is between 6 and 12, including 6 and 12 |

# *Using the Top Values Property*

You often need to determine the best and worst, highest and lowest, youngest and oldest. In the Stuffed Animals table, for example, you might need to find the five highest or lowest priced animals. If you keep a database of movies, you can create a query that would display the movies that won the most Oscars. In a Customers table, you might want to find those customers who generate the most revenue.

The Top Values Property finds a certain number of records (for example, the top 5) or a percentage (for example, the top 5%). You usually use this property with sorted fields. Depending on how you sort, you can also use Top Values to find the worst or lowest. Descending sorts with Top Values display the topmost records in the dynaset. Ascending Top Values sorts display the records at the bottom.

## EXERCISE 7-11 Find the Top Values

1. Return to Design View. Delete the existing criteria on the design grid.
2. Click in the Sort row for the HireDate column.
3. Click the drop-down arrow and choose a Descending sort to show dates most recent to least recent.
4. View the dynaset. Notice that the most recently hired employees are listed first.
5. Return to Design View. Click the Top Values box on the toolbar and set the number to 5 to display the five most recent hires.

**FIGURE 7-13**
The Top Values property is set from a drop-down list box.

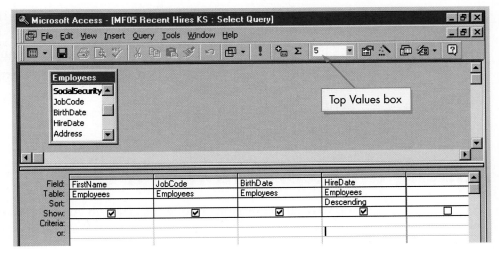

 **NOTE:** The Top Values property is listed on the properties sheet for the query. Select the query by clicking anywhere in the top pane outside the field list box. Choose Properties from the View menu.

**6.** View the dynaset. The five most recent hires are listed.

**TIP:** If you wanted to know the five employees who have been with the company the longest, you would choose an Ascending sort. The dates are listed least recent to most recent.

**7.** Return to Design View. Reset the Top Values box to All. Close the query without saving it.

 **NOTE:** Remember to reset the Top Values property to All. If you forget to reset the Top Values property to All and prepare a query to show employees hired after 1984, you would see only the five most recent hires.

**EXERCISE 7-12 Find the Bottom Percent**

The Top Values property can also be used for the top or lowest percent. For example, you could find the bottom 5% of products by list price.

**1.** Open the Animal Prices query in Design View. Delete the sorts for the ProductGroup and ProductName fields.

2. Sort the ListPrice field in ascending order. Switch to Datasheet View to view the dynaset. Return to Design View.

3. Click the Top Values box on the toolbar and set the number to 5%.

4. Switch to Datasheet View. The records for the least expensive 5% of products are displayed.

5. Close the query. Do not save the changes.

# Adding an Expression to a Query

You've used expressions in queries. The job code MF05 was a simple expression that consisted of a simple text string. Some expressions have operators, such as the ">" sign in >1/1/85, which you used to find employees who were hired after January 1, 1985. You can also use expressions to create a calculated field in a query. These expressions are the same as those you used for the calculated controls in forms and reports in Lessons 4 and 5.

 **TIP:** You can use the Expression Builder in a query by right-clicking the empty column for the expression and then selecting the Build button.

## EXERCISE 7-13 Create a Calculated Field

1. Open the **Animal Prices** *[your initials]* query in Design View.

2. Double-click the QuantityOnHand field in the field list box to add it to the first empty column of the design grid.

3. Delete the KitNumber field. Maximize the Query Design window (or click once on the horizontal scrollbar) to see the next empty column.

4. In the Field row of the first empty column, key **ListPrice*QuantityOnHand**.

5. View the dynaset. Notice that the last column shows the list price multiplied by the quantity on hand for each product, its wholesale value. The field is named **Expr1**.

6. Return to Design View. Notice that Access applied its standard format and enclosed the field names in brackets.

7. Give the new field a more descriptive name. Replace "Expr1" with **Wholesale Value**. The entire expression should read *Wholesale Value: [ListPrice]*[QuantityOnHand]*.

**FIGURE 7-14**
Give the calculated
field a more
descriptive name.

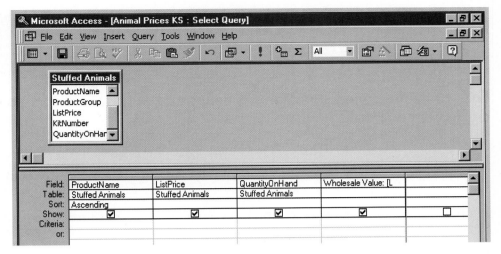

 **NOTE:** You must include a colon after the text to be used as the column title.

 **TIP:** You can press Shift+F2 to open the Zoom window when you cannot see the contents of a row in the design grid.

**8.** View the dynaset again. The last column has the new field name. Widen the column slightly so you can see the full name.

**9.** Save and close the query.

**COMMAND SUMMARY**

| FEATURE | BUTTON | MENU | KEYBOARD |
|---|---|---|---|
| Create query | | Insert, Query | |
| Run query | | View, Datasheet View<br>Query, Run | |
| Design View | | View, Design View | |
| Top Values | All | | |

# Concepts Review

Each of the following statements is either true or false. Indicate your choice by circling either **T** or **F**.

T  F  **1.** You cannot enter new records in the dynaset of a query.

T  F  **2.** When you edit data in a dynaset, the data in the underlying table is also changed.

T  F  **3.** You can't use a query as the source of records for a report.

T  F  **4.** You can add a field to a query in Design View by double-clicking it in the Field List window.

T  F  **5.** To sort on two fields in a query, the main sort field should be immediately to the left of the field that is sorted second.

T  F  **6.** You can use the Top Values property to find the bottom 5% of values for any field.

T  F  **7.** In the design grid, "OR" criteria go in the same row in the Criteria section, while "AND" criteria go on different lines.

T  F  **8.** You cannot use multiplication in an expression.

Write the correct answer in the space provided.

**1.** What is the name of the grid where you tell Access how to sort data in a query?

_____

**2.** In what view do you see the dynaset of a query?

_____

**3.** What property allows you to see the highest and lowest values in a field?

_____

**4.** What type of criteria do you use when you want two conditions to be true at the same time?

_____

**5.** If you want names sorted in alphabetical order, what kind of sort do you use?

_____

**6.** Where do you choose fields to add to the design grid?

_____

**7.** Where do you choose a table or tables on which to base a query?

_____

**8.** What symbol do you use in an expression to multiply values?

_____

## CRITICAL THINKING

**Answer these questions on a separate page. There are no right or wrong answers. Support your answers with examples from your own experience, if possible.**

**1.** Think of your favorite hobby or interest, like music, sports, movies. Think of some examples of how queries could help you find out something you wanted to know.

**2.** In this lesson you used "AND" criteria and "OR" criteria. How could these be used in a database for a hobby or interest?

# Skills Review

## EXERCISE 7-14

**Create a query in Design View. Make changes to the dynaset.**

**1.** Create a query in Design View by following these steps:

**a.** If necessary, open the file *[your initials]***CC3.mdb**.

**b.** Click the Queries tab. Click the New button.

**c.** Select Design View from the New Query dialog box and click OK.

**d.** Click the Tables tab in the Show Table dialog box. Select Customers from the list. Click Add and click Close.

**e.** In the Query Design window, double-click CustomerID in the Customers field list to add the field to the design grid.

**f.** Add the CompanyName and ContactName fields to the design grid.

*g.* Switch to Datasheet View. Save the query. Name the query **Company Contacts *[your initials]*.**

    *h.* Click the Database Window button 🖻. Click the Queries tab. Notice that the query was added to your database.

    *i.* Select Company Contacts[your initials]: Select Query from the Window menu.

**2.** Edit a record by following these steps:

    *a.* In the Company Contacts *[your initials]* dynaset, change the text in the first record in the Contact Name field from "Sharon" to **"Sally."**

    *b.* Close the Company Contacts *[your initials]* query.

    *c.* Open the Customers table. Notice that in the first record the Contact Name "Sharon" is changed to "Sally."

    *d.* Change "Sally" back to **Sharon** and close the table.

## EXERCISE 7-15

## Modify a query. Sort on multiple fields.

**1.** Add a sort to a query by following these steps:

    *a.* Open the **Company Contacts *[your initials]*** query in Design View. If necessary, maximize the window.

    *b.* In the design grid, click in the Sort row for the CompanyName field.

    *c.* Click the drop-down arrow and choose Ascending from the list.

    *d.* Switch to Datasheet View to see the dynaset. The records are sorted by Company Name.

**2.** Add more fields to a query by following these steps:

    *a.* Return to Design View. Add PhoneNumber to the design grid.

    *b.* Switch to Datasheet View and note that the PhoneNumber field is now part of the dynaset.

**3.** Delete a field by following these steps:

    *a.* Switch to Design View. In the design grid, move the pointer toward the column selector for the PhoneNumber field.

    *b.* When the pointer is a down arrow, click to select the column.

    *c.* Press Delete to delete the field from the design grid.

**4.** Resize the Field List window and the columns of the design grid by following these steps:

    *a.* Move the pointer to the right border of the Customers Field List window.

> **b.** Drag the right border until all the field names are in full view.
>
> **c.** Move the pointer to the line that separates the column selector boxes for the CompanyName and ContactName columns of the design grid. The pointer changes to a double arrow.
>
> **d.** Drag the border to the right about ¼ inch.
>
> **e.** Resize the CompanyName column to its original width.
>
> **f.** Save your changes and close the **Company Contacts** *[your initials]* query.

5. To sort on multiple fields, follow these steps:

> **a.** Open the **Animal Prices** *[your initials]* query in Design View.
>
> **b.** Move the pointer to the column selector box of the ProductName field. When the pointer is a down arrow, click to select the column.
>
> **c.** Move the pointer again to the column selector box. Drag the column right until the border between the ListPrice and QuantityOnHand fields is a heavy black line. The field columns are in the following order: ProductGroup, ListPrice, ProductName, QuantityOnHand, and Wholesale Value.
>
> **d.** Choose Ascending sorts for the ProductGroup and ListPrice fields. Keep the Ascending sort for ProductName.
>
> **e.** Switch to Datasheet View. Notice that the fields are sorted by Product Group, by List Price within the Product Group, and then alphabetically by Animal Name.
>
> **f.** Save your changes. Close the Animal Prices *[your initials]* query.

## EXERCISE 7-16

## Specify selection criteria in a query. Use "AND" and "OR" criteria.

1. To specify criteria follow these steps:

> **a.** Open the **MF05 Recent Hires** *[your initials]* query in Design View. Maximize the window.
>
> **b.** Delete all criteria in the Criteria section of the design grid.
>
> **c.** In the Criteria row of the LastName column, key **Clark.** Switch to Datasheet View. Notice that only those employees whose last name is Clark, Martin and Diane Clark, are displayed.
>
> **d.** Return to Design View. Delete the "Clark" criteria in the LastName field.
>
> **e.** In the Criteria row of the HireDate field, key **>12/31/92**. View the dynaset. Only records for those employees hired after 1992 are included.

**2.** To include "AND" criteria follow these steps:

  **a.** Return to Design View. In the LastName column, key **Clark** in the Criteria row. Criteria for both the LastName and HireDate fields are in the same line.

  **b.** Switch to Datasheet View. Since you are using "AND" criteria, only those records for employees named "Clark" hired after 1992 are included in the dynaset. Diane Clark is in the dynaset. Martin Clark, hired before 1992, is not.

**3.** To include "OR" criteria, follow these steps:

  **a.** Return to Design View. Cut >#12/31/92# from the Criteria row of the HireDate column to the Clipboard.

  **b.** Paste **>#12/31/92#** in the Or row of the HireDate column, directly below the Criteria row.

  **c.** Switch to Datasheet View. The dynaset includes records in which either the employee is named Clark or he or she was hired after 1992. Note that Martin Clark was hired in 1991.

## EXERCISE 7-17

### Use the Top Values property. Add an expression to a query.

**1.** To use the Top Values property, follow these steps:

  **a.** Return to the Design View of the **MF05 Recent Hires** *[your initials]* query.

  **b.** Delete the existing criteria on the design grid.

  **c.** Click in the BirthDate column in the Sort line.

  **d.** Choose an Ascending sort from the drop-down list.

  **e.** View the dynaset. Notice that oldest employees (the employees who have the earliest birth date) are listed first.

  **f.** Return to Design View. On the toolbar, click the Top Values box and set the number to 5.

  **g.** View the dynaset. Only the five oldest employees are listed.

  **h.** Return to Design View. Click the Top Values box and select 25%.

  **i.** View the dynaset. The oldest 25% of employees are displayed.

  **j.** Return to Design View. Reset the Top Value box to All. Close the query and don't save the changes.

**2.** To create an expression in a query:

  **a.** Open the **Animal Prices** *[your initials]* query in Design View.

***b.*** In the Field row of the first empty column, key **ListPrice\*.1**. This expression calculates the additional revenue from each product with a 10% price increase.

***c.*** View the dynaset. The last column shows the list price multiplied by 10%. It is called *Expr1*.

***d.*** Return to Design View to give the new field a more descriptive name. Replace Expr1 with **Price Increase**. You must include the colon.

***e.*** Right-click the Field row for Price Increase and select Properties. Click the General tab and click the Format row. Select Currency. Close the properties sheet.

***f.*** View the dynaset. Note that Price Increase is now the caption for the field and the numbers are in currency format. Save and close the query.

# Lesson Applications

## EXERCISE 7-18

**Create a query, specify selection criteria, do multiple sorts, use "AND" and "OR" criteria.**

1. Start Access, if necessary, and open your database file.

2. Create a query based on the Stuffed Animals table that includes the following fields: ProductName, ProductGroup, ListPrice, and QuantityOnHand.

3. Sort the query by ascending ProductName. Save it as **Product Queries** *[your initials].*

4. Find animals with a list price above $11 and greater than 200 units in inventory.

5. Find animals with a list price of $10.75 and greater than 150 units in inventory.

6. Find the dinosaurs ("D" group) that have a list price of $11. Print the dynaset. Clear the query grid of all criteria.

7. Find animals that either have a list price of greater than $11 or greater than 250 units in inventory.

8. Find animals with a list price of $10.75 or greater than 200 units in inventory. Alphabetize them.

9. Find animals with a list price of less than $11 and greater than 150 units in inventory. Sort them first by group, then by name. Print the dynaset. Resave and close the query.

## EXERCISE 7-19

**Create a query. Perform multiple sorts. Use "AND" and "OR" criteria. Use the Top Values property.**

Create queries based on the Payroll Information table to find the following. Save the queries as **Pay Info** *[your initials]***1**, **Pay Info** *[your initials]***2**, and so on. Print the dynasets.

- Employees who are paid on a monthly salary basis and make more than $2,100 a month. Show their ID# and Social Security #, along with the salary. Sort by ID.

- Employees who are paid on an hourly basis and make more than $8.25 an hour. Show their ID#, Social Security #, hourly wage rate, and the federal tax per month. Sort first by hourly rate, from lowest to highest, and then by ID#.

- Employees who earn more than $9 per hour or are paid more than $2,600 a month on a salary basis. Show their ID#, Social Security #, and monthly salary or hourly wage. Sort by ID.

- Employee(s) who earn an hourly wage of $8.25 per hour and also pay more than $190 per month in federal tax (not including FICA). Show their ID#, Social Security #, hourly wage, and federal tax.

- The top five earners at the company, all of whom are paid on a monthly basis. Show their ID#, Social Security #, and salary.

## EXERCISE 7-20

**Create a query. Sort fields. Add an expression to a query.**

Carolina Critters is thinking of increasing the inventory it keeps on hand for certain products. Using the Stuffed Animals table as your source, create a new query that shows how many additional dinosaurs with a price of less than $11 they would have if they increased the current inventory by 20%. Your dynaset will have the following fields: ProductName, ProductGroup, ListPrice, QuantityOnHand, and AdditionalInventory (calculated field). Alphabetize the dinosaur names. Save the file as **Dinosaur Inventory** *[your initials]* and print it.

# 8

# Creating and Using Relationships

**OBJECTIVES**

After completing this lesson, you will be able to:

1. **Create a lookup field.**
2. **Edit records with a lookup field.**
3. **View relationships in the Relationships window.**
4. **Establish a relationship in the Relationships window.**
5. **Edit relationships.**
6. **Create a multiple table query.**
7. **Use the Expression Builder.**

 Estimated Time: 1½ hours

Y ou've been working with a single table or query. The Carolina Critters database, however, is a relational database. You might compare a relational database to a symphony orchestra. Although each instrument can play on its own, the result is considerably more vibrant when they play together. Individual tables are useful on their own. When you use them together, however, the power of the database increases.

Relationships are essential for good database management. They allow you to use more than one table in a query, form, or report and to combine or assemble information in useful ways.

In this lesson you learn about relationships between tables. You can create, edit, and delete these relationships. You also learn the relationship rules that are essential to good database management.

# *Creating a Lookup Field*

Information needed for a particular table is often part of another table. In the Stuffed Animals table, for example, one field shows the product code or line. The Product Lines table also contains a field with product codes or lines. The Kit Contents table includes a field with the Supplier's ID (AA-01, BB-02, etc.).The Kit Suppliers table also includes this field.

A *lookup field* allows you to select data for one table from a field with similar data in another table. For example, when you enter the Supplier's ID in the Kit Contents table, you can "look it up" from the Kit Suppliers table. You don't have to key it.

---

**EXERCISE 8-1 Compare Tables with the Same Data**

---

The Kit Suppliers and Kit Contents tables contain similar information. Compare them to see how to use a lookup field.

1. Open the file *[your initials]*CC3.mdb.

2. Open the Kit Suppliers table from the Database window. Notice the type of information contained in the Supplier ID field.

3. Click 📖 and open the Kit Contents table. The table is sorted by ascending Kit Number. Minimize the Database window.

4. Choose Tile Horizontally from the Window menu. Notice that the SupplierID field of the Kit Contents table contains the same type of information as the Supplier ID field in the Kit Suppliers table.

**FIGURE 8-1**
Both tables contain
Supplier IDs.

| Kit Number | Supplier ID | Cost | Kit Contents |
|---|---|---|---|
| Bear001 | DD-04 | $7.29 | This kit contains |
| Bear002 | DD-04 | $7.71 | This kit contain |
| Bear003 | DD-04 | $6.71 | This kit contains |
| Bear004 | AA-01 | $6.97 | This kit contains |
| Bear005 | AA-01 | $8.05 | This kit contains |
| Cat004 | BB-02 | $6.03 | This kit contains |

Record: 1 of 25

| Supplier ID | Supplier Name | Contact Name | Address | City |
|---|---|---|---|---|
| AA-01 | Mills Fabric & Notion Supply | Mary Kay Smith | 1642 Industrial Drive | McHenry |
| BB-02 | Waternam Fabric Works | John Anders | 1019 Grant Street | Denver |
| CC-03 | Cosby Manufacturing, Inc. | Peter Johnson | 628 South Street | Raleigh |
| DD-04 | Robinson Mills, Inc. | Your Name Here | 481 Lafayette Avenue | Passic |
| EE-05 | Southern Fabrics, Inc. | Randolph C. Pete | 2600 Patterson Street | Greensboro |
| FF-06 | Northeast Fabric Supply | Patrice Davis | 562 Industrial Parkway | Wallingford |

Record: 1 of 7

5. Close the Kit Suppliers table.

6. Restore the Database window.

## EXERCISE  8-2  Create a Lookup Field

You can create a lookup field for the Supplier ID field in the Kit Contents table. To enter the Supplier ID, you choose it from a drop-down list box that displays the IDs in the Kit Suppliers table. The Lookup Wizard guides you step-by-step through the process of creating the lookup field.

1. Open and maximize the Kit Contents table. Switch to Design View.

2. Click in the Data Type column for the SupplierID row. Click the drop-down arrow and select Lookup Wizard.

3. In the first dialog box of the Lookup Wizard, choose "I want the lookup column to look up the values in a table or query." Click Next.

4. In the next dialog box, select Tables from the View option group near the bottom of the dialog box. Choose Kit Suppliers from the tables displayed and click Next.

5. In the dialog box that asks which values to include in the lookup column, select SupplierID and click > to transfer it to the Selected Fields list. Click Next.

6. The next dialog box shows the SupplierID field with all its values from the Kit Suppliers table. You can make the column wider or narrower here. Click Next.

**FIGURE 8-2**
Lookup column
contains
SupplierIDs.

**Lookup Wizard**

How wide would you like the columns in your lookup column?

To adjust the width of a column, drag its right edge to the width you want, or double-click the right edge of the column heading to get the best fit.

| SupplierID |
| --- |
| AA-01 |
| BB-02 |
| CC-03 |
| DD-04 |
| EE-05 |
| FF-06 |

[ Cancel ]   [ < Back ]   [ Next > ]   [ Finish ]

7. In the next dialog box, change the label to **Supplier** and click Finish.

8. A message box appears saying "The table must be saved before relationships can be created." Click <u>Y</u>es.

9. Click the Lookup tab in the Field Properties section. The Lookup tab includes more properties than the other fields.

10. Save the table.

# *Editing Records with a Lookup Field*

To enter data in a lookup field, click the drop-down arrow and select a value from the drop-down list box or lookup column.

**EXERCISE**    **8-3**    ## Using a Lookup Column and the Zoom Window

You now enter a new record to see how the lookup field works. You also review how to enter text into a Memo field using the Zoom window when you press Shift + F2. Besides word wrap, you can correct errors using regular Cut, Copy, and Paste commands in this window.

1. Switch to Datasheet View. Click the New Record button ▶*.

2. Don't key the Supplier ID. Click the drop-down arrow that appears and select the ID from the lookup values. When you reach the Kit Contents field, press Shift + F2.

| Kit Number: | **Ele007** |
|---|---|
| Supplier: | **BB-02** |
| Cost: | **$5.27** |
| Kit Contents: | **This kit contains tusks, eyes, a tail, dark gray parachute, and cotton fill.** |

**FIGURE 8-3**
Choose the value from the lookup column.

| Kit Number | Supplier | Cost | Kit Contents |
|---|---|---|---|
| Dog003 | CC-03 | $6.62 | This kit contains |
| Ele004 | BB-02 | $4.32 | This kit contains |
| Gos002 | BB-02 | $3.81 | This kit contains |
| Lam001 | AA-01 | $4.50 | This kit contains |
| Lin003 | BB-02 | $6.96 | This kit contains |
| Pig004 | CC-03 | $3.79 | This kit contains |
| Shp001 | DD-04 | $4.50 | This kit contains |
| Tig002 | EE-05 | $6.73 | This kit contains |
| Whl005 | FF-06 | $4.24 | This kit contains |
| Zeb001 | GG-07 | $6.71 | This kit contains |
| Ele 007 | | $0.00 | |
| * | | $0.00 | |

3. Click OK to close the Zoom window.

4. Delete the record you just added and close the table.

# Viewing Relationships in the Relationships Window

When you created the lookup field, Access identified a relationship between the Kit Contents and Kit Suppliers tables based on a common or similar field containing Supplier IDs.

You can create, view, and edit relationships in the Relationships window. You can also add and remove tables from the Relationships window and save the layout of the window. The layout is a snapshot of the tables in the Relationships window at a particular time. It may not show all the relationships that actually exist in the database. Even if you don't save the layout, you don't change the actual relationships.

**EXERCISE** 8-4 Open the Relationships Window

In the Relationships window, you see field lists for tables and existing relationships between those tables. You can make changes to the appearance of this window by deleting, adding, sizing, and moving the field lists for the tables.

1. Click the Relationships button .

TIP: You could also use the Relationships command on the Tools menu.

2. The Relationships window should be empty. If it is not, click the Clear Layout button ⊠ and select Yes.

3. Click the Show Table button. If necessary, click the Tables tab.

4. Select the Kit Contents table and click Add. It appears in the window under the Show Tables dialog box.

5. Select Kit Suppliers in the Show Tables dialog box and click Add. It is added to the window.

TIP: You can add more than one table at a time by selecting the tables' names in the Show Tables dialog box. Hold down Ctrl and click each name to be added.

6. Click <u>C</u>lose to close the Show Tables dialog box. There is a connecting line between the Kit Suppliers field list and the Kit Contents field list. This line demonstrates that a relationship exists between the two tables.

**FIGURE 8-4**
The line between the Supplier ID fields shows a relationship exists between the tables.

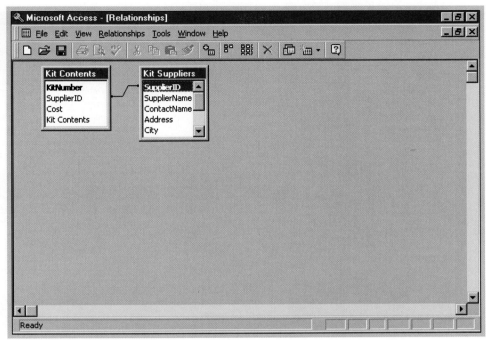

7. Point at the title bar of either field list and drag it to a new location. Size the Kit Suppliers field list so you can see all the fields.

8. Close the Relationships window. A message box asks if you want to save the changes to the layout. Click Yes.

# *Establishing a Relationship in the Relationships Window*

Different types of relationships can exist between or among tables in a database. The most common type of relationship is *one-to-many*. The Customers and Sales Orders tables have this type of relationship. The Customers table has a unique field for each customer, the Customer ID field. Each customer can have only one ID, and an ID number can be used only once in that table. The Customer ID field is the primary key in this table. This is the *one* side of the relationship to the Sales Orders table.

The Sales Orders table has a record for every order, and each order includes the Customer ID. If a customer orders many times, his or her ID can appear several times in the Sales Orders table, the *many* side of the relationship. The Customer ID field in this table is called the *foreign key*, and the Sales Orders table is called the *related table*.

**FIGURE 8-5**
Compare the Customer ID field in the two tables.

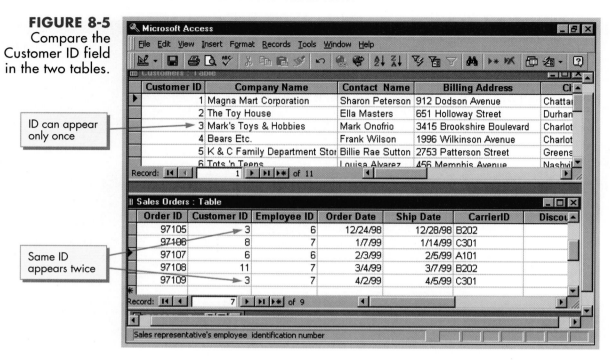

ID can appear only once

Same ID appears twice

---

**EXERCISE 8-5 Establish a One-to-Many Relationship**

When you created a lookup field in the Kit Contents table, you established a relationship between the Kit Suppliers and Kit Contents tables. You can also create relationships directly in the Relationships window. The primary key for each table appears in bold. Create the relationship by dragging the common field name from one table to another. As soon as you release the mouse button, the Relationships dialog box opens so you can define the relationship.

**1.** Click the Relationships button 🖼. The relationships layout for Kit Suppliers and Kit Contents appears.

**2.** Click the Clear Layout button ☒ and click Yes.

**3.** Click 🖼.

**4.** Choose the Customers table and click Add. Choose the Sales Orders table and add it to the window. Click Close.

**TIP:** You can add a table to the Relationships window by double-clicking its name in the Show Tables dialog box.

5. Drag the CustomerID field from the Customers field list to the CustomerID field in the Sales Orders field list. You dragged the primary key to the foreign key. Release the mouse button.

**FIGURE 8-6**
Dragging a field to create a relationship.

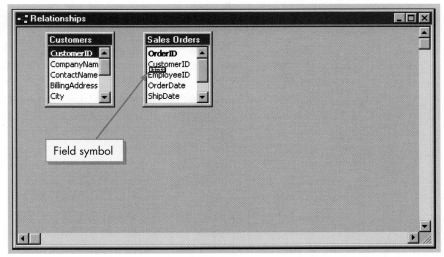

6. The Relationships dialog box opens. The primary table is shown on the left; the related table is on the right. The Relationship Type is One-To-Many, shown near the bottom of the dialog box.

7. Do not check a checkbox. Click Create.

8. The relationship is shown in the window. Click Close and save the layout. This layout replaces the one with Kit Suppliers and Kit Contents.

**FIGURE 8-7**
Relationships dialog box

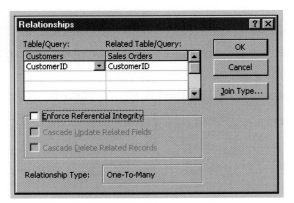

# Editing Relationships

You can create, edit, or delete relationships between tables. You already created a relationship by dragging the common field. Access created a relationship when you ran the Lookup Wizard. If a relationship exists between two tables and you want to delete one of those tables, you must first delete the relationship.

You can edit a relationship to use referential integrity. *Referential integrity* is a set of Access rules. You can turn these rules on or off in the Relationships dialog box. These rules tell Access to check what you're doing so you don't accidentally delete data that shouldn't be deleted or change information that shouldn't be changed.

To review: The Customer ID field in the Customers table is the primary key, which is unique for each record. The Sales Orders table has the same field, but it isn't the primary key. It's a foreign key. When you established the relationship between these two tables, you linked the primary key in the primary table (Customers) to the foreign key in the related table (Sales Orders).

Here's an example of what referential integrity does for these two tables. You can't add a sales order (in the Sales Orders table) that uses a nonexistent customer ID. The customer ID must already be in the Customers table (primary table) before you can complete the related record in the Sales Orders table. If you were able to add a sales order without a customer ID, the company could easily be cheated.

Here's another example of referential integrity. You can't delete a customer from the Customers table if the customer has outstanding orders in the Sales Orders table. If you could delete such a record, you could delete your customer information before you get paid for the order.

## EXERCISE 8-6 Enforce Referential Integrity

You can enable referential integrity for two tables if:

- The related fields have the same type of data (Text, Number, etc.).
- The tables are in the same database.
- The common field in the primary table is the primary key in that table.

To enforce referential integrity between two tables that have a relationship:

*1.* Click the Relationships button ⊞ to open the Relationships window.

*2.* Right-click the sloping portion of the jagged line between the two field lists to select it.

*3.* Choose Edit Relationship from the shortcut menu. The Relationships dialog box opens.

**TIP:** You can double-click the sloped portion of the line between the field lists to open the Relationships dialog box.

4. Check the <u>E</u>nforce Referential Integrity box and click OK.

5. The relationship line now has a "1" and an infinity sign at opposite ends. The "1" is closest to the Customers field list, the table on the "one" side of the relationship. The infinity sign is closest to the Sales Orders list, the table on the "many" side.

**FIGURE 8-8**
A one-to-many
relationship with
referential integrity
enforced

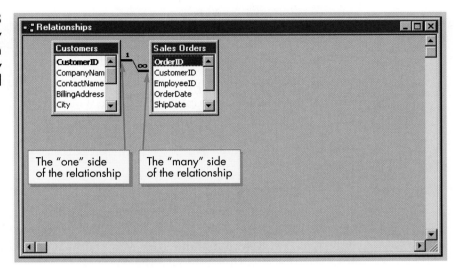

6. Close the Relationships window and save the layout.

7. Open the Customers table in Datasheet View. Open the Sales Orders table in Datasheet View.

8. Minimize the Database window.

9. From the Window menu, choose Tile Vertically. You can see there is no Customer ID 12 in the Customers table.

10. Click in the Sales Orders table and enter a new record with the following information:

| | |
|---|---|
| Order ID: | **97110** |
| Customer ID: | **12** |
| Employee ID: | **7** |
| Order Date: | **5/10/99** |
| Ship Date: | **5/26/98** |
| Carrier ID: | **B202** |
| Discount: | **.1** |

**11.** As soon as you try to move the pointer past this new record you see an error message. You can't move forward until you fix the problem. Click OK in the error box.

**FIGURE 8-9**
Error message for
violation of
referential integrity

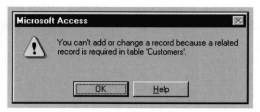

**12.** Press Shift+[Tab] to move the insertion point back to the Customer ID field. Change the ID for the new record to **3**.

**13.** Move the pointer to any other record. You can add the record.

**14.** Close both tables. Restore the Database window.

## EXERCISE 8-7 Set the Cascade Update Related Fields Option

When you set referential integrity, you cannot make certain types of changes. Suppose you changed the customer ID numbering system and now need to change all IDs. Referential integrity won't allow it. You could, of course, turn off referential integrity and make the changes. But then you need to make the changes in both the Customers and Sales Orders tables. You can override the rule about changing related records when you enable the Cascade Update Related Fields option. You can then edit the ID in the Customers table and Access automatically changes all the related records in the Sales Orders table.

To select the Cascade Update Related Fields option:

**1.** Click the Relationships button ⬚.

**2.** Right-click the sloping part of the relationships line.

**3.** Choose Edit Relationship from the shortcut menu.

**4.** Check Cascade Update Related Fields to turn on the option.

**5.** Click OK and close the Relationships window.

**6.** Open the Customers table in Datasheet View. Open Sales Orders in Datasheet View. Minimize the Database window.

**7.** From the Window menu, choose Tile Vertically.

**8.** In the Customers table, double-click 2 in the Customer ID field and change it to **12**. You see the related change in the Sales Order table as a cascade update after you move the pointer to another record.

9. In the Customers table, double-click 12 in the Customer ID field and change it to **2.** Look for the change in the Sales Order table as another cascade update.

10. Close both tables and restore the Database window.

**EXERCISE 8-8 Set the Cascade Delete Related Fields Option**

Suppose you want to delete a customer record in the Customers table. The customer has one or more outstanding orders in the Sales Orders table. Under the rules of referential integrity, you cannot delete the record. Access finds there are associated records in the Sales Orders table with the existing customer ID and prohibits the deletion.

If you set the Cascade Delete option, you *can* delete the customer record in the Customers table. In fact, *all* the orders for that customer are deleted from the Sales Orders table, too.

It is important that you are careful when deleting records if Cascade Delete Related Fields is turned on. If you delete a particular customer from the Customers table, all the customer's sales orders are deleted, too. This may be acceptable if the customer is up-to-date with payments, but it's certainly not acceptable if the customer owes money. Suppose your school keeps your records in two related tables—Students and Classes. A cascade delete option would allow someone to delete you from the Students database as well as all the classes you have taken.

To select the Cascade Delete option:

1. Click the Relationships button.

2. Right-click the sloping part of the relationships line.

3. Choose Edit Relationship from the shortcut menu.

4. Check Cascade Delete Related Fields to turn on the option.

5. Click OK and close the window.

6. Open the Customers table and the Sales Orders table in Datasheet View. Minimize the Database window.

7. From the Window menu, choose Tile Vertically.

8. In the Customers table, click in the record selector for Bears, Etc. to select it. There is one sales order for this customer in the Sales Orders table.

9. Click the Delete Record button. A warning message box appears. (See Figure 8-10 on the next page.)

10. Click Yes. You can see the change in the Sales Order table because the record is marked as deleted. This indicator is removed as soon as you close the table.

**FIGURE 8-10**
Warning message
for Cascade Delete
option

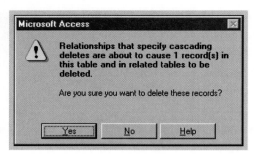

**11.** Close both tables. Restore the Database window and open the Sales Orders table. The record is deleted. Close the table.

---

**EXERCISE** **8-9** **Delete a Relationship**

---

To delete a relationship in the Relationships window:

**1.** Choose Relationships from the Tools menu to open the Relationships window.
**2.** Right-click the sloping portion of the relationships line.
**3.** Select Delete.
**4.** A confirmation message box appears. You would click Yes to delete the relationship, but for now click No to keep this relationship for future use.
**5.** Close the Relationships window.

# *Creating a Multiple Table Query*

Relationships allow you to combine data from two tables. Good database management requires that you use small, manageable tables rather than big unmanageable tables. That's why there's a Kit Contents table with information about kits. This table includes a code for the supplier. It doesn't, however, include the name and address of the supplier. If it did, you would need to enter that name and address for every kit from that supplier. Not only would that be a lot of extra work, but you might be much more likely to make an error. And if a supplier's address changed, you would have to change many records.

The Kit Suppliers table lists the name and address of suppliers. You only need to key the supplier's name once. If the address changes, you only need to change it here. But suppose you need a report that shows the kit number, the kit cost, *and* the supplier's name. Two of those fields are in the Kit Contents table, but the name is in the Kit Suppliers table. You can create a query that uses both tables.

**FIGURE 8-11**
Required fields are
in two separate
tables.

Kit number and kit
cost are in this table.

Supplier's name
is in this table.

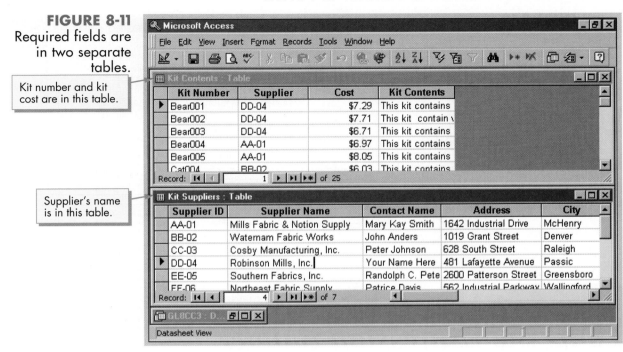

**EXERCISE 8-10 Create a Query with Two Tables**

To create a query with two tables, you add both tables to the Query Design grid, add the fields to the grid, set the sort option, and enter criteria.

1. Click the Queries tab in the Database window and click New.
2. Select Design View and click OK.
3. In the Show Table dialog box, double-click Kit Contents to add it to the grid. Double-click Kit Suppliers. Close the Show Tables dialog box.
4. If necessary, maximize the window. You can see the relationship in the Query window. (See Figure 8-12 on the next page.)
5. Double-click the KitNumber field to add it as the first field in the design grid.
6. Double-click the SupplierName field. Double-click the Cost field. The Table row in the grid identifies which table has supplied the field.
7. Click the Sort line for KitNumber and select Ascending.
8. Click the View button to see the dynaset.
9. Save the query. Name it **Kit Suppliers/Costs** *[your initials]*.

259

**FIGURE 8-12**
The jagged line shows the relationship between the two tables.

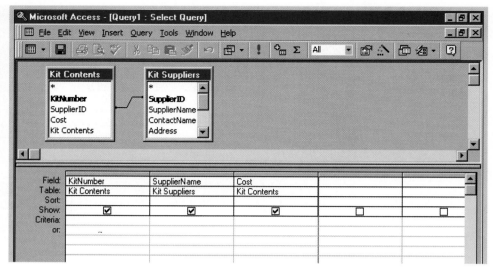

# Using the Expression Builder

In Lesson 6 you used the Expression Builder to create an expression by choosing the elements of an expression rather than keying them.

An expression is usually a combination of identifiers, operators, and values. The *identifier* in an expression usually refers to a field in the underlying table. An *operator* is often an arithmetic symbol such as + or =. You may remember the expression you used earlier, *QuantityOnHand*ListPrice,* to determine the wholesale value of inventory. A *value* is a number, such as 5 or 1.36.

 **NOTE:** There are other types of operators for more sophisticated math and logic.

**EXERCISE** **8-11** **Build an Expression**

You can add a calculated field using an expression in the Kit Suppliers/Costs query. This calculated field determines what the kits would cost if the cost were increased by 8 percent.

**1.** Click the View button 📉 to return to the design grid.
**2.** Right-click the Field row for the first empty column and select Build. The leftmost panel shows that you are in the Kit Suppliers/Costs query. The middle panel lists the fields already in that query.

3. Double-click Cost in the middle panel to paste it in the preview area of the builder. Access adds brackets around the field name as standard formatting.

4. Click * in the row of buttons below the preview to paste the multiplication operator.

5. Key **1.08** after the * symbol.

**FIGURE 8-13**
Using the
Expression Builder

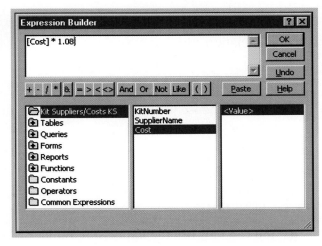

6. Click OK to close the Expression Builder. The expression appears in the Field row.

7. View the dynaset. The label for the calculated field is *Expr1*.

8. Return to the design grid.

9. Point at the *Expr1* field, right-click, and select <u>P</u>roperties.

10. Click the General tab. Click the Format row, click its drop-down arrow, and select Currency.

11. Close the properties sheet.

12. Select *Expr1* and replace it with **New Cost**. Remember to leave the colon after the column name.

13. View the dynaset again. Save and close the query.

**COMMAND SUMMARY**

| FEATURE | BUTTON | MENU | KEYBOARD |
|---|---|---|---|
| Create, view, edit relationships | | Tools, <u>R</u>elationships | |
| Clear Layout | | <u>E</u>dit, Cl<u>e</u>ar Layout | |
| Show Table | | Tools, <u>R</u>elationships, Show Table | |

# Concepts Review

## TRUE/FALSE QUESTIONS

Each of the following statements is either true or false. Indicate your choice by circling either **T** or **F**.

T  F  **1.** When you clear the Relationships window, you delete all existing relationships.

T  F  **2.** The most common kind of relationship is a one-to-one relationship.

T  F  **3.** You can choose the Cascade Delete option only when you enforce referential integrity.

T  F  **4.** When you create a query with two tables, a jagged line connects the matching fields in the field lists.

T  F  **5.** In a one-to-many relationship, the foreign key is in the related table, which is on the many side of the relationship.

T  F  **6.** You can only use the Expression Builder when referential integrity is enforced.

T  F  **7.** A Lookup field allows you to select values for data entry rather than keying them.

T  F  **8.** When you create a query with more than one table, you add the tables you need from the Show Table window.

## SHORT ANSWER QUESTIONS

Write the correct answer in the space provided.

**1.** In a one-to-many relationship, what do you call the field with matching data in the related table?

_____

**2.** What is the name given to the set of rules governing relationships that help protect data from accidental changes and deletions?

_____

**3.** In a one-to-many relationship, what do you call the table on the "one" side of the relationship?

_____

**4.** Where can you learn what relationships have been established among the tables in a database?

_____

**5.** What option enables you to update records in related tables, despite the enforcement of referential integrity?

_____

**6.** In the Relationships window, there is a one-to-many relationship with referential integrity enforced. How do you tell which table is on the "many" side of the relationship?

_____

**7.** What option enables you to delete the records in related tables despite the enforcement of referential integrity?

_____

**8.** What do you call the drop-down box in a lookup field from which you can select values?

_____

## CRITICAL THINKING

**Answer these questions on a separate page. There are no right or wrong answers. Support your answers with examples from your own experience, if possible.**

**1.** In this lesson you studied the concept of referential integrity. In what ways is referential integrity helpful in managing a database? Can you think of any problems connected with enforcing referential integrity?

**2.** What are some of the advantages and disadvantages of using the Cascade Update Related Fields and Cascade Delete Related Fields options?

# Skills Review

## EXERCISE 8-12

**Create a lookup field and enter records using it.**

**1.** To create a lookup field, follow these steps:

**a.** Open the file *[your initials]*CC3.mdb.

**b.** Open the Sales Orders table in Design View and maximize the window.

**c.** Click in the Data Type column for the CarrierID. Click the drop-down arrow and select Lookup Wizard.

**d.** In the first wizard dialog box, choose "I want the lookup column to look up the values in a table or query." Click Next.

**e.** Make sure Tables is selected in the View group in the next dialog box. Choose Carriers in the list of tables. Click Next.

**f.** In the next dialog box, select CarrierID and click > to move it to the Selected Fields list. Click Next.

**g.** The next dialog box shows the CarrierID field with all its values. Click Next.

**h.** As a label for the lookup field, use the default **CarrierID**. Click Finish.

**i.** The message box reminds you to save the table. Click Yes.

**j.** Switch to Datasheet View.

**k.** Click in the CarrierID column. The drop-down arrow shows it is now a lookup field.

**2.** To enter a record using the lookup field, follow these steps:

**a.** Click the New Record button ▶*.

**b.** For the CarrierID, click the drop-down arrow and choose the ID from the list. For the Order and Ship dates, enter your birthday with the year as shown.

| | |
|---|---|
| Order ID: | 97111 |
| Customer ID: | 6 |
| Employee ID: | 6 |
| Order Date: | *Enter your birthday and /99* |
| Ship Date: | *Enter your birthday and /99* |
| Carrier ID: | B202 |
| Discount: | 0 |

**c.** Close the table.

## EXERCISE 8-13

## View and establish relationships in the Relationships window.

**1.** To view relationships in the Relationships window, follow these steps:

**a.** Click the Relationships button ⊟.

**b.** Click the Clear Layout button ⊠ and click Yes.

*c.* Click the Show Table button 🔲. Select the Carriers table and click <u>A</u>dd. Select the Sales Orders table and click <u>A</u>dd.

*d.* Click Close to close the Show Table dialog box. The field lists appear with the relationship line between the CarrierID fields. (If necessary, make the Sales Orders field list taller to see the CarrierID field.)

*e.* Close the Relationships window and don't save the layout.

2. To establish a relationship in the Relationships window:

*a.* Click the Relationships button 🔲.

*b.* Click the Clear layout button ☒ and click Yes.

*c.* Click the Show Table button 🔲. Select the Sales Order Line Items table and click <u>A</u>dd. Select the Sales Orders table and click <u>A</u>dd.

*d.* Click <u>C</u>lose to close the Show Table dialog box. There is no relationship line.

*e.* Size the field lists so you can see all the field names. Size both field lists so you can see the table name in the title bar.

*f.* Drag the tables and rearrange them so the Sales Orders table is to the left of the Sales Order Line Items table.

*g.* Drag the OrderID field from the Sales Orders field list to the OrderID field in the Sales Order Line Items field list. When you release the mouse button, the Relationships dialog box opens.

*h.* The primary table is Sales Orders, on the left. The related table is Sales Order Line Items. This is a One-to-Many Relationship Type. Make sure Enforce Referential Integrity is not on. Click <u>C</u>reate.

*i.* The relationship line shows the relationship. Close the Relationships window and save the layout.

## EXERCISE 8-14

**Enforce referential integrity. Add records to related tables. Set Cascade Update Related Fields and Cascade Delete Related Fields options.**

*1.* To enforce Referential Integrity:

*a.* Click the Relationships button 🔲. The relationships layout opens with the Sales Orders and Sales Order Line Items tables.

*b.* Right-click the relationships line.

*c.* Choose Edit <u>R</u>elationship from the shortcut menu.

*d.* Click the Enforce Referential Integrity checkbox to enable the option. Click OK. There is a 1 symbol to mark the primary table and an infinity sign to mark the related table.

*e.* Close the Relationships window.

2. To add records to related tables, follow these steps:

   *a.* Open the Sales Orders table in Datasheet View. Click the Database Window button 🗗 and open Sales Order Line Items in Datasheet View.

   *b.* Minimize the Database window.

   *c.* From the Window menu, choose Tile Vertically. There is no Order ID 97113 in the Sales Orders table.

   *d.* Click in the Sales Order Line Items table and enter a new record with the following information:

   | Order ID: | **97113** |
   |---|---|
   | Product ID: | **T005** |
   | Quantity: | **20** |

   *e.* As soon as you try to move the pointer forward you see an error message. You can't continue until you fix the problem. Click OK in the error box.

   *f.* Press Shift+Tab to move the insertion point back to the Order ID field. Change the ID for the new order to **97110**.

   *g.* Move the pointer to any other record. Access allows you to add the record.

   *h.* Close both tables. Restore the Database window.

3. To set the Cascade Update and Delete options, follow these steps:

   *a.* Click the Relationships button 🗗.

   *b.* Right-click the sloping part of the relationships line.

   *c.* Choose Edit Relationship from the shortcut menu.

   *d.* Click Cascade Update Related Fields to turn on the option.

   *e.* Click Cascade Delete Related Fields to turn on the option.

   *f.* Click OK. Close the Relationships window.

   *g.* Open the Sales Orders table in Datasheet View. Open the Sales Order Line Items table in Datasheet View. Minimize the Database window.

   *h.* From the Window menu, choose Tile Vertically.

   *i.* In the Sales Orders table, double-click 97108 in the Order ID field and change it to **97104.** Move the insertion point away from the record to write the change in both tables. The related change appears in the Sales Order Line Items table as a cascade update.

   *j.* In the Sales Orders table, click in the Record Selector for Order ID 97107 to select that record. There are two line items for this sales order in the Sales Order Line Items table.

   *k.* Click the Delete Record button 🗙. A message box appears asking you to confirm the deletion.

*l.* Click <u>Y</u>es. The change appears in the Sales Order Line Items table because the record is marked as deleted. This indicator is removed as soon as you close the table.

*m.* Sort the Sales Order and Sales Order Line Items tables by Order ID.

*n.* Close both tables. Save the changes. Restore the Database window.

## EXERCISE 8-15

**Create a Query with two tables; use the Expression Builder to create an expression.**

*1.* To create a query with two tables:

*a.* Click the Queries tab and create a new query.

*b.* In the New Query dialog box, select Design View and click OK.

*c.* In the Show Table dialog box, select the Carriers table and click <u>A</u>dd. Select the Sales Orders table, click <u>A</u>dd, and close the Show Table window. Maximize the window.

*d.* Resize the field lists for both tables so you can see all the fields.

*e.* Double-click CarrierName in the Carriers field list to add it to the design grid. Double-click the OrderID and ShipDate fields in the Sales Orders field list.

*f.* Click the column selector at the top of the OrderID field to select the column.

*g.* Drag the OrderID column so it is the first column.

*h.* Click in the Sort row for the OrderID column and select Ascending.

*i.* Click the View button 🔲. The orders are listed in ascending order by order number with the carrier name and ship date.

*j.* Save the query and name it **Delivery Dates** *[your initials]*.

*2.* To use the Expression Builder to create an expression:

*a.* Return to Design View. Right-click in the Field row for the first empty column in the design grid. Select <u>B</u>uild to open the Expression Builder.

*b.* Double-click ShipDate in the middle panel to paste it to the Preview area.

*c.* Click + in the row of icons below the preview to paste the addition operator.

*d.* Key **7** after the addition operator. The expression reads **[Ship Date]+7**. This figures a new ship date a week later. Click OK.

*e.* Switch to Datasheet View to see the dynaset. Return to Design View.

**f.** Replace Expr1: with the title **New Delivery Date:** Keep the colon after the field name.

**g.** Click the View button 🔳. Widen the last column so you can see the title.

**h.** Save the query and close it.

# Lesson Applications

**Create a lookup field. Edit records with a lookup field. View the relationship cre-
ated by a lookup field.**

1. Open your Access database, if necessary. Open the Employees table in
   Design View.
2. Click in the Data Type column for the JobCode field and start the
   Lookup Wizard.
3. Look up the values in a table and use the Job Codes table.
4. Use the JobCode field for the lookup column. Label the column
   **JobCode**. Save the table.
5. Switch to Datasheet View. Do not sort any fields. In the last record,
   change the employee's name to your first and last name.
6. Print the table in landscape orientation and close it.
7. Open the Relationships window and clear the layout. Add the Job Codes
   and Employees tables.
8. Size the field lists so you can see all the fields and the relationship line.
9. Close the Relationships window and don't save the layout.

**Create a relationship with referential integrity. Add a record to related tables.**

1. Open the Stuffed Animals table and the Sales Order Line Items table.
   Minimize the Database window and vertically tile the table windows.
   The Product ID field is the primary key in the Stuffed Animals table and
   a foreign key in the Sales Order Line Items table.
2. Close both tables and restore the Database window.
3. Open the Relationships window and clear the layout.
4. Add the Stuffed Animals and Sales Order Line Items table to the
   Relationships window.
5. Size the field lists so you can see all the field names. If necessary,
   arrange the field lists so Stuffed Animals is on the left.
6. Drag the primary key from the Stuffed Animals table to the ProductID
   field in the Sales Order Line Items table.
7. Enforce Referential Integrity and create the relationship.

8. Close the Relationships window and save the layout.

9. Open the Stuffed Animals table. Open the Sales Order Line Items table. Minimize the Database window and vertically tile the windows.

10. Click in the Sales Order Line Items table and add the following record.

Order ID: **97111**

Product ID: **Q001**

Quantity: *Your birthdate (for example, March 3, 1978 would be 30378)*

11. As soon as you try to move forward, an error message appears. Click OK in the error box.

12. Press Shift + Tab to move the insertion point back to the Product ID field. Change the ID for the new record to **F004.** Move the pointer to any other record.

13. Print the Sales Order Line Items table. Close both tables and restore the Database window.

## EXERCISE 8-18

**Select Cascade Update and Cascade Delete Related Fields options. Add records to related tables.**

1. Open the Stuffed Animals table.

2. Attempt to delete the record for Product ID C001. You can't delete the record because of its referential integrity with the Sales Order Line Items table. Click OK. Close the table.

3. Edit the relationship between the two tables to turn on Cascade Update Related Fields and Cascade Delete Related Fields. Close the Relationships window.

4. Open the Stuffed Animals table. Open the Sales Order Line Items table. Minimize the Database window and vertically tile the windows.

5. Click in the Stuffed Animals table. Click the record selector for Product ID C001 in the Stuffed Animals table. Click the Delete Record button ⌧ and select Yes. The record and its related record in the Sales Order Line Items table are deleted.

6. Look at the Sales Order Line Items table and note which orders include Product ID T005. Find that Product ID in the Stuffed Animals table.

7. In the Stuffed Animals table, change T005 to **T006**. Move the insertion point away from the record to write the change in both tables.

8. Resort the Sales Order Line Items table by ascending Order ID. Print the table.

9. In the Stuffed Animals table, change T006 to **T005**. Move the insertion point away from the record to write the change in both tables.

10. Close both tables and restore the Database window.

## EXERCISE 8-19

### Create a multiple table query. Use the Expression Builder.

1. Click the Queries tab. Create a new query using Design View.

2. Add the Customers and Sales Orders tables to the Query window. Close the Show Table dialog box. Maximize the Query window.

3. Resize the field lists for both tables so you can see all the fields.

4. From the Customers table, add the CompanyName and State to the design grid. From the Sales Orders table, add OrderID and Discount.

5. Sort by OrderID in ascending order.

6. View the dynaset. Return to the Design window.

7. Save the query as **NC Discounts** *[your initials]*.

8. Right-click the Field row for the first empty column. Select Build. The left panel shows that you are in the NC Discounts query. The middle panel lists the fields in the query.

9. Double-click Discount in the middle panel to paste it in the Preview area of the builder.

10. Click * in the row of buttons to paste the multiplication operator.

11. Enter **2** after the * symbol. The expression is **[Discount]*2**. Close the Expression Builder.

12. Scroll in the Field row and select *Expr1*. Replace it with **Double Discount**. Leave the colon.

13. Point at the *Double Discount* field, right-click, and select Properties.

14. Click the General tab. Click the Format row and select Percent. Close the properties sheet to save this change.

15. Open the properties sheet again. Click the Decimal Places row and select 0. Close the properties sheet.

16. Check the dynaset. Widen the Double Discount column so you can see the title. Return to the Design window.

17. In the State field, enter **NC** as criteria to use this double discount only for customers in North Carolina.

18. Click the View button ⬚. Since some customers don't get a discount, they shouldn't be shown in the dynaset. Return to the Design window.

19. In the Discount field, enter **>0** as criteria to select only those customers who already have a discount greater than 0. Both criteria are on the same row.

20. View and print the dynaset. Resave and close the query.

21. Compact your database.

# Designing Advanced Queries

**OBJECTIVES**

After completing this lesson, you will be able to:

1. Select a range of records.
2. Edit a dynaset.
3. Select records that don't match a value.
4. Use the Total row in a query.
5. Create a parameter query.
6. Create an update query.
7. Create a delete query.
8. Create append and make table queries.

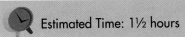 Estimated Time: 1½ hours

In Lesson 7, you learned how to create simple queries. In Lesson 8, you learned how to build a query that retrieves data from more than one table. Although tables are the building blocks of a database, queries give you the ability to work with data to accomplish business tasks. In this lesson, you learn how queries make data in tables accessible and valuable.

## Selecting a Range of Records

A *range* of records is a group of records in which the information for a particular field starts at one value in the first record and ends at another value in the last record in the group. In the Stuffed Animals table, for example, you could find the animals in the price range of $12.50 to $13.75. In the Customers table, you could find all customers whose ZIP codes are between 37200 and 37500. In the Sales Orders table, you could look for all customers whose discounts are between 5 and 10 percent.

## EXERCISE 9-1 Size the Query Grid

You can size the panes in the Query window by dragging the border between the parts of the window.

1. Open your file *[your initials]*CC3.mdb.
2. Click the Queries tab and click New to design a new query. Choose Design View in the New Query dialog box and click OK.
3. Choose Stuffed Animals from the Show Table dialog box, click Add, and click Close.
4. Maximize the Query window.
5. Position the pointer on the border between the top and bottom pane until it displays a double-headed arrow.
6. Drag the border down until the design grid (bottom) is about a third of the window.

FIGURE 9-1
Size the Query
grid.

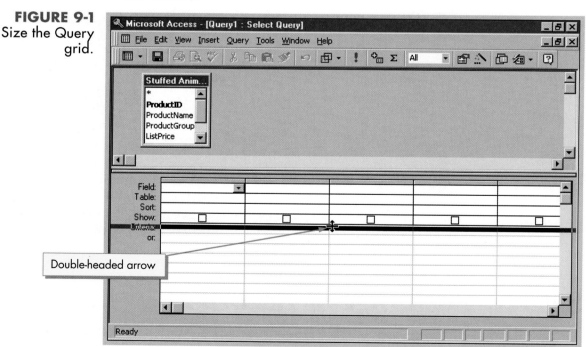

Double-headed arrow

7. Resize the field list for the table so you can see all the fields.

**EXERCISE** **9-2** **Select a Range of Records**

Suppose you need to determine which stuffed animals show current inventory between 250 and 325 units. This is a simple range. You can find this range of records by entering an expression as criteria in your query. There are two ways to write this expression: *>=250 and <=325* or *between 250 and 325*.

1. Double-click the ProductID, ProductName, ProductGroup, ListPrice, and QuantityOnHand fields to add them to the design grid.
2. In the QuantityOnHand column in the Criteria row, key **>=250 and <=325**.

**FIGURE 9-2**
Select a range of
records using
criteria.

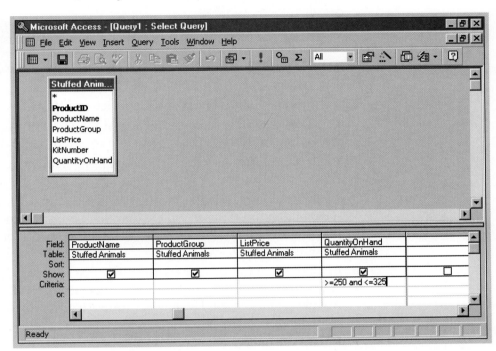

> ⭐ **TIP:** You can use the <, <=, >, and >= operators for dates and text. The expression ">=5/1/98 and <=5/31/98" displays records with dates in the month of May. The expression ">=B and <=L" finds all names beginning with a B, C, D, and so on through the letter L.

3. Display the dynaset and review the results.
4. Return to Design View. Select *>=250 and <=325* in the Criteria row and replace it with **between 250 and 325**.
5. View the dynaset. Both expressions display the same records.
6. Save your query as **Quantity Range *[your initials]*** and close it.

# *Editing the Dynaset*

You learned in Lesson 7 that you can make changes in the dynaset that are automatically reflected in the table. You can also make other types of changes in the dynaset, such as sorting records, rearranging fields, and renaming columns. These are layout changes and are not reflected in the table.

**EXERCISE** **9-3** **Sort Fields in a Dynaset**

As you know, you can sort the records in a query. After you run the query, you can also sort the records and move the fields in the dynaset.

1. Double-click Quantity Range *[your initials]* to run the query and display the dynaset.

2. For product F004, change the List Price to **$10.75**.

3. Click the column selector at the top of the List Price field. Click the Sort Ascending button ⬇. The records are sorted by price, lowest to highest.

4. Click the column selector for the List Price field. Drag the field so it is first in the dynaset.

5. Click the column selector for the Product Group field. Drag the field so it is second in the dynaset. Notice that there are two products with a list price of $10.75. The record with product group "F" appears before product group "D."

6. Click the column selector for the List Price field. Hold down Shift and click the column selector for the Product Group field. Click the Sort Ascending button ⬇. The records are sorted first by List Price and then by Product Group.

7. Resave the query.

**FIGURE 9-3**
Dynaset sorted by two fields

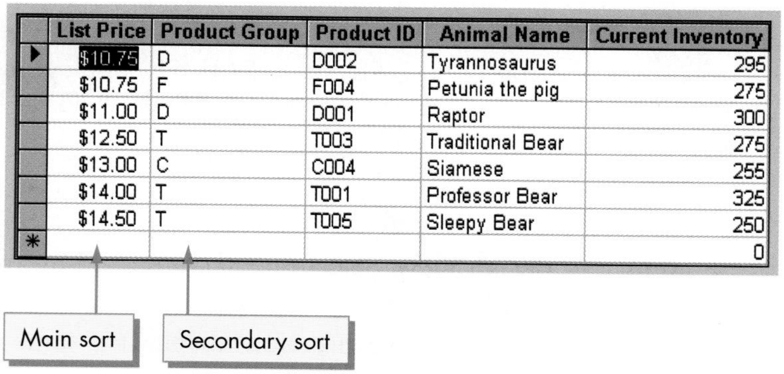

| List Price | Product Group | Product ID | Animal Name | Current Inventory |
|---|---|---|---|---|
| $10.75 | D | D002 | Tyrannosaurus | 295 |
| $10.75 | F | F004 | Petunia the pig | 275 |
| $11.00 | D | D001 | Raptor | 300 |
| $12.50 | T | T003 | Traditional Bear | 275 |
| $13.00 | C | C004 | Siamese | 255 |
| $14.00 | T | T001 | Professor Bear | 325 |
| $14.50 | T | T005 | Sleepy Bear | 250 |
| * | | | | 0 |

Main sort   Secondary sort

**EXERCISE** 9-4 **Edit a Caption**

The title for a field in a dynaset is the same as the caption for that field in the table. The caption is a field property in the table design window, and the query inherits most of these field properties. You can change the properties of the dynaset in the query design window. When you make these changes, they're not copied to the table.

1. Return to Design View.
2. Right-click anywhere in the QuantityOnHand column.
3. Choose Properties from the shortcut menu.
4. Click the General tab.
5. In the Caption row, key **Quantity** and close the properties sheet.

**FIGURE 9-4**
Use the field's properties sheet to change a caption.

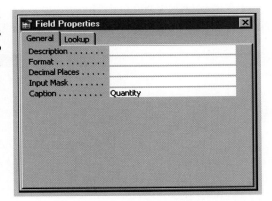

6. View the query. The title is changed to *Quantity* for the inventory column.
7. Save the query.

# *Selecting Records that Don't Match a Value*

Sometimes it is faster to find records that don't match a particular criteria. Suppose you want to find all customers who don't live in North Carolina. You could set criteria to find all customers who live in Alabama, Alaska, Arizona, Arkansas, California, Colorado, and so on, listing the other 49 states. A more efficient query, however, uses the "NOT" operator. You simply enter the word **not** before the criteria in the design grid.

**EXERCISE** **9-5** **Use the "NOT" Operator in a Query**

You can edit the Quantity Range query to exclude products that cost exactly $14 or products named "Lion."

1. Return to Design View. Delete all criteria in the Criteria row.
2. In the ListPrice field, click in the Sort row. Select Descending from the drop-down menu.
3. View the dynaset. Notice that there are two products—the Professor Bear and the Lion—that sell for $14.
4. Switch to Design View. Key **not 14** in the Criteria row of the List Price column.
5. View the dynaset. Notice that the two products selling for $14 are no longer in the dynaset.
6. Switch to Design View. Delete the criteria on the grid.
7. In the Criteria row of the ProductName field, key **not Lion**.

**FIGURE 9-5**
Use "NOT" criteria to exclude records from a dynaset.

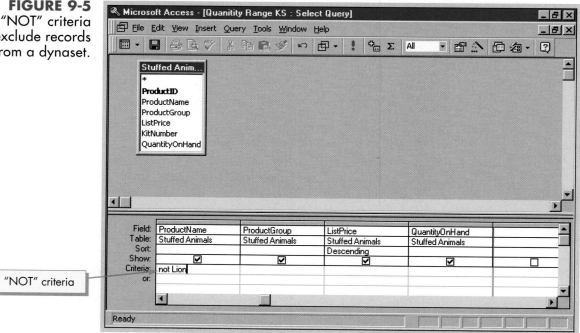

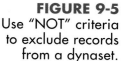 "NOT" criteria

8. View the dynaset. Notice that one of the products selling for $14, Professor Bear, is now in the dynaset. The Lion is excluded because of the "NOT" criteria.
9. Save and close the query.

# *Using the Total Row*

In the query grid, you can add a row that allows you to use certain total or aggregate functions. An *aggregate function* calculates a total, an average, a maximum, a minimum, or other values. Usually these special functions are used with a group of records.

A simple aggregate function is "Count." If you need to determine how many employees in the Employees table have each job code, you can use a query with the "Count" function.

When you use an aggregate function such as "Count," you must group the records by the field in the query. In this case, you would group records by job code because that is the field you want to count. You use the same or another field in the query grid for the "Count" function.

## EXERCISE 9-6 Use Group By and Count

To use the aggregate functions, you add the Total row to the query. When you add the Total row, all fields will show Group By.

1. Click the Queries tab and click New. Choose Design View and click OK.

2. Choose Employees from the Show Table dialog box. Click <u>A</u>dd and click <u>C</u>lose.

3. Maximize the window. Size the design grid so it occupies the bottom third of the window. Size the field list so you can see more of the field names.

4. Double-click JobCode to add it to the grid. Double-click it again to add it to the second column.

5. Click the Totals button . A Total row appears in the grid. All fields show Group By for this row.

> **NOTE:** The Totals button Σ toggles the Total row off and on. You can also toggle the <u>T</u>otal row off and on from the <u>V</u>iew menu.

6. In the first JobCode column, make sure Group By appears in the Total row. This is the column you want to group by because you want to determine how many employees are in each job title.

7. In the second JobCode column, click the Total row. Click the drop-down arrow to display the aggregate functions. (See Figure 9-6 on the next page.)

8. Select "Count" from the list. Rather than listing the job code, the Count function counts how many records belong to each job code.

**FIGURE 9-6**
Use "Count" to
count records.

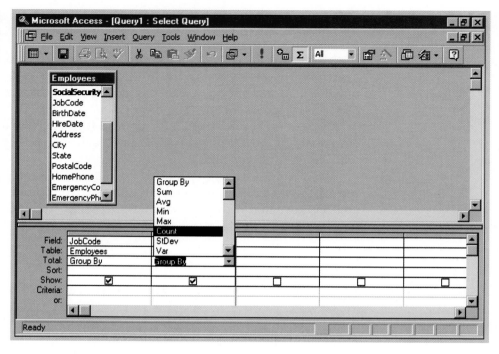

9. View the dynaset.

10. Return to Design View. Right-click the Total row for the second column
and select Properties.

**FIGURE 9-7**
Dynaset shows
count for each
job code.

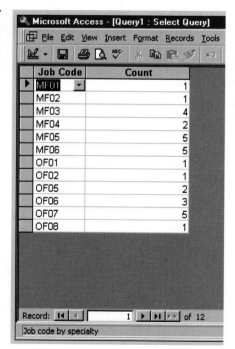

11. If necessary, click the General tab.
Key **Count** as the caption. Close the
properties sheet.

12. View the dynaset.

13. Save the query as **Job Code Count**
*[your initials]* and close it.

# *Creating a Parameter Query*

You used criteria in queries to identify and restrict records. To see records for customers in North Carolina, you include the State field in the design grid and key NC in the criteria row. Perhaps the next time, though, you need to see records for customers in Tennessee. You could open the query in Design View and edit the criteria to TN. You could use this query for all 50 states, editing the criteria row each time. Or you can use a parameter query to do this an easier way.

A *parameter* is a determining factor or characteristic. In a parameter query, the parameter is the criteria, such as NC or TN. Rather than opening a query in Design View and editing criteria, however, you enter new criteria in a small dialog box.

**EXERCISE** **9-7** **Use a Parameter Query**

There is a parameter query in the database. You can run it and see how it works before you create your own parameter query.

1. Click the Queries tab. Double-click the Employees by Job Code query to run it.
2. The Enter Parameter Value dialog box opens.

**FIGURE 9-8**
Enter Parameter
Value dialog box

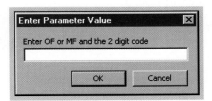

3. Key **MF04** in the dialog box and click OK.
4. The dynaset shows **MF04**, the job code for designers. This is what you see if you enter **MF04** in the Criteria row.
5. Switch to Design View and maximize the window. Click the Criteria row for the JobCode field. This is the prompt you saw in the Parameter Value dialog box.
6. Press Shift + F2 to open the Zoom window. The prompt for a parameter query is enclosed in square brackets. Click Cancel.
7. Click the View button . The query runs again and displays the parameter dialog box.

**8.** Key **MF03** and click OK.

**9.** This dynaset lists all the tailors. Close the query.

## EXERCISE 9-8 Create a Parameter Query

Now create a parameter query. You enter the prompt on the Criteria line and again in the Query Parameters dialog box.

**1.** Create a new query in Design View.

**2.** Choose the Employees table and add it to the grid. Close the Show Table dialog box.

**3.** Maximize the window. Size the design grid so it occupies the bottom one-third of the window. Size the field list so you can see more of the field names.

**4.** Double-click these field names in the order shown to add them to the grid: FirstName, LastName, and JobCode.

**5.** Click on the Criteria line for the JobCode field and press Shift+F2 to open the Zoom window.

**6.** Enter this text with the square brackets **[Enter OF or MF and the 2 digit code]** (Do not enter a period.)

**7.** Select all the text and the square brackets. Press Ctrl+C to copy this prompt to the Windows Clipboard.

**8.** Click OK to close the Zoom window.

**9.** Choose Parameters from the Query menu. Click in the Parameter column for the first row.

**10.** Press Ctrl+V to paste the text from the Clipboard.

**11.** Click in the Data Type column and select Text.

**FIGURE 9-9**
Choose a Data Type in the Query Parameters dialog box.

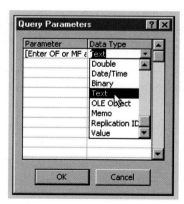

**12.** Click OK to close the Query Parameters dialog box.

**13.** Run the query. Key **MF02** in the dialog box and click OK.

**14.** Save the query as **Employee Parameter Query** *[your initials]* and close it.

# *Creating an Update Query*

The queries you have created so far are *select queries,* which select records based on the criteria you enter. Another type of query is an *action query.* Action queries do something to the data. An action query might change the area code for all customers in a particular state. You might also delete all kits made by a certain supplier.

You learn about four types of action queries. One of these is an *update query,* which revises the data in a field for many records with one command. If you have thousands of customers in New York City and the area code is changed, you don't need to edit each record individually. You update all the records with the old area code to the new one.

You create action queries the same way you create select queries. Be careful, though, because you can't undo an action query. If you changed thousands of records from New York City and then realized that you shouldn't have, you can't use the Undo command to reverse the action.

**EXERCISE** 9-9 **Create an Update Query**

You can see how an update query works by changing the job code for all designers in the Employees table. Then you can run a similar update query to change it back to the original job code. In an update query, you only need to add the field that is to be updated or changed.

*1.* Create a new query in Design View.

*2.* Choose the Employees table, add it to the grid, and close the Show Table dialog box.

*3.* Maximize the window. Size the design grid and the field list so you can see more of the field names.

 *4.* Click the drop-down arrow of the Query Type button . Select <u>U</u>pdate Query. The grid has a new row labeled "Update To."

> ★ **TIP:** Action queries appear in the Query Type list with an exclamation point as a reminder that you will be changing data.

*5.* Double-click JobCode to add it to the grid.

*6.* On the Update To row for the JobCode column, key **MF14**, the new job code.

7. On the Criteria row for the JobCode column, key **MF04**, the current job code.

**FIGURE 9-10**
Update query
includes Update To
row

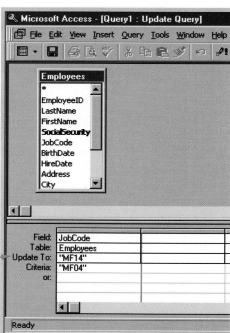

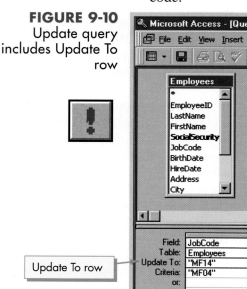

Update To row

8. Click the View button ⊞. This shows how many records will be changed. It doesn't run the query.

9. Click the View button ⊞ to return to the design grid. Click the Run button ❗ to run the update. A warning box tells you how many records will be changed. Click <u>Y</u>es.

10. Save the query. Name it **Job Code Update** *[your initials]*. Click OK and close the query.

11. Notice that the update query includes an exclamation point in its icon to remind you that this is an action query.

12. Open the Employees table.

13. Click anywhere in the JobCode column and click the Find button 🔍. Search for MF14, the new code for Designers. Close the Find dialog box and the table.

**EXERCISE** 9-10     **Edit an Update Query**

Many update queries are run once and don't need to be saved. Since you saved your update query, you can open it in Design View and change the criteria. In that way, you can return the job codes to the original number.

1. Click the Queries tab. Choose **Job Code Update** *[your initials]* and click <u>D</u>esign.

**NOTE:** If you double-click the update query, you run it and may accidentally change the data. A warning box appears to alert you.

2. On the Update To row for the JobCode column, key **MF04**, the original job code.

284

3. On the Criteria row for the JobCode column, key **MF14**.

4. Click the View button  to see how many records will be changed.

5. Return to Design View. Click the Run button ▐. The warning box opens. Click Yes.

6. Save and close the query.

# *Creating a Delete Query*

Another type of action query is a *delete* query, which deletes all records that match a criteria. For example, you could delete all the customers in a particular state. You can delete all records for a certain stuffed animal category. You could delete all sales orders from a particular date or from a range of dates.

You need to be especially cautious about delete queries if you have created relationships with referential integrity. You learned in Lesson 8 about the Cascade Delete Related Records option for referential integrity. If you delete records with a delete query from the primary table (on the "one" side of the relationship), those deletions can cascade from table to table.

**TIP:** Frequent backups of your database file can help you recover from accidental deletions.

**EXERCISE 9-11 Create a Delete Query**

You can create a delete query that removes all the records for cats and dogs from the Stuffed Animals table. You will first delete a relationship to ensure only records in the Stuffed Animals table are deleted.

1. Open the Relationships window.

2. If necessary, add the Stuffed Animals and Sales Order Line Items tables from the Show Table window.

3. Right-click the sloping line between the two tables. Choose Delete and click Yes.

4. Close the Relationships window.

5. Create a new query in Design View and click OK.

6. Choose the Stuffed Animals table and add it to the grid. Close the Show Table dialog box.

7. Maximize the window. Size the design grid and the field list so you can see all the field names.

**8.** Click the drop-down arrow of the Query Type button . Choose <u>D</u>elete Query. The "Delete" row appears in the grid.

**9.** You can add all the fields in the field list to the grid by double-clicking the asterisk (*) at the top of the field list. Double-click it.

> **TIP:** You need one field to specify which records to delete. However, showing other fields helps you identify which records will be deleted.

**10.** Stuffed Animals* appears in the first column. View the dynaset. All the fields appear. Return to the design grid.

**11.** Double-click ProductGroup to add it to the grid. You need this field for your criteria. The first column shows "From" in the Delete row to show from where you are deleting records. The ProductGroup column shows "Where." Access is building an expression like this: Delete all records *from* Stuffed Animals *where* the ProductGroup is C.

**12.** Enter **C** in the Criteria row for ProductGroup.

**FIGURE 9-11**
A delete query uses the Delete row on the design grid.

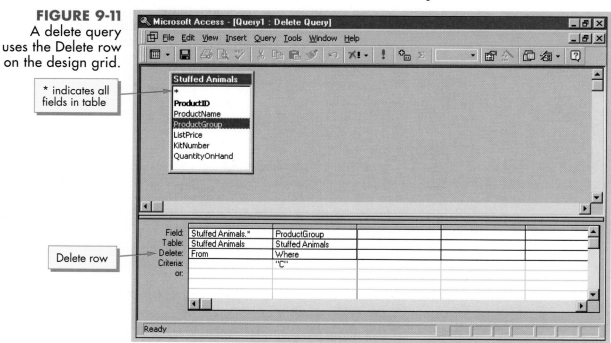

**13.** Click the View button 🔽 to preview the records to be deleted.

**14.** Click the View button 🔽 and then click the Run button ❗. Click <u>Y</u>es in the warning box.

**15.** Close the query without saving its design.

**16.** Click the Tables tab and open the Stuffed Animals table. All the cat and dog toys were deleted. Close the table.

# Creating Append and Make Table Queries

Two other types of action queries are *append* and *make table* queries. You use an append query to add records from an Access table to another existing table. The target table can be in the same database or another database. You use a *make table* query to create a new table that contains some or all of the fields of another table in your database. For both types of queries, you use criteria to select the records.

## EXERCISE 9-12 Create an Append Query

Suppose Carolina Critters purchased a cat and dog line of stuffed animals from another company. That other company gave Carolina Critters a copy of their database with a table that lists the new products. As long as their table has the same fields in the same order as Carolina Critters' Stuffed Animals table, you can append the new records to the existing table.

You can add a cat and dog line back to the Stuffed Animals table using an append query. When you use an append query, you use the table that is being added or appended. In this case, you are adding the Cats and Dogs table to the Stuffed Animals table.

1. Click the Tables tab and open the Cats and Dogs table. It has the same fields in the same order as the Stuffed Animals table. Close the table.

2. Create a new query in Design View. Select the Cats and Dogs table and add it to the grid. Close the Show Table dialog box.

3. Maximize the window; size the design grid and the field list.

4. Click the drop-down arrow of the Query Type button 📇 and choose Append Query. The Append dialog box opens. You can append records from the current database or from another database. Make sure Current Database is selected.

5. Click the drop-down arrow for the Table Name entry box and select Stuffed Animals.

**FIGURE 9-12**
Append dialog
box

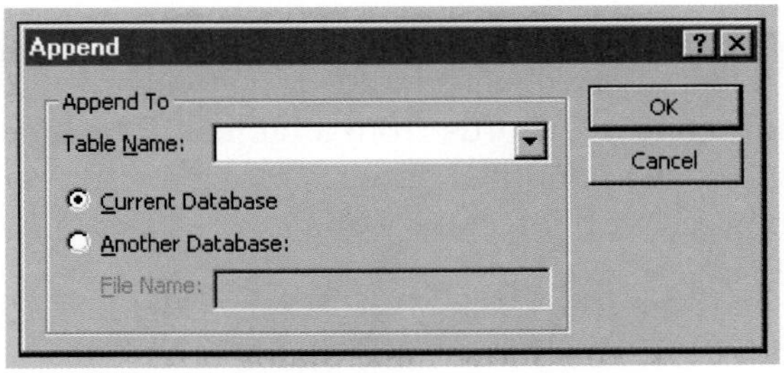

Append dialog box with:
- Append To
  - Table Name:
  - ⦿ Current Database
  - ○ Another Database:
    - File Name:
- OK
- Cancel

**6.** Click OK. An Append To row appears in the grid.

**7.** Double-click the asterisk at the top of the Cats and Dogs field list to add all the fields to the grid. The grid shows all the fields from Cats and Dogs added to the Stuffed Animals table.

**FIGURE 9-13**
The append query adds records to an existing table.

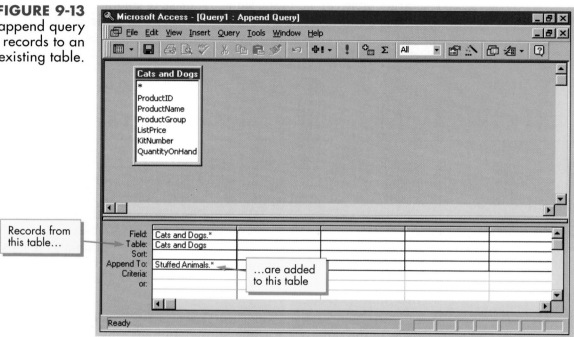

**8.** Click the View button 📊 to preview the records to be appended.

**9.** Click the View button 📊, click the Run button ❗ and click Yes.

**10.** Close the query. Don't save its design.

**11.** Click the Tables tab and open the Stuffed Animals table. Cats and dogs are now included in the product line. Close the table.

# EXERCISE 9-13 Create a Make Table Query

You usually use a query to select and display records from tables. Sometimes you may want to select records from a table and include them in a new table, perhaps for export to another database. Use a make table query to create a table of employees with job code MF06.

**1.** Create a new query in Design View. Select the Employees table and add it to the grid. Close the Show Table dialog box.

2. Maximize the window; size the design grid and the field list.

3. Click the drop-down arrow of the Query Type button and choose Make Table. The Make Table dialog box opens.

4. Key **MF06 Employees** *[your initials]* in the box. Make sure Current Database is selected. Click OK.

5. Double-click the asterisk to add all the fields of the Employees table. Double-click the JobCode field to add it to the second column.

**FIGURE 9-14**
The make table query creates a new table from existing records.

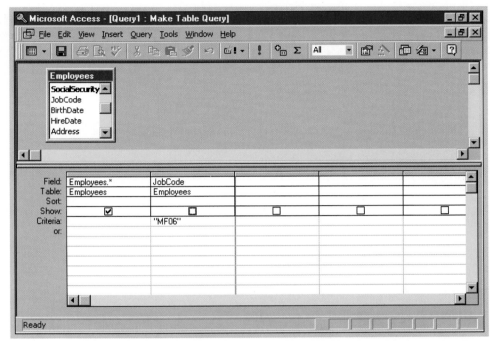

6. Key **MF06** on the Criteria row of the JobCode column. Click to deselect the Show checkbox in the same column.

 **NOTE:** The JobCode field is displayed in the new table because in the first column you selected all fields in the Employees table.

7. Click the View button to preview the records that will be in the new table.

8. Return to Design View, click the Run button , and click Yes.

9. Close the query and don't save it.

10. Open, review, and close the MF06 Employees table. Notice that the data in the new table you created does not inherit the field properties or the primary key setting from the original table.

**COMMAND SUMMARY**

| FEATURE | BUTTON | MENU | KEYBOARD |
|---|---|---|---|
| Show Total row | Σ | View, Totals | |
| Update Query | ▣ | Query, Update Query | |
| Append Query | ▣ | Query, Append Query | |
| Delete Query | ▣ | Query, Delete Query | |
| Make Table Query | ▣ | Query, Make-Table Query | |

# Concepts Review

Each of the following statements is either true or false. Indicate your choice by circling either **T** or **F**.

**T   F**   *1.* You use a select query to change many records at one time.

**T   F**   *2.* When you use a delete query, records from more than one table might be deleted.

**T   F**   *3.* You can sort a dynaset by more than one field.

**T   F**   *4.* In Query Design View, you can select all fields in a field list by double-clicking the primary key.

**T   F**   *5.* When used as criteria, the expression "<=250 and >=600" returns the same values as the expression "between 250 and 600."

**T   F**   *6.* You can use the "NOT" operator only when you use "AND" criteria.

**T   F**   *7.* When you run a parameter query, you must always change the criteria in Design View.

**T   F**   *8.* You use an append query to add records from one table to another table.

Write the correct answer in the space provided.

*1.* What kind of action query would you use to delete many records from a table?

_____

*2.* What is the name of the operator you use when you want to retrieve records that don't match a value?

_____

*3.* What is a fast way to add all the fields in a field list to the design grid?

_____

*4.* On the design grid, what row contains the words "Group By" and "Count" when you group and count records?

_____

5. When you open a parameter query, what is the name of the dialog box that appears?

_____

6. When you use an update query, what button do you click to see the records that will be changed?

_____

7. What appears with the icon for an action query in the Database window?

_____

8. To change the title of a column in a dynaset, what field property should you edit?

_____

## CRITICAL THINKING

**Answer these questions on a separate page. There are no right or wrong answers. Support your answers with examples from your own experience, if possible.**

1. In this lesson you learned about three action queries: update queries, delete queries, and append queries. Give examples of when it would be useful to use each type of query.

2. In general, what are the advantages of using action queries? What are the disadvantages, if any?

# Skills Review

## EXERCISE 9-14

**Select a range of records and edit a dynaset.**

1. Size the query grid by following these steps:

   a. If necessary, open the file *[your initals]*CC3.mdb. Click the Queries tab and click <u>N</u>ew. Choose Design View from the New Query dialog box and click OK.

   b. Choose Sales Orders from the Show Table dialog box, click <u>A</u>dd, and click <u>C</u>lose.

   c. If necessary, maximize the Query window. Position the pointer on the border between the top and bottom pane until it displays a double-headed arrow.

***d.*** Drag the border down until the design grid (bottom) is about a third of the window.

    ***e.*** Resize the field list for the table so you can see all the fields.

**2.** Select a range of records by following these steps:

    ***a.*** Double-click the OrderID, CarrierID, and ShipDate fields to add them to the design grid.

    ***b.*** In the Ship Date column on the Criteria row, key **>=1/1/99 and <=3/31/99** to select orders that will be or were shipped in the first three months of 1999.

    ***c.*** Sort the query by ship date in ascending order. Display the dynaset and review the results.

    ***d.*** Switch to Design View. Click the Criteria row for ShipDate and press Shift+F2. Replace *>=1/1/99 and <=3/31/99* with **between 1/1/99 and 3/31/99**. Click OK.

    ***e.*** Display the dynaset and review the results. Notice that both expressions gave you the same records. Save the query as **Ship Date*[your initials]***.

**3.** Sort a field in a dynaset by following these steps:

    ***a.*** Return to Design View. Delete the criteria on the grid.

    ***b.*** Switch to Datasheet View. Select the CarrierID column and click the Sort Ascending button ⚏↓. The records are now sorted by CarrierID.

    ***c.*** Rearrange the columns in the dynaset in this order: CarrierID, Order ID, and Ship Date.

    ***d.*** Select the CarrierID and Order ID fields and click the Sort Ascending button ⚏↓. The dynaset is now sorted first by CarrierID and then by Order ID.

**4.** Change a column name in a dynaset by following these steps:

    ***a.*** Return to Design View. Click anywhere in the CarrierID column.

    ***b.*** Click the right mouse button and choose Properties from the shortcut menu.

    ***c.*** Click the General tab. In the Caption row, key **Carrier ID.** Close the properties sheet.

    ***d.*** Switch to Datasheet View. Note that the column title CarrierID was changed to Carrier ID. Save the query and close it.

## EXERCISE 9-15

**Select records that do not match a value, use totals in a query.**

**1.** Select records that do not match a value by following these steps:

*a.* Create a new query in Design View. Add the Customers table from the Show Table dialog box.

*b.* Size the window, the grid, and the field list.

*c.* Add the CompanyName, City, State, and PhoneNumber fields to the design grid.

*d.* Sort the dynaset by ascending State name.

*e.* Switch to Datasheet View. Notice that there are three records for companies located in Tennessee, two for Magna Mart and one for Tots 'n Teens.

*f.* Return to Design View. Key **not TN** in the Criteria row of the State column.

*g.* Switch to Datasheet View. Notice that the records for companies in Tennessee are no longer included in the dynaset.

*h.* Save the query as **State Count *[your initials]*.**

2. Group and summarize data by following these steps:

*a.* Switch to Design View and choose Clear Grid from the Edit menu.

*b.* Double-click the State field to add it to the design grid. Double-click it again to add the same field to the second column of the grid.

*c.* Click the Totals button $\boxed{\Sigma}$.

*d.* In the first column, notice that the Total row shows "Group By." In the second column, click in the Total row. Click the drop-down arrow and select Count from the list. You want to count the number of customers in each state.

*e.* Switch to Datasheet View. Notice that the first column shows the state and the second column shows the number of customers in that state.

3. Rename the field with the Count total by following these steps:

*a.* Switch to Design View. Right-click in the second column and select Properties. If necessary, click the General tab.

*b.* On the Caption row, key **State Count**. Close the properties sheet.

*c.* Switch to Datasheet View. Notice the new field caption. Save and close the query.

## EXERCISE 9-16

### Create a parameter query. Create an update query.

*1.* To run a parameter query, follow these steps:

*a.* Select the Animals by Product Group query and click Open. The Enter Parameter Value dialog box opens with a prompt to Enter Product Code C, D, E, F, or T.

**b.** Key **E** and click OK. The dynaset displays only animals with Product IDs beginning with "E".

**c.** Close the query.

**2.** To create a parameter query, follow these steps:

**a.** Create a new query in Design View.

**b.** Add the Stuffed Animals table from the Show Table dialog box. Size the window, the grid, and the field list.

**c.** Add ProductID, ProductName, and ProductGroup to the grid.

**d.** Click the Criteria row for ProductGroup and press Shift+F2 to open the Zoom window.

**e.** Enter this text with the square brackets: **[Enter Product Code C, D, E, F, or T]** (Don't enter a period.)

**f.** Select the text and the brackets. Press Ctrl+C to copy the prompt to the Clipboard. Click OK to close the Zoom window.

**g.** Choose Parameters from the Query menu. Click in the Parameter column for the first row.

**h.** Press Ctrl+V to paste the text from the Clipboard.

**i.** Click in the Data Type column, select Text, and click OK.

**j.** Click the View button ⊠. Test the query by keying **E** in the dialog box. Click OK.

**k.** View the dynaset. All the Product IDs begin with the letter E. Notice that the Product Group field repeats the information and doesn't need to be shown.

**l.** Return to Design View. Click the Show check box in the ProductGroup field to deselect it.

**m.** Click the View button ⊠. Key **E** in the Enter Parameter dialog box. The ProductGroup field no longer appears in the dynaset. Save the query and name it **Product by Type *[your initials]***. Close the query.

**3.** To create an update query, follow these steps:

**a.** Create a new query in Design View. Add the Stuffed Animals table from the Show Table dialog box.

**b.** Size the window, grid, and field list.

**c.** Click the Query Type button ▦. From the drop-down list, choose Update.

**d.** Double-click ListPrice to add the field to the design grid. You will increase the price of items selling for $13 to $13.25.

**e.** On the Update To row, key **13.25**, the new price.

**f.** On the Criteria row, key **13**, the current price.

**g.** Click the Run button ⚠. Access warns you that three records will be updated. Click Yes to confirm the change.

  **4.** To save an update query, follow these steps:

    **a.** Click 🖫. In the Save text box, key **Price Increase *[your initials]*** and click OK. Close the query.

    **b.** Notice that the Price Increase update query icon includes an exclamation mark to remind you that it is an action query.

    **c.** Open the Stuffed Animals table. Notice that there are no items selling for $13; they now sell for $13.25. Close the table.

---

**FIGURE 9-17**

## Create delete, append, and make table queries.

  **1.** To create a delete query, follow these steps:

    **a.** Create a new query in Design View. Add the Employees table from the Show Table dialog box. Size the grid and field list.

    **b.** Click the Query Type button 🔲 and choose Delete Query. The Delete row appears in the design grid.

    **c.** Add *all* the fields in the Employees table by double-clicking the asterisk (*) in the field list.

    **d.** Double-click the JobCode field to add it to the grid.

    **e.** Key **MF06** on the Criteria line of the JobCode column.

    **f.** Click the View button 🔲 to preview the records that will be deleted.

    **g.** Return to Design View. Click the Run button ⚠ to delete the records. Confirm the delete by clicking Yes in the message box.

    **h.** Close the query and don't save your changes.

    **i.** Open the Employees table. Notice that employees with job code MF06 were deleted from the table. Close the table.

  **2.** To create an append query, follow these steps:

    **a.** Click the Tables tab in the Database window and open the **MF06 Employees *[your initials]*** table. Notice that it has the same fields as the Employees table. Close the table.

    **b.** Create a new query in Design View. Add MF06 Employees to the query window. Size the grid and field list.

    **c.** Click the Query Type button 🔲 and choose Append Query. The Append dialog box opens.

    **d.** In the lower half of the Append dialog box, choose Current Database.

*e.* Click the drop-down arrow for the Table Name and choose Employees. Click OK. Notice that the Append To row appears on the design grid.

  *f.* Double-click the asterisk at the top of the MF06 Employees field list to add all the fields to the design grid. Notice that the Append To row says *Employees.\**.

  *g.* Click the View button 🖳 to preview the records that will be added to the Employees table.

  *h.* Return to Design View. Click the Run button 🔳. Click Yes when Access asks you to confirm the addition of records.

  *i.* Close the query. Don't save your changes.

  *j.* Open the Employees table. Notice that the MF06 employee records were added back to your table. Close the table.

**3.** To create a make table query, follow these steps:

  *a.* Create a new query in Design View.

  *b.* Add the Stuffed Animals table to the grid.

  *c.* Maximize the window; size the design grid and the field list.

  *d.* Click the drop-down arrow of the Query Type button 🔲 and choose Make-Table Query. The Make Table dialog box opens.

  *e.* Key **Bears** *[your initials]* in the box. Make sure Current Database is selected. Click OK.

  *f.* Double-click the asterisk to add all the fields of the Stuffed Animals table. Double-click the ProductGroup field to add it to the second column.

  *g.* Key **T**, the code for bears, in the Criteria row of the ProductGroup column. Click to deselect the Show checkbox in the same column.

  *h.* Click the View button 🖳 to preview the records of the new table.

  *i.* Return to Design View, click the Run button 🔳, and click Yes.

  *j.* Close the query and don't save it.

  *k.* Open, review, and close the Bears table.

# Lesson Applications

## EXERCISE 9-18

**Select a range of records, select records that don't match a value, and use the Total row.**

1. Create a new query and add the Stuffed Animals table to the Query window.

2. Add the ProductGroup, ProductName, and ListPrice fields to the design grid, in that order.

3. Add the Total row to the grid.

4. Choose options in the Total row to count the number of products in each product group.

5. Add criteria to find products that don't sell for a price between $9.50 and $10. Choose Where on the Total row and don't show the ListPrice field in the dynaset.

6. Change the caption for the field that shows the number of products to "Number of Products." In dynaset view, widen the column to make the title fully visible.

7. Save the query as **Product Breakdown** *[your initials]*. Print the dynaset and close the query.

## EXERCISE 9-19

**Create a parameter query.**

1. Create a new query and add the Sales Orders table to the Query window.

2. Add the following fields to the design grid: OrderID, EmployeeID, OrderDate, ShipDate.

3. The prompt in the Enter Parameter Value dialog box should be [Enter Employee ID]. The Data Type is Long Integer.

4. Run a query that finds the sales made by Employee #6.

5. Save the query as **Sales Orders by Employee** *[your initials]*. Print the dynaset and close the query.

## EXERCISE 9-20

### Create an update query. Select records that don't match a value.

1. Open the Sales Orders table. Change the discount for sales order 97111 from 0% to 5%. Close the table.
2. Create a new query in Design View and add the Sales Orders table to the Query Window.
3. Add the CarrierID and Discount fields to the design grid.
4. Make this an update query. Save the query as **New Discounts** *[your initials]*.
5. Key an expression to double the discount for all orders that have a discount. You must enclose the field name in square brackets.
6. Use criteria to exclude orders that used CarrierID C301.
7. Preview the dynaset. Six records will be updated.
8. Run the query and close it.
9. Open the Sales Orders table and print it in landscape orientation. Close the table.
10. Open the New Discounts query in Design View. Edit the expression to *[Discount]*.5 to return the records to the original discount.
11. Save, run, and close the query.

## EXERCISE 9-21

### Choose a range of records, create delete, make table, and append queries.

1. Create a new Query in Design View. Add the Sales Orders table from the Show Table dialog box.
2. Make this a make table query.
3. Key **Fourth Quarter Orders** *[your initials]* in the Make Table dialog box. Choose the Current Database.
4. Add all the fields in the Sales Orders table to the first grid column. Add Order Date to the second grid column and deselect its Show option.
5. Include records in which the order date is between 10/1/98 and 12/31/98.
6. Preview the records in the new table. Create the table. Close the query without saving it.
7. Create a new query in Design View for the Sales Orders table.
8. Make this a delete query.

9. Add all the fields in the Sales Orders table. Add the OrderDate field to the grid.

10. Include records in which the order date is between 10/1/98 and 12/31/98.

11. Preview the records to be deleted. Run the query and delete the records. Close the query without saving it.

12. Open and print the Sales Orders table in landscape orientation. Close the table.

13. Create a new query in Design View for the Fourth Quarter Orders table.

14. Make it an append query. You will append records to the Sales Orders table in the Current Database.

15. Add all the fields from the Fourth Quarter Orders table to the grid.

16. Preview the records to be appended. Run the query and append the records. Close the query without saving it.

17. Open and print the Sales Orders table. Close the table.

18. Compact your database and exit Access.

# Unit 3 Applications

## APPLICATION 3-1

**Create a query. Use "AND" and "OR" criteria. Select a range of records. Sort on multiple fields. Add an expression to a query. Edit a dynaset.**

1. Open the file *[your initials]***CC3.mdb**.
2. Create a new query in Design View for the Kit Contents table. Size the window, grid, and field list.
3. Add the KitNumber, SupplierID, Cost, and Kit Contents fields to the design grid.
4. Add criteria to select kits that cost between $6 and $8 and aren't supplied by SupplierID BB-02. As the "OR" criteria, select all records from SupplierID CC-03, regardless of cost.
5. In Datasheet View, move the Supplier and Cost fields so they are the first and second columns in the dynaset.
6. In Design View, sort in ascending order by SupplierID. Then sort by cost so the most expensive items are listed first.
7. View the dynaset and save the query as **Cost Increase** *[your initials]*. Print the dynaset. You see only a few words of the Kit Contents field.
8. Add the records in Figure U3-1 to the dynaset. For the Supplier field, use the lookup column. For the Kit Contents field, press [Shift]+[F2] to open the Zoom window for easier typing.

**FIGURE U3-1**

| Supplier | Cost | Kit Number | Kit Contents |
|---|---|---|---|
| CC-03 | $4.26 | Cat006 | This kit contains green stripe acrylic, a cloth collar, feline eyes/nose, and pellet fill. |
| CC-03 | $6.35 | Dog004 | This kit contains blue acrylic, a collar, eyes/nose, and fiberfill. |
| AA-01 | $6.75 | Bear006 | This kit contains reddish brown acrylic, 45mm plastic joints, eyes/nose, and fiberfill. |
| DD-04 | $7.35 | Dog005 | This kit contains vermilion acrylic, a collar, eyes/nose, and fiberfill. |

9. Return to Design View. Right-click in the first empty column and use the Expression Builder to add a calculated field showing the increase in cost if the cost of each product in the dynaset is increased by 15%.

10. View the dynaset. In the Design window, change the name of the calculated field to **Cost Increase**.

11. Use the properties sheet for this column to format the field as Currency. View the dynaset.

12. In Design View, use the Expression Builder to add a second calculated field showing the new cost with the 15% increase. Multiply the existing cost by 115%.

13. View the dynaset. In the Design window, change the name of the calculated field to **New Cost**. Format the field as Currency.

14. View the dynaset and print it. Resave the query and close it.

## APPLICATION 3-2

**Create a lookup field. View a relationship. Create a query using multiple fields. Use Totals.**

1. Open the Product Lines table in Design View. Change the primary key to ProductGroup. Save and close the table.

2. Open the Stuffed Animals table in Design View. Maximize the window. Delete the Validation Rule and the Validation Text for the ProductGroup field and save the table.

3. Create a lookup column for the ProductGroup field that "looks to" the ProductGroup field in the Product Lines table for its data. Label the lookup column **Product Group.**

4. Save and close the table.

5. Open the Relationships window and clear the layout.

6. Add the tables to the Relationships window and view the relationship established by the lookup column. Close the window and save the layout.

7. Create a query in Design View for the Product Lines and Stuffed Animals tables.

8. Add the ProductLine field from the Product Lines table. Add the ProductID and ListPrice fields from the Stuffed Animals table to the grid.

9. Add the Total row to the grid.

10. Group on the ProductLine field and count the number of products. Count only products where the list price is above $10.75.

**TIP:** Select "Where" in the Total row of the ListPrice field. Don't show the ListPrice field in the dynaset.

11. Run the query and view the dynaset.

12. Return to Design View. Change the name of the column that counts the number of products to **Product Count**.

13. Save the query as **Product Count *[your initials]***. Print the dynaset. Close the query.

## APPLICATION 3-3

**Establish and edit a relationship. Select a range of records. Create a multiple table query. Delete records from related tables.**

1. Open the Stuffed Animals table and add the following record. Select the Product Group from the lookup column you created in Application 3-2:

| | |
|---|---|
| Product ID: | **E006** |
| Animal Name: | **Gorilla** |
| Product Group: | **E** |
| List Price: | **$13.25** |
| KitNumber: | **Gor006** |
| Current Inventory | **240** |

2. Open the Sales Order Line Items table and add the records shown in Figure U3-2.

**FIGURE U3-2**

| Order ID | Product ID | Quantity |
|---|---|---|
| 97104 | E006 | 100 |
| 97106 | E006 | 75 |
| 97110 | E006 | 40 |

3. Open the Relationships window and clear the layout.

4. Establish a one-to-many relationship between the Stuffed Animals and Sales Order Line Items table.

5. Enforce referential integrity between the two tables.

6. Close the Relationships window and save the layout changes.

7. Create a new query in Design View.

8. Add the Stuffed Animals and Sales Order Line Items tables to the Query window.

9. Add the ProductID, ProductName, and ListPrice fields from the Stuffed Animals table to the grid. Add the OrderID and Quantity fields from the Sales Order Line Items table.

10. Specify criteria to select records for products with a list price greater than $10.75.

11. Sort the query by ascending Product ID and then by ascending Quantity. Make these the first two columns in the Design window.

12. View the dynaset. Save the query as **Sales by Product [your initials]**. Print the dynaset and close the query.

13. Open the Stuffed Animals table and try to delete Product ID E006. Click OK when Access tells you that you can't delete the record. Close the table.

14. Open the Relationships window.

15. Edit the relationship between the Stuffed Animals and Sales Order Line Items tables so you can delete record E006 while maintaining referential integrity. Close the Relationships window.

16. Open the Stuffed Animals table. Delete record E006. Confirm the change in the message box. Close the table.

17. Open the Sales Order Line Items table. Notice that any records with Product ID E006 are deleted. Close the Sales Order Line Items table.

## APPLICATION 3-4

Select a range of records. Use the Expression Builder. Create update and parameter queries. Save an action query. Modify a query.

1. Open the Stuffed Animals table and add the records shown in Figure U3-3 (include the changes shown):

**FIGURE U3-3**

| Product ID | Product Name | Product Group | List Price | Kit Number | Current Inventory |
|---|---|---|---|---|---|
| C006 | Abyssinian | C | $15.75 | Cat006 | ~~275~~ 225 |
| E006 | Lioness | E | $15.25 | Lin004 | ~~350~~ 325 |
| T006 | Baby Bear | T | $14.75 | *Bear006* ~~Ted006~~ | ~~150~~ 125 |
| C007 | Beagle | ~~T~~C | ~~$14.25~~ $15.25 | Dog005 | ~~225~~ 190 |

2. Create a new query in Design View for the Stuffed Animals table.

3. Add the ProductName, ProductGroup, ListPrice, and QuantityOnHand fields to the design grid.

4. Save the query as **Stuffed Animals Value** *[your initials]*. View the dynaset.

5. Use the Expression Builder to create a calculated field in the first empty column that shows the total wholesale value (list price multiplied by quantity on hand) for all products. View the dynaset.

6. Return to Design View. Rename the calculated field *Total Value*.

7. View and print the dynaset. Save the changes and close the query.

8. Create a new query in Design View for the Stuffed Animals table.

9. Add the ListPrice field to the design grid.

10. Save the query as **10% Price Increase** *[your initials]*.

11. Make this an update query. In the Update row, use the Expression Builder to create an expression that computes a new list price that is 10% higher (110% of the current price). This price increase applies only to products that cost between $15 and $16.

12. Run the query and confirm the changes when asked.

13. Save and close the query. Make sure you saved the query by viewing its title in the Queries tab of the Database window.

14. Open the Stuffed Animals Value query in Design View.

15. Use the Zoom window to enter this parameter query prompt: **[Enter Product Code C, D, E, F, or T]**. Copy the prompt to the Clipboard.

16. Paste the prompt in the Query Parameters dialog box and set the Data Type to Text.

17. Click the View button <View>. Type **C** in the Enter Parameter Value dialog box and click OK to select records of cats and dogs (Product Group C).

18. Alphabetize the Animal Name field. Notice that the list prices of the Abyssinian and Beagle products are raised by 10%.

19. Print the dynaset and save your changes. Close the query.

## APPLICATION 3-5

**Use the Top Values property. Create make table, delete, and append queries.**

1. Create a new query in Design View for the Employees table.

2. Make this a Make Table Query.

3. Name the table **Late 1980s Hires** *[your initials]* and include it in the current database. The new table should contain all fields in the

Employees table for staff hired after 1984 and before 1990. Include the HireDate field only once in the table. Preview the table before you create it. Do not save the query.

4. Open the table you made and print it in landscape orientation. Close the table.

5. Create a new query in Design View for the Employees table.

6. Create a Delete query.

7. Enter information on the design grid that tells Access to eliminate the records of all staff hired after 1984 and before 1990 from the Employees table. Preview the changes. Run the Delete query and confirm the deletions.

8. Close the Delete query without saving.

9. Open the Employees table and sort by ascending Employee ID. Print the table (landscape). Save and close the table.

10. Create a new query in Design View for the Late 1980s Hires table.

11. Create an Append query that adds records to the Employees table.

12. Enter information on the design grid that adds all records in all fields of the Late 1980s Hires table to the Employees table. Run the query and confirm the additions. Don't save the query.

13. Open the Employees table and make certain the late 1980s hires are added back to the Employees table. Close the table.

14. Create a new query in Design View for the Employees table.

15. Add the FirstName, LastName, and HireDate fields to the grid. Use a sort and the Top Values property to show the 25 most recent hires.

16. Save the query as **25 Recent Hires** *[your initials]*.

17. Print the dynaset and close the query.

18. Compact your database and exit Access.

# Printing Information from a Database

# Additional Report Features

**OBJECTIVES**

After completing this lesson, you will be able to:

1. Create an AutoReport.
2. Modify controls.
3. Group records in a report.
4. Move controls between sections.
5. Use page breaks in a report.
6. Use AutoFormat.
7. Create mailing labels.

 Estimated Time: 1½ hours

Tables are the building blocks of databases, but reports are an important element in good database management. As you learned in Lesson 6, a report prints information from a database. You can control which fields and records are printed, as well as the style or design of the report. In this lesson, you work with AutoReport and AutoFormat, features that make designing a report faster and easier.

You also work with labels. Although you may not think of mailing labels as reports, Access includes many styles of labels on the Reports tab because labels are printed data. You can design and print labels, selecting and sorting the records and fields as you wish.

# *Creating an AutoReport*

An AutoReport is a basic report. Access includes all the fields and selects a style for the report. All you do is select the table to be used as the basis for the report. There are two AutoReports listed in the New Report dialog box. A *tabular report* resembles most of the reports you have designed or printed so far. Each record is on a separate line with the labels at the top of the column. Tabular reports usually print many records on the same page.

A *columnar report* prints each field on a separate line with its own label. The columnar style is also called a *vertical report*. This type of report is often used when there are many fields in a table and a tabular report would be too wide. You might use this type of report when you want each record to print on a separate page.

You can print either style of report (tabular or columnar) in portrait or landscape orientation.

**EXERCISE** **10-1** **Create a Columnar AutoReport**

A columnar AutoReport displays each field on a separate line. All the information for a particular record is in its own section.

1. Make a copy of CC4.mdb and name it *[your initials]CC4.mdb.* Open the file.
2. Click the Reports tab. Click <u>N</u>ew.
3. From the New Report dialog box, choose AutoReport: Columnar.

**FIGURE 10-1**
New Report
dialog box

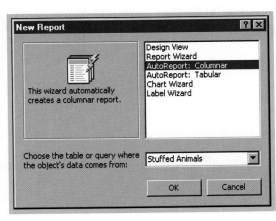

4. Click the down arrow for "Choose the table or query where the object's data comes from" and choose Stuffed Animals. Click OK.
5. Maximize the window.
6. Point and click anywhere in the report to change to a full-page view. This view fits the report to the window. Each record is shown in its own segment marked by horizontal lines.

7. Click the Last Page button  to see how many pages are included in the report.

**309**

**TIP:** When the report is in a full-page (Fit) view, you can use ⌈PgUp⌉ and ⌈PgDn⌉ to move to the previous and next pages.

**8.** Click the First Page button ⧏ to return to page 1.

**FIGURE 10-2**
Columnar Report

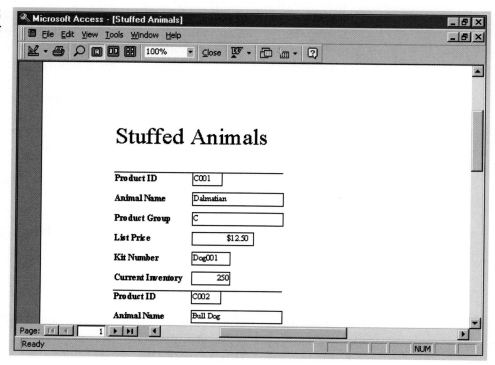

**9.** Close Print Preview. The report opens in Design View.

**10.** Save the report as **Animals Columnar AutoReport** *[your initials]*. Close the report.

# EXERCISE 10-2 Create a Tabular AutoReport

You can use an AutoReport to prepare a default tabular report.

**1.** Click the Reports tab. Click <u>N</u>ew. From the New Report dialog box, choose AutoReport: Tabular.

**2.** Choose Stuffed Animals as the table. Click OK.

**3.** Maximize the window. Change to a full-page view. This AutoReport uses landscape orientation.

**4.** Click the Last Page button ▶⧐ to see how many pages are included in this report.

5. Return to Design View.

6. Save the report as **Animals Tabular AutoReport** *[your initials]* and close it.

# *Modifying Controls*

A basic report consists of the Detail, Report, and Page sections. Some reports have a Group section. Each section can include bound controls (text boxes), unbound controls (labels), and calculated controls. A field control consists of its unbound control (label), if any, and its bound control (text box).

AutoReports don't include a Group section or calculated controls. They have Report, Detail, and Page sections. You can edit controls in any of these sections.

**EXERCISE 10-3 Move Controls**

1. Open the Animals Columnar AutoReport in <u>D</u>esign View. Maximize the window.

2. Scroll the window and place the pointer at the top edge of the Page Footer bar to display a double-headed arrow.

3. Drag the border to the 2-inch mark on the vertical ruler. This makes the Detail section taller.

 **TIP:** When you can't see the ruler marker, release the mouse button and drag the bar several times until you can see its position.

4. Use Shift +click to select each control in the Detail section.

5. Point at any selected control to display the open-hand pointer. Drag the group so the top edge of the group is at the 0.25-inch mark on the vertical ruler.

6. Deselect the controls in the Detail section.

7. Select the Kit Number control and drag it next to the Product ID control so its left edge rests on the 2-inch mark on the horizontal ruler.

 **NOTE:** The vertical and horizontal lines in Design View in the layout gird indicate 1-inch marks on both rulers.

8. While the Kit Number control is selected, press [Shift]+click the Product ID control.

9. Choose Format, Align, Top to align these two controls at their top edges.

10. Select the Current Inventory control and move it closer to the List Price control.

11. Select the Kit Number label.

12. Use the right middle sizing handle to resize the label so the right edge is at the 3-inch mark.

13. Select the KitNumber text box. Point at the top left handle until it displays a pointing-finger. Drag the text box closer to its label.

14. Deselect all controls. Save the report, but don't close it.

**FIGURE 10-3**
Report
(in Design View)

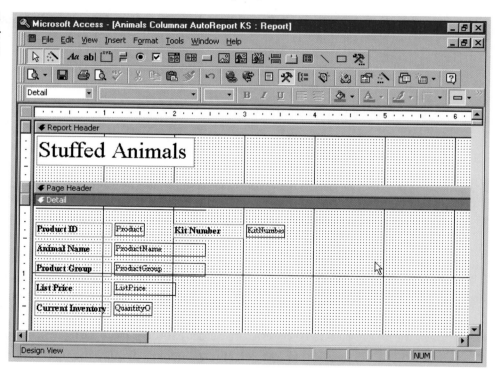

# EXERCISE 10-4 Change a Caption

You can change the caption for a control by editing its properties sheet.

1. Right-click the Current Inventory label. Select Properties.

2. Click the Format tab. On the Caption row, key **Inventory on Hand** as the new caption.

**FIGURE 10-4**
Changing the
caption

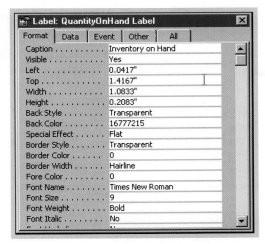

3. Close the properties sheet.

4. Change to Print Preview to see the report. Return to Design View and save the report.

## EXERCISE 10-5 Change Borders and Colors

The text boxes in this AutoReport show a hairline border (a thin box) around the data. You can edit or remove the border.

1. Use Shift+click to select all the text boxes, but not the labels. Right-click one of the selected text boxes. Select Properties.

2. Click the Format tab. Click Border Width row to display the down arrow. Click the arrow.

**FIGURE 10-5**
Choosing a
transparent
border style

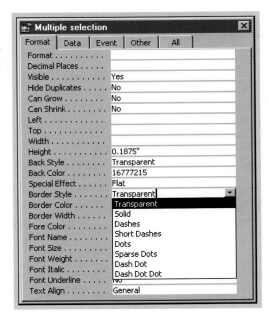

3. Select 2 pt. All the text boxes display a thicker border. Close the properties sheet.

4. Change to Print Preview. Use a 100% view size. Return to Design View.

5. Make sure all the text boxes are still selected. Right-click one of the controls.

6. Select Properties.

7. Click the Format tab. Click the down arrow in the Border Style row. Choose Transparent.

8. Close the properties sheet and view the report. Return to Design View.

9. While the text box controls are selected, change the font to 12-point Times New Roman. Use the Formatting toolbar.

10. View the report. Changing the font and size also requires changing the width and height of the text boxes so all the text is visible in the printed report.

11. Return to Design View. Make sure all the text box controls are selected.

 **NOTE:** You can double-click an object to open its properties sheet.

12. Right-click one of the controls and select Properties. Click the Format tab.

**FIGURE 10-6**
Width and Height settings

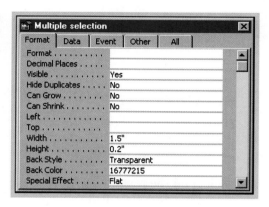

13. Set the Width for the multiple controls to 1.5 inches. Set the Height to .2 inches. Close the properties sheet.

 **TIP:** You don't need to key the inches mark (") when you key a measurement.

14. It appears that the Kit Number control overlaps the Product ID control. Change to Print Preview. Since the data in the Product ID text box is short, the fields don't overlap when printed.

15. Return to Design View. Deselect all controls.

16. Select the Kit Number control and move it to the right.

17. Select the Product ID text box and drag its right middle sizing handle to the 2-inch mark.

18. Move the Kit Number control closer to the Product ID text box. Save your report.

 **TIP:** Left align labels and text in a report. Right align numbers.

**19.** Select all the text boxes. Click the drop-down arrow for the Special Effect button and select Sunken.

**20.** Select the label in the Report Header section.

**21.** Click the down arrow for the Font/Fore Color button [A]. Select white. You can't see white text on a white background, however, so you need to change the background color.

**22.** Click the down arrow for the Fill/Back Color button [🖌]. Select a medium blue. The text is visible again.

**23.** Click the down arrow for the Special Effect button [🔲]. Select Raised.

**24.** Save the report. Preview it and return to Design View.

## EXERCISE 10-6 Modify a Horizontal Line

The AutoReport includes a horizontal line at the top of the Detail section. Anything in the Detail section prints with each record, so the line repeats with each record. Since your report is now wider than the initial AutoReport, you need to increase the length of the line to match the width of the text.

**1.** Double-click the horizontal line at the top of the Detail section in Design View. The properties sheet for the line appears.

**2.** Click the Format tab. Change the width to 5 inches.

**FIGURE 10-7**
Line
properties sheet

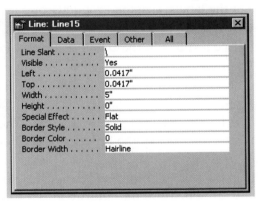

**3.** Close the properties sheet and preview the report. The line is a bit too long. Return to Design View.

**4.** You can also change the width (length) of a line by dragging the handle, just as you drag a handle to size a control. As you drag, keep the line straight by holding down Shift. Drag the right handle of the line to the 4.5-inch mark on the horizontal ruler, keeping the line straight.

**5.** Preview the report. Save and close it.

# EXERCISE 10-7 Use a Line Break and Align Text

Use the tabular AutoReport to learn about a few other properties you can set for a control. Using the Line Break feature allows you to divide a long single line label into two lines for easier spacing and reading.

1. Open the Animals Tabular AutoReport in Design View.

2. The Animal Name label and text box are both wider than necessary. Select the label and use Shift+click to select the text box. Right-click either selected control and choose Properties.

3. Set the width to 1.25 inches and close the properties sheet. Deselect the controls.

4. Select the Animal Name label in the Page Header. Click again to place the insertion point before "Name." Press Ctrl+Enter to force a line break. Press Enter to select the label. A line break splits the label to display on two lines. Deselect the label.

5. The horizontal line didn't move. Select the line and press Delete. You can redraw it later.

6. Select the Product Group label in the Page Header. Click again to place the insertion point before "Group." Press Ctrl+Enter to force a line break.

7. Repeat these steps to split each of the remaining labels in the Page Header, including ProductID. Scroll the window as necessary.

8. Before you align the labels, size the ProductGroup text box in the Detail section so it is the same width as its label in the Page Header section.

9. Select the ListPrice text box in the Detail section and drag the right middle handle to make it narrower.

10. Select the List Price label and move it over the List Price text box.

11. Select the List Price label in the Page Header. Press Shift+click to select the ListPrice text box in the Detail section. Display the open-hand pointer and move the controls closer to the Product Group controls. Deselect the controls.

12. Select the Kit Number label in the Page Header and the Kit Number text box in the Detail section. Move the controls closer to the List Price controls. Deselect the controls.

13. Select the Current Inventory text box and drag the right middle handle to make it narrower.

14. Select the Current Inventory label and move it over its text box.

15. Select the Current Inventory label and its text box. Move the controls closer to the Kit Number controls. Deselect the controls.

16. Select all the labels in the Page Header. Select Format, Align, and Top.

**17.** While the labels are selected, click the Center ■ button in the Formatting toolbar.

**18.** Preview the report. Return to Design View and save the report.

---

**E X E R C I S E** | **10-8** | **Set Page Header Properties and Draw a Horizontal Line**

---

You can draw the horizontal line that you deleted earlier. Before you do so, you should make the Page Header section taller so you have more room to add the line. You can drag the border to size the section, or you can use the Page Header properties sheet.

A line is an object. You can move and size it like a control. It also has its own properties.

**1.** Place the pointer at the top edge of the Detail bar to display a double-headed arrow.

**2.** Drag the border down about ½ inch. This makes the Page Header section taller.

**FIGURE 10-8**
Page Header properties sheet

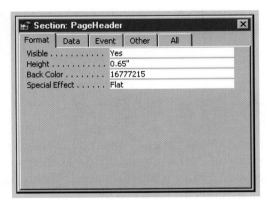

**3.** Right-click the Page Header bar. Select Properties.

 **NOTE:** Each section of the report has its own properties sheet.

 **4.** Set the Height to .65 inch. Close the properties sheet.

**5.** Click the Line button ⬊ in the toolbox. Position the pointer at the left edge under the first label in the Page Header.

**6.** Hold down Shift and drag the pointer to draw a line that ends at the 6-inch mark on the horizontal ruler.

 **NOTE:** If you aren't satisfied with the line, select it, press Delete, and try again.

7. Preview the report. Return to Design View.

8. You can edit the length of a line by pointing at either end handle and dragging that handle (hold down Shift while doing this). You can move a line by pointing anywhere other than a handle to display the open-hand pointer. Edit and position the line.

9. Select the line and right-click. Select Properties.

10. Set the width to 6 inches. Close the properties sheet.

11. The line in the Page Footer should be the same width (length). Select the line in the Page Footer and right-click. Select Properties.

12. Set the width to 6 inches and close the properties sheet.

13. Preview the report. Return to Design View.

14. Scroll the window to see the text box with the page number in the Page Footer. This was added as part of the AutoReport. Select the control and right-click.

15. Select Properties and set the width to 2 inches. Close the properties sheet.

16. Display the open-hand pointer and move the page number control so its right edge aligns with the horizontal line in the footer.

17. Select the date control (=Now) and the page number control. Select Format, Align, and Top.

18. Save, print, and close the report.

# *Grouping Records in a Report*

The Animals Tabular AutoReport is sorted by Product Group so all the Cs are together, followed by all the Ds, and so on. You can group the records in a report so they appear to be in their own section. When you use grouping, you can also show calculations for each group.

**EXERCISE 10-9 Save a Report with a Different Name**

You can keep your original tabular report and make a copy of it by saving it with a different name.

1. In the Database window, click the Reports tab.

2. Click the Animals Tabular AutoReport to select it. If you accidentally display a text cursor with the name, click away from the file and select it again.

3. Select File, Save As/Export. You can save a table in the current database, or you can export it to another database.

**NOTE:** You can export Access tables to other database software such as Paradox and FoxPro. You can also import tables from these programs into Access.

**FIGURE 10-9**
Save As
dialog box

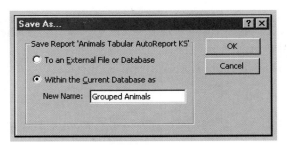

4. Click Within the Current Database As.

5. Enter **Grouped Animals** as the new name. Click OK. The copied report appears in the Database window.

 EXERCISE **10-10** Add Grouping and Sorting

Sorting and Grouping is a command in the View menu, as well as a button on the toolbar. For each field you select, you can decide whether to sort, to group, or both. The Group Properties include a Group Header and Group Footer. The Group On property allows you to set when each new group starts. This property is usually set to Each Value so each time there's a new value in the field, a new group starts. The Group Interval property sets how many characters in the field are used for grouping.

1. Open the Grouped Animals report in Design View.

2. Click the Sorting and Grouping button 🔳.

3. Click in the first row in the Field/Expression column and display the drop-down list. Select ProductGroup.

**FIGURE 10-10**
Sorting and
Grouping
dialog box

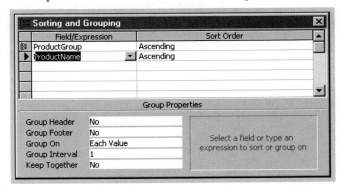

4. The default sort order is Ascending, but there is no grouping yet. Click the Group Header row in the Group Properties and set it to Yes. This creates a group for the ProductGroup field.

5. You can further sort your group so the animals within the group are in alphabetical order by the name of the animal. Click in the second row of the Field/Expression column and display the drop-down list. Select

ProductName. The sort order is Ascending, but you won't use grouping for this field.

6. Close the dialog box. The report has a ProductGroup Header with nothing in it.

7. Preview your report in a size that allows you to see the groups based on the product line.

8. Return to Design View and save the report.

# Moving Controls Between Report Sections

Groups should be identified. Often when you use a group, you don't need the field on which the grouping is based within the report itself. If the controls are already in the report, you can move them into the ProductGroup Header as a means of identifying individual groups.

**TABLE 10-1**  **Sections of a Report**

| NAME OF SECTION | GENERAL DESCRIPTION |
|---|---|
| Report Header | Prints once at the top of report. It often includes a main title, a company logo, author, and so on. |
| Page Header | Prints at the top of every page. It usually includes column headings but might also display a date and page number. |
| Group Header | Prints at the start of each group. It can display a label for the group as well as the actual group field. |
| Detail Section | Prints each record from the table. |
| Page Footer | Prints at the bottom of every page. It can include dates and page numbers as well as other text. |
| Group Footer | Prints at the end of every group. It can display a total, a count, or other calculation for the group. |
| Report Footer | Prints once at the end of the report. It is generally used for report totals or summaries. |

**EXERCISE** `10-11` **Move Controls to the Group Header**

1. Select the Product Group label in the Page Header.

2. Drag the control to the left edge of the ProductGroup section. The section expands to accommodate the label.

3. Drag the right middle handle to make the control wider.

4. Click to place an insertion point after the word "Product" in the label. Press Delete to delete the forced line break and set the label text on one line. Insert a space between the words. Deselect the label.

 **NOTE:** You may need to press Delete more than once to remove the line break. You also need to insert a space and resize the label.

5. Select the ProductGroup text box in the Detail section. Drag it to the ProductGroup section to the right of the label.

## EXERCISE 10-12 Fine-Tune the Appearance of a Report

You already formatted reports and forms using the Formatting toolbar and the appropriate properties sheet. Like the controls, each section in a report has its own properties. To change section properties, you can click anywhere in the section to select the bar at the top of the section. You can also right-click the section bar.

1. Select the Product Group label. Click the Format Painter button ⌖. Click the ProductGroup text box to copy the format.

2. Use Shift+click to add the ProductGroup text box to the selection. Right-click either control and select Properties. Set the width to 1 inch and the Height to .25 inch. Close the properties sheet.

3. While both controls are selected, select Format, Align, and Top.

4. Preview the report. When you moved the ProductGroup control from the Detail section, it was removed as a column in the report. The group heading identifies the groups.

5. Return to Design View. Save the report.

6. Click anywhere in the Report Header. Click the down arrow for Fill/Back Color ▩. Select a light blue. The entire section is blue.

7. Scroll the window and click anywhere in the Page Footer but not on a control. Click the Fill/Back Color ▩ button to select the same blue.

8. Preview and save your report.

9. Select the List Price, Kit Number, and Current Inventory labels in the Page Header. Select the ListPrice, KitNumber, and QuantityOnHand text boxes in the Detail section so all six controls are selected.

10. Drag the controls so the left edge is at 2.5-inch on the horizontal ruler. Deselect the controls.

11. Select all the text boxes in the Detail section. Change the font to 11-point Times New Roman.

12. To put more space before the Group Header so each group is set apart, right-click the ProductGroup Header bar. Select Properties. Set the height of the section to .45 inch. Close the properties sheet.

13. Select the controls in the ProductGroup header and move them close to the bottom of the section, just above the Detail bar.

14. Select and delete the horizontal line in the Page Footer.

15. Save the report, preview it, and return to Design View.

# Using Page Breaks in a Report

Access places a page break at the end of a printed page, based on the margins in the Page Setup dialog box. You have some additional control over page breaks through the properties for each section. You can, for example, set a property to start a new page for each group.

## EXERCISE 10-13 Force a Page Break for a Group

1. Double-click the ProductGroup header bar to open its properties sheet.

2. Click the Format tab. Click the Force New Page row and display its drop-down list.

3. Select Before Section. This forces the start of a new page each time a new animal group starts. Close the properties sheet.

**FIGURE 10-11**
Forcing a new page before each section

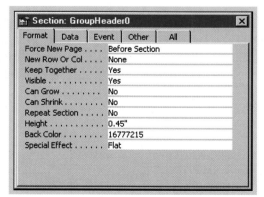

4. Preview the report. Each group is on a separate page.

5. Return to Design View. Save the report and close it.

# Using AutoFormat for a Report

When creating a report with a wizard, you select a style for the report. These styles are available for all reports as Report AutoFormats. When you apply an Autoformat to a report, Access reformats the report using a preset style.

**EXERCISE 10-15 Modify a Report with AutoFormat**

1. Open the Animals Tabular AutoReport in Design View.
2. Click the Select Report box, the etched square to the left of the horizontal ruler. A small black rectangle appears in the box to show that the entire report is selected.
3. From the Format menu, select AutoFormat.

 **TIP:** The Report Wizard also uses these styles.

4. Choose Casual and click OK. Preview the report.
5. Return to Design View and click the AutoFormat button 🔄. Choose Soft Gray and click OK. Preview the report.
6. In Design View, size the controls as necessary. Then close the report without saving it.

# Creating Mailing Labels

The database includes the names and addresses of customers, employees, and suppliers. You already have all the data you need to create mailing labels using the Label Wizard.

The Label Wizard lists common label brands and sizes. Laser labels usually come in sheets with 20 to 30 labels per sheet. You can buy larger labels for packages, video cassettes, CDs, or file folders. The Label Wizard asks which fields to place on the label, which font to use, and how to sort the labels.

**EXERCISE 10-16 Create Mailing Labels**

1. Click the Reports tab and click New.

**2.** From the New Report dialog box, choose Label Wizard. Choose Customers as the table. Click OK.

 **NOTE:** Access uses Avery brand labels in the Label Wizard. Other brands use the same sizes, so you aren't limited to using only Avery labels.

**3.** The first wizard dialog box asks you which size label to use. Choose 5160 for labels that measure 1 inch by 2 5/8 inches, 3 labels across the page. Choose English as the Unit of Measure and Sheet Feed as the Label Type. Click Next.

**4.** The next dialog box asks you to set the font. Use black, 10-point Arial, Normal weight. Click Next.

**5.** The next dialog box asks you to select fields for the label. As you select fields, they appear in the label prototype, a preview of the actual label.

**6.** Double-click ContactName to place it on the first row in the prototype. It appears in brackets in the prototype.

**FIGURE 10-12**
Prototype for a
mailing label

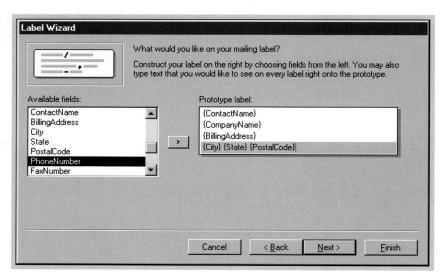

**7.** Press Enter to move the insertion point in the prototype to the next line.

**8.** Double-click CompanyName to place it on the second row in the prototype. Press Enter to move the insertion point to the next line.

 **NOTE:** If you place the wrong field in the prototype, double-click to select it and then press Delete to remove it.

**9.** Double-click BillingAddress and press Enter.

10. Double-click City. Press the Spacebar to insert a space.

11. Double-click State to insert the state field on the same line as the City. Press the Spacebar to insert a space after the State field.

12. Double-click PostalCode to place it in the prototype. Click Next.

13. Use the next dialog box to sort the labels. Double-click PostalCode and click Next.

14. The last wizard dialog box asks you to name the label report. Change the name to **Customer Labels** *[your initials]*. Select the option to the See the labels as they will look printed. Click Finish.

**FIGURE 10-13**
Mailing label in Design View

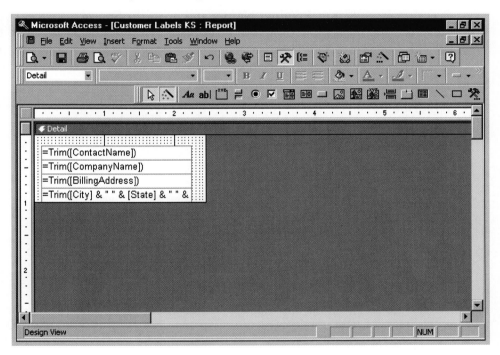

15. The labels are three across. Maximize the window to view the labels. Then return to Design View. The label is a report with only the Detail section. The "=Trim" command with each row eliminates extra spaces. The "&" in the last line joins the text fields on the same line.

16. Close the report.

## EXERCISE 10-17 Create Package Labels

1. Click the Reports tab and click New. From the New Report dialog box, choose Label Wizard. Choose the Stuffed Animals table and click OK.

**2.** In the first wizard dialog box, choose 5388 for labels that measure 3 inches by 5 inches, 1 label across the page. Choose English as the Unit of Measure and Sheet Feed as the Label Type. Click <u>N</u>ext.

**3.** Set the font in the next dialog box as black, 18-point Times New Roman Normal. Click <u>N</u>ext.

**4.** Press Enter once to create a blank line in the prototype.

**5.** Key **Product ID:** and press the Spacebar twice.

**6.** Double-click ProductID to place it in the prototype.

**7.** Press Enter twice to insert two blank lines in the prototype.

**8.** Key **Product Name:** and press the Spacebar twice. Double-click ProductName to place it in the prototype. Press Enter twice.

**9.** Key **Kit Number:** and press the Spacebar twice. Double-click KitNumber to place it in the prototype. Click <u>N</u>ext.

**FIGURE 10-14**
Prototype for
large labels

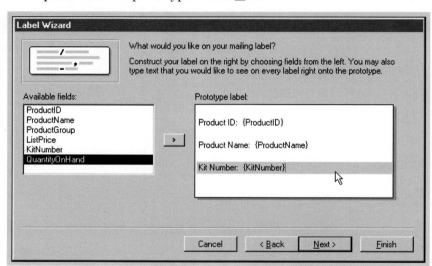

**10.** In the next dialog box, choose ProductGroup for the sort order and click <u>N</u>ext.

**11.** In the last wizard dialog box, change the name to **Animals Labels *[your initials]***. Select the option "See the labels as they will look printed." Click <u>F</u>inish.

**12.** The labels are one across and print on nine label sheets. Maximize the window to view the labels. View several pages. (See Figure 10-15 on the next page.)

**13.** Return to Design View. The blank lines in the label are marked with an Access expression (=" "). The "&" joins the data in the controls on the same line.

**14.** Preview the report, save it, and print the first two pages. Then close the report.

**FIGURE 10-15**
Design View for
large labels

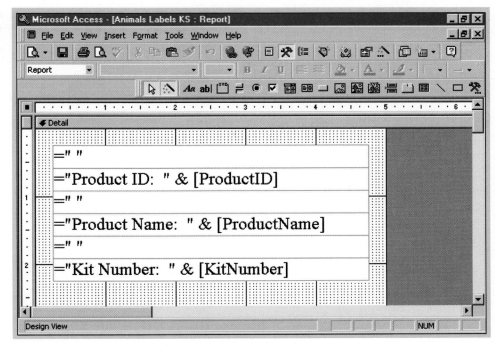

# Concepts Review

Each of the following statements is either true or false. Indicate your choice by circling either T or F.

**T  F  1.** A columnar report shows the data in vertical columns with titles at the top of the page.

**T  F  2.** You can change the properties of more than one control at a time.

**T  F  3.** If you group records on a field in a report, all records with the same value for that field appear in the same segment of the report.

**T  F  4.** You can place a forced page break in the report Page Header to print each group on a separate page.

**T  F  5.** Each section of a report has its own properties.

**T  F  6.** A line break is the same as a page break.

**T  F  7.** When you update a table with new data, you must also update the report to show that new data.

**T  F  8.** An AutoFormat won't overwrite any formatting you already applied.

Write the correct answer in the space provided.

**1.** Name three sections of a report.

_____

**2.** How can you create a default columnar report for any table?

_____

**3.** What property can you change to display a title for a control other than the field name?

_____

**4.** What border style will show no border?

_____

**5.** What is the command to force a line break?

_____

**6.** How do you delete a horizontal line in a report?

_____

**7.** What command do you use to save a report with a different name?

_____

**8.** What command allows you to create a group in a report?

_____

## CRITICAL THINKING

**Answer these questions on a separate page. There are no right or wrong answers. Support your answers with examples from your own experience, if possible.**

**1.** Most reports are done on a regular basis. For example, you might need to run a sales report every Monday or a payroll report every Friday. Explain how creating a report design can increase your productivity.

**2.** Many tables have thousands of records entered in random order. Suppose you need a report that shows all your customers organized by sales representative assigned to the customer. Explain the steps to create this report.

# Skills Review

## EXERCISE 10-18

**Create a columnar AutoReport and modify controls.**

**1.** Create a columnar AutoReport by following these steps:

**a.** Open the file *[your initials]***CC4.mdb.**

**b.** Click the Reports tab. Click New and choose AutoReport: Columnar.

**c.** Choose Employees as the table for this report. Click OK.

**d.** Maximize the window. See how many pages are in the report. Return to Design View.

**2.** Change the appearance of the report by following these steps:

**a.** Select and delete the LastName label.

***b.*** Drag the LastName text box so its left edge aligns at the 3-inch mark on the horizontal ruler. Leave it in the same vertical position.

***c.*** Drag the FirstName control box up to align horizontally with the LastName text box.

***d.*** Double-click the FirstName label to open its properties sheet. Change the caption to **Employee Name**. Close the properties sheet.

***e.*** Double-click the SocialSecurityNumber label and change the caption to **SS#**. Close the properties sheet.

***f.*** Select all the controls from SS# down to the bottom of the Detail section.

***g.*** When all the controls are selected, drag them up so there is one row of grid dots between them and the Employee Name control. Deselect the controls.

***h.*** Select the BirthDate and HireDate labels. Right-click either control and select Properties. Set the width to 1 inch and close the properties sheet. Deselect the controls.

***i.*** Move the BirthDate control to align at the 2-inch mark on the same line as the JobCode control.

***j.*** Move the HireDate control to align at the 4.25-inch mark on the same line as the BirthDate control.

***k.*** Move the Address control up so there is one row of grid dots between it and the JobCode control.

***l.*** Select the City, State, and PostalCode labels. Set the Width to 1 inch and close the properties sheet. Deselect the controls.

***m.*** Move the City control up so there is one row of grid dots below the Address control.

***n.*** Move the State control to align at the 3-inch mark on the same line as the City control.

***o.*** Select the State label and drag its middle right handle to size it to accommodate the label text.

***p.*** Drag the State text box closer to its label.

***q.*** Move the PostalCode control to align at the 4-inch mark on the same line as the City and State.

***r.*** Select the three controls at the bottom of the report and move them below the City control.

***s.*** Move the Page footer bar to the 3-inch mark.

***t.*** Place a label in the Report Header section with your first and last name. Change the font to 10-point Arial. Position the label at the right margin.

***u.*** Save the report as **Employees AutoReport**. Print the first page of the report and close the report.

## Change borders, align controls, and modify a horizontal line.

1. Change the borders by following these steps:

   a. Open the **Employees AutoReport** in Design View.

   b. Select all the text boxes, not the labels. Open the properties sheet.

   c. Set the Border Style to Transparent. Close the properties sheet.

   d. Select all the labels and apply the Raised special effect.

   e. Preview the report. Check that all the labels and text boxes have the correct style.

   f. Return to Design View.

2. Align controls by following these steps:

   a. Select all the text boxes in the first column of the report (EmployeeID, FirstName, SocialSecurity, and so on) and align them on the left.

   b. Select the EmployeeID controls and move it so its left edge aligns with the HireDate label on the same line as the employee's name. Resize the LastName text box.

3. Modify the horizontal line by following these steps:

   a. Select the horizontal line at the top of the Detail section.

   b. Hold down Shift and drag the right handle to make the line as long as the Detail section.

   c. Preview the report and make any other necessary changes. Save the report and print page 1. Close the report.

## Create a tabular AutoReport, modify controls, and use line breaks in a control.

1. Create a tabular report by following these steps:

   a. Click the Reports tab. Click New and choose AutoReport: Tabular.

   b. Choose Employees as the table for this report. Click OK.

   c. Maximize the window. Return to Design View.

   d. Save the report. Name it **Employees by Job Code** *[your initials]*.

2. Modify the controls and insert line breaks by following these steps:

   a. Right-click the Page Header bar and select Properties. Set the height to .75 inch. Close the properties sheet.

*b.* Select the horizontal line and drag it to the bottom of the Page Header section.

*c.* Select and delete the JobCode label in the Page Header and the JobCode text box in the Detail section.

*d.* Delete the EmployeeID controls in the Page Header and the Detail sections.

*e.* Delete the SocialSecurityNumber and the BirthDate controls in the Page Header and the Detail sections.

*f.* Select the LastName label in the Page Header. Click again to place the insertion point before "Name." Press Ctrl+Enter to force a line break.

*g.* Select the FirstName label in the Page Header. Click to place the insertion point and press Ctrl+Enter to force a line break.

*h.* Size the labels so all the text is visible.

*i.* Select the LastName label and text box. Drag them to the left edge of the Detail section. Size the text box so its right edge touches the 1-inch mark.

*j.* Size the FirstName text box so its right edge touches the 2-inch mark.

*k.* Select the HireDate label and text box and drag them to the 2.5-inch mark.

*l.* Select the label and split it into two lines. Select the label again and click Align Left in the toolbar.

*m.* Select the Address label and text box and drag them to the 3.25-inch mark. Select the label and click before the word "Address." Press Ctrl+Enter to insert a blank line.

*n.* Select and delete the City, State, and PostalCode controls in the Page Header and the Detail sections.

*o.* Preview the report and return to Design View. Size the Address text box in Design View so all the addresses are visible.

*p.* Drag the HomePhone controls to the 5.25-inch mark. Split the label into two lines. Size the controls.

*q.* Drag the EmergencyContact controls to the 6.5-inch mark. Split the label and size the controls.

*r.* Format the EmergencyPhone field to match the other controls and to fit the report.

*s.* Drag the horizontal line in the Page Header so there is one row of grid dots between the controls and the line. Drag the top of the Detail bar so there is one row of grid dots below the line.

*t.* Place a label at the right margin in the Report Header with your first and last name. Make it Arial 10 point.

*u.* Save and print the report. Then close the report.

## Group records in a report and force group page breaks.

**1.** Group records in a report by following these steps:

    **a.** Open the **Employees by Job Code** *[your initials]* report in Design View.

    **b.** Click the Sorting and Grouping button [≣].

    **c.** Click in the first row in the Field/Expression column and display the drop-down list. Select JobCode. The default sort order is Ascending

    **d.** Click the Group Header row in the Group Properties and set it to Yes.

    **e.** Click in the second row in the Field/Expression column and display the drop-down list. Select LastName. The sort order is Ascending. Don't use grouping for this field. Close the dialog box.

    **f.** Click the Field List button [▣] and drag the JobCode field to the 1-inch mark in the JobCode Header. Close the field list.

    **g.** Preview the report and return to Design View.

    **h.** Size the JobCode text box so all the text is visible.

    **i.** Right-click the JobCode Header bar. Select Properties.

    **j.** Set the height of the section to .5 inch. Close the properties sheet.

    **k.** Select the controls in the JobCode group header and move them close to the bottom of the section. Leave one row of grid dots below them.

    **l.** Select File and Page Setup. Change the left and bottom margins to .75 inch.

    **m.** Save your report.

**2.** Force a page break between each group by following these steps:

    **a.** Double-click the JobCode header bar to open its properties sheet.

    **b.** Set Force New Page to Before Section. Close the properties sheet.

    **c.** Preview the report. Save it and print the first page. Then close the report.

## Create mailing labels.

**1.** Create mailing labels by following these steps:

    **a.** Click the Reports tab and click New.

    **b.** Choose the Label Wizard and the Employees table. Click OK.

**c.** In the first wizard dialog box, choose 5160 for laser mailing labels. Choose English as the Unit of Measure and Sheet Feed as the Label Type. Click Next.

**d.** In the next dialog box, set the font as black, 10-point Arial, Normal weight. Click Next.

**e.** In the next dialog box, double-click FirstName to place it on the first row in the prototype.

**f.** Press the Spacebar to insert a space. Double-click LastName to place it on the same line as the first name.

**g.** Press Enter to move the insertion point in the prototype to the next line.

**h.** Double-click Address to place it on the second row in the prototype. Press Enter to move the insertion point to the next line.

**i.** Double-click City. Press the Spacebar.

**j.** Double-click State to insert the State field on the same line as the City. Press the Spacebar to insert a space after the State field.

**k.** Double-click PostalCode to place it in the prototype. Click Next.

**l.** In the next dialog box, sort the labels by PostalCode and click Next.

**m.** In the last wizard dialog box, name the label report as **Employee Labels** *[your initials]*. Select the option to the See the labels as they will look printed. Click Finish.

**n.** Maximize the window. Then print the labels on plain paper and close the report.

# Lesson Applications

## Create a Columnar AutoReport. Modify controls.

1. Open your database file, if necessary.
2. Create a columnar AutoReport for the Customers table.
3. Move the CustomerID control down to the same line as the CompanyName control, leaving one column of grid dots between the controls.
4. Place the City, State, and PostalCode controls all on one line. Size the labels and text boxes so they fit and all the data is visible.
5. Move the PhoneNumber, FaxNumber, and TaxStatus controls below the City control, leaving one row of empty grid dots.
6. Check the report to determine which controls need sizing and alignment.
7. Right-click the horizontal line at the top of the Detail section. Change its width (length of the line) to 6.5 inches.
8. Edit the label in the Report Header to show **Carolina Critters Customers**.
9. Open the Page Header and add a label with your first and last name at the right margin. Set the font to 10-point Arial normal.
10. Save the report as **Customers AutoReport** and print the first two pages.

## Create a tabular AutoReport, modify controls, use line breaks, and group records.

1. Create a tabular report for the Kit Contents table. Determine how many pages are included in the report.
2. Save the report as **Kit Contents AutoReport**.
3. Open the Page Header properties sheet. Set the height to .5 inch.
4. Drag the horizontal line in the Page Header to the bottom of the section.
5. Edit the KitNumber and KitContents labels in the Page Header to show the text on two lines. Insert a blank line before the word "Cost" in the label so it aligns with the other two labels.
6. Size the Cost text box to be wide enough for the prices. Move the Cost label so it aligns on the right with its text box.

7. Move the Kit Contents label and text box closer to the Cost controls. Size the Kit Contents text box so it extends to the right margin, even with the horizontal line in the Page Header or Footer.

8. Make the line in the Page Header section the same length as the section. Keep the line straight.

9. Add a label in the Page Header section at the right margin for your first and last name. Use 9-point Arial Normal.

10. Add a group header for SupplierID, sorted in ascending order. Use a second sort for KitNumber without a group header.

11. Move the SupplierID label from the Page Header to the left edge of the SupplierID Group Header section.

12. Move the SupplierID text box from the Detail section next to the label in the SupplierID Group Header section.

13. Align these two controls on the bottom.

14. Make the SupplierID text box the same format as the SupplierID label.

15. Move the Cost controls to the left.

16. Save the report and print it.

## EXERCISE 10-25

### Create mailing labels.

1. Create Avery 5160 labels for the **Kit Suppliers** table.

2. Select a 10-point normal font. Sort the labels by Postal code.

3. In the prototype, show the ContactName on the first line. Then show the SupplierName on the second line. Use normal address style for the rest of the label.

4. Name the report **Kit Suppliers Labels**. Print the labels.

# Using Expressions in a Report

LESSON

11

**OBJECTIVES**

After completing this lesson, you will be able to:

1. Use the Expression Builder in a report.
2. Calculate aggregate totals in Group Footers and Report Footers.
3. Calculate percentages in a report.
4. Build an underlying query for a report.
5. Use a query as the source of a report.
6. Add common expressions to a report.

 Estimated Time: 1½ hours

You've used the Expression Builder several times to add calculated controls to forms and reports. With the Expression Builder, you can use fields, operators, common expressions, and values to create a field that shows useful information. You learned how to use a calculated control to determine the value of the inventory (ListPrice*QuantityOnHand) for each animal in Lesson 6.

You've also seen that Access has several built-in functions and expressions that you can add to a report or a form. For example, the =(Now) expression displays the current date. In this lesson, you use the =Sum() function in the Group Footers and Report Footers to get a total for a particular group of records, as well as a grand total.

In this lesson you also use the Expression Builder to add calculated controls to a report, build a True/False Condition, use Count and Average, and show percentages in a report.

# Using the Expression Builder in a Report

An expression uses a combination of identifiers and operators. The identifiers are the field names that you can either key or select from a panel. You can key the operators or select them from the row of operators in the Expression Builder. The Expression Builder is a visual aid you use when building formulas or expressions. Once you know how to build formulas, you can enter them directly in the unbound control or on the Control Source row in the properties sheet.

## EXERCISE 11-1 Create a Report with the Report Wizard

1. Open the file *[your initials]***CC4.mdb.**
2. Click the Reports tab and click <u>N</u>ew.
3. Choose Report Wizard, choose Sales Representatives as the table, and click OK.
4. Double-click SocialSecurityNumber, Salary, and Region to place each one in the Selected Fields list. Click <u>N</u>ext.
5. Group the records by Region and click <u>N</u>ext.
6. Sort the records by SocialSecurityNumber and click <u>N</u>ext.
7. Use a Portrait, Stepped layout for this report. Click <u>N</u>ext.
8. Choose the Corporate style and click <u>N</u>ext.
9. Name the report **Sales Representatives Salaries** *[your initials]* and click Finish.
10. Maximize the window, view the report, and return to Design View.

## EXERCISE 11-2 Modify Controls and Entering an Expression

1. Select the Region label and its text box. Size both controls so the right edge touches the 1-inch mark on the ruler.
2. Select the SS# label and text box. Move them so the SS label is next to the Region label.

 **TIP:** Switch between Design View and Report View as you build a report to see if the data is completely displayed .

**3.** Select the Salary controls and move them next to the SS# controls. Size the controls to accommodate the data.

**4.** Size and position the controls so they don't extend past the 3-inch mark on the ruler. Save the report.

**FIGURE 11-1**
Report in Design
View

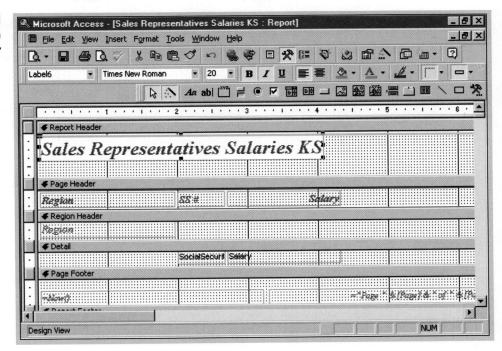

**5.** Click the Text Box button [abl] and draw a control that is 1 inch wide in the Detail section starting at the 4-inch mark.

**6.** Select the label for the new control and delete it.

**7.** Drag the unbound control next to the Salary text box at the 3-inch mark.

**8.** Right-click the unbound control and select Properties. Click the All tab.

**9.** Click the Name row and enter **Projected Salary** as the name of the control.

**10.** Click the Control Source row and click the Build button [...].

**11.** In the middle panel, double-click the Salary field, not the label.

**12.** Click the asterisk (*) for multiplication.

**13.** Key **1.1** after the asterisk to create the expression "Salary*1.1." This multiplies the current salary by 110 percent. (See Figure 11-2 on the next page.)

**14.** Click OK and close the properties sheet.

**15.** Select and align the controls in the Detail section at the top.

**16.** Change the font to 11-point Times New Roman. Deselect the controls.

**FIGURE 11-2**
Expression Builder

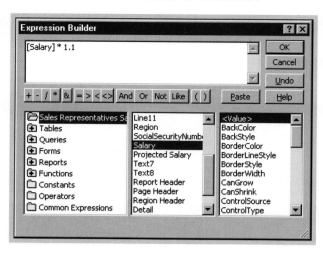

**17.** Open the properties sheet for the calculated control and format it to show Currency.

**18.** Select the Salary label in the Page Header. Click the Copy button 🔳 and then click the Paste button 🔳.

**19.** Drag the copied control to be the title for the new Projected Salary control. Replace the text with **10% Increase**.

**20.** Resize and reposition the new label as necessary.

**21.** Drag the top of the Region Header bar up so there is one row of grid dots beneath the horizontal line.

**22.** Preview your report. Resize and reposition controls so you can see all the data.

**23.** Save your report.

**TABLE 11-1** | **Parts of the Expression Builder**

| PART | FUNCTION |
|------|----------|
| Preview area | Area at the top of the dialog box that shows the expression as you build it. |
| Operator row | Set of buttons with mathematical symbols below the Preview area. |
| Left panel | Folders that contain objects or elements that you can paste into the expression. These folders include tables, reports, forms, or queries as well as Functions, Constants, Operators, and Common Expressions. A + symbol on a folder means it contains other folders and can be expanded. |
| Middle panel | Displays the contents of the current folder. |
| Right panel | Shows additional commands, properties, or objects for the element selected in the middle panel. |
| Paste | Copies selected object into the Preview area. You can also paste by double-clicking the object. |

**EXERCISE** **11-3** **Add a Check Box Control to a Report**

You can use an expression to determine if a value meets a condition. In the Sales Representatives Salaries report, for example, you can determine if a particular employee is eligible for a pension plan.

To enter this type of true/false or yes/no expression, you can use the Check Box button ☑. It places a label and an unbound control, similar to the Text Box tool.

1. Click the Check Box button ☑. Draw a control that is 1 inch wide in the Detail section, starting near the 4.5-inch mark on the ruler. Deselect the control.

2. Select the label for **CheckNN**. Press Delete to delete the label, but not the checkbox.

3. Right-click the check box control and choose Properties.

4. Click the Name row and enter **Eligibility** as the name of the control.

5. Click the Control Source row and the Build button.

6. In the middle panel, double-click the Projected Salary field.

7. Click the > operator (for "greater than").

8. Key **30000** after the greater than symbol (>) to create the expression "Projected Salary>30000." This checks if an employee's projected salary is greater than $30,000.

**FIGURE 11-3**
Expression Builder

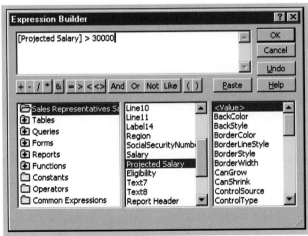

9. Click OK and close the properties sheet.

10. Preview the report and return to Design View.

11. Copy and paste the Salary label in the Page Header.

12. Drag the copied control to be the title for the eligibility control. Replace the text with **Eligible?**

13. Resize and reposition the new label as necessary and change its alignment to Center.

14. Drag the top of the Page Header bar up so there is one row of grid dots beneath the horizontal line.

15. Preview and save your report.

# Calculating Aggregate Totals in Group and Report Footers

You can now determine what the total salary cost would be if the company gives the sales representatives a 10% increase. You can also determine what the new cost would be for a particular region of the country. In both cases, use the =Sum() function. A *function* is a word or statement used in an expression to display or calculate a value. Functions you might recognize include Sum, Average, Maximum, and Minimum. These are known as *aggregate functions* because they calculate for a group.

Many functions require other elements to be complete, known as the argument(s). The Expression Builder guides you into using the correct form or syntax for your functions.

When you use the =Sum() function in a Group Footer, it calculates a total for the group. When you use the same function in a Report Footer, it calculates a total for the entire report.

## EXERCISE 11-4 Create Totals in the Report Footer

The Report Footer bar is in the report, but the footer is not open. After you open it, you can insert a text box to use the =Sum() function and total the new salaries.

**1.** Position the pointer on the bottom edge of the Report Footer bar. Drag the border down to make the footer about .5 inch tall.

**2.** Click the Text Box button  and draw a control that starts at the 3-inch mark and is 1 inch wide.

**3.** Right-click the label and select Properties. Click the Format tab and change the caption to **Total Payroll**. Close the properties sheet.

**4.** Size the label to see the caption.

**5.** Open the properties sheet for the text box. Click the Data tab, the Control Source row, and the Build button.

**6.** In the left panel, double-click the Functions folder. The folder expands to show the Built-In Functions folder and the folder for the database.

**7.** Double-click the Built-in Functions folder. The middle panel lists categories of functions. The right panel lists individual functions in each category.

> **NOTE:** If you don't know the category of a function, you can click the All category.

**FIGURE 11-4**
Expression Builder
with Sum
highlighted

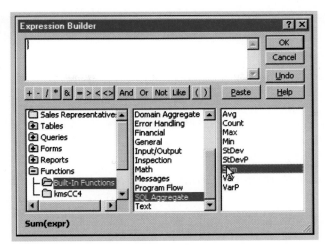

8. Click once to select SQL Aggregate in the middle panel. The Sum function appears in the right panel.

9. Double-click Sum to paste it to the Preview area. It appears with a placeholder <<expr>> to mark where you must enter the rest of the argument.

 **NOTE:** An argument is additional information required by some expressions or macros.

10. Click <<expr>> in the Preview area to select it. Don't select the parentheses.

 **TIP:** If you delete a parenthesis, re-key it and make sure the insertion point is between the two parentheses.

11. In the left panel, click the Sales Representatives Salaries folder. The controls appear in the middle panel.

12. In the middle panel, double-click Salary.

13. Key **\*1.1** after the Salary field in the Preview area.

**FIGURE 11-5**
Formula for salary
increase

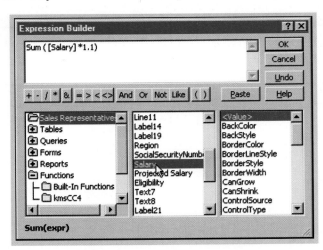

14. The expression shows square brackets around the field name and parentheses around the entire argument. Click OK.

15. Click the Other tab and change the Name to **Total Payroll**.

16. Click the =[Salary]*1.1 control in the Detail section and click Format Painter.

17. Paint the format to the Total Payroll text box in the Report Footer.

18. Open the properties sheet for the Total Payroll text box. Change the Format to Currency.

19. Align the two calculated controls on the right.

20. Preview your report and return to Design View.

## EXERCISE 11-5 Copy and Modify a Control for the Group Footer

You can now open the Group Footer and use the same basic function and expression to determine a payroll subtotal for each region. The report already has a group, so you only need to display its footer, copy the control from the Report Footer, and edit it as needed.

1. Click the Sorting and Grouping button 〖≡〗.

2. For the Region group, set the Group Footer property to Yes. Close the dialog box.

3. The Region Group Footer appears below the Detail section and before the Page Footer.

4. Copy and paste the Total Payroll label and text box in the Report Footer.

5. Drag the duplicate controls to the Region Group Footer.

6. Change the copied label to **Region Payroll**.

7. Preview the report. Because the Sum function is now in the Group Footer, it totals the salaries for each group.

**FIGURE 11-6**
Sales Representatives Salaries report

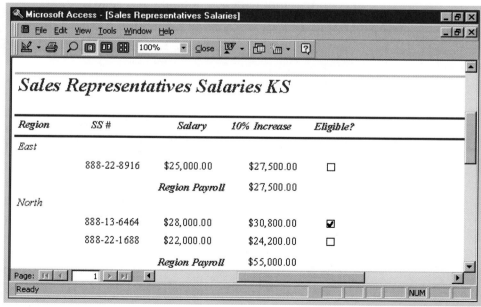

344

8. Return to Design View. Size the Report Footer section so there is one row of grid dots beneath the controls.

9. Align any controls that you moved, save the report, and close it.

## EXERCISE 11-6 Use the Count Function

In Lesson 9, you used the Count function to determine how many records were in a particular group. You can use this function in a report with similar results.

The Kit Costs report has a calculated control, similar to the one you used in the Sales Representatives Salaries report to compute a new cost with a 10% increase. The records are grouped by Supplier ID and sorted further by Kit Number.

1. Preview the Kit Costs report. Switch to Design View.

2. Position the pointer on the bottom edge of the Report Footer bar. Drag the border down to make the footer about .5 inch tall.

3. Click the Text Box button ab| and draw a control that starts at the 1-inch mark and is 2 inches wide, to align beneath the Kit Number control.

4. Right-click the label and select Properties. Click the Format tab and change the Caption to **Total Number of Kits**. Close the properties sheet.

5. Size the label to see more of the caption. Click the text insertion point after "Number" and press Ctrl + Enter to force a line break in the label. Deselect the label.

6. Select the label again and click the Center button ≣.

7. Open the properties sheet for the text box. Click the Data tab, the Control Source row, and the Build button ....

8. In the left panel, double-click the Functions folder and the Built-in Functions folder.

9. Find and click once to select SQL Aggregate in the middle panel.

10. Double-click Count to paste it to the Preview area. It appears with the placeholder. Click <<expr>> and delete it.

11. Open the Kit Costs folder in the left panel. Double-click Kit Number from the middle panel to paste it between the parentheses in the Preview area. Click OK.

12. Click the Other tab and name the control **Total Number of Kits**. Close the properties sheet.

13. Preview the report. The Count result is on page 2. Return to Design View.

**14.** Resize the label and the text box to show all the data. Align the text box beneath the KitNumber column in the report.

**15.** Save the report.

## EXERCISE 11-7 Use the Average Function

Use the same report to add another control that shows the average cost of the kits.

**1.** Copy and paste the Total Number of Kits label and text box in the Report Footer.

**2.** Drag the duplicate controls in the Report Footer to align beneath the New Cost controls.

**3.** Select the words "Total Number" in the copied label and enter **Average New**.

**4.** Click to place the text insertion point before "of" in the label and key **Cost** on the second line. The label should read **Average New Cost of Kits.**

**5.** Open the properties sheet for Average New Cost of Kits text box.

**6.** Click the Data tab, the Control Source row, and the Build button [⋯].

**7.** Delete the Count expression in the Preview area.

**8.** In the left panel, double-click the Functions folder. Double-click the Built-in Functions folder. Select SQL Aggregate in the middle panel.

**9.** Double-click Avg.

**10.** Delete <<expr>> in the Preview area, but not the parentheses.

**11.** In the left panel, click the **Kit Costs** report folder. In the middle panel, double-click Cost.

**FIGURE 11-7**
Text box with Avg expression

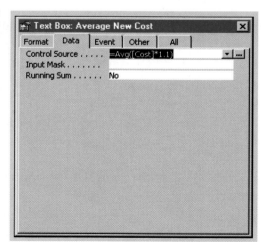

**12.** Key **\*1.1** after the Cost field in the Preview area. Click OK.

**13.** Click the Other tab and change the Name to **Average New Cost**.

**14.** Preview the report. The Count and Average numbers appear at the end of the report on page 2. Return to Design View.

**15.** Select all four controls in the Report Footer and align them on the Bottom.

**16.** Size the Report Footer section so there is one row of grid dots beneath the controls.

**17.** Format the Average Cost text box to show Currency. Align this control on the right with the calculated cost control.

**18.** Preview, save, and close the report.

**FIG 11-8**
Kit Costs report with Avg and Count

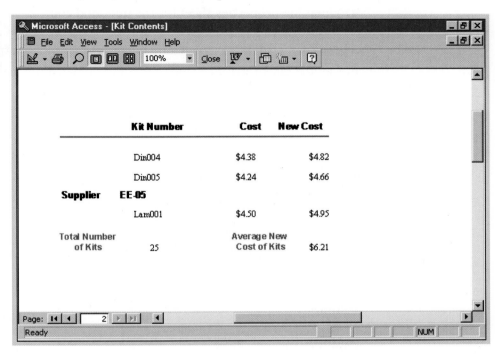

# Calculating Percentages in a Report

In addition to the common functions you used, you can calculate percentages. You designed a report in Lesson 6 that determined the dollar value of the inventory for each animal. It might be helpful to know what percent each animal's inventory value represents of your total inventory value.

**EXERCISE 11-8 Create a Percentage Expression**

The current version of Inventory Value includes a group total as well as the report total.

 **TIP:** Always work in a maximized window for better views of your work.

1. Preview the Inventory Value report. Look at the Group Footers and Report Footers and totals. Switch to Design View.

2. Draw a text box in the Detail section that starts at the 5-inch mark and is 1 inch wide.

3. Select the label for this control and delete it.

4. Open the properties sheet for the unbound control. Click the Data tab, the Control Source row, and the Build button [...].

5. Make sure the Inventory Value folder is open in the left panel.

6. Double-click Current Value in the middle panel to paste it in the Preview area.

7. Click / in the row of operators to paste the division symbol.

8. Double-click Total Inventory Value in the middle panel to paste it.

**FIGURE 11-9**
Expression Builder with percent calculation

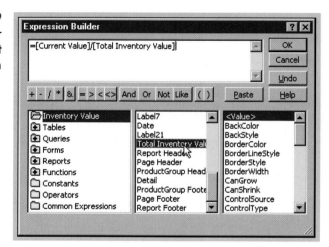

9. Click OK to close the Expression Builder.

10. Click the Other tab and name the control **Percent of Total**. Close the properties sheet.

11. Preview the report. The percentages need to be formatted. Return to Design View.

12. Select one of the controls in the Detail section and use the Format Painter to copy its format to the new control.

13. Open the properties sheet for the new control. Click the Format tab and the Format row. Select Percent. Close the properties sheet.

14. Click the Label button [Aa] and add a label in the Page Header for the percent column that reads **Percent of Total**. Copy the format from one of the other labels. Force this label to two lines.

15. Align the labels in the Page Header on the bottom. Return to Design View and save the report.

**EXERCISE** | 11-9 | **Add a Percentage Expression to the Group Footer**

You can add a similar percentage expression for the group as well. As you learned earlier in this lesson, you don't need to start from scratch. You can copy the current percent control. However, you need to edit the expression.

1. Select the percent control in the Detail section.
2. Click the Copy button 🖹 and click the Paste button 🖺.
3. Move the copied control to the ProductGroup Footer.
4. Resize the Detail section so there is one row of grid dots beneath the controls.
5. Right-click the new control and select Properties. Click the Data tab, the Control Source row, and the Build button ⸱⸱⸱.
6. The expression is almost correct. Scroll through the list of fields in the second panel to find the Group Value field. The percentage for the group needs to divide the Group Value by the Total Inventory Value, rather than the Current Value.
7. In the Preview area, select the word "Current." Key **Group**. The new expression is "=[Group Value]/[Total Inventory Value]." Click OK.
8. Click the Other tab and name the control **Group Percent**.
9. Align the controls in the Group Footer at the top.
10. Close the properties sheet and look at the report. The percent format was copied with the control. Save the report and close it.

**FIGURE 11-10**
Inventory Value Report

| Stock No. | Name | Price | Value | of Total |
|---|---|---|---|---|
| **Product Group** | **C** | | | |
| C002 | Bull Dog | $12.50 | $2,187.50 | 3.40% |
| C003 | Labrador | $12.50 | $2,812.50 | 4.37% |
| C004 | Siamese | $13.00 | $3,315.00 | 5.15% |
| C005 | Tiger cat | $13.00 | $3,120.00 | 4.84% |
| C001 | Dalmatian | $12.50 | $3,125.00 | 4.85% |
| | **Group Total** | | $14,560.00 | 22.60% |

**349**

# Building an Underlying Query for a Report

Reports are based on tables or queries. When a report uses a table as its source, you can use any field in that particular table. Although one table may contain many fields, you may need more data than is provided in that table.

In Lesson 8, you learned you can use more than one table in a query. For example, you already worked with the Kit Contents and Kit Suppliers tables. The Kit Contents table contains the kit number, a supplier code, the cost of the kit, and its contents. The Kit Suppliers table includes the name and address of the supplier. To see the name of the supplier with the kit number and cost, you can create a query using these two tables and use that query as the basis for a report.

To use two tables in the Simple Query Wizard, you must establish a relationship between the two tables. You established a relationship between the Kit Contents and Kit Suppliers tables when you created the lookup field in Lesson 8.

**EXERCISE** 11-10 **Create a Query using the Simple Query Wizard**

1. Click the Queries tab and click New.
2. Choose Simple Query Wizard and click OK.
3. In the first wizard dialog box, click the down arrow for Tables/Queries. Choose Table: Kit Suppliers. The fields are shown in the Available Fields list.
4. Double-click SupplierName to move it to the Selected Fields list.
5. Click the down arrow for Tables/Queries again to select the second table. Choose Table: Kit Contents.
6. In the Available Fields list, double-click KitNumber and Cost. Click Next. (See Figure 11-11 on the next page.)
7. The next dialog box asks if you want a Detail or a Summary query. A Detail query shows all the records. A Summary query uses the Sum, Avg, Min, Max, or Count functions to show only totals from the two tables. Select Detail and click Next.
8. Change the name of the query to **Kit Suppliers by Number and Cost** *[your initials]*. Click Finish.
9. Maximize the window to see the dynaset. The fields are from both tables.
10. Switch to the query design grid. You can see the two table field lists with the relationship.

**FIGURE 11-11**
Simple Query
Wizard

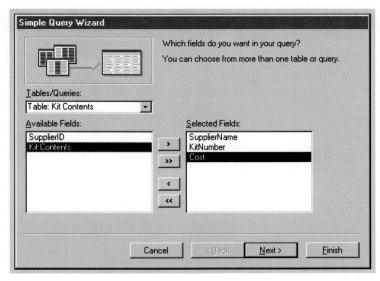

# EXERCISE 11-11 Modify the Query for the Report

1. Click the Sort row for the SupplierName field and select Ascending.
2. Click the Sort row for the KitNumber field and select Ascending.
3. Right-click in the Field row for the empty fourth column and choose Build.
4. Double-click Cost to paste it to the Preview area.
5. Key **\*1.1** in the Preview area to calculate a new cost with a 10% increase. Click OK.
6. Preview the dynaset and return to the design grid.
7. Right-click the Field row for the calculated field and choose Zoom to open the Zoom window.
8. Point anywhere within "Expr1" and double-click to select the word. Key **New Cost**. Click OK.

 **NOTE:** The colon identifies the text that follows as the caption for the field.

9. Right-click the New Cost field row and choose Properties. Change the Format to Currency and close the properties sheet.
10. Preview the dynaset. Save and close the query.

# Using a Query as the Source of a Report

You can now base a report on the query. Your report displays all the fields from the query and allows you to print fields from two tables. Once the report is created, you can modify it just like any report.

---

**EXERCISE** `11-12` **Select a Query for a Report's Data**

---

1. Click the Reports tab and click New.
2. Choose Report Wizard and click the drop-down list to show where the report's data comes from.
3. Choose **Kit Suppliers by Number and Cost** and click OK.
4. Click >> to transfer all the fields from the query to the Selected Fields list. Click <u>N</u>ext.
5. You can view your data organized by fields from either of the two tables in the query. Select by Kit Suppliers and click Next.
6. The report is grouped by Supplier Name because you chose the table in the previous dialog box. Do not add more grouping. Click Next.
7. The query is sorted by the supplier's name and the kit number, so you don't need to sort in the Report Wizard. Click Next.
8. Use a Stepped layout and Portrait orientation. Click Next.
9. Use the Formal style and click Next.
10. Name the report **New Kit Costs** and click Finish.
11. Maximize the window, view the report, and return to Design View.

---

**EXERCISE** `11-13` **Add a Group Footer with the Maximum Function**

---

The Report Wizard adds the Group Header for SupplierName. It does not, however, open the Group Footer.

1. Click the Sorting and Grouping button ▤.
2. Click the Group Footer row and set it to Yes. Close the dialog box.
3. Draw a text box that aligns in the Group Footer beneath the New Cost controls.
4. Change the caption for the label to **Maximum Cost for This Supplier**.

5.  Size the label to see the caption.

6.  Open the properties sheet for the unbound control. Click the Data tab, the Control Source row, and the Build button

7.  In the left panel, double-click the Functions folder. Click the Built-in Functions folder.

8.  Click once to choose SQL Aggregate in the middle panel.

9.  Double-click Max to paste it to the Preview area.

10. Select <<expr>> in the Preview area, but don't select the parentheses.

11. In the left panel, find and click the New Kit Costs report folder. In the middle panel, find the New Cost field, not the label. Double-click it. The expression reads "Max([New Cost])." Click OK.

12. Click the Other tab and name the control **Maximum Cost**. Close the properties sheet.

13. Preview the report, save it, and return to Design View.

## EXERCISE 11-14 Fine-Tune the Appearance of the Report

1.  Size the New Cost and Maximum Cost text boxes so they're both about 1 inch wide.

2.  Open the properties sheet for the Maximum Cost text box. Change the Format to Currency.

3.  Select both controls and align them on the right.

4.  Drag the top border of the SupplierName Group Header down to leave one row of grid dots below the horizontal line. This adds some space between the column titles and the first group on the page.

5.  Choose Select All from the Edit menu to select all the controls in the report.

6.  Point at the label in the Report Header, hold down Shift, and click to deselect this control.

7.  Format all the controls except the title to 11-point Times New Roman. Click in an unused area to deselect the controls.

8.  Preview the report to determine which controls need to be sized. Check the number of pages in the report. Return to Design View.

9.  Right-click the SupplierName Group Header bar and select Properties. Click the Format tab and the Force New Page row. Choose Before Section to place each group on a separate page.

10. Save, preview, and close your report.

**FIGURE 11-12**
New Kit Costs
report

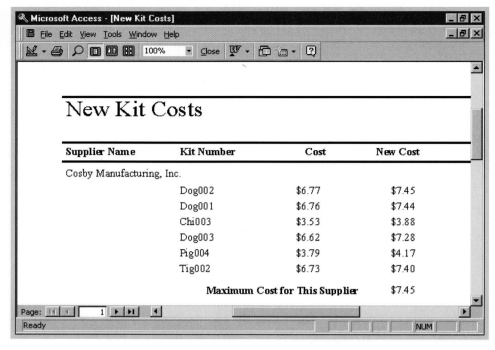

# Adding Common Expressions to a Report

The Expression Builder has several categories of commands you can use to build expressions. You already used some of the built-in functions. There is a Common Expressions category that adds date, time, and page number information to a control. You saw such controls in reports created by a wizard. Now you learn how to create these controls yourself.

**EXERCISE** **11-15** **Add a Date Expression to a Report**

1. Open the Employee's Date of Hire report in Design View. This report doesn't have any controls in the Page Footer. Right-click the Page Footer bar and choose Properties. Set the section height at 1 inch.

2. Draw a text box in the Page Footer that starts at the 1-inch mark and is about 1 inch wide.

3. Select and delete the label.

4. Open the properties sheet for the unbound control. Click the Data tab and open the Expression Builder.

5. In the left panel, click the Common Expressions folder. The expressions are shown in the middle panel. The Access programming commands for the expression are shown in the right panel when you select an expression in the middle panel.

**FIGURE 11-13**
Common
expressions in the
Expression Builder

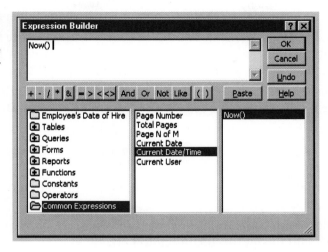

6. In the middle panel, double-click Current Date/Time to paste it. The Access command is Now() to display the date and time. Click OK.

7. Close the properties sheet and preview the report. Use a Fit % view size and then zoom in on the new control at the bottom of the page. Return to Design View.

8. Right click the =Now() control and select Properties. Click the Format tab and select the Long Date format.

9. Preview the report again. The Long Date format shows the date, not the time.

10. Return to Design View. Size the control so the date shows on one line.

11. Align the date control on the left with the label in the Report Header.

12. Use Format Painter to make this control the same as those in the Detail section.

13. Size the Page Footer section to show one row of dots above and below the control.

14. Preview the report, save it, and close it.

# EXERCISE 11-16 Add a Page Expression to a Report

1. Open the Stuffed Animals Products report in Design View. This report has the Now function in the Page Footer.

2. Draw a text box in the Page Footer that starts at the 4-inch mark and is about 1 inch wide. Select and delete the label.

3. Right-click the unbound control and open its properties sheet. Click the Data tab, the Control Source row, and the Build button ....

4. In the left panel, click the Common Expressions folder.

5. In the middle panel, double-click Page N of M to paste it. The Access command includes text within quotes to identify what actually prints. The ampersand (&) marks Access commands. Click OK.

6. Close the properties sheet and preview the report. Scroll to the bottom of the report so you can see the new control. Return to Design View.

7. Drag the bottom border of the Page Footer section down to make it taller.

8. Drag the page number control beneath the =Now() control. Align the controls on the left.

9. Copy the format from a control in the Detail section to both controls in the Page Footer.

10. Select both controls in the footer and open the properties sheet. Click the Format tab. Set the Text Align to Left.

11. Size the Page Footer section so there is one row of dots above and below the controls.

12. Preview the report. Save and close it.

# Concepts Review

**Each of the following statements is either true or false. Indicate your choice by circling either T or F.**

T  F  *1.* The Expression Builder verifies that controls and operators are correct and in the proper order.

T  F  *2.* The Sum function displays a total for the field used as the argument in the function.

T  F  *3.* A calculated control can perform addition, subtraction, multiplication, or division.

T  F  *4.* A built-in function displays <<expr>> when you paste it in the Expression Builder.

T  F  *5.* You can use a check box control for an expression that determines if a particular condition is true.

T  F  *6.* The Avg function calculates the average for a group if it is in the Group Footer.

T  F  *7.* You must use the Query Wizard to create a multiple table query.

T  F  *8.* Reports that are based on queries cannot be modified.

**Write the correct answer in the space provided.**

*1.* What common expression displays the date and time?

_____

*2.* Name two of the built-in aggregate functions.

_____

*3.* What operator do you use to determine a percentage?

_____

*4.* What two sections of a report often show totals or other sums?

_____

5. What row do you click in the Data tab of a properties sheet to build a calculated control?

_____

6. What is the placeholder when you paste a built-in function to the Preview area?

_____

7. If a control is in the Report Footer, where does it print?

_____

8. How do you display the Group Footer?

_____

## CRITICAL THINKING

**Answer these questions on a separate page. There are no right or wrong answers. Support your answers with examples from your own experience, if possible.**

1. The built-in functions in Access are similar to those in Excel. Give some examples of how you might use Avg, Min, and Max in reports or forms. Look up some of the Financial or Math functions in the Expression Builder and determine how some of them might be used.

2. Although tables are essential to working in a database, much of the work is handled through queries and reports. Based on your work so far, explain why queries and reports are so important to good database management.

# Skills Review

## EXERCISE 11-17

**Create a report with the Report Wizard. Modify controls and build an expression.**

1. Create a report with the Wizard by following these steps:
   a. Open the file *[your initials]***CC4.mdb.**
   b. Click the Reports tab and click New.
   c. Choose Report Wizard, choose Payroll Information as the table, and click OK.

**d.** Double-click SocialSecurityNumber, Monthly Salary, Federal Tax, State Tax, FICA, and Savings to place each in the Selected Fields list and click Next.

**e.** Don't group the records. Click Next.

**f.** Don't sort the records. Click Next.

**g.** Use a tabular layout, landscape orientation, for this report. Click Next.

**h.** Choose the Formal style and click Next.

**i.** Name the report **Payroll Deductions for Employees** *[your initials]* and click Finish.

**j.** Maximize the window and view the report in a Fit and a 100 percent size. Return to Design View.

**2.** Modify controls by following these steps:

**a.** Select the Monthly Salary label and text box. Size both controls so the right edge touches the 1.5-inch mark on the ruler.

**b.** Move both controls so the left edge aligns at the 1-inch mark.

**c.** Deselect the controls and size the label so you can see the text.

**d.** Size the SocialSecurityNumber text box so you can see the complete number in Print Preview.

**e.** Select the Federal Tax label and text box. Size both controls so the right edge touches the 3-inch mark on the ruler.

**f.** Select the State Tax label and text box. Size both controls so the right edge touches the 4-inch mark on the ruler.

**g.** Repeat these steps for the FICA (5-inch mark) and the Savings (6-inch mark) controls. The controls in the Detail section shouldn't extend past the 6.5-inch mark.

**h.** Save the report.

**3.** Build an expression by following these steps:

**a.** Click the Text Box button abl and draw a control that is 1 inch wide in the Detail section starting at the 6.5-inch mark.

**b.** Select the label for the new control and delete it.

**c.** Right-click the unbound control and select Properties. Click the All tab.

**d.** Key **Total Deductions** as the name of the control.

**e.** Click the Control Source row and click the Build button ....

**f.** In the middle panel, double-click the Federal Tax field, not the label.

**g.** Click the + operator for addition.

**h.** In the middle panel, double-click the State Tax field, not the label.

**i.** Click the + operator for addition.

**NOTE:** You cannot use the Sum function with the name of a calculated field. You must re-enter the expression used for the calculation.

    *j.* Continue to build this expression: [Federal Tax]+[State Tax]+[FICA] +[Savings]. Click OK.

    *k.* Click the Format row and use Currency for this control. Close the properties sheet.

    *l.* Select the Savings text box and the calculated control. Align them at the top.

    *m.* Move or size the calculated control so its right edge aligns with the horizontal line in the Page Header.

    *n.* Select the Savings label in the Report Header. Click the Copy button 🖺 and click the Paste button 🖺. Drag the copied control to be the title for the new Total Deductions control. Replace the text with **Total Deductions.**

    *o.* Drag the top of the Page Header bar up so there is one row of grid dots beneath the horizontal line.

    *p.* Size and position the new label as necessary.

    *q.* Insert a label at the right margin in the Report Header for your name.

    *r.* Preview and save the report. Print and close it.

## EXERCISE 11-18

**Add a check box control to a report. Copy a control. Show totals in the Report Footer.**

    *1.* Add a check box control to a report by following these steps:

      *a.* Open the Kit Contents report in Design View.

      *b.* Click the Check Box button 🗹. Draw a control that is about 1 inch wide in the Detail section, starting at the 4-inch mark on the ruler.

      *c.* Select the label for **CheckNN**. Delete the label, but not the check box.

      *d.* Right-click the check box control and choose Properties. Click the All tab.

      *e.* Key **Promotion** as the name of the control.

      *f.* Click the Control Source row and the Build button ⊡.

      *g.* In the middle panel, double-click the Cost field.

      *h.* Click the > operator ("greater than").

      *i.* Enter **6** after the greater than symbol to create the expression "Cost>6." This checks if cost is greater than $6.

      *j.* Click OK and close the properties sheet. Preview the report and return to Design View.

*k.* Select the Cost label in the Page Header. Click the Copy button 🖻 and click the Paste button 🖺.

     *l.* Drag the copied control to be the title for the Promotion control. Replace the text with **Promotion?**

    *m.* Size and position the new label. Change its alignment to Center.

    *n.* Move the check box so it appears centered beneath its title.

    *o.* Drag the top of the SupplierName Header bar up so there is one row of grid dots beneath the horizontal line.

    *p.* Preview and save the report. Close it.

2. Copy a control and add totals to a Report Footer by following these steps.

    *a.* Open the Payroll Deductions for Employees report in Design View.

    *b.* Drag the bottom edge of the Report Footer bar down to make the footer about .5 inch tall.

    *c.* Select the calculated control in the Detail section. Click the Copy button 🖻 and click the Paste button 🖺. Move the copied control to the Report Footer.

    *d.* Right-click the text box and open its properties sheet. Click the Data tab and the Build button ⨪.

    *e.* In the preview, key **Sum(** after the = sign. Then press End and key **)** after the last square bracket. Click OK. Be sure the expression has ( ).

    *f.* Click the Other tab and change the Name to **Grand Total**. Close the properties sheet.

    *g.* View the report in several view sizes. The Report Footer is at the end of the report. Return to Design View.

    *h.* Align the new calculated control with the calculated control in the Detail section on the right.

    *i.* Draw a label in the Report Footer that starts at the 4-inch mark and extends to the Grand Total control.

    *j.* Key **Total Deductions for Employees** and press Enter. Align this label at the top with the calculated control.

    *k.* Size the Detail section so there is not so much space between records.

    *l.* Preview the report. Save and print the report.

## EXERCISE 11-19

## Use the Average function in a report. Calculate percentages in a report.

1. Use the Average function in a report by following these steps:

    *a.* With the Payroll Deductions for Employees report open in Design View, select the label and text box in the Report Footer.

**b.** Click the Copy button 📋 and click the Paste button 📋. The duplicate controls are in the correct location. Deselect the copied controls.

**c.** Select the copied label and open its properties sheet. Change the caption to **Average State Tax**. Close the properties sheet.

**d.** Select the copied text box and open its properties sheet. Click the Data tab and the Build button ....

**e.** Delete everything in the Preview area.

**f.** In the left panel, double-click the Functions folder. Double-click the Built-in Functions folder. Click once to select SQL Aggregate in the middle panel.

**g.** Double-click Avg. Select <<expr>> in the Preview area, but not the parentheses.

**h.** In the left panel, click your report folder. In the middle panel, find the State Tax field, not the label, and double-click it. Close the Expression Builder.

**i.** Click the Other tab and change the Name to **Average State Tax**. Close the properties sheet.

**j.** Preview the report, save it, and close it.

**2.** Calculate percentages in a report by following these steps:

**a.** With the Payroll Deductions for Employees report open in Design View, select the State Tax text box in the Detail section.

**b.** Copy and paste the control. Drag the copied control to align its left edge at the 7.5-inch mark in the Detail section.

**c.** Open the properties sheet and the Expression Builder for the copied control.

**d.** Press Home and key **=[** before the control in the Preview area.

**e.** Press End and key **]** after the control.

**f.** Click **/** in the operator row for division.

**g.** Key the left parenthesis **(**.

**h.** In the middle panel, double-click the Federal Tax field, not the label.

**i.** Click **+** and then double-click the State Tax field. Click **+** again and double-click the FICA field.

**j.** Key the right parenthesis **)**. Your formula should read "=[State Tax]/ ([Federal Tax]+[State Tax]+[FICA])." Close the Expression Builder.

**k.** Click the Format tab and format the control as Percent. Close the properties sheet.

**l.** Drag the top of the Page Footer bar up so there is one row of grid dots beneath the controls in the Detail section.

*m.* Select the State Tax label in the Page Header and copy/paste it. Drag the copied control to be the title for the percent control.

*n.* Edit the copied label to show **State Tax %**.

*o.* Select the horizontal line, hold down Shift, and drag the handle to extend the line to the new label.

*p.* Drag the top of the Detail section bar up to show one row of grid dots beneath the line.

*q.* Preview the report and align controls as needed. Save, print, and close the report.

## EXERCISE 11-20

**Build a query for a report. Base a report on a query. Add common expressions to a report.**

*1.* Build a query for a report by following these steps:

   *a.* Click the Queries tab and click New. Choose Simple Query Wizard and click OK.

   *b.* In the first wizard dialog box, click the down arrow for Tables/Queries. Choose Table: Payroll Information.

   *c.* Click **>>** to move all the fields to the Selected Fields list.

   *d.* Select EmployeeID and click **<** to move it out of the Selected Fields list. Remove Hourly Rate from the Selected Fields list. Click Next.

   *e.* The next dialog box asks if you want a Detail or a Summary query. Select Detail and click Next.

   *f.* Change the name of the query to **Payroll Information Query [your initials]** and click Finish.

   *g.* Maximize the window to see the dynaset. The employees with Hourly Rates, as well as those with Monthly Salaries, appear in the dynaset.

   *h.* Return to the design grid. Click the Criteria row for the Monthly Salary field and key **>0**.

   *i.* Preview the dynaset. Save and close the query.

*2.* Base a report on a query by following these steps:

   *a.* Click the Reports tab and click New. Choose Report Wizard.

   *b.* Key **Payroll Information Query** for the query data and click OK.

   *c.* Click **>>** to transfer all the fields from the query to the Selected Fields list. Click Next.

   *d.* Don't group the records. Click Next. Don't sort the records. Click Next.

   *e.* Use a Tabular layout and Portrait orientation. Click Next.

*f.* Use the Formal style and click Next.

*g.* Name the report **Salaried Workers** *[your initials]* and click Finish.

*h.* Maximize the window and view the report. Save the report, print it, and close it.

**3.** Add common expressions to a report by following these steps:

*a.* Open the Employee's Date of Hire report in Design View.

*b.* Select the control in the Page Footer. Copy and paste it.

*c.* Drag and size the copied control to align on the right with the HireDate control.

*d.* Open the Expression Builder for the copied control.

*e.* Delete the expression in the Preview area.

*f.* Click the Common Expressions folder. Double-click Page Number to paste it. Click OK.

*g.* Close the properties sheet and view the report. Save and close it.

# Lesson Applications

## EXERCISE 11-21

**Build and use a query for a report. Format the report and add an expression.**

1. Start Access, if necessary, and open *[your initials]*CC4.mdb.

2. Design a new query in Design View for the Sales Orders, Sales Order Line Items, and Stuffed Animals tables.

3. Maximize the window and size the grid and the field lists.

4. From the Sales Orders table, add the OrderID field to the grid.

5. From the Stuffed Animals table, add the ProductName and the ListPrice fields to the grid.

6. From the Sales Order Line Items table, add the Quantity field to the grid.

7. Save your query as **Order Summary** *[your initials]*.

8. Right-click the Field row for the fifth column and open the Expression Builder. Build an expression to multiply the list price by the quantity.

9. Change the name of the calculated field to **Total**. Format the field to show Currency.

10. Sort the dynaset first by OrderID and then by ProductName.

11. Add Discount from the Sales Orders table as the sixth column.

12. View the dynaset. Then save and close the query.

13. Use the Report Wizard to create a report for the **Order Summary** *[your initials]* query.

14. Use all the fields and group the report by OrderID. Don't use sorting. Use a Stepped layout and Landscape orientation. Use the Formal style. Name your report **Order Summary** *[your initials]*.

15. With the **Order Summary** *[your initials]* report open in Design View, size the OrderID controls so they are 1 inch wide.

16. Size and position the Animal/Product Name controls to be 1.5 inches wide with the left edge aligned at the 1-inch mark. Move the ListPrice controls to align the left edge at the 2.5-inch mark.

17. Move the Quantity controls to align the left edge at the 3.5-inch mark. Size them to be 1 inch wide. Move the Total controls to the 4.75-inch mark and make them 1 inch wide. Move the Discount controls to the 6-inch mark.

18. Add a text box in the Detail section at the 7-inch mark that is 1 inch wide. Delete the label.

19. Build an expression for the unbound control to compute the net price after the discount. The expression is "Total*(1-[Discount])." Format the control as Currency and align it at the Top with other controls in the Detail section.

20. Copy the Total label in the Page Header to be the title for the new control. Edit it to show **Total Due**.

21. Adjust the amount of space below the horizontal line in the Page Header.

22. Select all the controls except the label in the Report Header. Change them to 11-point Times New Roman.

23. Adjust all controls to show all data.

24. Insert a label at the right margin in the Page Header for your first and last name.

25. Save the report and print it.

## EXERCISE 11-22

**Calculate totals in the Report Footer. Open the Group Footer. Calculate a group total.**

1. With the **Order Summary [your initials]** report open in Design View, size the Report Footer to be 1 inch tall.

2. Draw a text box that starts at the 7-inch mark, about three rows of grid dots down in the Report Footer. Make the control 1 inch wide.

3. Copy the control and paste it twice so you have three controls in the Report Footer.

4. Change the caption for the first label to **Number of Products** without a colon. Move the label away from the unbound control and size it, if necessary.

5. Set the Caption for the second control to **Gross Sales**. Set the caption for the last control to **Net Sales**. Align the three controls on the left.

6. Open the properties sheet for the Number of Products unbound control. Build an expression to count the ProductName.

7. Open the properties sheet for the Gross Sales unbound control. Build an expression to sum the Total. Format the control to show currency.

8. Open the properties sheet for the Net Sales unbound control. Build this expression to calculate the total net sales: "Sum([Total]*(1-[Discount]))." Format the control to show currency.

9. Select all the controls in the Report Footer and change them to 11-point Times New Roman. Align the text boxes on the right with the Total Due control in the Detail section. Align the labels on the left with each other.

10. Open the Sorting and Grouping dialog box and turn on the Group Footer for the Order ID.

11. Copy and paste the Total Due text box in the Detail section. Drag the copied control to the Group Footer.

12. Open the properties sheet and the Expression Builder for the copied control.

13. Edit the preview to insert the Sum function and the parentheses. The expression should read: **=Sum([Total]\*(1-[Discount]))**.

14. Close the extra space in the Detail section.

15. Add and align a label that shows **Total This Order** to the left of control in the Group Footer.

16. Save, print, and close the report.

## EXERCISE 11-23

### Design a query and a report.

1. Design a new query in Design View for the Payroll Information table.

2. Add these fields to the design grid: SocialSecurityNumber, Hourly Rate, Federal Tax, State Tax, and FICA.

3. View the dynaset. Save the query as **Hourly Workers *[your initials]*** and return to Design View.

4. In the first empty column, build an expression that adds the Federal Tax, State Tax, and FICA fields to determine an employee's total tax deductions.

5. Change the name of the calculated field to **Tax Deductions**. Format it to Currency.

6. In the Criteria row for Hourly Rate, key **>0** to remove any salaried workers from the dynaset.

7. View the dynaset. Save and close the query.

8. Use the Report Wizard to create a report based on the Hourly Workers query. Select the SocialSecurityNumber, Hourly Rate, and Tax Deductions fields. Use no grouping and no sorting. Use a tabular, portrait layout and the Formal style. Name the report **Hourly Workers *[your initials]***. Click Finish.

9. Move the Tax Deductions controls so the left edge aligns at the 3.5-inch mark.

10. Draw a text box between the Hourly Rate and Tax Deductions controls in the Detail section. Delete the label.

11. Build an expression for the unbound control to multiply the Hourly Rate field by 173.3 to determine an employee's monthly pay based on an average number of hours per month. Format this control as Currency and name it **Typical Gross Pay**.

12. Add a label for this control that displays **Typical Gross Pay**. Position the control so the text appears centered over the amount in Print Preview.

13. Draw another text box to the right of the Tax Deductions control in the Detail section. Delete the label.

14. Build an expression for the unbound control to subtract Tax Deductions from Typical Gross Pay. Format this control as Currency and name it **Net Pay**.

15. Add a label for this control that displays **Net Pay Before Savings**. Position the control so the text appears centered over the amount in Report View.

16. Select all the controls except the label in the Report Header. Set them to 11-point Times New Roman. Deselect the controls.

17. Lengthen the line in the Page Header to match the line in the Page Footer. Keep the line straight.

18. Size, position, and align the controls.

19. Add a label at the right margin in the Report Header for your name.

20. Save, print, and close the report.

## EXERCISE 11-24

### Create a report with an expression.

1. Use the Report Wizard to create a report based on the Payroll Information table. Select the SocialSecurityNumber, Monthly Salary, and Hourly Rate fields. Use no grouping and no sorting. Use a tabular, portrait layout and the Formal style. Name the report **Hourly Rate for All Workers** *[your initials]*.

2. Move the Hourly Rate controls so the left edge aligns at the 4-inch mark.

3. Draw a text box between the Monthly Salary and Hourly Rate controls in the Detail section. Delete the label.

4. Build an expression for the unbound control to multiply the Monthly Salary field by 12, then divide the total by 2080 to determine the employee's hourly rate based on monthly salary. Format this control as Currency and name it **Calculated Hourly Rate**.

5. Add a label for this control. Position the control so the text appears centered over the amount in Report View.

6. Change all the controls except the label in the Report Header to 12-point Times New Roman. Size and position the controls.

7. Extend the horizontal line in the Page Header.

8. Add a label for your name at the right margin in the Report Header.

9. Save, print, and close the report. Compact the database and exit Access.

# LESSON 12

# Using Queries and Main Reports

**OBJECTIVES**

After completing this lesson, you will be able to:

1. **Identify and create relationships.**
2. **Create a query for the main report.**
3. **Create a subreport query.**
4. **Create a main report.**
5. **Use a text expression and a concatenated field.**
6. **Complete the main report.**

 Estimated time: 1½ hours

Y ou can use reports within reports. For example, you might want a report that lists basic information about each stuffed animal using fields from the Stuffed Animals and Kit Contents tables. Each animal record might be printed on a separate page in this type of report. As a small section on each page, you might want to identify the supplier's name and address. This data is in the Kit Suppliers table.

One way to prepare this type of report is to create a main report and a subreport. The main report is based on the query that uses fields from the Stuffed Animals and Kit Contents tables.

A *subreport* is a separate report, often based on its own query, that is inserted into the main report. In this example, you wouldn't need a query for the subreport to display the supplier's name and address. When you insert the subreport into the main report, it appears as an object that you can select and edit. You work with subreports in Lesson 13. In this lesson, you create the underlying queries and main reports.

# *Identifying and Creating Relationships*

In Lesson 8 you learned that a relationship is a link between two tables that allows them to be used in other Access commands. The relationship is established between fields that are common to the two tables. These fields must have the same data type and size. They don't need to have the same name, but it's helpful if they do so you can identify them easily. The fields also don't need to have the same caption.

You also learned in Lesson 8 that the most common type of relationship is one-to-many. The table on the *one* side of the relationship shows the data for the common field in only one record. The same data, however, can appear many times in the table on the *many* side of the relationship. In the Carolina Critters database, a particular OrderID number can appear only once in the Sales Order table. However, that same OrderID number can appear several times in the Sales Order Line Items table.

Table 12-1 reviews the tables in the Carolina Critters database.

**TABLE 12-1**     Tables in Carolina Critters Database (by Category)

| NAME OF TABLE | CONTENTS |
| --- | --- |
| **Employee Information Tables** | |
| Employees | Lists each employee's ID, social security number, name, address, hire and birth dates, job code, and emergency information |
| Job Codes | Lists job codes and titles |
| Payroll Information | Lists employee's ID, social security number, monthly salary or hourly rate, and pay deductions |
| Sales Representatives | Lists employee's social security number, base pay, and region |
| **Product Information Tables** | |
| Kit Contents | Lists kit number, supplier ID, cost, and contents |
| Kit Suppliers | Lists the supplier ID, name, contact person, and address information |
| Product Lines | Lists each product line and code |
| Stuffed Animals | Lists product ID, name, group code, list price, kit number, and current stock |

*continues*

**371**

**TABLE 12-1**   Tables in Carolina Critters Database   *continued*

| NAME OF TABLE | CONTENTS |
|---|---|
| **Sales Information Tables** | |
| Carriers | Lists carrier ID, name, contact person, address, and delivery methods |
| Customers | Lists customer ID, name, contact person, address information, and tax status |
| Sales Campaigns | Lists campaign ID, name, dates, notes, and supplier |
| Sales Order Line Items | Lists the OrderID, each Product ID, and the quantity ordered |
| Sales Orders | Lists the OrderID, CustomerID, employee ID, dates, carrier, and discount |

# EXERCISE 12-1 Identify and Create Relationships

You can prepare sales invoices for customers by establishing a relationship between the Sales Orders and Customers tables, between the Sales Orders and Sales Order Line Items tables, and between the Sales Order Line Items and the Stuffed Animals tables.

1. Open the file *[your initials]*CC4.mdb..
2. Click the Relationships button ⊞.
3. If there are relationships in the window, click the Clear Layout button ⊠ to clear them.
4. Maximize the Relationships window. Click the Show Table button ⊞.
5. In the Show Table dialog box, choose Customers and click Add.
6. Double-click Sales Orders, Sales Order Line Items, and Stuffed Animals. Click Close.
7. Drag the border of the field lists so all the field names and table names are visible.
8. Review the relationships between these tables.
9. Close the Relationships window and save the layout.

**EXERCISE** 12-2 **Create a Relationship for a Multiple-Table Query**

Another useful relationship for Carolina Critters is one that identifies which carrier ships an order, along with the sales representative who wrote the order. You use this query as the basis for another main report.

1. Open the Relationships window and clear the layout.
2. Click the Show Table button 🔳. Add the following tables to the layout: Carriers, Sales Orders, and Employees. Close the Show Table dialog box.
3. Size the field lists to see all the field names.
4. Right-click the relationships line and enforce referential integrity for the Carrier ID fields.
5. Drag the EmployeeID field from the Employees table to the Sales Orders table. Do not enforce referential integrity.
6. Add the Stuffed Animals and the Sales Order Line Items tables to the window.
7. Move the field lists so you can see all the relationships.

**FIGURE 12-1**
Relationship
Window

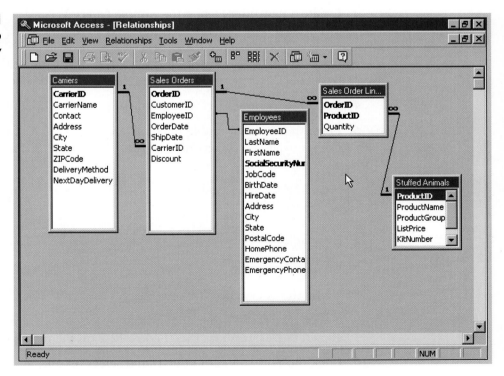

8. Close the Relationships window and save the layout.

# Creating a Query for the Main Report

The Sales Invoice is a report because it's printed. Unlike the other reports you created, it prints each record on a separate page so you can mail an invoice to each customer with only that customer's data.

To create an invoice, you first need to create a query that lists the necessary customer information and the basic sales order information. This query uses the Customers and the Sales Orders tables, but it doesn't include all the information you need for a complete invoice. The rest of the information comes from the subreport, which is based on a separate query.

When you use the Simple Query Wizard and more than one table, the relationship between tables must already be established. If you start to design a query for tables without relationships, an error message appears telling you the tables aren't related. You then need to end the query, establish the relationships, and start over.

---

**EXERCISE** **12-3** **Create a Multiple-Table Query for the Main Report**

1. Create a new query using the Simple Query Wizard.

2. From the Tables/Queries drop-down list, select Table: Sales Orders.

3. From the list of Available Fields, double-click each of the following fields: OrderID, CustomerID, OrderDate, ShipDate, and Discount.

4. From the Tables/Queries drop-down list, select Table: Customers.

5. From the list of Available Fields, double-click each of the following fields: CompanyName, BillingAddress, City, State, and PostalCode.

 **TIP:** If you forget to make a selection in a wizard dialog box, click the Back button.

6. Click Next.

7. Choose the option for a Detail query and click Next.

8. Name the query Sales Invoice Query [your initials]. Click Finish.

9. Notice the record order and switch to Design View. The relationship is shown in Design View. (See Figure 12-2 on the next page.)

10. Click the Sort row for OrderID and select Ascending.

11. Save the query and close it.

**FIGURE 12-2**
Sales Invoice
Query

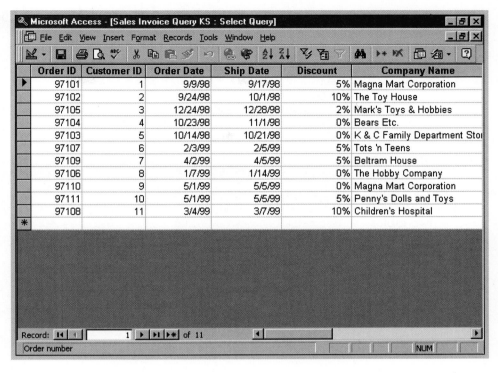

| Order ID | Customer ID | Order Date | Ship Date | Discount | Company Name |
|---|---|---|---|---|---|
| 97101 | 1 | 9/9/98 | 9/17/98 | 5% | Magna Mart Corporation |
| 97102 | 2 | 9/24/98 | 10/1/98 | 10% | The Toy House |
| 97105 | 3 | 12/24/98 | 12/28/98 | 2% | Mark's Toys & Hobbies |
| 97104 | 4 | 10/23/98 | 11/1/98 | 0% | Bears Etc. |
| 97103 | 5 | 10/14/98 | 10/21/98 | 0% | K & C Family Department Stor |
| 97107 | 6 | 2/3/99 | 2/5/99 | 5% | Tots 'n Teens |
| 97109 | 7 | 4/2/99 | 4/5/99 | 5% | Beltram House |
| 97106 | 8 | 1/7/99 | 1/14/99 | 0% | The Hobby Company |
| 97110 | 9 | 5/1/99 | 5/5/99 | 0% | Magna Mart Corporation |
| 97111 | 10 | 5/1/99 | 5/5/99 | 5% | Penny's Dolls and Toys |
| 97108 | 11 | 3/4/99 | 3/7/99 | 10% | Children's Hospital |

Record: ◄◄ ◄  1  ► ►► ►* of 11

Order number                                    NUM

---

**EXERCISE** 12-4 **Create a Second Report Query**

This query allows you to create a shipping report with fields from the Sales
Orders, Carriers, and Sales Representative tables. You complete this report in
Lesson 13.

 **NOTE:** You can rearrange the field lists in the Query Design window to
eliminate the crossed relationship lines.

1. Create a new query using the Simple Query Wizard.
2. From the Tables/Queries drop-down list, select Table: Sales Orders.
3. From the list of Available Fields, double-click OrderID.
4. From the Tables/Queries drop-down list, select Table: Carriers.
5. Double-click each of the following fields: CarrierName, DeliveryMethod,
   and NextDayDelivery.
6. Click Next.
7. Choose the option for a Detail query and click Next.

8. Name the query **Shipments Query** *[your initials]*. Click Finish.

9. Switch to Design View to see the relationship.

10. Click the Sort row for OrderID and select Ascending.

**NOTE:** You sort by OrderID so new orders added at a later date are added in ascending order.

11. Save the query and close it.

**FIGURE 12-3**
Simple Query
Wizard after
selection from
two tables

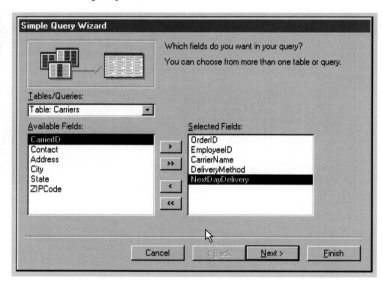

# Creating Subreport Queries

The two queries you designed so far in this lesson are used for the main part of a report. Your sales invoice report lists the customer's name and address, the order number, and related dates. The subreport lists the line items for that order number. In addition, the subreport shows the name of the product and the list price so the customer knows exactly what is billed in the invoice.

Access can link the report and the subreport because the OrderID number is a field in both the query for the main report and the query for the subreport.

Since the subreport uses two tables, it needs its own query. Designing the subreport query follows the same steps as designing any query.

**EXERCISE** 12-5 **Create a Query for the Subreport**

1. Create a new query using the Simple Query Wizard.

2. From the Tables/Queries drop-down list, choose Table: Sales Order Line Items.

3. Click >> to select all the available fields.

4. From the Tables/Queries list, choose Table: Stuffed Animals. Add ProductName and ListPrice to the Selected Fields list.

5. Click Next and select a Detail query. Click Next.

6. Name the query **Sales Invoice Subreport Query** *[your initials]*. Click Finish.

7. In Design View, sort by OrderID in ascending order.

8. Right-click in the Field row for the first empty column, next to the ListPrice column. Click the Build button [...].

9. Check that the query folder is open in the left panel. Paste "Quantity" from the middle panel. Click * for multiplication. Paste "ListPrice" after the multiplication symbol.

10. Press [Home] to position the insertion point in front of the left bracket.

11. Key the name for the calculated field in the preview, key **Total:** (include the colon).

12. Click OK to close the Expression Builder.

13. Right-click in the second row of this new field and choose Properties. Change the format to Currency and close the properties sheet.

14. Click the column selector for the ProductName field. Drag the field next to the ProductID field.

15. View the dynaset. Save and close the query.

**EXERCISE  12-6  Create a Second Query for a Subreport**

This query is the basis for the Shipments subreport.

1. Click the Queries tab and New. Choose Simple Query Wizard and click OK.

2. From the Tables/Queries drop-down list, choose Table: Stuffed Animals.

3. Add ProductID, ProductName, ListPrice to the Selected Fields list.

4. From the Tables/Queries drop-down list, choose Table: Sales Order Line Items. Add OrderID to the selected fields.

5. Click Next and select a Detail query. Click Next.

6. Name the query **Shipments Subreport Query** *[your initials]*.

7. Select the option to view the information and click Finish.

**8.** Switch to Design View and move the OrderID column so it is the first field in the query. Sort by OrderID in ascending order.

**9.** Save the query and close it.

# Creating the Main Report

When you create a report that has two reports in it, one must serve as the main report. The *main report* is usually based on a query or a table, but it can also just be a container for other reports. In your sales invoice, the main report is the top part of an invoice form. It includes the fields you used in the Sales Invoice Query. The subreport uses the Sales Invoice Subreport Query. You create the main report in this lesson and add the subreport in the next lesson.

**EXERCISE** **12-7** **Design a Report in Design View**

**1.** Create a new report in Design View for the Sales Invoice Query.

**2.** Click the Field List button 🔳 if you don't see the list of field names. Size the field list so you can see all the field names. Maximize the window.

**3.** Drag the top border of the Detail bar to make the Page Header section 1 inch tall.

**FIGURE 12-4**
Two fields selected
in Field List

**4.** Select CompanyName in the Field List. Hold down Ctrl and click to select BillingAddress in the Field List. Both fields are selected.

**5.** Drag both fields to the 2-inch mark in the Detail section. Deselect the controls.

**6.** To draw a selection marquee, click and hold the left mouse button above the first label and drag it below the second label as shown in Figure 12-5 (on the next page). This selects both labels.

**7.** Press Delete to delete the labels.

**8.** Move the CompanyName control so it is one row of grid dots down from the Detail bar and aligns at the .5-inch mark on the horizontal ruler.

**9.** Move the BillingAddress control two grid dot rows beneath the CompanyName control.

**10.** Align the controls on the left.

**11.** View the report to determine if the controls need to be sized.

**12.** Save your report as **Sales Invoice Main Report** *[your initials]*.

**FIGURE 12-5**
Marquee or lasso
of labels

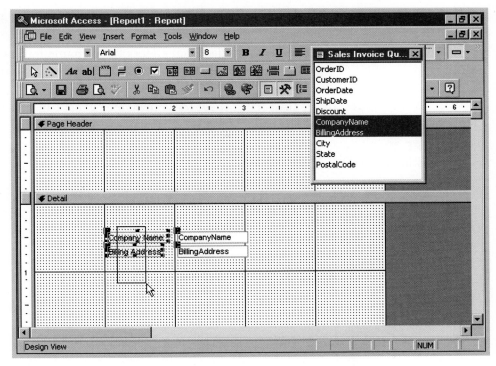

**NOTE:** A "marquee" is a box drawn around objects to select them. It is sometimes called a "lasso."

**EXERCISE** **12-8** **Complete the Page Header and Page Footer**

1. Click the Label button [Aa] and draw a label in the Page Header that starts at the 0.25-inch mark and extends to the 3.5-inch mark on the horizontal ruler. Make the box about 0.75 inch tall.

2. Key **Carolina Critters Sales Invoice** and press [Enter].

3. Change the font size to 18-point bold italic. Size the box so the label fits on one line.

4. Display the drop-down list for Font/Fore Color [A] and select blue from the first row in the palette.

5. Display the drop-down list for the Special Effect button [⊟] and select Shadowed.

6. Display the drop-down list for Fill/Back Color [⬛] and select light gray.

7. Right-click the label and select Properties. Click the Format tab and change the height of the label to 0.35 inch. Close the properties sheet.

**379**

**8.** Add a label in the Page Footer at the right margin for your first and last name.

**9.** Make the color and special effect of your name the same as the label in the Page Header, but set your name to 10 point. Size the label, if necessary.

**10.** In the properties sheet for your name, select Right Text Align. Move your name so the label ends at the right margin.

**FIGURE 12-6**
Sales Invoice

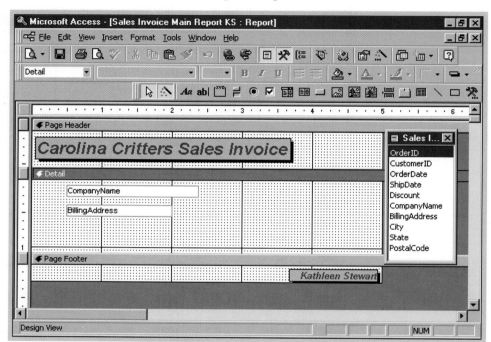

**11.** Save the report and preview it. Return to Design View.

# EXERCISE 12-9 Check the Page Width

When you prepare a portrait report, the paper size is 8.5 by 11 inches. The default report margins are 1 inch all around. This means that 6.5 inches are available for the width of the report. If you place a control outside this area, the width of the report is too wide for the margins. This generally causes the part that doesn't fit to print on the next page. An error message may appear if this happens.

**1.** Place your cursor on the right side of the design grid and expand the design area to the 9-inch mark. Your report is now very wide.

**2.** Click the Print Preview button 📇.

3. You see the message box shown in Figure 12-7. Click OK.

4. Use a Fit zoom size.

5. Click the Two Page button  to see two pages, side-by-side. The report does not fit on one page. Since the part that does not fit has no controls, it appears as a blank page.

**FIGURE 12-7**
Message indicates report is too wide for page margins.

Microsoft Access

ⓘ The section width is greater than the page width, and there are no items in the additional space, so some pages may be blank.

For example, the report width may be wider than the page width.

[ OK ]  [ Cancel ]

**TIP:** The section width error message may not always appear, but if a report prints with blank pages, that is often the problem.

6. View the other pages of the report.

7. Return to Design View. Drag the right margin to 4.5 inches on the ruler. Notice the right margin will move no further than the rightmost control. You need to move the rightmost object if you want to size this report any narrower.

8. Drag the right margin to 5.5 inches on the ruler.

9. Choose Page Setup from the File menu. Set the left and right margins to .75 inch.

10. Move your name to the new right margin. Save and close the report.

## EXERCISE 12-10 Create a Second Main Report

1. Create a new report in Design View for the **Shipments Query**.

2. Drag the top border of the Detail bar to make the Page Header 1 inch tall.

3. Draw a label in the Page Header that starts at the 0.25-inch mark and extends to the 2-inch mark.

4. Key **Shipments** and press Enter. Set the font to 18-point bold italic.

5. Draw a text box in the Page Header that starts at the 4-inch mark and ends at the right margin.

6. Delete the label and open the properties sheet for the unbound control.

7. Open the Expression Builder.

8. Open the Common Expressions folder and paste the Current Date. Close the Expression Builder.

9. Click the Format tab and use a Medium Date format. Close the properties sheet.

10. Set the font for the date to 18-point bold italic. Size the control so you can see the date in the preview.

11. Select both controls and open the properties sheet. Set the Height to .35 inches. Align these two controls at the top.

12. Adjust the height of the Page Header section so there's one row of grid dots beneath the controls.

13. Save the report as **Shipments Main Report** *[your initials]*.

14. Click the Field List button  to display the field list if necessary.

15. Drag the OrderID field to the 1-inch mark in the Detail section about 2 rows of grid dots down.

16. Change the label caption to **Order Number**. Move the controls so the left edge of the label starts at the 0.25-inch mark, even with the label in the header.

17. Drag the EmployeeID field to align at the 4-inch mark on the same line as the OrderID controls.

18. Drag the CarrierName field to align beneath the OrderID controls, leaving two rows of grid dots.

19. Drag the DeliveryMethod field to align beneath the CarrierName controls.

20. Drag the NextDayDelivery field to align at the 3-inch mark on the same line as the DeliveryMethod controls.

**FIGURE 12-8**
Shipment report

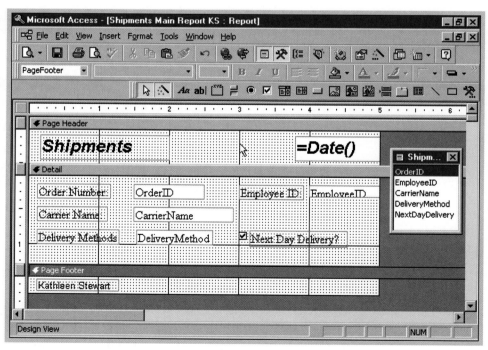

382

**21.** Lasso all the controls in the Detail section and change them to 12-point Times New Roman. Deselect the controls.

**22.** Size and move the controls so you can see all the data. You need to move the text boxes away from the labels so you can make the labels wider. You may also need to make some of the controls taller.

**23.** Set the OrderID text box to Align Left.

**24.** Align and space the controls as needed.

**25.** Add a label in the Page Footer to show your name in 10-point Arial. Place the control at the left margin.

**26.** Save the report and close it.

# Using a Text Expression and a Concatenated Field

A text expression is similar to the expressions you created so far. Rather than multiplying or dividing numbers, however, a text expression displays text as you want it to appear. You could, for example, create a simple text expression to say "Hello, how are you?" Use the Expression Builder and enter the text in the Preview area enclosed in quotation marks.

A *concatenated expression* is an expression that joins fields so they appear to be one field. For example, the city, state, and ZIP codes are separate fields in all the tables. When you use these fields in a report, you can position the controls as close together as possible, but it still doesn't quite look like a normal envelope address. You can make these three fields appear to be one field in a printed report if you concatenate them.

 **NOTE:** The + symbol is a math operator and can't be used with text fields.

When you concatenate text fields, you use the ampersand (&) to connect the fields. When there is text in a concatenated expression, it is enclosed in quotation marks. The comma and the space between the city and the state are considered text in a concatenated expression for the address.

**EXERCISE** **12-11** **Create a Concatenated Field**

**1.** Open the Sales Invoice Main Report in Design View. Display the Field List if necessary.

2. Draw a text box in the Detail section that starts at the 1.5-inch mark and ends at the 3-inch mark. You move it later.

3. Delete the label. Open the Expression Builder for the unbound control.

4. Click <Field List> in the middle panel. The field list shows all the fields in the underlying query in the right panel.

5. Paste **City** from the right panel.

6. Click **&** in the row of operators to paste it. This joins the next element in your expression.

7. Key **", "**(quote, comma, space, quote). This displays a comma and a space after the city.

 **NOTE:** For proper US Post Office protocol do not put the comma in the address between city and state.

8. Click **&** again.

9. Double-click **State** in the right panel. Click **&**.

10. Key **" "** (quote, space, quote). This displays one space after the state.

11. Click **&**. Double-click **PostalCode**.

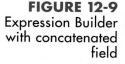
**FIGURE 12-9**
Expression Builder with concatenated field

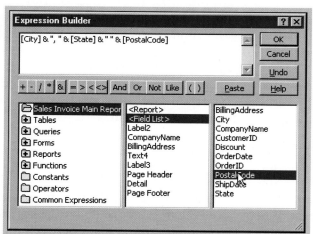

12. Close the Expression Builder and the properties sheet.

13. Size the text box so the concatenated expression fits on one line in Print Preview.

14. Position and align the control to complete the address.

15. Save and close the report.

# *Completing the Main Report*

You completed the main report for Shipments. It includes the OrderID and delivery information about that order. You add a subreport with details about the order in Lesson 13. You need to complete the Sales Invoice main report to add the fields that allow you to add its subreport in the next lesson.

## EXERCISE 12-12 Complete the Main Report

1. Open the **Sales Invoice Main Report** in Design View.
2. Click the Field List button 🗉, if necessary.
3. Scroll the window and drag the right border of the report to the 6.5-inch mark.
4. Select the OrderID field in the field list. Hold down Ctrl and select the OrderDate, ShipDate, and Discount fields. Drag all four fields to the 5-inch mark in the Detail section.
5. Drag the OrderID control to vertically align it with the CompanyName control. Align the OrderDate control with the BillingAddress control. Align the ShipDate control with the city control. Align the Discount control to match the others below the ShipDate.
6. Draw a new text box below the Discount controls in the Detail section.
7. Change the label to **Total Due**. (You complete this control in the next lesson, calculating the total amount due for each invoice.)
8. Size and align this control to match the others.
9. Draw a marquee around all the controls in the Detail section to select them. Change the font to 12-point Times New Roman.
10. With all the controls selected, choose Format, Size, and To Fit. This sizes the controls to fit the new font size.
11. Check the sizes in Print Preview. Then adjust them if necessary.
12. Click the Rectangle tool in the toolbox. The pointer changes to a + with a small rectangle.
13. Draw a rectangle around the name and address fields, leaving one row of grid dots as a border between the rectangle and the text.

 **NOTE:** A rectangle is an object and has its own properties. You can size and move it like a control.

14. The rectangle is on top of the controls. While the rectangle is selected, select Send to Back from the Format menu. This places the rectangle behind the controls.

15. While the rectangle is selected, change its Fill/Back Color to light gray to match the label in the report header. Change its Special Effect to Shadowed.

16. Deselect the rectangle. Select the three controls in the rectangle and click the drop-down arrow for Fill/Back Color. Select Transparent.

17. Size the Detail section to show two rows of grid dots below the controls.

**FIGURE 12-10**
Sales Invoice
Main Report

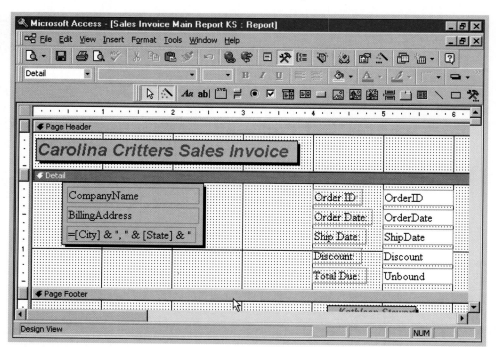

18. Preview the report. Size the controls, if necessary.

19. Print the first page of the report. Then save and close the report.

# Concepts Review

Each of the following statements is either true or false. Indicate your choice by circling **T** or **F**.

**T   F**   ***1***. All relationships are automatically established when you create a table.

**T   F**   ***2***. A one-to-many relationship is used when a table has one record that can occur many times in another table.

**T   F**   ***3***. A main report and a subreport are always linked by a connecting form.

**T   F**   ***4***. If you are using two tables to create a query, a relationship between the tables is required.

**T   F**   ***5***. You can select all controls in a report by pressing Ctrl+D.

**T   F**   ***6***. The ampersand (&) in an expression joins one element to the next one.

**T   F**   ***7***. To place a comma in a concatenated expression you need to enclose it in brackets.

**T   F**   ***8***. A subreport needs to take all its data from the same source as the main report.

Write the correct answers in the space provided.

***1***. In what window do you establish a link between tables?

_____

***2***. If you create a report that actually consists of two reports, what are those two parts called?

_____

***3***. What is the term used to describe an expression that joins fields so they look like one field?

_____

**4.** How can you include regular text in an expression?

_____

**5.** What command places one object behind another in the Design window?

_____

**6.** Why might part of a report print on the next page?

_____

**7.** How do you delete a relationship between two tables?

_____

**8.** What menu command attempts to size the controls to fit the data?

_____

## CRITICAL THINKING

**Answer these questions on a separate page. There are no right or wrong answers. Support your answers with examples from your own experience, if possible.**

**1.** Describe how you would create a concatenated expression to build this salutation for a letter: Dear Mr. Smith. Assume that your table has first and last name fields.

**2.** Describe the various types of commands you can use to design an attractive report. What types of changes do you use for the controls? What objects can you add to the report?

# Skills Review

## EXERCISE 12-13

**Identify links between tables and create relationships.**

**1.** Identify links between tables by following these steps:
  **a.** Open the file *[your initials]*CC4.mdb.
  **b.** Click the Relationships button. Clear the layout.
  **c.** Maximize the window. Click the Show Tables button.
  **d.** Add all the tables that show something about the product: Kit Contents, Kit Suppliers, Product Lines, Sales Order Line Items, Sales Orders, and Stuffed Animals. Close the Show Table dialog box.

*e.* Rearrange the field lists so the relationships are easy to see with a minimum of crossed lines. Size the field lists so you can see all the fields.

*f.* Review the lists to determine which common fields could still be linked. Notice that the Product Lines table isn't related to any table.

2. Create the relationships by following these steps:

*a.* Drag the ProductGroup field from the Stuffed Animals table to the same field in the Product Lines table.

*b.* Create the relationship without referential integrity.

*c.* Drag the KitNumber field in the Stuffed Animals table to the same field in the Kit Contents table. Enforce referential integrity.

*d.* Close the Relationship window without saving the layout.

### EXERCISE 12-14

**Create a query for a main report. Modify the query and create a subreport query.**

1. Create a query for related tables by following these steps:

*a.* Create a new query in Design View.

*b.* In the Show Table dialog box, double-click Kit Contents, Stuffed Animals, Sales Order Lines Items, and Sales Orders. Close the Show Table dialog box.

*c.* Size the design grid so you can make the field lists taller to see all the fields. Verify that the tables are related.

*d.* From the Sales Orders table, add the OrderID field to the grid.

*e.* From the Stuffed Animals table, add ProductID, ProductName, and ListPrice.

*f.* From the Sales Order Line Items table, add Quantity.

*g.* From the Kit Contents table, add KitNumber.

*h.* View the dynaset.

*i.* Save the query as **Sales Review Query** *[your initials]*.

*j.* Return to Design View.

2. Modify the query by following these steps:

*a.* Click in the Sort row for OrderID and sort in ascending order.

*b.* Right-click in the Field row for the first empty column and choose Build.

*c.* Paste the ListPrice field to the Preview area.

*d.* Click * for multiplication.

*e.* Paste the Quantity field to the Preview area.

    *f.* Click to place the insertion point at the beginning of the expression in the Preview area. Key **Total Due:** and click OK.

    *g.* Right-click in the second row of the Total Due column and open the properties sheet. Change the format to Currency and close the properties sheet.

    *h.* To save the query with a new name, choose Save As/Export from the File menu.

    *i.* Select the option to save the query within the current database.

    *j.* Click after the "w" in "Review" and key a space and **Main**. Click OK. Close the query.

**3.** Create a subreport query by following these steps:

    *a.* Create a new query using the Simple Query Wizard.

    *b.* Use Table: Kit Contents for this query.

    *c.* Place all the fields in the Selected Fields list and click Next.

    *d.* Use a Detail query.

    *e.* Name the query **Sales Review Subreport Query** *[your initials]*.

    *f.* Click Finish and close the query.

## EXERCISE 12-15

## Create a main report in Design View. Modify the report and change the page setup.

**1.** Create a main report in Design View by following these steps:

    *a.* Create a new report in Design View for the Sales Review Main Query.

    *b.* Maximize the window and display the Field List.

    *c.* Increase the height of the Page Header section to 1 inch.

    *d.* Drag the OrderID field to the 1-inch mark in the Detail section, about two rows of grid dots down.

    *e.* Draw a text box in the Detail section that starts at the 1-inch mark, is 1 inch wide, and is two rows of grid dots below the OrderID controls.

    *f.* Drag the KitNumber, ListPrice, and Quantity fields so they align at the 1-inch mark and are all two rows of dots apart.

    *g.* Draw another text box that matches beneath the Quantity controls.

    *h.* Save the report as **Sales Review Main Report** *[your initials]*.

**2.** Modify the controls by following these steps:

    *a.* Change the label for the top unbound control to **Product**.

    *b.* Change the label for the bottom unbound control to **Total Value**.

**c.** Draw a marquee around all the controls to select them.

**d.** Change the font to 11-point Times New Roman.

**e.** While the controls are selected, choose Size, To Fit from the Format menu.

**f.** Deselect the controls.

**g.** Draw a marquee to select all the text boxes (not the labels). Right-click any one of the selected controls and open the properties sheet.

**h.** Click the Format tab and the Left row. Change the location to 1.5 inches and close the properties sheet.

**i.** Draw a marquee to select all the labels. Right-click and change the Left location to .25 inch. Close the properties sheet.

**j.** Click the Rectangle tool and draw a rectangle around all the controls, leaving at least one row of grid dots between the rectangle and the controls.

**k.** While the rectangle is selected, choose Send to Back from the Format menu. Change its background color to light blue.

**l.** Draw a label in the Page Header that starts and ends evenly with the rectangle in the Detail section.

**m.** Key **Sales Review Main Report** and press [Enter].

**n.** Change the font to 14-point Arial bold italic. Size the label so the title appears on one line.

**o.** Change the background color to match the rectangle. Add the Shadowed special effect.

**p.** Open the properties sheet for the label and set the Height to .35 inches. Set the Text Align to Center.

**q.** Align the label on the left with the rectangle. Show two rows of dots above and below the label.

**r.** Add a label in the Page Footer that ends at the 5-inch mark. Key *[your first and last name]*. Use Text Align, Right for your name.

**s.** Save the report.

**3.** Change the page setup by following these steps:

**a.** Choose Page Setup from the File menu.

**b.** Change the left and right margins to 2 inches. Close the dialog box.

**c.** Preview the report. Your name is split because the report is too wide for the margin settings.

**d.** Choose Page Setup from the File menu. Change the margins to 1 inch.

**e.** Return to Design View. Save the report.

## EXERCISE 12-16

## Create a concatenated expression and build an expression.

*1.* Add a concatenated expression to the report by following these steps:

*a.* Double-click the Product unbound control to open the properties sheet. Open the Expression Builder.

*b.* Check that the report folder is open in the left panel. Click <Field List> in the middle panel.

*c.* Paste ProductID from the right panel to the Preview area.

*d.* Click **&** to join the next part of the expression.

*e.* Key " " (quote, space, space, quote) to add two spaces after the ProductID field.

*f.* Click **&** to join the next part of the expression.

*g.* Paste ProductName to the preview.

*h.* Close the Expression Builder and the properties sheet.

*i.* Preview the report. Return to Design View and size the control so you can see the product ID with the product name.

*j.* Size the rectangle so it extends to the 3.25-inch mark.

*k.* Save the report.

*2.* Build an expression by following these steps:

*a.* Double-click the Total Value unbound control to open the properties sheet. Open the Expression Builder.

*b.* Check that the report folder is open in the left panel. Click <Field List> in the middle panel.

*c.* Paste ListPrice to the preview. Click * for multiplication. Paste Quantity and close the Expression Builder.

*d.* Change the format to Currency. Close the properties sheet.

*e.* Save the report. Print the first page and close the report.

# Lesson Applications

**Identify and create relationships. Create queries for main reports and subreports.**

1. Open *[your initials]***CC4.mdb**, if necessary.
2. Open the Relationships window and clear the layout. Maximize the window.
3. Click the Show Table button 🔲.
4. Add the Payroll Information and Employees tables to the window. Close the dialog box.
5. Size the field lists so you can see the field names.
6. Drag the SocialSecurityNumber field from the Employees table to the Payroll Information table. This is a one-to-one relationship because a social security number can appear only once in both tables.
7. Enforce referential integrity.
8. Close the Relationships window and save the layout.
9. Create a new query in Design View for the Employees table.
10. Add these fields to the design grid: SocialSecurityNumber, FirstName, LastName, Address, City, State, and PostalCode.
11. Sort by SocialSecurityNumber in ascending order.
12. Save the query as **Payroll Main Query** *[your initials]*.
13. Choose Clear Grid from the Edit menu.
14. Click the Employees table title bar and press Delete .
15. Click the Show Table button 🔲 and add Payroll Information to the query. Close the dialog box.
16. Add these fields to the design grid: SocialSecurityNumber, Monthly Salary, Hourly Rate, Federal Tax, State Tax, FICA, and Savings.
17. Sort by SocialSecurityNumber in ascending order.
18. Select Save As/Export from the File menu.
19. Save this query as **Payroll Subreport Query** *[your initials]* in the current database. Close the query.

**Create a main report. Create a text expression.**

1. Create a new report in Design View for the Payroll Main Query.

2. Make the Page Header section 1 inch tall.

3. Draw a label in the Page Header and key **Confidential Payroll Information**. Set the font to 20-point Arial bold. Size the label so the title fits on one line.

4. Change the font/fore color to red. Set the Height to .35 inches.

5. Position the label to start at the second column of grid dots. Size the section to show two rows of grid dots above and below the label.

6. Draw a label at the left edge of the Page Footer for your name.

7. Draw a text box at the right edge of the Page Footer. Delete the label and open the Expression Builder for the unbound control.

8. Open the Common Expressions folder and paste the Current Date. Close the Expression Builder. Format the date as Long Date. Set its Border Style to Transparent. Set the Text Align to Right. Close the properties sheet.

9. Align the controls in the Page Footer at the top. Make the Page Footer tall enough for the labels with one row of grid dots below the controls.

10. Save the report as **Payroll Main Report** *[your initials]*.

11. Drag the SocialSecurityNumber field from the Field List to the Detail section at the 2-inch mark, two rows of grid dots down.

12. Drag the FirstName field two rows of grid dots below the SocialSecurityNumber field. Change the label to **Employee's Name**.

13. Drag the LastName field immediately to the right of the FirstName text box. Delete its label and align the controls.

14. Drag the Address field two rows of grid dots below the name, aligned at the 2-inch mark.

15. Draw a text box two rows of grid dots below the Address field. Delete the label.

16. Open the Expression Builder for the unbound control.

17. Make sure your report folder is open. Click <Field List> in the middle panel.

18. Paste City from the right panel. Click **&**.

19. Key **", "** (quote, comma, space, quote) in the Preview area.

20. Click **&** and paste State from the right panel.

21. Click **&** and key **" "** (quote, space, quote).

22. Click **&** and paste PostalCode.

23. Return to the report. Size the control to better see its contents.

24. Select all the controls in the Detail section and change to 12-point Times New Roman. While the controls are selected, choose Size to Fit from the Format menu.

**25.** Move the labels to align at the .5-inch mark. Move the text boxes to align at the 2-inch mark.

**26.** Size the controls to display all the data. Save your report.

## EXERCISE 12-19

**Draw a rectangle to frame the controls, change the page setup, and create a concatenated expression.**

**1.** With the **Payroll Main Report** open in Design View, draw a rectangle around the controls in the Detail section to frame them with one row of grid dots as an inside border.

**2.** Change the color of the rectangle to pale gray and send it to the back.

**3.** Change the Page Setup to use .75 inch left and right margins.

**4.** Delete the Employee Name label, the FirstName text box, and the LastName text box.

**5.** Draw a new text box where the name text boxes were located. Delete the label and open the Expression Builder.

**6.** Click <Field List> in the middle panel and paste FirstName.

**7.** Click **&.** To concatenate a space key " " (quote, space, quote). Click **&** again and paste LastName. Close the Expression Builder and the properties sheet.

**8.** Use the Format Painter to copy the format for this new control.

**9.** Delete the SS# and Address labels.

**10.** Move all text boxes to the 1.5-inch mark.

**11.** Save the report. Print the first two pages of the report.

**12.** Close the report. Compact the database and exit Access.

# Adding Subreports and Graphics to Reports

**OBJECTIVES**

After completing this lesson, you will be able to:

1.  **Create a subreport.**
2.  **Use built-in functions in a subreport.**
3.  **Combine the main report and subreports.**
4.  **Edit subreports.**
5.  **Carry expressions from the subreport to the main report.**
6.  **Use a forced page break.**
7.  **Add graphics to a report.**
8.  **Proofread reports.**

 Estimated Time: 1½ hours

In Lesson 12, you designed queries and built reports. Those reports were identified as "main reports." They will include subreports that you create in this lesson. Some of the queries you built in Lesson 12 were also intended for the subreports you are about to build.

The main report is the section that is most constant or unchanging. In a sales invoice, for example, the customer's name and address would stay the same from month to month. The actual purchases and amounts due, however, would change more often. The name and address portion is the main report; the sales details are in the subreport.

You can include graphics in a report to customize it. Graphics might include a company logo, a photograph, or other images.

**NOTE:** You can embed graphics in a form, too. You can also embed other objects such as sound or video clips in a form.

# *Creating a Subreport*

Technically, a subreport is not really a subreport until it is inserted into another report. Up to that point, it is just a report like any other report. You can use the Report Wizard, one of the AutoReports, or Design View to create the subreport. After the subreport is designed, it is embedded, or placed, in the main report. You can edit the main report and the subreport after the subreport is embedded.

A main report and its subreport are linked by a common field. So although you can use a simple report as a subreport, it must have an established relationship with the main report.

## EXERCISE 13-1 View Queries for Reports and Subreports

1. Open the file *[your initials]***CC4.mdb**.

2. Click the Reports tab. Check that you have the following main reports: CC Invoice Main Report, CC Payroll Main Report, CC Products Main Report, CC Sales Review Main Report, CC Sales Review Subreport, and CC Shipments Main Report. These reports are similar to the ones you created in Lesson 12.

3. Click the Queries tab. Check that you have the following queries: CC Invoice Main Query, CC Invoice Subreport Query, CC Payroll Main Query, CC Payroll Subreport Query, CC Product List Main Query, CC Product List Subreport Query, CC Sales Review Main Query, CC Sales Review Subreport Query, CC Shipments Main Query, and CC Shipments Subreport Query. These queries are similar to the ones you created in Lesson 12.

4. Open the **CC Invoice Main Query**. It includes basic information about each order and customer.

5. Switch to Design View. The query uses the Customers and Sales Orders tables. Close the query.

6. Open the **CC Invoice Subreport Query**. It includes details about each order.

7. Switch to Design View. This query uses the Stuffed Animals and Sales Order Line Items tables. The common field for these two queries is the OrderID. Close the query

## EXERCISE 13-2 Create a Subreport

1. Create a new report in Design View for the CC Invoice Subreport Query.
2. Maximize the window. Click the Field List button 🔲, if necessary.
3. Drag the right border of the design grid to the 6.5-inch mark.
4. Drag the ProductID field to the 1-inch mark in the Detail section, three rows of grid dots down.
5. Delete the label and right-click the text box. Choose Properties.
6. Change the Left property to 0.125 inch. Close the properties sheet.
7. Select these four fields in the Field List: ProductName, Quantity, ListPrice, and Extension.
8. Drag these fields anywhere in the Detail section. Deselect the controls.
9. Draw a marquee to select the labels and delete them.
10. Drag the ProductName text box next to the ProductID text box.
11. Drag and place the other text boxes in this order: Quantity, ListPrice, and Extension to create a horizontal set of controls.
12. Use Ctrl + A to select all the text boxes. Align them at the top.
13. Draw a label in the Page Header as a title for the ProductID text box.
14. Key **Product ID** and press Enter.
15. Create the following labels over the appropriate text boxes: **Animal Name, Quantity, List Price, Extension**.
16. Align the labels at the top. Show one row of grid dots below the labels.
17. While the labels are selected, apply bold formatting.
18. Check your work in Print Preview. Since numbers are right-aligned and text is left-aligned, some of the labels appear off balance.

 **TIP:** Bold makes characters larger, so you usually need to size the control after applying bold formatting.

19. Return to Design View.
20. Select the Quantity label and its text box. Align the controls on the right. Then open the multiple control properties sheet and set Text Align to Right. Repeat these steps for the List Price and Extension controls.
21. Size the Detail section to show two rows of grid dots below the controls.
22. View your report. Save it as **CC Invoice Subreport** *[your initials]*.

**FIGURE 13-1**
Invoice subreport
in Design View

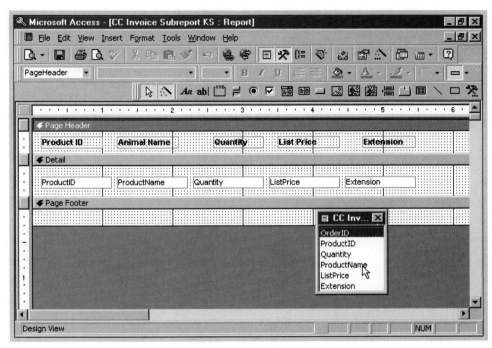

EXERCISE 13-3 Group Records

The subreport lists each product, how many were ordered, and the costs. This isn't particularly helpful for an invoice, however. You need to see which products belong with which order. The OrderID field is not currently part of the report. You can still use it for grouping, though.

1. With the **CC Invoice Subreport** open in Design View, click the Sorting and Grouping button [≣].
2. Click the down arrow for the first Field/Expression row and choose OrderID. The default sort order is ascending.
3. Click the Group Header row in the Group Properties and set it to Yes.
4. Close the Sorting and Grouping dialog box.
5. Drag the top border of the Detail bar up until it meets the Order IDGroup Header bar. This closes the Group Header section, but leaves it in effect for the report.
6. Save and close the report.

**EXERCISE** **13-4** **Create a Second Subreport**

1. Create a new report in Design View for the CC Shipments Subreport Query. Click the Field List button , if necessary.

2. Drag the OrderID field to the 1-inch mark in the Detail section, two rows of grid dots down.

3. Drag the fields in this order to align beneath the OrderID controls: ProductID, ProductName, and ListPrice. Leave one row of grid dots between controls.

4. Drag the top of the Detail bar until it meets the Page Header bar. This closes the Page Header section.

5. Size the Detail section to show two rows of grid dots below the last control.

6. Drag the right border of the Design section to the 2.5-inch mark.

7. Save the report as **CC Shipments Subreport *[your initials]*.** Close the report.

**FIGURE 13-2**
Shipments report
in Design View

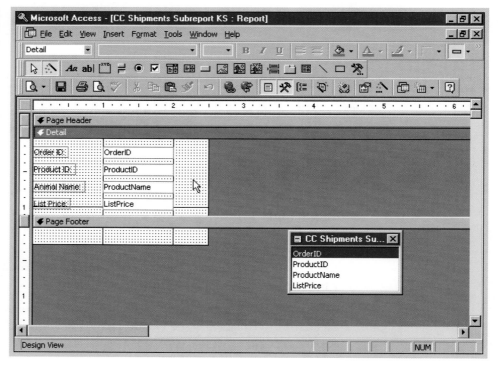

# Using Built-In Functions in a Subreport

Since a subreport is a report like any other, you can use calculated fields as well as all Access functions and common expressions.

In the following subreport, you place a calculated control in the Report Footer to total the extensions. In the subreport itself, it will total the extension amounts for all orders. However, when the subreport is combined with the main report, the link on the OrderID field causes the subreport to display the total for each order.

## EXERCISE 13-5 Add the Sum Function to a Subreport

1. Open the **CC Invoice Subreport** in Design View.
2. Choose Report Header/Footer from the View menu to open the Report Header/Footer sections.
3. Draw a text box in the Report Footer that aligns beneath the Extension text box in the Detail section.
4. Open the properties sheet for the label.
5. Change the caption to **Total Sales**. Close the properties sheet.
6. Size the label to show the text.
7. Open the properties sheet for the unbound control. Open the Expression Builder.
8. Open the Functions folder and then the Built-in Functions folder.
9. Click SQL Aggregate in the middle panel.
10. Double-click Sum in the right panel.
11. Select <<expr>> in the preview, but not the parentheses.
12. Click the CC Invoice Subreport folder in the left panel. Click <Field List> in the middle panel.
13. Paste Extension from the right panel. This expression totals the extensions for each order number in the final report.
14. Click OK to close the Expression Builder.
15. Click the Format tab and change the format to Currency.
16. Click the Other tab and name the control **Total Sales**. Close the properties sheet.
17. Select the calculated control you just created and the Extension text box in the Detail section. Align them on the right.
18. Drag the top of the Page Header bar up until it meets the Report Header bar. Drag the Report Footer bar up until it meets the Page Footer bar.

*19.* Save and close the report.

**FIGURE 13-3**
CC Invoice
Subreport in
Design View

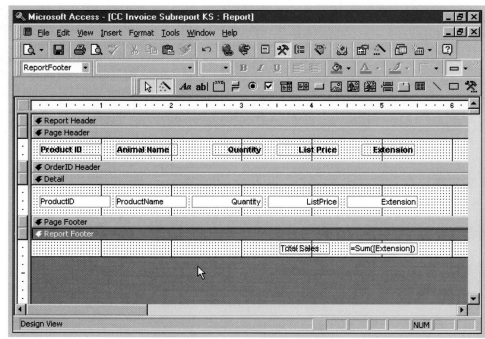

## EXERCISE 13-6 Add the Count Function to a Subreport

The Count function counts or tallies how many times any entry or any value appears in a table in a particular field. When you add this function to the Shipments subreport, it counts how many products were ordered. In the final report, it will show how many products were ordered per order.

*1.* Open the **CC Shipments Subreport** in Design View.

*2.* Choose Report Header/Footer from the <u>V</u>iew menu to open the Report Header/Footer sections.

*3.* Draw a text box in the Report Footer that starts at the 1-inch mark and is 1 inch wide.

*4.* Open the properties sheet for the label.

*5.* Change the caption to **Number of Orders** and close the properties sheet.

*6.* Select Size, to <u>F</u>it, from the Format menu.

*7.* Open the properties sheet and the Expression Builder for the unbound control.

*8.* Open the Functions folder and then the Built-in Functions folder.

9. Find and paste Count from the right panel.
10. Select <<expr>> in the preview, but not the parentheses.
11. Click the CC Shipments Subreport folder in the left panel. Click <Field List> in the middle panel.
12. Paste ProductID from the right panel. This expression counts how many products are listed on each order number.
13. Close the Expression Builder and the properties sheet.
14. Close the Page Footer and Report Header sections by dragging the appropriate borders.
15. Preview, save, and close the report

# *Combining the Main Report and Subreports*

You can use the Control Wizards as you add certain controls to the report. One of these controls is a subreport control. The Control Wizards button ▨ in the toolbox must be pressed or activated.

The report that you identified as the subreport is placed or embedded in the main report. When you place a subreport, you draw a box for the location of the subreport. Then the Subreport/Subform wizard starts and you make choices in the dialog boxes. Once the subreport is placed in the main report, it appears as a control that can be moved, sized, and edited.

Like all reports, the subreport and its main report display changes made in any of the underlying tables. The CC Invoice Main Report is based on a query that uses the Customers and Sales Orders tables. The report will always show the most current data from those tables. The CC Invoice Subreport is based on a query that uses the Stuffed Animals and Sales Order Line Items tables, so it always displays the most current data from those tables.

## EXERCISE 13-7 Embed a Subreport in a Main Report

1. Open the **CC Invoice Main Report** in Design View.
2. Drag the top of the Page Footer bar down to the 3-inch mark to make the Detail section taller.
3. Make sure the Control Wizards button ▨ is activated.
4. Click ▦. The insertion point displays a crosshair cursor with a form icon.
5. Position the pointer at the 2-inch mark on the vertical ruler and the .5-inch mark on the horizontal ruler, below the main report controls.

**403**

**6.** Draw a box that extends to the 5-inch mark on the horizontal ruler and the 3-inch mark on the vertical ruler.

**7.** The first wizard dialog box asks if you want to use one of the existing reports or forms or build a new one. You already created the subreport, so choose Reports and forms. Click the down arrow to display the list of reports and forms in the database.

**8.** Choose **CC Invoice Subreport** and click Next.

**FIGURE 13-4**
Subform/Subreport
Wizard dialog box

**9.** The next wizard dialog box asks about linking the subreport to the main report. You can define a link now if the relationships are created. Access also lists possible links based on the controls in the two reports. Choose "Choose from a list." Then Choose "Show CC Invoice Subreport Query for each record in CC Invoice Main." Click Next.

**FIGURE 13-5**
Subform/Subreport
Wizard with
established links

**10.** The next wizard asks for the name of the report. This appears as the name for the subreport control in the main report. The default name is the name of the report you are embedding. Click <u>F</u>inish.

**11.** The subreport control appears in the main report. Maximize the window.

**12.** Switch to Print Preview. If you see the error message about the section width and blank pages, click OK. View the report in a 100 percent size to check the data.

**13.** Return to Design View. Save and close the main report.

**FIGURE 13-6**
CC Invoice Main
Report

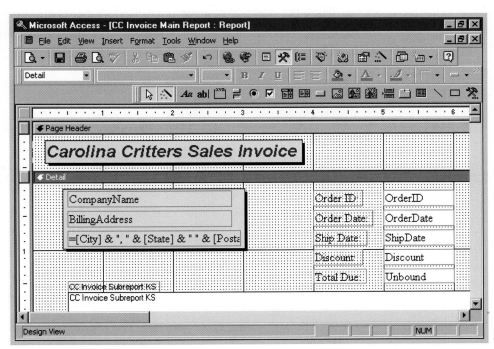

## EXERCISE 13-8 Define a Link for a Subreport

As you place a subreport in a main report, you can define the link if there is a common field.

**1.** Open the **CC Shipments Main Report** in Design View.

**2.** Right-click the Detail bar and open its properties sheet. Set the Height at 4 inches.

**3.** Click 🖩.

**4.** Position the pointer at the 2-inch mark on the vertical ruler aligned left with the main report controls.

5. Draw a box that extends to the 3-inch mark on the horizontal ruler and the 3½-inch mark on the vertical ruler.

6. The first wizard dialog box asks if you want to use an existing report or form or build a new one. Choose Reports and forms and click the down arrow to display the list of reports and forms.

7. Choose CC Shipments Subreport and click <u>N</u>ext.

8. The next wizard dialog box asks about linking the subreport to the main report. Choose "Define my own."

9. Click the down arrow for Form/Report fields and choose OrderID.

10. Click the down arrow for Subform/Subreport fields and choose OrderID. Click <u>N</u>ext.

**FIGURE 13-7**
Subform/Subreport
Wizard with
defined links

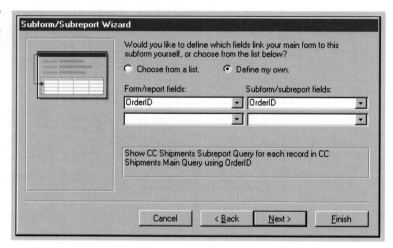

11. The default name is the name of the report you are embedding. Click <u>F</u>inish.

12. The subreport control appears in the main report.

13. Change to Print Preview. Use a Fit and a 100 percent view size to check the data. Save and close the report.

# *Editing Subreports*

As with any report, you may notice that something is missing from a subreport after you place it in the main report. You may notice that the controls aren't sized properly to show the data or you may decide to change a caption, delete a field, or add another field.

Since the subreport is a report, you can edit it like any report from the Reports tab. You can also edit a subreport from within the main report to see more quickly the changes in the main report. To do this, double-click the subreport control to open Design View for the subreport. Then make the changes as usual. When you close the report, you're back in the main report.

## EXERCISE 13-9 Edit a Subreport from the Main Report

1. Open the **CC Invoice Main Report** in Design View. Maximize the window and close the Field List, if necessary.
2. Scroll the screen so you can see the subreport control.
3. Double-click the subreport control to open it in Design View.

**TIP:** Before you double-click a subreport control to open the subreport, make sure it isn't selected. If it is selected and you double-click, you open the subreport properties sheet.

4. Press Ctrl/A to select all the controls. Change the font to 12-point Times New Roman.
5. Choose Size, To Fit from the Format menu while the controls are selected.
6. While the controls are selected, move them to the left edge of the design grid. Deselect the controls.
7. Drag the right edge of the design grid to the 5.5-inch mark or as close as possible to your rightmost control.
8. Select the controls in the Detail section. Move them and size the section so there is one row of grid dots above and one row below.
9. Make sure the data is aligned properly and that you can see all the data. Check the Extension controls in the Detail and Report Footer sections.

**NOTE:** If you see the section width error message, click OK. You'll fix that later.

10. Save the report. Close the subreport to return to the main report.
11. View the main report in Print Preview. Return to Design View and save the main report.

## EXERCISE 13-10 Edit the Subreport Control

You can format some of the basic appearance of the subreport from within the main report. Changes to the format of the data, however, are done in the subreport itself.

1. Click the label at the top left edge of the subreport control. Press `Delete`.

2. Select the subreport control.

3. Display the Line/Border Color palette and choose Transparent. This removes the border.

4. Click the Label button ▣ and draw a label box just above the subreport control, aligned at the left with the control.

5. Key **Items Ordered** and press `Enter`.

6. Set the font for the label to 18-point Times New Roman. Size the control to fit.

7. Select the label and the subreport control. Align them on the left. Position both controls so they are just below the Total Due controls. The Items Ordered label should start on the grid row below Total Due.

8. Choose Page Setup from the File menu. Click the Columns tab. Set the Column Size Width at 6.5 inches. Close the dialog box.

9. Preview the main report. Then save and close the report.

## EXERCISE 13-11 Use Design View to Edit a Subreport

You can edit a subreport from the Database window, too. Just open it in Design View like any report.

1. Open **CC Shipments Subreport** in Design View. Maximize the window.

2. Select the calculated field (=Count ([ProductID])) in the Report Footer and the ListPrice text box in the Detail section.

3. Use the properties sheet and Align Text to align them on the right.

4. Select all the text boxes in the report and change the Special Effect to Sunken.

5. Select all the labels in the report and change the special effect to Raised.

6. Preview the report and return to Design View.

7. Select all the controls on the report and change them to 10-point Times New Roman. Size them to fit.

8. Preview the report and return to Design View. Check the last page of the report. You can make the text box for the calculated control less wide to make room for its label.

9. Deselect all the controls. Size controls that still are not wide enough.

10. Save and close the report.

11. Open the **CC Shipments Main Report** in Preview to see the updated subreport. Close the report.

12. Open the **CC Shipments Main Report** in Design View.

**13.** Select the label at the top left edge of the subreport control and delete it.

**14.** Right-click the subreport control and open its properties sheet.

**15.** Click the Format tab and change the Border Style to Transparent. Close the properties sheet.

**16.** Move the subreport control two rows of grid dots below the main report controls. Move it so it appears centered within the design grid.

**17.** Choose Page Setup from the File menu. Set the left and right margins at 1.5 inches. Click OK.

**18.** Size the Detail section to show 1 row of grid dots below the subreport control.

**FIGURE 13-8**
CC Shipments
Main Report in
Print Preview

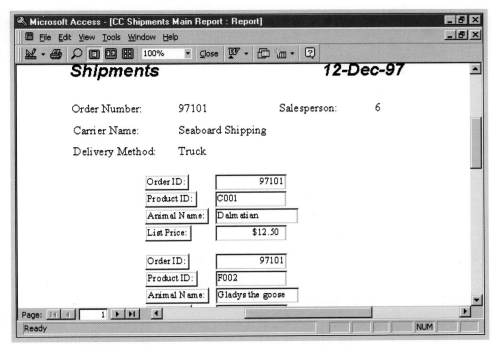

**19.** Preview the report to see if you need to make additional adjustments. Then save and close it.

# Carrying an Expression from the Subreport to the Main Report

Your CC Invoice Main Report shows the total sales in the subreport control. It currently doesn't show the total amount due with the discount for each customer. You can use the total sales computed in the subreport to calculate the total due in the main report. This is the total sales minus the dollar value of the discount.

## EXERCISE 13-12 Calculate the Total Due in the Main Report

1. Open the **CC Invoice Main Report** in Design View.

2. Open the properties sheet and the Expression Builder for the unbound Total Due control.

3. Double-click the CC Invoice Main Report folder in the left panel to open it. The name of the subreport folder is shown.

4. Click the name of the subreport folder to open it. Its fields and controls appear in the middle panel.

5. In the middle panel, double-click Total Sales to paste it to the Preview area. The expression in the preview is [CC Invoice Subreport].[Report]! [Total Sales]. This means the control shows the total sales field from the subreport report.

6. Close the Expression Builder.

7. Click the Format tab and change the format to Currency. Close the properties sheet.

8. View the report. The Total Due in the main report is now the same as the Total Sales in the subreport. Return to Design View.

9. Right-click the Total Due text box and open the Expression Builder.

10. The insertion point should be after the existing expression in the preview. Click to place it there if necessary.

11. Click * for multiplication. Then click ( for the left parenthesis.

12. Key 1- after the left parenthesis.

**FIGURE 13-9**
Expression Builder with discount calculation

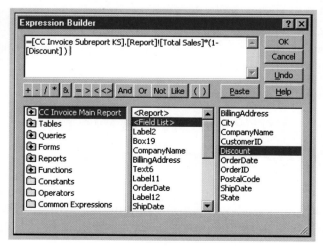

13. Click <Field List> in the middle column.

14. Paste Discount from the right panel to the preview.

15. Click ) for the right parenthesis.

16. The expression should read [CC Invoice Subreport].[Report]![Total Sales]*(1-[Discount]). This computes the total due including the discount.

**17.** Close the Expression Builder and the properties sheet.

**18.** View the report. Return to Design View. Save and close the report.

**EXERCISE** **13-13** Use the Count Function in the Main Report

In the CC Shipments Subreport, you used the Count function to count the number of animals. This tallies each product in the dynaset from the CC Shipments Subreport Query. When you use this control in the main report, it counts the number of products per order. Then you can show on your shipments report how many products were shipped. It is easier to identify controls from different reports when you name them.

**1.** Open the **CC Shipment Subreport** in Design View. Open the properties sheet for the calculated control in the Report Footer.

**2.** Click the Other tab. Name this control **Number of Animals**. Close the properties sheet.

**3.** View the report. Close and save the subreport.

**4.** Open the **CC Shipments Main Report** in Print Preview. Look at the report and find the Number of Animals controls in the subreport.

**5.** Click the View ⬛ button to return to Design View.

**6.** Draw a text box in the Detail section beneath the Salesperson controls.

**7.** Change the label to **# of Animals**.

**8.** Open the Expression Builder for the unbound control.

**9.** Double-click the CC Shipments Main Report folder in the left panel to open it. You see the name of the subreport folder.

**10.** Click the name of the subreport folder to open it. Its fields and controls appear in the middle panel.

**11.** In the middle panel, double-click Number of Animals to paste it to the Preview area. The expression in the preview is [CC Shipments Subreport].[Report]![Number of Animals]. This control in the main report shows the number of animals per OrderID.

**12.** Close the Expression Builder and the properties sheet.

**13.** View the report. Return to Design View.

**14.** Click one of the other controls in the Detail section. Double-click the Format Painter button ⬛ to lock it. Copy the format to the new label and text box. Click ⬛ again to turn it off.

**15.** Align these controls at the top with the Carrier Name controls. Size them as needed. Save the report.

# EXERCISE 13-14 Make a Control Invisible

The report and the subreport both show the number of animals. You only need to show that information in the main report, so you can hide the control in the subreport. You need the control in the subreport to calculate, but it doesn't need to be visible.

1. Double-click the subreport control.
2. Double-click the Number of Animals text box to open its properties sheet.
3. Click the Format tab and the Visible row. Choose No. Close the properties sheet.
4. View the subreport. Save and close it.
5. View the main report. Save and close it.

**FIGURE 13-10**
CC Shipments
Main Report in
Design View

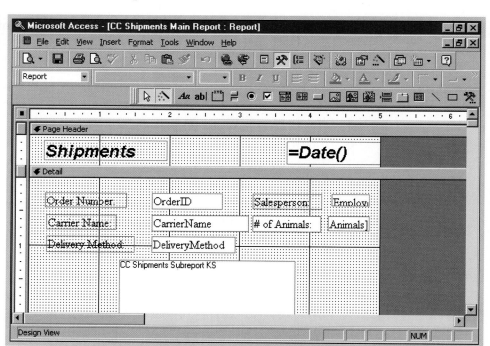

# *Using a Forced Page Break*

When you send or review Invoice and Shipments reports, each invoice and each shipment report should print on its own page. Depending on the amount of data per record, this might happen by coincidence. When the invoice or order is short, however, the page breaks are not correct. You can force a page break for each record.

## EXERCISE 13-15 Insert Page Breaks in the Main Reports

1. Open the **CC Invoice Main Report** in Design View.
2. Right-click the Detail bar and open its properties sheet.
3. Click the Format tab.
4. Set the Force New Page property to After Section. Close the properties sheet.
5. Preview the report. Save and close the report.
6. Open the **CC Shipments Main Report** in Design View.
7. Right-click the Detail bar and open its properties sheet.
8. Click the Format tab.
9. Set the Force New Page property to After Section. Close the properties sheet.
10. Preview the report. Save and close the report.

# *Adding Graphics to a Report*

You can add a control to a report or a form that holds a graphic image. A company logo is a typical example of an image that might appear on reports and forms. In a Stuffed Animals report, you might include a photograph of each product. In an Employees form, you might show a photograph of each worker. Access can use most popular graphics formats, such as PCX, TIF, GIF, and JPEG.

When you use an image, you can place it as a separate control on the report. Then it has properties similar to the ones you've been using. You can size and move the image like other controls. This type of picture is considered a foreground image.

You can place a foreground picture in an image frame or an unbound object frame. An image frame is best for pictures that are placed once and not changed. If the picture is one that you will often need to edit in another application such as Paint, you can use an unbound object frame. This type of control allows you to double-click and launch the other application.

When you use an image frame, you can size the image itself in three ways. *Clip mode* shows the picture at its original size as it was drawn or scanned. If the image is bigger than the control, it is cut off. *Stretch mode* sizes the picture to fit the control and can distort the image by changing its proportions. *Zoom mode* sizes the image to fill the height or width of the control, without changing the proportions.

 **NOTE:** You can also embed or link an image as a background or watermark. Use the Picture property for the report or form.

# EXERCISE **13-16** Add an Image Frame to the Main Report

In this exercise, you use the Image control to add an image in BMP format to the main reports.

*1.* Open the **CC Invoice Main Report** in Design View.

*2.* Size the Page Header to twice its current height.

*3.* Click 🖾.

*4.* Position the pointer at the 4-inch mark in the Page Header, two rows of grid dots down.

*5.* Draw a box that extends to the 6-inch mark and is about 1 inch tall.

*6.* The Insert Picture dialog box opens. Find the appropriate folder and **Critters.bmp**. Click 🖽.

**FIGURE 13-11**
Critters.bmp ready
to be inserted

*7.* Select the filename and click OK to load it. It may not be the right size for the report.

**8.** Double-click the image control to open its properties sheet.

**FIGURE 13-12**
Image properties sheet

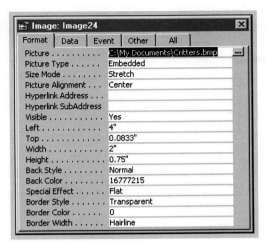

**9.** Click the Format tab and the Size Mode row. Choose Stretch and close the properties sheet.

**10.** Deselect the image control.

**11.** Save, view, and close the report.

# *Proofreading Reports*

Your final task in the preparation of a report is to make sure the data is complete and appears attractive. You've already seen how controls need to be sized and aligned after changes. You may have realized that the Design View is an approximation of what the report will look like when printed. You need to switch between Design View and Print Preview many times when you design a report. Controls may appear to be the right size in Design View, but data is missing in Print Preview. The controls may appear to overlap in Design View, but the data is visible in Print Preview.

It is a trial-and-error process, perhaps a bit tedious. However, once a report is finalized, it often will not need to be edited again.

**EXERCISE 13-17 Review and Edit the Main Report**

**1.** Open the **CC Invoice Main Report** in Design View. Switch to Print Preview.

**2.** In a 75% view size, arrange the window so you can see the top part of the invoice and the items ordered section.

**415**

3. Navigate through the pages of the report. Verify that the company names and addresses aren't cut off. Check that product names are all visible.

4. If company names or addresses are cut off, return to Design View and size the appropriate text box. If items ordered are truncated, double-click the subcontrol to make the change.

5. In Design View for the main report, align the label in the Page Footer with the right edge of the subreport control. Edit the text to show *[your first and last name]*.

6. Draw a text box in the Report Header below the label. Delete its label and align the unbound control with the label on the left.

7. Open the Expression Builder for the unbound control.

8. Double-click the Common Expressions folder. Paste the Current Date and close the Expression Builder.

9. Format the date to show a Medium Date. Close the properties sheet.

10. Copy the format from the label to the Date control.

11. Size and align the controls as needed.

12. Save the report. Print the first page of the invoice. Save and close the report.

13. Open the CC Shipments Main Report in Design View.

14. Edit the label in the Page Footer to show your name.

15. Review the report to determine if controls need to be sized or aligned.

16. Print pages 2 and 3 of the report. Save and close the report.

# Concepts Review

Each of the following statements is either true or false. Indicate your choice by circling either **T** or **F**.

T  F     *1.* A subreport has the same field information as the main report.

T  F     *2.* You can add fields to a subreport the same way you add them to any report.

T  F     *3.* The main report and the subreport are linked by the linking tool on the tool bar.

T  F     *4.* It is possible to have a value calculated in the subreport appear in the main report.

T  F     *5.* You can hide a control to make it invisible in a report, even though it is needed for calculation.

T  F     *6.* The image box accepts bitmapped images as its graphic format.

T  F     *7.* When you set the Zoom size mode for an image, the graphic fills the control but distorts the image.

T  F     *8.* You can add built-in functions to a main report or a subreport.

Write the correct answer in the space provided.

*1.* What is the name for a report that is embedded in another report?

_____

*2.* What button do you click to insert one report into another?

_____

*3.* What are the three size modes for a graphic image?

_____

*4.* What built-in function tallies the number of entries in a table?

_____

*5.* Which report section determines how much space appears between records?

_____

**6.** What property allows you to print a report on separate pages based on a section in your report?

_____

**7.** If an image is not likely to change, which button should you click to place it in the report?

_____

**8.** How can you edit a subreport?

_____

## CRITICAL THINKING

**Answer these questions on a separate page. There are no right or wrong answers. Support your answers with examples from your own experience, if possible.**

**1.** Creating reports is a trial-and-error process in which you switch views often. Explain the types of edits or changes that you look for when proofreading a report.

**2.** There are three size modes for an image in an Access report. Why do you think this might be helpful?

# Skills Review

## EXERCISE 13-18

**View a query. Create a subreport.**

**1.** View a query for a subreport by following these steps:

    ***a.*** Open the **CC Product List Subreport Query**. It includes basic information about each kit.

    ***b.*** Switch to Design View. The query uses the Kit Contents table. Close the query.

**2.** Create a subreport by following these steps:

    ***a.*** Create a new report in Design View for the CC Products List Subreport Query.

    ***b.*** Click the Field List button 📇, if necessary. Maximize the window.

    ***c.*** Drag the KitNumber field to the 1-inch mark in the Detail section, two rows of grid dots down.

**d.** Place the SupplierID, Cost, and Kit Contents fields in a column below the KitNumber field with two rows of grid dots separating each.

**e.** Drag the right border of the design grid to the 2.5-inch mark.

**f.** Drag the top border of the Detail bar up to close the Page Header section.

**g.** Drag the bottom border of the Page Footer section to close it.

**h.** Double-click the Kit Contents text box to open its properties sheet. Set the Width at 1.25 inches and the Height at 0.75 inch. Close the properties sheet.

**i.** Size the Detail section so there are two rows of grid dots below the Kit Contents controls.

**j.** Preview your report.

**k.** Save your report as **CC Products Subreport** *[your initials]*. Close the report.

## EXERCISE 13-19

## Use functions in a subreport.

**1.** Add functions to a subreport by following these steps:

**a.** Open **CC Sales Review Subreport** in Design View. Maximize the window.

**b.** Draw a text box in the Report Footer to align beneath the Quantity text box.

**c.** Change the label to **# of Items**. Change the font size to 12 point.

**d.** Open the properties sheet and the Expression Builder for the unbound control.

**e.** Open the Functions folder in the left panel and then open the Built-in Functions folder.

**f.** Click SQL Aggregate in the middle panel.

**g.** Double-click Sum in the right panel.

**h.** Select <<expr>> in the preview, but not the parentheses.

**i.** Click the CC Sales Review Subreport folder in the left panel.

**j.** Paste Quantity from the middle panel. This expression sums the number of items for each order number.

**k.** Close the Expression Builder and the properties sheet.

**l.** Change the font size to 12 point.

**m.** View the report. Align and size the controls as needed.

**n.** Save and close the report.

## EXERCISE 13-20

### Embed a subreport in a main report.

**1.** Place a subreport in a main report by following these steps:

    **a.** Open the **CC Products Main Report** in Design View.

    **b.** Close the field list box if necessary.

    **c.** Click 🔳.

    **d.** Position the pointer at the 3.75-inch mark in the Detail section. Draw a box that extends to the 6-inch mark and is about the same height as the rectangle in the Detail section.

    **e.** In the first wizard dialog box, choose Reports and forms. Click the down arrow and choose CC Products Subreport. Click Next.

    **f.** The link in the list is correct, so click Next.

    **g.** The report name should also include your initials. This is the name of the subreport control. Click Finish.

    **h.** Maximize the window. View the report.

    **i.** Save the report and close it.

    **j.** Open the **CC Sales Review Main Report** in Design View. Close the field list box if necessary.

    **k.** Click 🔳.

    **l.** Position the pointer at the 3-inch mark in the Detail section. Draw a box that extends to the 4.5-inch mark and is about 2 inches tall.

    **m.** In the first wizard dialog box, choose Reports and forms. Click the down arrow and choose CC Sales Review Subreport. Click Next.

    **n.** The link in the list is correct, so click Next.

    **o.** The report name is the name of the subreport control. Add your initials to the report name. Click Finish.

    **p.** View the report. Then save and close it.

## EXERCISE 13-21

### Edit a subreport in Design View. Edit a subreport from the main report.

**1.** Edit a subreport in Design View by following these steps.

    **a.** Open the **CC Products Subreport** in Design View.

    **b.** Select all the controls.

    **c.** Change the font to 12-point Times New Roman.

    **d.** While the controls are all selected, choose Size, to Fit, from the Format menu. Deselect the controls.

*e.* Drag the right border of the design grid to the 3-inch mark.

  *f.* Drag the middle right handle of the Kit Contents text box until it almost reaches the 3-inch mark. Leave two columns of dots as a margin.

  *g.* Save and close the report.

 **2.** Edit a subreport from the main report by following these steps:

  *a.* Open the **CC Sales Review Main Report** in Design View.

  *b.* Double-click the CC Sales Review Subreport control.

  *c.* Drag the right border of the design grid to the 3-inch mark.

  *d.* Open the properties sheet for the calculated control.

  *e.* Click the Format tab and change the format to Standard.

  *f.* Choose 0 (zero) Decimal Places. Close the properties sheet.

  *g.* Open the properties sheet for the Quantity control in the Detail section. Change its format to Standard with 0 (zero) decimal places.

  *h.* Close the properties sheet and view the report.

  *i.* Align the Quantity control and the calculated control on the right.

  *j.* Save and close the report to return to the main report.

  *k.* Preview the main report. Save and close it.

## EXERCISE 13-22

## Add an image to the main report.

 **1.** Add an image frame to a report by following these steps:

  *a.* Open the **CC Products Main Report** in Design View.

  *b.* Position the label in the Page Header so its right border touches the 6-inch mark.

  *c.* Click ▣.

  *d.* Position the pointer at the 0.25-inch mark in the Page Header and draw a box for the image that almost reaches the label and is about 1 inch tall.

  *e.* In the Insert Picture dialog box, find the appropriate folder and the **Critters.bmp** file.

  *f.* Select the filename and click OK.

  *g.* Right-click the image and open its properties sheet.

  *h.* Click the Format tab and the Size Mode row. Choose Zoom. Close the properties sheet.

  *i.* Save and close the report.

UNIT 4 ■ **PRINTING INFORMATION FROM A DATABASE**

## EXERCISE 13-23

## Review and edit the reports.

**1.** Modify a subreport control and the report by following these steps:

   ***a.*** Open the **CC Sales Review Main Report** in Design View.

   ***b.*** Scroll the screen to find the right border.

   ***c.*** Drag the right middle handle of the subreport control to the 4.75-inch mark.

   ***d.*** Drag the right edge of the design grid to the 5-inch mark.

   ***e.*** Select the subreport label and delete it.

   ***f.*** Right-click the subreport control to open its properties sheet.

   ***g.*** Click the Format tab and set the Border Style to Transparent. Close the properties sheet.

   ***h.*** View the report and return to Design View.

   ***i.*** Drag the subreport control so its bottom border rests on the 1-inch grid line.

   ***j.*** Add a label above the subreport control. Key **ID and Quantity**.

   ***k.*** Click the OrderID label and the Format Painter button .

   ***l.*** Copy the format to the new label. Make the new label italic also.

   ***m.*** Align the OrderID label, its text box, and the new label at the top.

   ***n.*** Adjust the height of the Detail section so there are two rows of grid dots as a bottom margin.

   ***o.*** Choose PageHeader/Footer from the View menu to add the Page Header/Footer to the report.

   ***p.*** Close the Page Header and the Report Footer.

   ***q.*** Add a label in the Page Footer at the right margin. Key *[your name]*.

   ***r.*** Save, print, and close the report.

**2.** Modify the page setup and page breaks by following these steps:

   ***a.*** Open the **CC Products Main Report** in Design View.

   ***b.*** Preview the report to see that part of the report is truncated.

   ***c.*** Choose Page Setup from the File menu while in Print Preview.

   ***d.*** Click the Columns tab. Set the Width to 6.5 inches.

   ***e.*** Click the Margins tab. Set the left and right margins at 0.5 inch, if necessary. Close the dialog box.

   ***f.*** Check the report in a Fit view size. Return to Design View.

   ***g.*** Right click the Detail bar and select Properties.

*h.* Click the Format tab and the Force New Page row. Choose After Section. Close the properties sheet.

3. Make final edits to the report by following these steps:

*a.* Select all the labels in the gray rectangle. You may need to deselect the rectangle first.

*b.* Right-click any selected label to open the Multiple selection properties sheet. Set the width to 1.25 inches. Close the properties sheet.

*c.* Deselect the labels. Drag each label by its pointing-finger pointer to be closer to its text box.

*d.* Select the labels again and align them on the right.

*e.* Select the rectangle and drag its middle left handle so you can see two columns of grid dots as a margin.

*f.* Select and delete the subreport label.

*g.* Click to select the subreport control if necessary. Move the right border to 6.25 inches.

*h.* Click the Line/Border Color down arrow and change the color to Transparent.

*i.* Deselect the subreport control. Then double-click it to open it in Design View.

*j.* Click the Detail bar to select the section. Click the Fill/Back Color down arrow and select the last gray tile in the fourth row.

*k.* Select all the labels. Align them on the right.

*l.* While they are selected, open the properties sheet and set the Text Align to Right.

*m.* In the properties sheet, change the Special Effect to Raised. Close the properties sheet.

*n.* Select all the text boxes and change the Special Effect to Sunken.

*o.* While the text boxes are selected, change the font to 10 point.

*p.* Preview the report. Then save and close the subreport.

*q.* View the main report to determine what other changes you need to make. You may need to return to the subreport. Change the Page Setup in the main report if the controls are truncated. You can change the width of the subreport control.

*r.* Align the label in the Page Header on the right with the subreport control.

*s.* Add a label to the Page Footer with your first and last name.

*t.* Save the report and print its first page. Then close the report.

# Lesson Applications

## EXERCISE 13-24

**View queries. Create a subreport.**

1. Open *[your initials]CC4database* file if necessary.
2. Look at the dynaset and Design View for the CC Payroll Main Query and the CC Payroll Subreport Query. Close the queries.
3. Create a new report in Design View for the CC Payroll Subreport Query.
4. Display the field list. Select all the fields.
5. Drag the fields to the 1-inch mark in the Detail section.
6. While the controls are selected, change the font to Times New Roman 10 point. Size them to fit.
7. Deselect the controls and preview the report. Return to Design View and size individual controls as necessary.
8. Draw a marquee to select all the text boxes and change the Special Effect to Sunken.
9. Open the properties sheet for the SocialSecurityNumber control and change the Visible setting to No. Preview the report again.
10. Drag the right border of the design grid to the 3-inch mark.
11. Select all the controls and move them so they appear to be horizontally centered in the Detail section with one row of grid dots above and below them.
12. Save the report as **CC Payroll Subreport** *[your initials]* and close it.

## EXERCISE 13-25

**Embed a subreport in a main report. Edit the main report and the subreport.**

1. Open the **CC Payroll Main Report** in Design View. Preview the report and return to Design View.
2. Close the field list and maximize the window.
3. Place a subform/subreport control to the right of and aligned at the top with the blue rectangle.
4. In the first wizard, click the Reports and forms option and choose CC Payroll Subreport.
5. In the next wizard, click the Define my own option.

6. In the first row for Form/report fields, choose SocialSecurityNumber. In the first row for the Subform/subreport fields, choose SocialSecurityNumber.

7. You can use the same report name. Click Finish.

8. Preview the report and return to Design View.

9. Select and delete the subreport label. You may need to separate the label slightly from the subreport control to select it. Deselect the subreport control.

10. Double-click the subreport control to open it in Design View.

11. Press Ctrl+A to select all the controls. Drag them to be flush with the top of the Detail section.

12. Adjust the height of the Detail section so there are no grid dots below the last control.

13. Close both the Page Header and the Page Footer sections.

14. Save and close the report to return to the main report.

15. Preview the main report and return to Design View.

16. Align the subreport control at the top with the rectangle. Size the control to the same height as the rectangle.

17. Preview the report to see if the page width is too small. Navigate the pages to see if some pages are blank. Return to Design View.

18. Drag the middle right handle of the subreport control to the 6.5-inch mark.

19. Open the Page Setup dialog box. Set the margins to 0.75 inch. In the Columns tab, set the width to 7 inches

20. Select the subreport control and change its line/border color to Transparent. Move it so there is one column of dots between it and the rectangle.

21. Click the Line button. Draw a horizontal line two rows of grid dots below the rectangle and the subreport control. Hold down Shift as you drag to keep the line straight. The line should be as long as the rectangle and the subreport control.

22. Right-click the line and open its properties sheet. Change its Border Width to 1 point.

23. Adjust the height of the Detail section so there are two rows of grid dots below the line.

24. Select the date and time control in the Page Footer and change its font to 10-point Arial. Align this control on the left with the Confidential label in the Page Header.

**25.** Draw a label in the Page Footer that aligns on the right with the subreport control. Key your first and last name and set it to 10-point Arial.

**26.** Save the report.

## EXERCISE 13-26

### Edit concatenated controls. Add an image to the report.

**1.** In Print Preview for the CC Payroll Main Report, notice that there is a comma between the city and state.

**2.** In Design View, select the text box with the address concatenated field. Open the Expression Builder.

**3.** Click in the Preview area after the ampersand (&).

**4.** Delete the comma but not the space.

**5.** Close the Expression Builder and the properties sheet. Preview the report.

**6.** Open the Expression Builder for the date/time control in the Page Footer.

**7.** Replace the expression with a new common expression for the current date. Set it to use a Medium Date format.

**8.** Size the date control to be 1- inch wide.

**9.** Draw an image control in the Page Footer that starts at the 2-inch mark between the date control and your name. Extend it to the 4-inch mark.

**10.** Find the appropriate folder and the **Critters.bmp** file.

**11.** Open the properties sheet for the image. Set the Size Mode to Zoom. Set the Height to .75 inches. Close the properties sheet.

**12.** Save the report. Print the first two pages.

**13.** Close the report. Compact the database. Exit Access.

# Unit 4 Applications

## APPLICATION U4-1

Create a columnar AutoReport. Modify controls and group records. Use AutoFormat.

1. Open the file *[your initials]*CC4.mdb.

2. Create a columnar AutoReport using the Customers table. Maximize the window and switch to Design View.

3. Delete the control (label and text box) for ContactName.

4. Select the Billing Address and City controls and drag them below the Company Name controls.

5. Drag the State control next to the City control. Drag the ZIP Code control next to the State control. Align these three controls as needed.

6. Move the Phone Number control below the City control. Move the Fax Number control next to the Phone Number control. Align these controls. Delete the Tax Exempt control.

7. Edit the label in the Report Header to show **Customers by State *[your initials]***. Set the font to 24-point Times New Roman. Select a fill/back color and font/fore color for the label.

8. Open the Page Header section. Move the label in the Report Header to the Page Header with two rows of dots below the label. Then close the Report Header.

9. Use Sorting and Grouping to group the records by State with a Group Header.

10. Select the State label and text box. Drag them to the left edge of the State Group Header section.

11. Open the properties sheet for the State group section and force a page break before the section so each state is on a separate page.

12. Change the font of the State label in the Group Header to 14-point Times New Roman bold. Use the same fill/back and font/fore colors you used for the label in the Page Header.

13. Copy the format from the label in the State Group Header to the State text box in the Group Header. Adjust the height of the group section so there are two rows of grid dots below the controls.

14. Select and delete the horizontal line at the top of the Detail section.

15. Move the ZIP Code control closer to the City. Align the ZIP Code with the Fax Number.

**16.** Select all the controls in the Detail section and change them to 11 point. While the controls are selected, size them to fit.

**17.** Preview the report to see which controls need to be sized and positioned. Make those changes.

**18.** Select all the labels in the Detail section and change the Special Effect to Raised.

**19.** Select all the text boxes and change the Line/Border Color to Transparent.

**20.** Size the Detail section to show six empty grid dot rows below the controls.

**21.** Size the controls in the Page Footer so you can enter a label with your first and last name in the middle of the section. Align your name with the controls and use the same font and size.

**22.** Save the report as **New Customers AutoReport**. Print the pages for the North Carolina customers.

**23.** In Design View, click the Report Selector button so it displays a small rectangle.

**24.** Apply the Soft Gray AutoFormat. Make any other adjustments to improve the report format. Check for blank pages and adjust the Page Setup, if necessary.

**25.** Print the page(s) for the Tennessee customers.

**26.** Close the report without saving it.

## APPLICATION U4-2

**Create a report with the Report Wizard. Use line breaks in the labels. Build calculated controls. Use Access functions to show a summary in the footer.**

**1.** Use the Report Wizard to create a report using the Stuffed Animals table.

**2.** Use all the fields and group on the ProductGroup field. Sort by ProductID. Use a Stepped layout, Portrait orientation. Use the Corporate style.

**3.** Name the report **Stuffed Animals Retail Value** *[your initials]*.

**4.** In Design View, edit each two-word label in the Page Header to show on two lines using a line break Shift+Enter. As you do this, the horizontal line will be in the way.

**5.** Make the Page Header section taller. Select and drag the horizontal line below the labels.

**6.** Delete the ProductGroup label. Center all the labels.

7. Size the ProductGroup text box in the Group Header to be as small as possible and still show the letter.

8. Draw a label next to the ProductGroup text box and key **Group**. Move this label as close as possible to the text box. You can even allow the label to overlap the text box. Use the Format Painter to copy the font from the text box to the label.

9. Size the Group Header section so there are no rows of grid dots above and one row below the controls.

10. Select all the text boxes in the Detail section and make them 11-point Arial. Size them to fit.

11. Preview the report. Size individual controls as needed.

12. Select the text boxes and their labels in the Detail section. Move them to start at the 1-inch mark to make room for two more columns at the right.

13. Draw a text box to the right of the QuantityOnHand text box in the Detail section. Select and delete the label.

14. Open the Expression Builder for the unbound control.

15. Build the following expression to show a retail value that reflects a 50 percent markup: **[ListPrice]*1.5**. Format the control as Currency. Name this control **Retail Value**.

16. Copy the format from one of the other controls in the Detail section to this new control.

17. Add a label in the Page Header for this control that shows **Retail Value**.

18. Size and align these controls as needed.

19. Draw another text box to the right of the Retail Value text box in the Detail section. Select and delete the label. Open the Expression Builder.

20. Build the following expression to show the total retail value of the inventory: **[Retail Value]*[QuantityOnHand]**. Format the control as Currency. Name the control **Total Value**.

21. Format the control to match the others.

22. Add a label in the Page Header for this control that shows **Total Value**.

23. Size and align the controls as needed. Save the report.

24. Size the =Now() control in the Page Footer to be 1 inch wide. Then move it to the Report Header section. Place it near the right border of the report and align it with the label. Size it so you can see the entire date.

25. Delete the page number control. Add a label in its place with your first and last name. Right-align your name at the right border of the report.

26. Open the Report Footer section. Draw a text box in this section that is 2 inches wide and starts at the 2-inch mark. Change the label to **Total Number of Animals**.

27. Open the Expression Builder for the unbound control. Use the Count function to tally the number of animals. Name the control **Number of Animals**. Copy the format from a control in the Detail section. Leave one row of grid dots above and below this control.

28. Draw another text box to align beneath the Retail Value control. Change its label to **Total Retail Value**.

29. Open the Expression Builder. Use this formula to compute the total retail value of the inventory: **Sum([ListPrice]\*[QuantityOnHand]\*1.5)**. Format the control as Currency. Format and align the control.

30. Save and print the report.

31. Edit the appropriate controls to determine what the retail values would be if the markup or margin were changed to 75 percent instead of 50 percent. Print page 2 of this revised report.

32. Close the report without saving.

## APPLICATION U4-3

**Establish and edit relationships. Build queries for a report and a subreport. Use calculated fields in a query.**

1. In the Relationships window, create a relationship between the Stuffed Animals and Kit Contents tables using the KitNumber field if it does not already exist. Check for a second relationship between the Kit Contents and Kit Suppliers tables using the SupplierID field. Create it if necessary. Edit existing relationships so you do not enforce referential integrity for either relationship.

2. Use the Simple Query Wizard to create a query with the following fields:

| Table | Field |
|---|---|
| Stuffed Animals | **KitNumber** |
| | **ProductID** |
| | **ProductName** |
| | **ListPrice** |
| Kit Contents | **SupplierID** |
| | **Cost** |

3. Name the query **Mark-up Main Query** *[your initials]*.

4. Add a calculated field to the query titled **Mark Up**. The expression is **([ListPrice]-[Cost])/[Cost]**. Remember that you can enter the label in the preview of the Expression Builder with the colon. Change the format to percent with 0 (zero) decimal places.

5. Save the query and close it.

6. Create another query in Design View using the Kit Contents and Kit Suppliers tables.

7. From the Kit Contents table, add the KitNumber and SupplierID fields to the design grid. From the Kit Suppliers, add SupplierName, Address, City, State, PostalCode, and PhoneNumber.

8. Save the query as **Mark-up Subreport Query** *[your initials]*. Close the query.

## APPLICATION U4-4

**Create a main report. Create a subreport with a concatenated expression. Combine the reports.**

1. Create a report in Design View using the Mark-Up Main Query.

2. Show the Field List. Select all the fields and drag them to the 1-inch mark in the Detail section.

3. While the fields are all selected, change the font to 10-point Arial. Then size the controls to fit. Do the same for the labels.

4. Position the controls so there is one row of grid dots between each pair.

5. Right-align all the text boxes to better balance the text with the numbers.

6. Enter a label at the left margin in the Page Header that says **Stuffed Animals Suppliers**. Choose a font, size, and color.

7. Enter a label at the left margin in the Page Footer for your first and last name.

8. Use a text box at the right margin to place the long date in the Page Footer.

9. Save the report as **Mark-up Main Report** *[your initials]*. Close the report.

10. Create a report in Design View using the Mark-Up Subreport Query.

11. Show the Field List. Select and drag these fields to the 1-inch mark in the Detail section: KitNumber, SupplierID, SupplierName, PhoneNumber, and Address.

12. Change the font to 10-point Arial for all the controls. Size them to fit. Position the controls to show one row of grid dots between each pair.

13. Arrange the controls so Phone Number is below Supplier Name and Address is below Phone Number.

14. Draw a text box that aligns beneath the Address text box. Delete the label.

15. Use the Expression Builder to create a concatenated text expression to show the city, state, and ZIP code on a single line.

16. Size the Detail section to show row one of empty grid dots. Close the Page Header and Footer sections.

17. Size the controls to see all the data and make all the controls the same font and size.

18. Save the report as **Mark-Up Subreport** *[your initials]*. Close the report.

19. Open the **Mark-Up Main Report** in Design View.

20. Place a Subform/Subreport control to the right of the existing controls. Use Reports and forms to find your **Mark-Up Subreport**.

21. Define the link using KitNumber from both reports. Use the default name.

22. Right-click the subreport control and open its properties sheet. Change the Width to 3 inches.

23. Drag the right border of the design grid to the 6-inch mark.

24. Delete the subreport label. Deselect the subreport control.

25. Edit the subreport to make the SupplierID control invisible. Then move it to the top right edge of the design grid.

26. Move the other controls up so the top control is flush against the Detail bar. Keep one row of grid dots between controls. Adjust the height of the Detail section. Save and close the subreport.

27. Change the Border Style of the subreport so there is no border.

28. Preview the report to see what other changes you might make.

29. As a design element, add a horizontal line or an image to the report.

30. Save the report and print page 5. Close the report.

## APPLICATION U4-5

### Create and sort mailing labels.

Create Avery 5096 mailing labels for the Carriers table. Sort the labels by State. Open the Page Header/Footer sections. Add a label with your first and last name in the Page Footer. Close the Page Header. Save the labels as **Carriers Labels** *[your initials]*. Print the labels on plain paper.

# Appendices

## APPENDIX A

# Windows Tutorial

If you're unfamiliar with Windows, we suggest that you review this Windows tutorial.

If you've never used Windows before, you may need additional help with some basic Windows actions. At appropriate points in this Tutorial, a Note will guide you to one of the two Appendixes covering basic Windows actions (Appendix B: "Using the Mouse," and Appendix C: "Using Menus and Dialog Boxes").

# *Starting Windows*

Individual computers may be set up differently. In most cases, however, when you turn on your computer, Windows will load and the Windows desktop will appear.

The desktop contains *icons*, or symbols representing windows. If you double-click an icon, the window represented by that icon opens. Two icons are especially important:

- My Computer
  Opens a window that contains icons representing each input and output device on your printer or in your network.

- Recycle Bin
  Opens a window listing files you have deleted. Until you empty the Recycle Bin, these files can be undeleted.

 **TIP:** If you don't know how to use the mouse to point, click, double-click, or drag and drop, see Appendix B: "Using the Mouse."

# *Using the Start Menu*

 The Start button  on the taskbar at the bottom of the desktop is probably the most important button in Windows. Clicking displays the Start menu from which you can perform any Windows task.

**NOTE:** If Microsoft Office is installed on your computer, additional options may appear on your Start menu.

**1.** Turn on the computer. Windows will load, and the Windows desktop will appear.

 **NOTE:** When you start Windows, you may be prompted to log on to Windows or, if your computer is attached to a network, to log on to the network. If you are asked to key a user name and a password, ask your instructor for help.

**2.** Click 🏁Start on the Windows taskbar. The Start menu appears.

 **TIP:** If you don't know how to choose a command from a menu, see Appendix C: "Using Menus and Dialog Boxes."

**FIGURE A-1**
Windows desktop

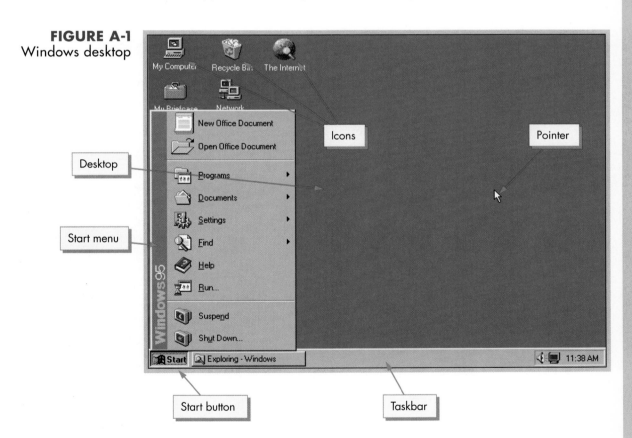

**TABLE A-1**  **Start Menu**

| COMMAND | USE |
| --- | --- |
| Programs | Displays a list of programs you can start. |
| Documents | Displays a list of documents that you've opened previously. |
| Settings | Displays a list of system components for which you can change settings. |
| Find | Helps you find a folder or a file. |
| Help | Starts Help. You can then use Help to find out how to perform a task in Windows. |
| Run | Starts a program or opens a folder when you type an command. |
| Shut Down | Shuts down or restarts your computer, or logs you off (if you are on a network). |

# Using the Programs Command

The Programs command is the easiest way to open a program.

1. Click 🏁Start.
2. Point to Programs. The Programs submenu appears, listing the programs present on your computer. Every computer will have a different list of programs.

**FIGURE A-2**
Programs submenu

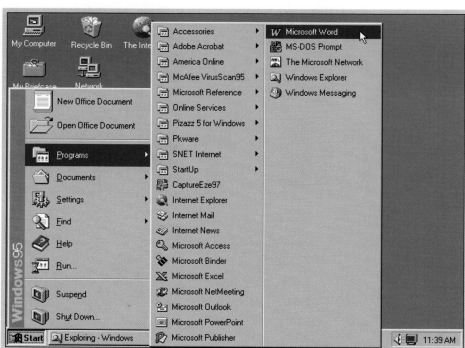

3. Point to a program that you want to open and then click. In a few seconds, the program will load and its first screen will appear. Notice that a button for the program appears in the taskbar. Keep the program open.

**NOTE:** Many items on the Program menu represent names for groups of programs. These group names have an arrow ▶ across from them on the right side of the menu. When you point to the group name, a submenu will appear listing programs that you can click to select.

# Using the Taskbar

One of the major features of Windows is that it enables you to work with more than one program at a time. The taskbar makes it easy to switch between open programs.

The window in which you are working is called the *active* window. The title bar for the active window is highlighted, as is its taskbar button.

1. The program you opened in the preceding procedure should still be open. (If it's not, open a program now.) Open a second program using the Program command. Notice how the second program covers the first. The window containing the second program is now active. Its title bar is highlighted and its button on the taskbar is highlighted.

**FIGURE A-3**
Active window

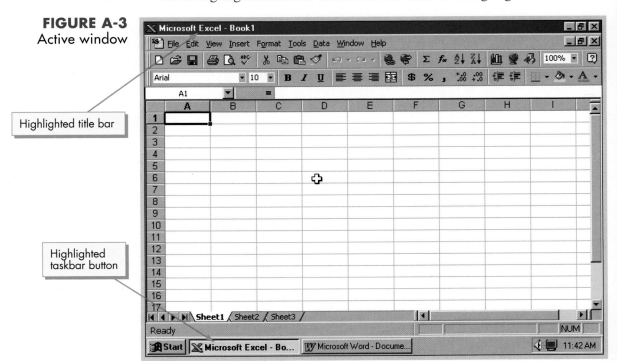

Highlighted title bar

Highlighted taskbar button

**2.** Click the button on the taskbar for the first program you opened. The program appears again.

**3.** Click the button on the taskbar for the second program to switch back to it.

# Changing the Sizes of Windows

In Windows it's easy to adjust the size of your windows using the pointer. You can also use the Minimize button [_], the Maximize button [□], and the Restore button [▣] to adjust the size of windows.

**TABLE A-2**    **Sizing Buttons**

| NAME | BUTTON | USE |
|------|--------|-----|
| Minimize button | [_] | Reduces the window to a button on the taskbar. |
| Maximize button | [□] | Enlarges the window to fill the desktop. |
| Restore button | [▣] | Returns the window to its previous size. (Appears when you maximize a window.) |

**1.** In the open window, click [▣] at the right side of the title bar of the window. (If [□] appears instead of [▣], the window has already been reduced. In that case, go on to step 2.)

**2.** Move the pointer to a window border. The pointer changes to a double-headed arrow ↔.

 **TIP:** Sometimes the borders of a window can move off the computer screen. If you're having trouble with one border of a window, try another border.

**3.** When the pointer changes shape, you can drag the border to enlarge, reduce, or change the shape of the window.

**4.** Make the window smaller. Notice that the other open program appears behind the currently active window.

5. Click the window that had been behind the first window. It now appears in front of the first window because it has become the active window.

6. Click ▬ to minimize the window to a button on the taskbar. The other program becomes active.

7. Click the Close button ✕ at the top right corner of the window to close the current program. The desktop should now be clean.

8. Click the button on the taskbar for the other program you have open. Close the program by clicking . You have a clean desktop again.

# Using the Documents Command

You can open an existing document by using the Document command on the Start menu. This command allows you to open one of the last 15 documents previously opened on your computer.

1. In the Start menu, point to Documents. The Documents submenu appears, showing documents that have been previously opened.

2. Click on a document. The document opens, along with the program in which the document was written (for example, if the document were a Word document, it would open within Word). A button for the document appears on the taskbar. You could now work on the document, if you wanted.

3. To close the document, click ✕ on the document window. Click ✕ to close the program window that contained the document.

**FIGURE A-4**
Close buttons

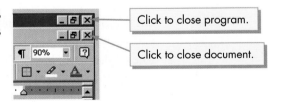

Click to close program.

Click to close document.

# Using the Settings Command

You can change the way Windows looks and works by using the Settings command. Be very careful when changing settings. Don't change them unless it's really necessary.

 **NOTE:** Before changing any settings, talk to your instructor.

**FIGURE A-5**
Settings submenu

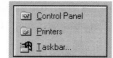

1. Open the Start menu, and point to Settings. The Settings submenu appears.
2. Click the option that relates to the settings you want to change. Close any open windows and clear your desktop.

**TABLE A-3**    Settings options

| OPTION | USE |
|--------|-----|
| Control Panel | Displays the Control Panel, which allows you to change screen colors, add or remove programs, change the date or time, and change other settings for your hardware and software. |
| Printers | Displays the Printer window, which allows you to add, remove, and modify your printer settings. |
| Taskbar | Displays the Taskbar Properties dialog box, which allows you to change the appearance of the taskbar and the way it works. |

# Using the Find Command

If you don't know where a document or folder is, you can use the Find command to find and open it.

**FIGURE A-6**
Find Submenu

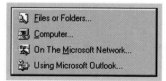

1. On the Start menu, point to Find. The Find submenu appears.
2. Click Files or Folders. The Find: All Files dialog box appears.

**FIGURE A-7**
Find: All Files
dialog box

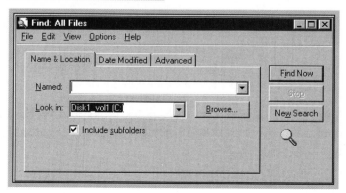

3. In the <u>N</u>amed box, key the name of the file or folder you want to find.

4. Click the arrow next to the <u>L</u>ook In box to specify where to search. (You could also check <u>B</u>rowse.)

 **TIP:** You can use the Advanced tab to search files for specific text.

5. Click F<u>i</u>nd Now to start the search. Any matches for the file will be shown at the bottom of the dialog box.

6. To open a file that was found, double-click on the filename.

7. When you have finished viewing the file, close all open windows and clear your desktop.

# *Using the Run Command*

If you know the name of the program you want to use, you can use the Run command to start it easily. This command is often employed to run a "setup" or "install" program that installs a new program on your computer.

1. In the Start menu, click <u>R</u>un. The Run dialog box appears.

**FIGURE A-8**
Run dialog box

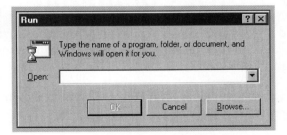

2. If you know the name of a program you want to run, key the name and click OK. The program you specified will start. Otherwise, you can click Browse to look for the program.

3. When you're finished, close the program.

# *Using the Right Mouse Button*

When the pointer is on an object in Windows and you click the right mouse button, a shortcut menu will typically appear. This menu provides you with the commands that would be most useful in working with the object to which you were pointing.

A shortcut menu is available for . The shortcut menu options for  are described in Table A-4.

**FIGURE A-9**
Shortcut menu for
the Start button

> **Open**
> Explore
> Find...

**1.** Click  with the right mouse button. The right mouse button Start menu appears.

**2.** Investigate the options on the right mouse button menu, and then close any open programs.

**TABLE A-4**

| Shortcut menu for the start button | |
|---|---|
| OPTION | USE |
| Open | Opens the Start Menu window. Double-click the Programs icon to open the Program window. Then, double-click the icon for the program you want to open. |
| Explore | Opens Windows Explorer (see Appendix E: "File Management"). |
| Find | Opens the Find: All Files dialog box. |

# Using the Shut Down Command

You should always shut down Windows before you turn off or restart your computer. You can then be sure that your work will be saved and no files will be damaged.

**1.** In the Start menu, click Shut Down. The Shut Down Windows dialog box appears.

**FIGURE A-10**
Shut Down
Windows
dialog box

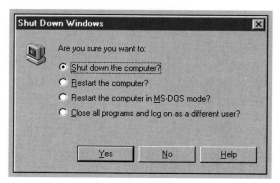

**2.** Click Yes. Windows will prompt you to save changes to any open documents, and will then shut down your computer.

## APPENDIX B

# Using the Mouse

Although you can use a keyboard with Windows, you'll probably find yourself using the mouse. Typically, you roll the mouse on a *mouse pad* (or any flat surface). A *pointer* shows your on-screen location as the mouse moves.

To select items on the computer screen using a mouse, you usually press the left button on the mouse. (Whenever you're told to "click" or "double-click" the mouse button, use the left mouse button. In those cases where you should use the right button, you'll be told to do so.)

When using a mouse, you'll need to become familiar with these terms.

**TABLE B-1**

**Mouse Terms**

| TERM | DESCRIPTION |
|------|-------------|
| Point | Move the mouse until the tip of the on-screen pointer is touching an item on the computer screen. |
| Click | Press the mouse button and then quickly release it. |
| Double-click | Press and quickly release the mouse button twice. |
| Triple-click | Press and quickly release the mouse button three times. |
| Drag (or drag-and-drop) | Point to an object, hold down the mouse, and move the mouse to a new position (dragging the object to the new position). Then release the mouse button (and drop the object in the new position). |

The mouse pointer changes appearance depending on where it's located and what you're doing. Table B-2 shows the most common types of pointers.

**TABLE B-2**

**Frequently Used Mouse Pointers**

| POINTER NAME | POINTER | DESCRIPTION |
|--------------|---------|-------------|
| Pointer | ▷ | Used to point to objects. |
| I-beam | I | Used when keying, inserting, and selecting text. |
| 2-headed arrow | ↖ | Used to change the size of objects or windows. |
| 4-headed arrow | ✛ | Used to move objects. |
| Hourglass | ⧗ | Indicates the computer is processing a command. |
| Hand | ☜ | Used in Help to display additional information. |

## APPENDIX C

# Using Menus and Dialog Boxes

## *Menus*

Menus throughout Windows applications use common features. To open a menu, click the menu name. An alternative method for opening a menu is to hold down [Alt] and key the underlined letter in the menu name.

 **TIP:** If you open a menu by mistake, click the menu name to close it.

**FIGURE C-1**
Edit menu (Excel)

**FIGURE C-2**
View menu (Word)

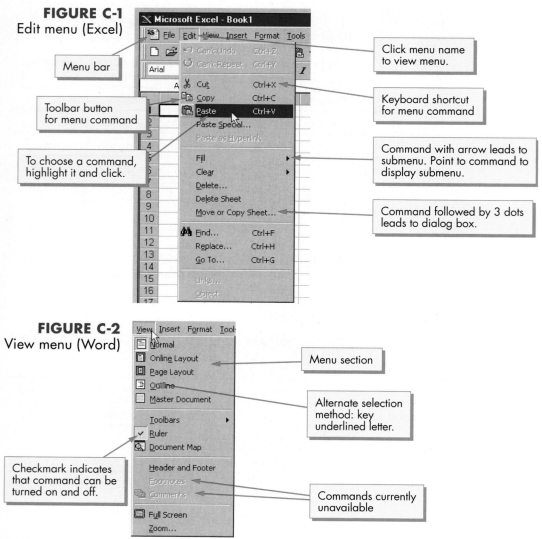

Menu bar

Toolbar button for menu command

To choose a command, highlight it and click.

Click menu name to view menu.

Keyboard shortcut for menu command

Command with arrow leads to submenu. Point to command to display submenu.

Command followed by 3 dots leads to dialog box.

Menu section

Alternate selection method: key underlined letter.

Checkmark indicates that command can be turned on and off.

Commands currently unavailable

**A-12**

# *Dialog Boxes*

Dialog boxes enable you to view all of the current settings for a command, as well as change them. Like menus in Windows, dialog boxes share common features. The following examples show the most frequently seen features.

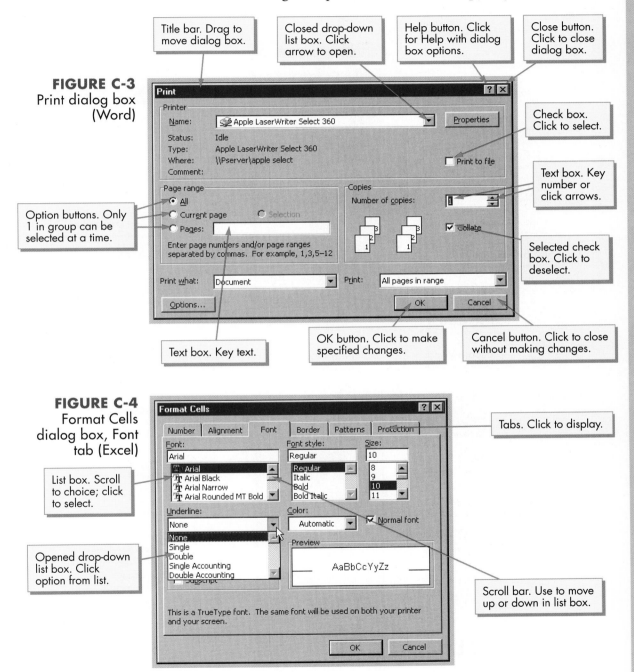

Title bar. Drag to move dialog box.

Closed drop-down list box. Click arrow to open.

Help button. Click for Help with dialog box options.

Close button. Click to close dialog box.

**FIGURE C-3**
Print dialog box (Word)

Check box. Click to select.

Text box. Key number or click arrows.

Option buttons. Only 1 in group can be selected at a time.

Selected check box. Click to deselect.

Text box. Key text.

OK button. Click to make specified changes.

Cancel button. Click to close without making changes.

**FIGURE C-4**
Format Cells dialog box, Font tab (Excel)

Tabs. Click to display.

List box. Scroll to choice; click to select.

Opened drop-down list box. Click option from list.

Scroll bar. Use to move up or down in list box.

**A-13**

# APPENDIX D
# Access Toolbars

**FIGURE D-1**  Table Datasheet Toolbar

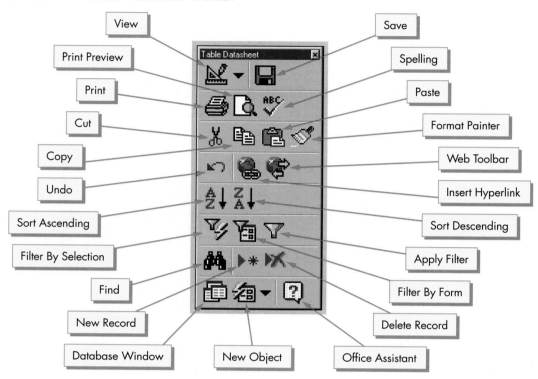

**FIGURE D-2**  Table Design Toolbar

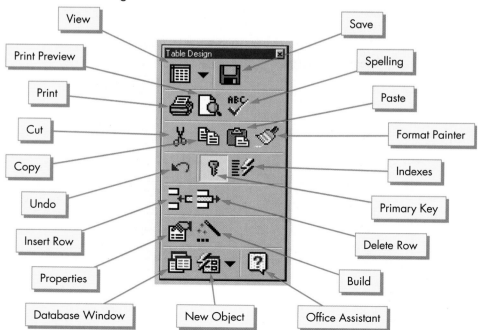

**FIGURE D-3**  Form View Toolbar

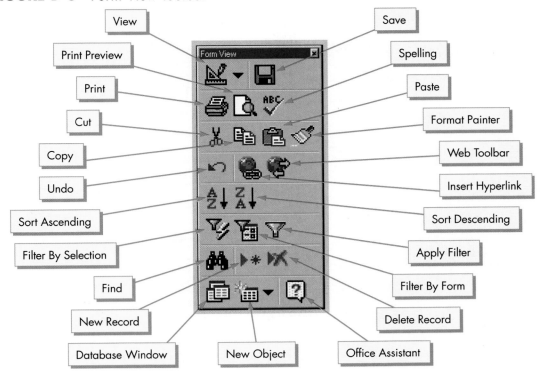

**FIGURE D-4**  Form Design Toolbar

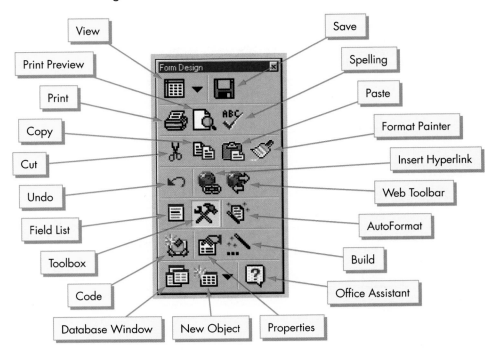

**FIGURE D-5** Query Datasheet Toolbar

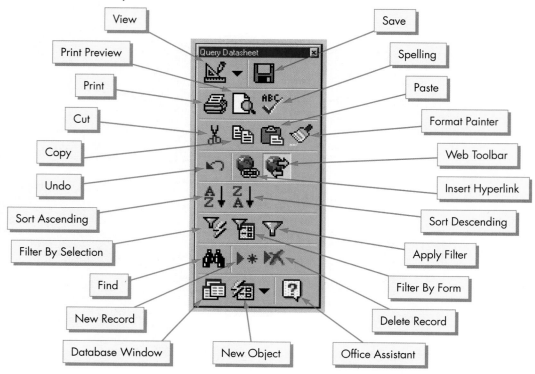

**FIGURE D-6** Query Design Toolbar

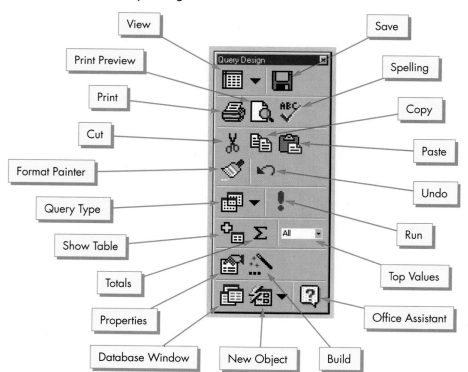

**FIGURE D-7** Toolbox

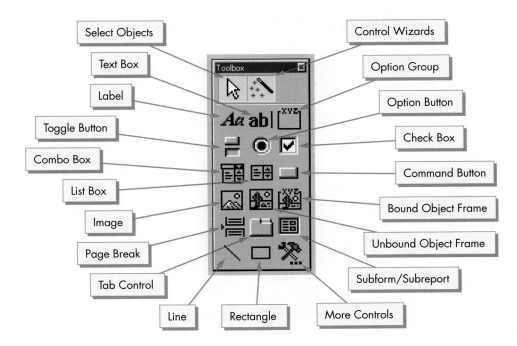

Select Objects

Text Box

Label

Toggle Button

Combo Box

List Box

Image

Page Break

Tab Control

Line

Rectangle

Control Wizards

Option Group

Option Button

Check Box

Command Button

Bound Object Frame

Unbound Object Frame

Subform/Subreport

More Controls

**FIGURE D-8** Formatting (Form/Report) Toolbar

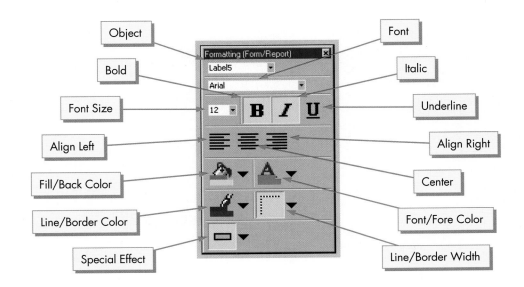

Object

Bold

Font Size

Align Left

Fill/Back Color

Line/Border Color

Special Effect

Font

Italic

Underline

Align Right

Center

Font/Fore Color

Line/Border Width

**FIGURE D-9** Database Toolbar

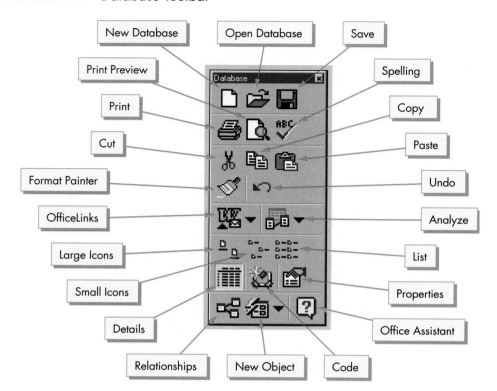

New Database
Open Database
Save
Print Preview
Spelling
Print
Copy
Cut
Paste
Format Painter
Undo
OfficeLinks
Analyze
Large Icons
List
Small Icons
Properties
Details
Office Assistant
Relationships
New Object
Code

## APPENDIX E

# File Management

This Appendix briefly explains how information is stored in Windows. It also introduces one of the most useful tools for managing information in Windows—the Windows Explorer.

# *Files, Folders, and Paths*

In Windows, the basic unit of storage is a *file*. The documents you create and use are files, as are the programs you use. These files are stored in *folders*, which can also contain other folders.

Windows supports filenames that can contain up to 250 characters. A filename also has a three-letter extension, which identifies the type of file. For example, the extension "doc" identifies a file as a Word document. The extension is separated from the filename by a period. For example: "Birthdays.doc."

**NOTE:** In this course, we assume that your machine displays file extensions. If it doesn't, open Windows Explorer, select <u>O</u>ption from the <u>V</u>iew menu, and make sure that the following option is *not* selected: "Hide MS-DOS file extensions for file types that are registered."

A file's *path* is its specific location on your computer or network. A file's path begins with the drive letter, followed by a colon and a backslash (example: c:\). The path then lists the folders in the order you would open them. Folders are separated by backslashes. The last item in the path is the filename.

For example: c:\My Documents\Letters\Reservations.doc

# *Windows Explorer*

One of the most useful tools in Windows for managing files is the *Windows Explorer*, which gives you a view of your computer's components as a hierarchy, or "tree." Using Windows Explorer, you can easily see the contents of each drive and folder on your computer or network.

To open Windows Explorer, click the Start button 🏁Start with the right mouse button. Then click <u>E</u>xplore in the Start button shortcut menu.

Table E-1 describes how to accomplish common file management tasks using Windows Explorer and shortcut menus.

**FIGURE E-1**
Windows Explorer

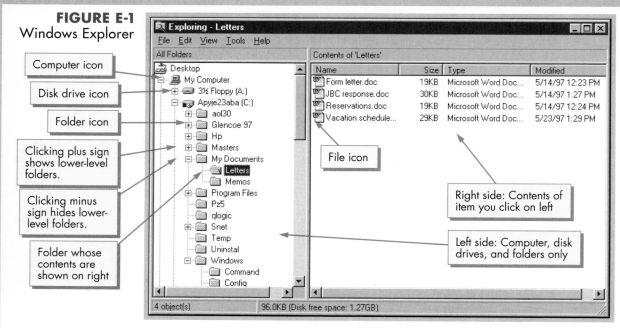

Computer icon

Disk drive icon

Folder icon

Clicking plus sign shows lower-level folders.

Clicking minus sign hides lower-level folders.

Folder whose contents are shown on right

File icon

Right side: Contents of item you click on left

Left side: Computer, disk drives, and folders only

**TABLE E-1**  **Common File Management Tasks**

| TASK | HOW TO DO |
|------|-----------|
| Copy file or folder | Right-click file or folder to be copied and click Copy, then right-click folder in which you want to copy file and click Paste. (Alternative: Drag and drop a file from one folder to another.) |
| Move file or folder | Same method as above, but using Cut and Paste. |
| Delete a file or folder | Point to icon for file to be deleted and press Delete. |
| Create a new folder | Choose New from File menu, and then choose Folder. Creates new folder at current position. |
| Copy file to floppy disk | Point to icon for file to be copied and press right mouse button. Point to Send To and click floppy disk drive in submenu. |
| Edit/rename file | Point to icon for file you want to rename, press right mouse button, and click Rename. |
| Open file | Double-click icon for file. |
| Print file | Point to icon for file to be printed, press right mouse button, and click Print. |

# Glossary

**&** Ampersand operator used to join or connect fields in a concatenated expression. (12)

**Action query** Query type used to update, append, or delete records without individual editing of each record. (9)

**Append query** Action query that adds records from one table to the end of another table. (9)

**Argument** Element required to complete a function. (11)

**AutoCorrect** Microsoft feature that corrects spelling and capitalization errors as you type. (2)

**AutoFormat** Feature used to apply a style for automatic reformatting of a report. (10)

**AutoReport** Default report created by a wizard that lists all fields in either columnar or tabular style. (10)

**Calculated field** Field in a report, form, or query that uses an expression rather than stored data. (4)

**Cascade Delete** Exception to referential integrity rules that allows you to delete a record from a table which has related records in another table. All related records are deleted. (8)

**Cascade Update** Exception to referential integrity rules that allows you to update a record in a table which has related records in another table. All related records are updated. (8)

**Check Box Control** Control in a report or a form that displays the values from a Yes/No field. (11)

**Clip mode** Sizing property for an image control that shows the picture at its original size. (13)

**Columnar report** Printed representation of records with each field on a separate line. Labels, when used, are often to the left of the field. (10)

**Common Expressions** Category of Access commands that adds date, time, and page number information to a control. (11)

**Concatenated expression** Expression that joins two fields so that they appear to be one field. (12)

**Control Source** Property of a control that indicates what data appears in that control. (6, 8, 11)

**Criteria** Text, values, or expressions used to filter or limit records. (3, 7)

**Current record pointer** Triangular arrow or pencil in the record selector area that marks the active record. (2)

**Database** Collection of objects such as tables and queries that tracks information for a business or individual. (1)

**Database Properties** Dialog box that provides descriptive information about the database. It includes attributes such as all the filenames and objects, the date the database was last edited, the author, and the size of the database. (1)

**Datasheet view** Way of looking at a table that displays the records in rows and columns, similar to a spreadsheet. (1)

**Delete query** Action query that removes records from a table based on criteria. (9)

**Design grid** Lower pane of the Query Design window with fields, sort instructions, and criteria for displaying the dynaset. Known as the QBE (query-by-example) grid in earlier versions of Access. (7)

**Design view** Screen used for determining, formatting, and editing the basic structure or layout of a table, a form, a query, or a report. (1)

**Dynaset** Results of a query shown in Datasheet view. It is dynamically linked to the table so that changes are reflected in the table. (7)

**Expression** Combination of field names, text, operators, or constant values that results in a single value. Expressions are used as the basis for calculated fields. (7, 8)

**Expression Builder** Window for entering expressions by pasting elements from tables, queries, and other Access lists. (6, 8, 11)

**Field** Individual piece of information in a record represented by a column in a table. (1)

**Foreign key** Key or field in a related table that is the same as the primary key (field) in the primary table. (8)

**Form** Database object that displays information from the table in an attractive, easy-to-read screen format. Forms can be used to edit and add records. (1)

**Form view** Screen layout for a record that is easy to read and often resembles the paper source. (2)

**Function** Word or statement used in an expression to display or calculate a value. (11)

**Group header** Section on a report that identifies a category of records based on the field selected in the Grouping and Sorting dialog box. (10)

**Identifiers** Field names that you can type or select from a panel in the Expression Builder to create a formula or expression. (11)

**Image frame** Control on a report or a form that holds a graphic file. (13)

**Insertion point** I-beam cursor that marks the next location for text that you enter. (2)

**Line break** Command that forces text to a new line. (10)

**Lookup field** Field in a table that looks up its values or data from a field in another table or from a list that you enter. (8)

**Main report** Report that serves as the container for other reports, known as subreports. A main report may have its own data based on its own query. (12)

**Marquee** Small box drawn around objects to select them. (12)

**Navigation buttons** Icons that move to the next, previous, first, and last record or page. They are available in Datasheet and Form view as well as Print Preview. (2)

**NOT operator** Element used in an expression to select records that do not match or are not equal to a value. (9)

**Object** Element in a database. Objects include tables, queries, forms, and reports. (1)

**Operator** Symbol or word used in expressions. Common operators are =, +, *, /, >, and <. The word OR is also an operator. (7)

**Page break** Command that starts a new printed page. (10, 13)

**Page footer** Section on a report that prints at the bottom of every page. (6, 10)

**Page header**   Section on a report that prints at the top of every page. (6, 10)

**Page Setup**   Command that allows you to change margins and the print orientation. (2, 12)

**Page width**   Amount of space available for a report, determined by the paper size and the left and right margins. (12)

**Parameter query**   Query that displays a dialog box with a prompt for the criteria each time it is run. (9)

**Primary table**   Table on the "one" side of a one-to-many relationship. It has a primary key. (8)

**Print Preview**   Command that displays the table, form, or report as it will print. (2)

**Query**   Database object that extracts information from the table. A query uses a design grid to set which fields should be displayed and what criteria should be met. (1)

**Query view**   Toggle button that switches from the Query Design window to the dynaset. (7)

**Record**   One entity (person, place, or thing) in a table, shown as a row. (1)

**Record selector**   Icon that marks the current or active record. It changes shape depending on the status of the record. (1)

**Referential integrity**   Set of rules that protects data in related tables from accidental changes and deletions. (8)

**Related table**   Table on the "many" side of a one-to-many relationship. It has the foreign key. (8)

**Relational Database Management System (RDBMS)**   Application for creating tables, queries, forms, and reports as objects in a database.

Tables are broken down to include necessary data without duplication. When tables are related, though, the application can use multiple tables to assemble, compile, and analyze data that otherwise would be not available. (1)

**Relationship**   Link between two tables that allows them to be used with several special Access features such as referential integrity and multiple table queries. The link is made on a field that is the same in both tables.(8).

**Report**   Database object that lays out the printed page for information from the database. (1)

**Report header**   Section on a report that prints once at the bottom of the report. (6, 10)

**ScreenTip**   Identifying information that appears when you point to a screen object such as a toolbar button. (1)

**Select query**   Query that displays records in a dynaset based on criteria. (9)

**Sort**   Command to place records in ascending (A-Z) or descending (Z-A) order. (3, 7)

**SQL Aggregate Functions**   Predefined expressions that calculate totals for a group. Aggregate functions include Sum, Avg, Count, Min, and Max. (11)

**Stretch mode**   Sizing property for an image control that fits the picture to the control, possibly distorting the image by changing its proportions. (13)

**Subreport**   Report that is inserted into another report. (12, 13)

**Table**   Basic database object consisting of an individual record for each person, place, or thing. Each record is represented as a row with fields (columns) for individual bits of data. (1)

**Table Properties**   Dialog box that provides de-scriptive information about the table including the type of object and a description that can be entered by the user. (1)

**Table view**   Toggle button that switches from De-sign view to the Datasheet view. (1)

**Tabular report**   Printed representation of records with each record on a single line and each field in a column. Labels usually print as column titles (10)

**Text expression**   Expression that displays text only. Text must be enclosed in quotation marks. (12)

**Top Values**   Access property that limits a dynaset to the topmost or bottommost records. (7)

**Update query**   Action query that changes data in the records. (9)

**Zoom**   Command that enlarges or reduces the screen size of the print preview. (2)

**Zoom mode**   Sizing property for an image con-trol that fits the picture to the height or width of the control without changing the image's propor-tions. (13)

**Zoom window**   Expanded text entry box used for memo fields and many text editing boxes. Open the Zoom window by pressing Shift/F2. (8)

# Index

# Photo Credits

Page 1: Losh/FPG, Rathe/FPG, Laubacker/FPG, Chris/FPG, Telegraph Color Library/FPG; Page 2: Fritz/FPG; Page 4: PhotoDisc, Inc. Page 9: Green/FPG; Page 109: Laubacher/FPG; Page 307: Chris/FPG; Page A-1: Telegraph Color Library/FPG